CONFEDERATE PATTON

CONFEDERATE PATTON

RICHARD TAYLOR AND THE RED RIVER CAMPAIGN

2ND (EXPANDED) EDITION

DR. SAMUEL W. MITCHAM, JR.

CONFEDERATE PATTON: Richard Taylor And The Red River Campaign

Copyright© 2012, 2023 by Dr. Samuel W. Mitcham, Jr.

(Originally published as *Richard Taylor and the Red River Campaign* [Gretna, Louisiana: Pelican Publishing, 2012]).

ALL RIGHTS RESERVED. No part of this publication may be reproduced, distributed, or transmitted in any form or by any means, including photocopying, recording, or other electronic or mechanical methods, or by any information storage and retrieval system without the prior written permission of the publisher, except in the case of very brief quotations embodied in critical reviews and certain other noncommercial uses permitted by copyright law.

Produced in the Republic of South Carolina

SHOTWELL PUBLISHING LLC

Post Office Box 2592

Columbia, So. Carolina 29202

www.ShotwellPublishing.com

Cover Design by Boo Jackson. Images used are Public Domain.

ISBN: 978-1-947660-92-2

REVISED EDITION

10 9 8 7 6 5 4 3 2

Contents

Introduction ix

Chapter I 1
Yankees

Chapter II 39
The Rebels

Chapter III 73
Opening Moves

Chapter IV 107
Taylor Reorganizes

Chapter V 123
Up The River And Through The Woods:
The Battle Of Henderson Hill

Chapter VI 159
The Battle Of Mansfield

Chapter VII 197
The Battle Of Pleasant Hill

Chapter VIII 221
Bouncing Down The River

Chapter IX 233
The Camden Expedition

CHAPTER X 271
MONETT'S FERRY AND THE RETREAT TO ALEXANDRIA

CHAPTER XI 301
OVER THE FALLS

CHAPTER XII 323
ACROSS THE ATCHAFALAYA

CHAPTER XIII 335
EPILOGUE AND POSTSCRIPT:
WHAT HAPPENED TO THE MEN OF THE RED RIVER EXPEDITION

APPENDIX 1 357
ORDER OF BATTLE, THE ARMY OF WESTERN LOUISIANA

APPENDIX 2 361
ORDER OF BATTLE, THE ARMY OF THE GULF APRIL 8, 1864

BIBLIOGRAPHY 369

LIST OF MAPS AND TABLES

1.1	Halleck's Strategy	34
1.2	Grant's Strategy	34
2.1	The Lafourche And Teche Regions	59
3.1	The Red River Campaign: The Union Plan	78
3.2	The Red River Valley	87
3.3	The Simmesport-Fort Derussy Sector	92
5.1	The Alexandria Sector	122
5.2	The Shreveport Sector	139
5.3	The Approaches To Mansfield	142
6.1	The Battle Of Mansfield	170
7.1	The Battle Of Pleasant Hill	203
9.1	The Camden Expedition	236
10.1	Monett's Ferry	279

Table 3.1	Order Of Battle, Walker's Texas Division	91
Table 5.1	The Cavalry Corps, Army Of Western Louisiana	147
Table 9.1	Order Of Battle, Union Vii Corps And The Department Of Arkansas	241
Table 9.2	Order Of Battle, Department Of Arkansas	249
Table 10.1	Confederate Order Of Battle, Monett's Ferry	284

I do not fear an army of lions led by a sheep.

I do fear an army of sheep led by a lion.

—Alexander the Great

Introduction

The United States Army has had many brilliant, glorious, and successful campaigns in its illustrious history. The Red River Campaign of 1864 was not one of them.

Leadership matters. The Confederates were led by Richard Taylor who, more than anyone else in American history, resembled George S. Patton. He was equally brilliant (and probably more so); tougher (Patton slapped people; Taylor hanged them, often without a trial); and was perhaps more profane. Both were loved by their men. The Yankees were led by Nathaniel P. Banks, the former speaker of the U.S. House of Representatives. If you can imagine one army commanded by George Patton and the other directed by Nancy Pelosi, you have a pretty solid grasp of the Red River campaign.

Outnumbered 8,800 to 32,000, but led by a lion, the ragged and ill-equipped Confederate Army of Western Louisiana threw itself at the throat of the Union Army of the Gulf, routed it, surrounded it twice, starved it half to death, and chased it for 200 miles, all the way across Louisiana, while simultaneously inflicting heavy losses on the Union Navy's inland flotilla, which also fled for its life. From the Northern point of view, it is not a pretty tale.

Thanks go to everyone who helped with the completion of this task, especially my long-suffering wife, Donna, who took time away from her own proofreading and editing business to assist in the editing of this manuscript.

Dr. Samuel W. Mitcham, Jr.

August 2023

Chapter I

YANKEES

The Civil War (a/k/a the War for Southern Independence) began on April 12, 1861, when Abraham Lincoln successfully provoked Confederate President Jefferson Davis into firing on Fort Sumter.[1] Initially, both sides expected a brief, glorious war, ending in a swift victory for their respective side. The Northern political leadership did not even remotely grasp the reality of the situation until July 21, 1861, when Confederate Generals G. T. Beauregard, Stonewall Jackson, et al, routed their main army in the 1st Battle of Bull Run (Manassas). The Southern leadership did not wake up until after that.

The Rebel victory at Manassas put New England in a bad position economically. Its main employer was the textile industry and, in 1861, textiles could not be produced without cotton. By the fall of 1861, northern cotton reserves were nearly exhausted, with no hope of renewal, unless a Southern cotton growing region could be seized. As a result, as early as November 1861, Massachusetts Governor John

---

[1] For the run-up to this event, see Samuel W. Mitcham, Jr., *It Wasn't About Slavery* (Washington, D.C.: 2020), pp. 130-153. For the documentary evidence, see Lieutenant Commander Richard Rush and Robert H. Woods, *Official Records of the Union and Confederate Navies in the War of the Rebellion* (Washington, D.C.: 1880-1891), Series 1, Volume I, Part 2, Vol. IV, pp. 90, 107-119, 223-225, 244-251, 380 (hereafter cited as "O.R.N."). All Official Records citations are from Series 1 unless otherwise noted.

A. Andrew was calling for the invasion of Texas.² He was joined by Major General Benjamin Butler, the commander of the Department of New England. From his headquarters in Boston, Butler wrote General George B. McClellan, then the general-in-chief of the Union Army and suggested that 15,000 Federal troops—led by Butler himself—land on the Texas coast at Indianola. He would then drive north and seize San Antonio and the Texas cotton producing region to the northeast. Simultaneously, he would arm supposedly pro-Union German immigrants in the region, who were just waiting for Yankee forces to arrive. They would then rise up, overthrow their Rebel oppressors, and join the Union Army in droves.³ (The overconfidence which led to the disaster at Bull Run had yet to be fully dissipated.) On January 19, 1862, Butler met with Edwin M. Stanton, Lincoln's newly appointed secretary of war, to discuss the project. Butler and Stanton were political allies and close personal friends,⁴ and the secretary gave serious consideration to Butler's idea.

Although not actually abandoned until 1864, the Butler proposal was soon relegated to the back burner by men who actually understood something about military strategy. A Northern military professional, Commodore David D. Porter, presented a detailed operational plan to capture New Orleans to Secretary of the Navy Gideon Welles on November 12, 1861.⁵ The Porter plan was not a half-baked scheme to plunder Texas cotton—rather, it was an idea which might actually do military and economic harm to the Confederacy. Welles approved it

---

2   John A. Andrew (born 1818) was governor of Massachusetts from 1861 to 1866. A fervent abolitionist, he organized legal defense funds for John Brown in 1859 and was instrumental in forming the 54th Massachusetts, a celebrated black regiment, among others. He died in office in 1866 due to a sudden attack of apoplexy while having tea.

3   Robert N. Scott, chief compiler, *The War of the Rebellion: A Complication of the Official Records of the Union and Confederate Armies*, Series 1 (Washington, D.C.: 1880-1901), Volume LIII, p. 507-509 (hereafter cited as "O.R."). All citations are from Series 1 unless otherwise noted.

4   Ludwell H. Johnson, *The Red River Campaign* (Baltimore: 1958), p. 10 (hereafter cited as "Johnson").

5   David D. Porter, "The Opening of the Lower Mississippi," in Robert U. Johnson and Clarence C. Buel, ed.s, *Battles and Leaders of the Civil War* (New York: 1887-1888), Vol. II, pp. 23-25 (hereafter cited as "B & L"); David D. Porter, *Incidents and Anecdotes of the Civil War* (New York: 1885), pp. 63-66 (hereafter cited as "Porter").

Benjamin F. "Beast" Butler after the war, when he was a United States senator.

and delegated the task of executing it to David Farragut, the North's top admiral. When Farragut captured the South's largest city on April 28, 1862,[6] Porter commanded his mortar schooners. Benjamin Butler, now commander of the Department of the Gulf, assumed command of the occupation forces in Louisiana. He headquartered in New Orleans.

The Crescent City was the nation's largest cotton exporting port in 1860, when it shipped out 2,000,000 bales. Those who thought that its capture would solve New England's economic problems were doomed to disappointment, however, because the city itself grew no

---

6   Farragut arrived at New Orleans on April 25 but the city would not surrender until April 28, when Farragut threatened to bombard it if did not capitulate immediately.

cotton, and its hinterland remained mainly in Rebel hands. By the end of 1862, New Orleans had exported only 38,000 bales to the North. Meanwhile, New England lapsed into a severe economic recession.

In 1862, the six New England states had 100,000 looms and 4,745,750 cotton spindles. They needed 700,000 bales of cotton per year to keep them all producing. With Nashville supplying 36,000 bales that summer and New Orleans providing only slightly more, production plummeted. By June 1, 1862, 3,252,000 of the spindles were idle. Another seven percent ceased operation that month. By July 1862, at least 80% of all Northern cotton mills had closed down.[7] Unemployment was rampant.

New England's economic distress had grave political implications for the Lincoln administration. Although many Americans today view Abraham Lincoln as a larger-than-life and an almost God-like genius of the highest order, his contemporaries did not hold the same opinion. He was, in fact, an astute and practical politician who realized that he was a minority president. He was elected in 1860 after having received less than 40% of the popular vote and would have lost the election had the Democratic Party not split and placed two candidates on the ballot. No one in 1862 could envision a scenario in which Lincoln and his Republican Party could lose New England in the 1864 election and retain the White House. For this reason, Lincoln appointed several prominent New England politicians to high military commands—including Democrats. Benjamin Butler, for example, fervently supported Jefferson Davis for president of the United States and voted for him 57 times in the deadlocked Democratic Convention of 1860.[8] The "Great Emancipator" was vitally interested in mitigating

---

7   A. Sellew Roberts, "The Federal Government and Confederate Cotton," *American Historical Review*, Vol. 32 (January 1927), pp. 262-275.

8   Benjamin Franklin Butler (1818-1893) was born in New Hampshire and grew up in modest circumstances in Lowell, Massachusetts. He became an outstanding criminal attorney who was elected to the state legislature as a Democrat in 1853 and to the state senate in 1859. He supported the states' rights candidate, U.S. Vice President and future Confederate Major General John C. Breckinridge against Lincoln in the 1860 election. During the war, he was also called "Spoons" Butler because he stole the silverware from the houses in which he headquartered. See Ezra J. Warner, *Generals in Blue* (Baton Rouge: 1964), pp. 60-61.

the economic suffering in Massachusetts and surrounding states. Stanton, Secretary of State William H. Seward, and Secretary of the Treasury Salmon P. Chase also had a healthy interest in Louisiana and Texas cotton.

Meanwhile, back in New Orleans, Benjamin Butler proved to be an ineffective military governor and a mediocre military commander. His corruption and his infantile behavior toward the citizens of Louisiana (and especially toward the ladies) alienated the very people Lincoln wanted to placate, so that they would voluntarily embrace the Grand Republic and bring Louisiana back into the Union. Lincoln wanted to make Louisiana his Reconstruction showcase state, and he realized that willing subjects would produce more cotton than outraged civilians whose sympathies would naturally lie with the Confederacy. For this reason, "Beast" Butler had to go. Lincoln replaced him with Nathaniel P. Banks.

*

It is not possible to understand the Civil War, and especially the Union side of the war, without having at least some understanding of the political soldier, which Lincoln felt compelled to appoint to high command. Jefferson Davis appointed political soldiers also, but at lower levels than Lincoln, presumably because, as a West Point graduate, a regimental commander and hero in the Mexican War, and former secretary of war, he had a better appreciation of the dangers involved. Lincoln, on the other hand, had served fewer than 90 days' active duty during the Black Hawk War, and all he accomplished was getting demoted from captain to private.[9] Basically, he was a military illiterate who learned "on the job." His healthy common sense sometimes mitigated his dearth of military training or the fact that he lacked innate military skill, but by no means all the time. Certainly he was never the military genius some of his acolytes aver

---

[9] Ironically, the two met during the Black Hawk War, when Lieutenant Davis sore Captain Lincoln's company into Federal service. The meeting was largely perfunctory and made no impression on either man. Davis only made one patrol during this war, when he personally captured Chief Black Hawk and ended the war. Neither Davis nor Lincoln heard a shot fired in anger.

that he was.[10] Unlike Davis, he did not hesitate to appoint neophyte politicians to army and corps-level commands. This significantly increased the Union's casualty lists. For this reason, it is impossible to understand the Red River disaster without knowing something of Nathaniel P. Banks, the arch-typical political soldier.

Nathaniel Prentiss Banks was born on January 30, 1816, in Waltham, Massachusetts, a factory town which grew around the Boston Manufacturing Company, a cotton textile mill. He was the first of eight children of a mill worker. Nathaniel was a healthy, active boy and a born talker. Educated in a one-room schoolhouse, he dropped out against his will at age 14 to go to work as a bobbin boy at the Waltham Mill. His job was to remove bobbins from cotton spindles when they were full of thread and replace them with empty spools. He was paid $2 per week.[11] As a result of this early job, he was nicknamed "the Bobbin Boy" for the rest of his life.

Dissatisfied with his situation, Banks decided to rise above his working class origins. He attended the lectures held by the Rumford Institute (which was owned by the Boston Manufacturing Company) and heard Daniel Webster, Caleb Cushing, and Charles Sumner, among others, speak. He even tried his hand at acting, but this was not considered a Christian profession in Waltham. He also set up a dancing school but was forced to close it when the Boston Manufacturing Company announced that it would fire any of its female employees who attended the facility.

Meanwhile, Banks found his first cause: total abstinence. He became the leading speaker for the temperance movement in Waltham. Banks never drank hard liquor in his life, although he would occasionally have a beer or a glass of wine with a meal. Soon he became a strong speaker for the Democratic Party, and he gained a certain local prominence. He quit the mill and became a newspaper

---

10   For an objective look at the 16th president, his character, his politics and his agenda, see Thomas DiLorenzo, *The Real Lincoln* (New York: 2002), and *Lincoln Unmasked* (New York: 2006), by the same author.

11   James G. Hollandsworth, Jr., *Pretense of Glory: The Life of General Nathaniel P. Banks* (Baton Rouge: 1998), p. 4 (hereafter cited as "Hollandsworth").

Nathaniel P. Banks, circa 1861.

editor but failed in this profession. He also ran for the Massachusetts legislature in 1844 but lost.

About this time, Banks found his mentor: Robert Rantoul, Jr.[12] Smart and enthusiastic, Rantoul backed progressive causes such as pacifism, reform of prisons and insane asylums, temperance, the end of capital punishment, and the abolition of slavery. Banks joined him in his causes and even copied his oratorical style, which allowed Banks to use his booming voice to maximum advantage. Rantoul, who became a U.S. senator, occasionally compromised his principles. Sometimes, he worked for interests he professed to hate, including the Illinois Central Railroad. This lesson was not lost on Banks, who later did the same thing.

On April 11, 1847, after an eight-year engagement, the "Bobbin Boy" married Theodosia Palmer. Very much in love, he remained faithful and happily married for 47 years. They had four children. During the war, Nathaniel Banks had a special pocket sewn into his shirt, where he kept nothing but pictures of his wife and children. He and his wife did have a common flaw, however: both tended to overspend. Mr. and Mrs. Banks were sharp dressers and loved expensive clothes, fine food, high society and glittering parties.

---

12   Robert Rantoul, Jr. (1805-1852) was briefly a U.S. senator in 1851. He became a member of the U.S. House of Representatives on March 4, 1851 and held office until his death on August 7, 1852. He had previously been a United States Attorney and a member of the Massachusetts legislature.

By concentrating his campaign on non-factory workers, Banks was finally elected to the legislature in November 1848. Here he played down his support of workers' rights so as not to offend the moneyed interests. He even backed a liquor dealer who was running for state senator—an early indication of his willingness to place politics above principles. Meanwhile, as the Massachusetts electorate became more and more anti-slavery, Banks drifted toward abolitionism. He was reelected in 1850 and became speaker of the Massachusetts House of Representatives in 1851. To supplement his income, he worked in Washington, D.C., as a lobbyist for the state and as a publicist for the Massachusetts Board of Education.

Meanwhile, Nathaniel Banks educated himself. He had decided early that education was the key to upward mobility and he studied law, history, economics, foreign languages, and political science on this own. Visitors to his home commented that it was full of books. He was a voracious reader and throughout his life, kept a notebook in his pocket, to record data he found interesting or of note.

In 1852, Banks was narrowly elected to the U.S. House of Representatives. Here, he generally avoided controversy and voted with the Pierce administration. (Banks wanted to be all things to all people.) He was reelected in 1854. Shortly after, he switched over to the G.O.P., where there was more opportunity for advancement.

In Congress, the likeable Banks combined "Know Nothing" Americanism with opposition to slavery.[13] This potent combination propelled him to the speakership as a compromise candidate in early 1856, when he was elected on the 133rd ballot. This was considered the first national victory for the Republican Party. Personally charming, he did his best to please everyone and was always civil and courteous. He was praised by Alexander Stephens, the future vice president of the Confederacy, and Howell Cobb, the former speaker and future rebel general, even though he was working to reduce the political power of the agrarian South in favor of the industrial and commercial North by building a transcontinental

---

13   The "Know Nothings" were an anti-immigrant group which briefly grew into a political party. They held beliefs similar to the Whigs.

railroad across the northern states. He did, however, support compromise and moderation on the slavery issue and opposed the radical abolitionists. Even Banks' enemies considered him to be a successful speaker of the U.S. House of Representatives.

In November 1856, James Buchanan was elected president of the United States, and the Democratic Party won a majority of the seats in the House, which cost Banks his speakership. Undeterred, the ambitious Bobbin Boy ran for governor and in November 1857, defeated the incumbent, Henry J. Gardner. One of his first acts was to remove a judge who enforced the Fugitive Slave Law. He also flip-flopped on his previous pro-labor positions and became an advocate of the interests of big business and the large corporations. He was reelected in 1858 and 1859. He ran for the Republican nomination for president in 1860 but was defeated by Abraham Lincoln.

In late 1860, Banks received a lucrative offer from the Illinois Central Railroad. He took the job recently vacated by George B. McClellan and started out making twice as much as he made as governor. He also received a rent-free house. He left office on January 3, 1861, and moved to Chicago. When the Civil War began, however, the president of the railroad (a Republican) gave Banks a full release from his contract.

On May 16, 1861, Banks accepted a commission as a major general of volunteers, despite the fact that he had never served a day in the military in his life. His appointment was purely political. He was outranked only by Winfield Scott, John C. Fremont, and George McClellan. The move, however, did bring a measure of additional popular support to the administration.

Banks' first post was commander of the Department of Maryland. He replaced Benjamin Butler, who had, as usual, mishandled the situation completely. Initially, Banks continued the administration's policy of cooperation and even allowed the citizens of Baltimore to fly the Confederate flag. When he realized that this policy would not work, however, he gradually clamped down and restricted civilian travel in and out of Baltimore, arrested the chief of police, placed the police department under the command of a Union colonel, and incarcerated much of the state legislature. Overall, he dealt with a potentially volatile situation with tact and skill, and prevented Maryland (which was then a Southern state) from seceding. As a result, he was named commander of the Department of the Shenandoah, headquartered in Harpers Ferry.

In early October 1861, Banks met with Lincoln and Stanton at Harpers Ferry. Banks lobbied for a cabinet position, but Lincoln was pleased with his performance in Maryland, unlike the case with Fremont in Missouri or Butler in Virginia. (Fremont issued his own emancipation proclamation, which Lincoln forced him to revoke, and Butler put slaves to work around Fort Monroe.) The president persuaded Banks to stay in the military, to the eventual ruin of the former governor's career.

Banks, who fully realized that military victories would further his presidential aspirations, liked the army and looked impressive in a uniform. He surrounded himself with a bodyguard of Zouaves, who wore red fezzes, white leather leggings, and scarlet trousers. He was not an effective soldier, however, because he could not impose discipline. He lacked a military background or education, and he appointed staff officers who were not only military illiterates but who were also "tactless and arrogant."[14] He could not command the respect of his officers and men, and his orders against looting and soliciting prostitution were ignored. (About that same time, Confederate Brigadier General Richard Taylor, Banks' future opponent in Louisiana, faced a similar problem. Then two enlisted men were disrespectful to one of his officers. Taylor had them court-martialed and shot. He had few problems with discipline after that, but the Massachusetts politician was not the type of man to take this kind of action.)

General Banks' first experience in combat was commanding an army in the Shenandoah Valley against Stonewall Jackson, who tore him limb from limb. The Rebels captured so many supplies and

---

14 Willoughby M. Babcock, *Selections from the Letters and Diaries of Brevet-Brigadier General Willoughby M. Babcock of the Seventy-Fifth New York Volunteers* (Albany, New York: 1922), p. 74.

provisions that they called him "Commissary Banks," a nickname that crossed the lines. Banks' staff officers urged him to blame the War Department and to criticize the administration for his defeat, but this Banks refused to do. He took his beating like a man, earning him a measure of respect in Washington. Secretary Stanton wrote: "On this occasion as at other times General Banks has obeyed the orders from the War Department without one selfish complaint and was the only General of his rank of whom it could be said."[15] On the negative side, Banks felt he did well to escape with his army and his trains. More seriously, he was not a man to learn from his mistakes.

On the morning of August 9, 1862, near Cedar Mountain, Virginia, Dr. Hunter McGuire, Jackson's surgeon, asked the general if he expected a battle that day. Stonewall smiled and said: "Banks is in our front and he is generally willing to fight. And he generally gets whipped."[16] Sure enough, Banks fought. He committed his units piecemeal instead of all at once and was again chewed up by the Rebels. Banks lost 2,400 men (500 of them killed)—1/3rd of his command. Jackson lost about half as many. That night, Banks and his chief, General John Pope, were nearly captured by Southern cavalry. Banks himself was painfully injured when a Southerner shot and killed his aide. The lieutenant was on his horse, which reared, and caught the dismounted general in the chin with its hoof.

That evening, Jackson commented to Jeb Stuart, the commander of Lee's cavalry, that Banks had fought well. Stuart replied that Jackson would be ungrateful indeed if he complained about Banks, "for he has been the best commissary and quartermaster you have ever had."[17]

Despite his defeats, Banks was still popular in the North because he was popular with the Northern newspapers. (Media "spin" was certainly prevalent in the 19th Century, even though the term would not be invented for another century.) On November 9, 1862, Lincoln

---

15 Hollandsworth, p. 69.

16 *Ibid*, pp. 74-75.

17 Kyd Douglas, *I Rode With Stonewall* (Chapel Hill, North Carolina: 1940; reprint ed., Chapel Hill, 1968), p. 50.

ordered him to replace Butler as commander of the Department of the Gulf. Banks left New York for New Orleans on December 4, traveling with a fleet of 50 transports. He was not prepared for what he found there because the corruption was incredible. "Everybody connected with the government has been employed in stealing other people's property," he wrote to his wife.[18]

Historians consider the 1870s one of the most corrupt eras in the history of American politics. This phenomenon did not develop overnight. There was plenty of corruption in the 1860s as well, and much of it occurred in wartime New Orleans, which has never been known for its pristine politics. War brings out the best in some people and the worst in others, and the war drove the price of cotton from $.06 per pound to $1.09 per pound. Quick and large fortunes could be made buying and selling "White Gold," and as the port nearest the cottonfields, New Orleans naturally attracted the worst kind of speculator. The fact that these speculators would have to deal with Confederates or slave owners (whom many of them professed to despise) did not bother them particularly. One of these speculators was Andrew Butler, the brother of the general, who offered General Banks a $100,000 bribe. Banks, who was not personally corrupt at this stage of his career, turned down the money, but there were others who were more than willing to accept. Andrew Butler would die a rich man.

Southerners, of course, took bribes also, but there seems to have been fewer of them. Banks tried to bribe Rebel officers into not burning cotton and/or handing it over to Union speculators for a handsome profit. Naturally, exact figures are lacking, but this effort did not produce as much in the way of results as Banks hoped. It was not that certain Southerners were more morally upright or were averse to making a dollar on the sly, as long as it was in gold or Greenbacks and not worthless Confederate script. It was just that the new Rebel commander in Louisiana was General Taylor, and he ordered his officers to burn the cotton, rather than sell it for personal profit or let it fall into Yankee hands. Unlike Banks, Richard Taylor

---

18 Hollandsworth, p. 89.

was respected. More to the point, Taylor was feared. Nathaniel Banks spoke coldly to people who disobeyed his orders. Dick Taylor had them hanged or shot, which was a much more effective deterrent. Even so, some were willing to risk it.

Meanwhile, the Confederate military government was doing exactly what it ordered its citizens not to do: it was trading with the enemy.

J. H. McKee and Banks had an understanding. McKee's cousin, Major A. W. McKee, held an important position in the Cotton Bureau of the Confederates' Trans-Mississippi Department, of which Taylor's Army of Western Louisiana was a part. (Because he was on the staff of General Edmund Kirby Smith, Taylor's superior, McKee was beyond Taylor's reach.) McKee undertook to see that Confederate cotton was not burned as the Federals approached. For this service, he received $.18 per pound. The money was deposited in a New Orleans bank, in a joint account with McKee and Colonel Samuel B. Holabird, chief quartermaster of Banks' Department of the Gulf.[19]

Another speculator was Gardner Banks, the Bobbin Boy's brother. He resigned his commission in the 16th Massachusetts due to a bad knee and showed up in New Orleans, seeking favors. He ended up making huge profits, mainly in sutlers' goods. One of General Taylor's brothers-in-law was also reportedly a cotton speculator.[20] He did not, however, receive any support or encouragement from Taylor.

One of the most prominent speculators was George S. Denison, a young relative of Secretary of the Treasury Salmon P. Chase. He was a high-ranking treasury official in New Orleans and took bribes and sold permits for other speculators to deal with the Rebels.

---

19 Johnson, pp. 56-57.
20 J. Michael Parrish, *Richard Taylor: Soldier Prince of Dixie* (Chapel Hill, North Carolina: 1992), p. 326 (hereafter cited as "Parrish").

At this time, Banks did not take monetary bribes personally, as far as we know. "His thirst is not for money, but for power," Major Pellet wrote.[21] Even so, he was certainly willing to associate with dubious characters. When he arrived to assume command in New Orleans, several cotton speculators were on the ship with him. He allowed A. S. Mansfield, a representative of the Boston financial power brokers, and Jacob Barker of the New Orleans Bank of Commerce, to carry $45,000 in gold beyond Union lines to deal with Confederate officials. In his isolated department, Confederate General Edmund Kirby Smith was perfectly willing to let his agents sell cotton to the Yankees for gold. He then sent other agents to Europe via Mexico, where they bought all manners of military equipment, hardware, ammunition, shoes, food, medicine, liquor, and other supplies and had them shipped back home—all under the protection of the British or Mexican flags.

The United States War Department issued General Order 88 on March 31, 1863, instructing military commanders to turn over all captured and abandoned Confederate property (including cotton) to treasury agents, except that required by the army. Banks ignored the order. He was selling the property to help defray the expenses of his department—and continued to do so.[22]

Although Banks may not have pocketed tainted money, he did live large while in New Orleans. He brought his wife to town and held many lavish parties. One costume ball alone cost more than a $1,000. Her confectioner's bill for three months was $637. The general's pay at this time was less than $600 a month.

A thriving trade certainly existed between the cotton speculators, the Confederates, and the Quartermaster of the Department of the Gulf. The chief quartermaster, Colonel Holabird was found intoxicated and partially dressed in the residence of one of his staff officers, who kept six to eight mulatto girls. These officers could

---

21 Elias P. Pellet, *History of the 114th Regiment, New York State Volunteers* (Norwich, New York: 1866), p. 239 (hereafter cited as "Pellet").

22 Johnson, p. 55.

not have afforded such luxuries on their salaries. They (and others) were bribed into certifying cotton speculators and allowing them to operate freely, both inside and beyond Union lines. Exactly how much General Banks knew about this trade is subject to conjecture, but he certainly had to be aware of it. He even sent Federal officers in civilian clothes behind Rebel lines to buy cotton. Later, several Texans captured in the Battle of Pleasant Hill recognized some of these "cotton buyers" as they were being sent to the Union rear: they were officers on Banks' staff.[23]

Even President Lincoln, who was under tremendous pressure, sometimes granted special trading permits to certain people. On other occasions, he steadfastly refused to do so. He certified William Butler, an old friend from his Springfield days, and several others with the authority to buy cotton. He ordered Banks and Admiral David D. Porter, the senior naval officer in the department, to assist them in any way necessary. Lincoln was also duped at least once. John A. Stevenson, a director of the Louisiana State Bank, bought 19,000 bales of cotton and shipped them to Europe via New Orleans. His permit to do this was personally signed by Abraham Lincoln. Stevenson, however, was a loyal Confederate and was apparently a captain in the Confederate Secret Service. Little documentation concerning this shady deal is extant, so some of the details are missing, but we do know that Stevenson's operation had the full approval of General Kirby Smith, who was aware of everything. The cotton was provided by Colonel W. A. Broadwell, the chief of the Cotton Bureau of the Trans-Mississippi Department (i.e., by the Confederate government), and Jefferson Davis was fully briefed on what was transpiring. Davis, in fact, knew more about the deal than did Lincoln. The funds from the sale were reportedly transferred from the bank to Stevenson's personal account in Europe, and he transferred them to a Confederate treasury account. Apparently, Stevenson did not keep any money for himself and did not make a dime off the transaction.[24]

*

---

23 John Q. Anderson, *A Texas Surgeon in the Confederate States Army* (Tuscaloosa, Alabama: 1957), p. 92 (hereafter cited as "Anderson"); p. 92; J. P. Blessington, *The Campaigns of Walker's Texas Division* (New York: 1875), p. 162 (hereafter cited as "Blessington").

24 Johnson, pp. 68-69.

Whatever else he may have bungled, Benjamin Butler realized that the Union was failing to utilize a major potential source of manpower: the African-American. He created a stir within Federal ranks when he allowed them to enlist in already existing units, so to avoid controversy he began forming all black units on a large scale.[25] As soon as he arrived, Banks cancelled this policy, on the grounds that many Union soldiers felt it degraded the uniform to have black troops in the army. Apparently this was the general's view as well.[26] Shortly after, however, Lincoln announced that he was in favor of recruiting Negroes. Banks, ever the political chameleon, promptly reserved himself and resumed recruiting former slaves. He did, however, discontinue Butler's policy of commissioning black officers. He wrote Lincoln and asserted that they were simply "unsuited" to be officers. He set up a Board of Examiners to investigate the African Americans that Butler had commissioned to determine if they were qualified and could keep their commissions. The board was stacked; very few black officers were allowed to retain their ranks.

Before he departed, Butler begun organizing three United States Colored Troops (U.S.C.T) regiments. Banks allowed the process to continue and indeed organized a fourth, but he did nothing to improve the quality of officers, which was very poor. Mediocre Union officers who found their way to promotion in white units blocked by their own poor performance often volunteered for duty in "Colored" regiments because this was the only avenue of advancement left to them. Also, some were transferred to U.S.C.T. units against their will. Commanders of white regiments found it convenient to off-load their troublemakers and other problem officers on black regiments. The excellent black sergeants and corporals partially compensated

---

25 Senator James Lane created an African-American regiment in his state over Lincoln's objections, and General David Hunter formed an all African-American unit, the 1st South Carolina Volunteers.

26 Hollandsworth, p. 150. This view was by no means universally held within the Union Army. Sergeant Onley Andrus of Illinois, for example, wrote that "the n***ers had as good a right to be shot as anybody." Onley Andrus, *The Civil War Letters of Sergeant Onley Andrus*, Fred Albert Sharmon, ed. (Urbana, Illinois: 1947), pp. 115-116, 128).

for this huge deficiency, but it was usually not enough. Although there were some exceptions, black formations were generally worse led than any other units in the entire Civil War.

A good example of the incompetent white officer was Lieutenant Colonel Augustus W. Benedict. He was "a tactless and unstable man," noted for his foul language. He was transferred to the 4th Regiment, Corps d'Afrique, in Baton Rouge, where his sadistic tendencies came to the fore, and he vented his spleen on what he thought were helpless soldiers. In August 1863, two black soldiers were caught stealing corn. Benedict had them staked to the ground and covered with molasses to attract ants. When other Union soldiers objected to his torture, Benedict refused to release them, stating that he did not care if they died. They were not released for two days. A brutal tyrant, Benedict frequently struck African-American soldiers in the face with his fists and kicked them for minor infractions, such as not having their brass polished properly or failing to shine their boots.[27]

Benedict continued to abuse and humiliate black soldiers until December 9, 1863. (By this time, the 4th had been transferred from Baton Rouge to Fort Jackson, on the Mississippi River, south of New Orleans.) That day, two black soldiers appeared for a formation without their coats. Colonel Benedict assembled the unit and had the men beaten 15 to 20 times with a teamster's bullwhip. Then he had them thrown in the guardhouse. The result was a riot and a mutiny. The African Americans maintained a silent fury until they were dismissed. Shortly after, all hell broke loose. More than 250 blacks (i.e., more than half of the understrength regiment) joined the mutiny. Colonel James R. Drew, the regimental commander, tried to restore order but without success. The mutineers stormed the stockade and released all the prisoners. They also seized the regimental armory, issued themselves weapons, fired guns into the air, and started looking for Benedict. The colonel fled to a nearby steamboat and barely escaped with his life. Fortunately for him, the mutineers stormed the wrong steamer, yelling: "Kill the son of a

---

27   John D. Winters, *Louisiana in the Civil War* (Baton Rouge: 1963), p. 312 (hereafter cited as "Winters").

bitch!" Gradually, however, it dawned on the leaders that Benedict had escaped. With the cause of the riot gone, order was restored by the company grade white officers, who persuaded the African-Americans to return to their barracks.[28]

Banks was embarrassed by the riot, ordered an investigation, and summoned Benedict to New Orleans. The lieutenant colonel offered to resign, but Banks court-martialed himself instead. He was found guilty and dishonorably discharged from the service. Thirteen of the African Americans were also court-martialed. Four were acquitted, two were sentenced to death by firing squad, six were sentenced to hard labor, and one got 30 days in the guardhouse. Banks refused to confirm the death sentences and ordered the release of the man in the guardhouse.[29]

In the spring of 1863, Lincoln ordered Brigadier General Daniel Ullmann to recruit a U.S.C.T. brigade in the Department of the Gulf. Another political general, Ullmann was a Know Nothing candidate for governor of New York in 1854. Later, he joined the Republican Party and supported Abraham Lincoln for president. When the war broke out, he helped recruit the 78th New York (Highlander) Regiment and, as its colonel, led it in Virginia in 1862, where it formed part of Nathaniel Banks' ill-fated army. The two men quickly formed a mutual dislike for each other, at least in part because Banks was a teetotaler and Ullmann was a drunkard. Partially due to Banks' mismanagement, Ullmann was wounded and captured at Cedar Mountain. This did nothing to improve the relationship between the two men. Lincoln required Banks to provide Ullmann with 200 officers from his department further exacerbated the bad situation. Although Banks was surprised and very pleased by his black regiments' fine performance during the Siege of Port Hudson in June and July 1863, he nevertheless did all he could to undermine Ullmann. The former Highlander raised five regiments, mainly by

---

28   Winters, p. 313; O.R., Vol. XXVI, Part 1, pp. 456-457.

29   O.R., Vol. XXVI, Part 1, pp. 457-459. For the details of the Benedict court-martial, including testimony and individual verdicts, see O.R., XXVI, Part 1, pp. 459-479. Also see Hollandsworth, pp. 146-147.

impressing slaves or former slaves against their will, but Banks and his staff saw to it that they were poorly supplied and not used in major operations.

Not to be outdone by Ullmann, in September 1863, Banks ordered that all able-bodied Negro males between 20 and 30 years of age be drafted into the Corps d'Afrique. He also ordered that African American regiments be 500 men in size (i.e., smaller than the white regiments, which theoretically had 1,000 men.)[30] By October 1863, there were 20 regiments in the Corps.

African-American units still did not measure up to the standards of other Northern units because of their poor equipment and poorer officers. "The lack of discipline found among some of the Negro troops often could be blamed on their inefficient, lazy, or corrupt officers," historian John D. Winters wrote.[31] Brigadier General George L. Andrews, the commandant of Port Hudson and a regular army officer, was one of many Union officers who realized that the quality of officers in black regiments needed to be vastly improved. Unlike some of the other generals, however, Andrews actually did something about it. He set up a school for white officers assigned to the Corps d'Afrique and personally supervised the instruction. The entire Union effort to train and employ African American regiments and their officers, however, suffered from a total lack of uniformity.[32]

*

---

30 O.R., Vol. XXVI, Part 1, pp. 736-737.

31 Winters, p. 312.

32 George L. Andrews (1828-1899) was born in Bridgewater, Massachusetts, and graduated at the head of his West Point class in 1851. He left the service in 1855 to pursue a career in civil engineering but rejoined the army in 1861 as a lieutenant colonel in the 2nd Massachusetts. He became the regiment's colonel in June 1862 and was given command of a brigade that fall. Promoted to brigadier general on November 10, he served under Banks at Cedar Mountain and also fought at Sharpsburg (Antietam). Banks took him to Louisiana, and Andrews was Banks' chief of staff during the Siege of Port Hudson (1863). He later commanded the Baton Rouge District until early 1865, when he took part in the offensive against Mobile. After the war, he was a U.S. marshal in Massachusetts and a professor of French at West Point. He retired in 1892 and moved to Brookline, Massachusetts, where he died. He is buried in Arlington National Cemetery. Warner, *Generals in Blue*, p. 9.

During the Civil War, 191,000 African-Americans served in the Union Army. By the end, 12% of the 1,000,000 men in the United States Army were African-American. Banks' Department of the Gulf (which included Ullmann) raised 28 regiments by September 1864—more than any other department. In all, the United States Colored Troops (U.S.C.T.) totaled 145 infantry regiments, 12 regiments of heavy artillery, 10 batteries of light artillery, and seven regiments of cavalry. Union African-Americans fought in 449 battles during the Civil War, including 39 major engagements and 68,178 died from wounds, exposure or disease—more than 37% of the total.[33]

*

It will probably come as a surprise to many, and some will consider it "politically incorrect" to say so, but there was another side to this coin: tens of thousands of African-Americans fought for the Confederacy as well. Private James G. Bates of the 13th Iowa Volunteers was certainly surprised when a black Confederate sniper shot some of his comrades. He wrote to his father: "I can assure you of a certainty, that the rebels have negro soldiers in their army. One of their best sharp shooters, and the boldest of them all here is a negro ... . You can see him plain enough with the naked eye."[34] In fact, the first Union officer killed in action in the Civil War was Major Theodore Winthrop, the son of a prominent New England abolitionist family. He was shot down in the Battle of Big Bethel by a black Confederate sniper.[35]

The Yankees were warned. Frederick Douglass, a former slave, told Abraham Lincoln to his face that, unless he guaranteed the slaves freedom, "they would take up arms for the rebels." The president—for the moment—did not listen. As a result, Douglass wrote in

---

33 Ronnie A. Nichols, "The Changing Role of Blacks in the Civil War" in Mark K. Christ, ed., *"All Cut to Pieces and Gone to Hell": The Civil War, Race Relations, and the Battle of Poison Spring* (Little Rock: 2003), pp. 71-72 (hereafter cited as "Nichols").

34 www.svc-kirby.smith.org/Black%20Confederate.htm. Accessed 2012.

35 Frank Moore, *The Civil War in Song and Story* (New York: 1865), p. 481. Also see Richard Rollins, "Black Southerners in Gray," in Richard Rollins, ed., *Black Southerners in Gray: Essays on Afro-Americans in Confederate Armies* (Redondo Beach, California: 1994), p. 16 (hereafter cited as "Rollins").

September 1861: "There are at the present moment, many colored men in the Confederate Army doing duty not as cooks, servants and laborers, but as real soldiers, having muskets on their shoulders and bullets in their pockets ready to shoot down loyal troops and do all that soldiers may do to destroy the Federal government."[36]

Horace Greeley essentially agreed in 1863 when he wrote: "For more than two years, Negroes have been extensively employed in belligerent operations by the Confederacy. They have been embodied and drilled as rebel soldiers and had paraded with white troops at a time when this would not have been tolerated in the armies of the Union."[37]

In September 1862, Robert E. Lee ordered a staff officer to determine for him how many armed slaves were serving in the ranks of the Army of Northern Virginia. There were more than 3,000 under arms, carrying "rifles, muskets, sabers, Bowie knives, dirks" and all sorts of other weapons.[38] This report was delivered shortly after the Battle of Antietam. Three thousand men would equal more than seven percent of his army. Lee later commented that "When you eliminate the black Confederate soldier, you eliminate the history of the South."[39]

Other generals would have agreed with Lee. "There is no better soldier anywhere in the world than the black Confederate soldier." These words were uttered by Nathan Bedford Forrest. He was a slave trader before the war, a Confederate lieutenant general during the war, and the head of the Ku Klux Klan after the war. He also said of his black soldiers: "These boys stayed with me ... and better Confederates never lived."[40]

---

36 Frederick Douglass, *Douglass' Monthly*, Vol. IV (September 1861), p. 516.
37 www.jewishworldreview.com/; www.forrestescort.org/blacks.htm. Accessed 2012.
38 Thomas C. Mendes, "Blacks, Jews Fight on the Side of the Sout," Washington *Times*, June 15,2002.
39 See Richard Rollins, ed., *Black Southerners in Gray: Essays on Afro-Americans in Confederate Armies* (Murfreesboro, Tennessee: 1994).
40 "Papers," Old City Courthouse Museum, Vicksburg, Mississippi.

Richard Taylor would have agreed. He recalled the leader of several black Southerners telling him: "Give us guns and we'll fight for you, too. We would rather fight for our own white folks than for strangers." Esteemed historian Robert Selph Henry wrote: "That large numbers of slaves would have fought with their masters, if given the chance, cannot be doubted."[41] Even today, there is a significant black membership in the Sons of Confederate Veterans.

The Rebels were enrolling African-Americans in their ranks from Day One, despite the edict from their government, forbidding the recruitment of Negroes into the Confederate Army, unless they were musicians. The company commanders ignored this regulation. (Being Confederates, they tended to ignore a great many regulations anyway.) Typically, the potential African American recruit was asked only one question. "Will you fight?" If the answer was "Yes, sir," he immediately received his first order: "Fall in!" The graycoats were using blacks in combat more than a year before Brigadier General David Hunter in South Carolina, Senator James H. Lane of Kansas, and General Butler pioneered their use on the other side.[42] One of history's ironies is that the Civil War was fought by an integrated army and a segregated army. The Confederate Army was integrated. The Union Army was largely segregated.

One man who was acutely aware that the Southerners had stolen a march on the North in using African-Americans as combat troops was Henry Halleck, the general-in-chief of the Union Army. On March 31, 1863, he called upon Ulysses S. Grant to recruit African-Americans when he wrote: "Again, it is the policy of the Government to use the Negroes of the South, as far as practicable, as a military force, for the defense of forts, depots, & etc... . In the hands of the

---

41 Robert S. Henry, *The Story of the Confederacy* (New York: 1931; reprint ed., Old Saybrook, Connecticut: 1999), p. 440 (hereafter cited as "Henry").

42 General Hunter organized the 1st South Carolina Volunteers—the first black regiment—on May 9, 1862. Senator Lane, the Union recruiting commissioner in Kansas, organized the 1st Kansas Colored Volunteer Infantry Regiment in August 1862, over the objections of President Lincoln. Butler issued the first call for African-American volunteers in Louisiana on August 22, 1862. Jefferson Davis condemned him as a felon deserving of capital punishment for this and other acts.

A squad of Confederate infantry. Notice the 3rd man from the left. He seems to be the only one who knows how to wear a uniform.

enemy, they (Negroes) are used with much effect against us; in our hands, we must try to use them with the best possible effect against the rebels."[43]

So how many African-Americans fought for the South? Confederate records are, as usual, too inadequate to give us precise numbers. Thanks to the blockade, the South had no paper, and by the end of the war, its people were writing letters on the back of wallpaper. Older letters were also reused. The new sentences were written between the lines of older letters. By 1864, most military units did not have written rosters. In addition, many Confederate records were destroyed by Appomattox Day. Estimates of the number of African American combat soldiers vary from 65,000 to 100,000,

---

43   Ronnie A. Nichols, "The Changing Role of Blacks in the Civil War" in Christ, *"All Cut to Pieces and Gone to Hell,"* p. 69; Joseph T. Glatthaar, *Forged in Battle: The Civil War Alliance of Black Soldiers and White Officers* (New York: 1990), p. 29.

Members of Nathan Bedford Forrest's Escort Company at a 1901 Reunion. Forrest used his Escort Company in the most dangerous situations. Private George Dance, an African-American, is in the center of the second row. (Photo courtesy Danyon McCarroll).

with 80,000 to 96,000 being the best estimates, in my view, based on the report to General Lee. Ed Kennedy, a historian, a graduate of Command and General Staff College and a retired colonel, seems to agree. He estimated that 7% to 8% of the Confederate forces were

African-American.[44] This estimate coincides with my own estimates. Incidentally, the black Rebels were much better led than their Union counterparts because they had the same officers as the white Rebels.

There were a great many other blacks who served the Southern Army in non-combatant roles as mule skinners, cooks, hospital orderlies, and the like. Many of these deserted or went over to the Union when they got the chance. African-American combat soldiers, on the other hand, tended to stay with their units at least as well as their white counterparts.

Why, the question must be asked, did they fight for the South? Some of these Confederate slaves substituted for their owners and would receive freedom if they survived the war. Others were free men fighting for their homes and families. Southern blacks were Southerners too, and slave cabins were burned by the Yankees, just like the plantation houses (see Chapters V and following). The number of African-Americans in Taylor's army may have exceeded 8%. As early as the spring of 1861, an entire black militia regiment formed in New Orleans and volunteered to serve the Confederate State of Louisiana, and Governor Thomas O. Moore accepted them.

By 1864, Banks' recruiters closed the gap, and the number of African-Americans serving in the Army of the Gulf outnumbered the number of African-Americans fighting for the South. Banks, however, did not make very good use of his black regiments. Their main tasks were to guard the wagon trains and rear area posts. To the north, however, Major General Frederick Steele, a professional soldier, used his "Colored" soldiers as combat troops and with some excellent results, as we shall see (Chapter VII).

*

---

44 http://www.scvcamp469.nft.com/theblackconfederatesoldier.htm. Also see J. H. Segars and Charles K. Barrow, *Black Southerners in Confederate Armies* (Gretna, Louisiana: 2001), p. 203ff.

Although theoretically a military commander, there was a definite political component in Banks' job, and he was much more comfortable working in that area than in the military sphere. Banks, in fact, sometimes let political considerations delay and even undermine military operations. To a lesser degree, so did Abraham Lincoln.

In December 1862, Lincoln asked the military governor of Louisiana, Brigadier General George F. Shepley, to hold elections in the two congressional districts behind Northern lines.[45] The turnout was gratifyingly high, and Michael Hahn and Benjamin F. Flanders were elected to Congress.[46] Lincoln, meanwhile, decided to make Louisiana the first Southern state to be reconstructed.

Banks agreed with Lincoln on this matter and tried to play poor whites against planters in occupied Louisiana. His attempts to create and then benefit from class warfare failed, however, because both classes united against the Northern invader. The Yankees and their sympathizers were far from united themselves. With Hahn and Flanders gone to Washington, leadership of the Louisiana Republicans devolved on Thomas Jefferson Durant, a lawyer and a Philadelphia native. Durant had radical ideas for 1863. He favored

---

45   George F. Shepley (1819-1878) was the son of a U.S. senator and chief justice of the Supreme Court. He graduated from Dartmouth at age 18 and was a highly successful lawyer and district attorney. He was commissioned colonel of the 12th Maine Infantry Regiment in 1861 and accompanied his close personal friend, Benjamin Butler, to Louisiana in 1862. He became Butler's right-hand man and was promoted to brigadier general in July 1862. In the spring of 1864, he was transferred to Virginia and was chief of staff of the XXV Corps at the end of the war. Briefly military governor of Richmond, he was appointed U.S. Circuit Court judge for Maine in 1869. He reportedly died of Asiatic cholera.

46   George Michael Decker Hahn (1830-1886) was born in Klingenmuenster, Palatinate (now Rhineland-Palatinate), Germany. His widowed mother immigrated to the United States and settled in New Orleans in 1840. He attended the University of Louisiana (now Tulane), received a law degree, and became director of the New Orleans public schools while still in his twenties. Originally a Douglas Democrat, Hahn opposed succession and became a moderate Republican. He was a Congressman for four months and served as governor from March 4, 1864 to March 4, 1865. He was said to be the first ethnic Jewish governor in the United States, although he had converted to Episcopalianism by 1864. He was elected to the U.S. Senate in 1865 but was denied his seat by the Radical Republicans. Post-war, he was a member of Congress from 1885 to 1886. He was shot and seriously wounded in a New Orleans race riot in 1866. Hahn also served several terms in the Louisiana legislature in the 1870s. Unlike many of the Republican officeholders in the South during Reconstruction, Hahn was admired for his integrity.

universal suffrage—even to the point of allowing African Americans and women to vote. He soon came into conflict with Banks, who feared that Durant's ideas would scuttle his efforts to set up a Free State of Louisiana.

On December 9, 1863, Abraham Lincoln instituted the 10% rule. He (and the Federal government) would recognize the legitimacy of any Free State government in which the number of people taking the oath of loyalty exceeded 10% of the number of people who voted in the 1860 election. On January 11, 1864, Banks ordered a gubernatorial election. Only men who signed the oath of loyalty would be allowed to vote. Election day was set for February 22.

There were three main candidates for governor: Flanders (the radical); Hahn (the moderate) and J. Q. A. Fellows (the conservative). Hahn, who was Banks' man, attacked Flanders' views on black suffrage and hammered on the fact that Flanders considered blacks equal to whites. Eleven thousand people cast ballots—including Union soldiers, who were allowed to vote by General Banks. By thus stuffing the ballot boxes, Banks was able to double Lincoln's 10% requirement and made himself look good. With the election over, Banks was able to abolish General Shepley's position and transferred Butler's lieutenant to Virginia. Hahn, meanwhile, joined a group of New England financiers and committed himself to backing the Bobbin Boy for president of the United States in 1864, so Banks won all the way around.

Sometimes Nathaniel P. Banks' skills as a political operator can only be marveled at.

*

Banks' department extended from Pensacola to Baton Rouge, and his area of responsibility extended from Florida to Brownsville, Texas, on the Mexican border. In late 1862, it controlled 36,000 soldiers, 22,000 of whom were in New Orleans. The Confederate Department of Louisiana had only 4,000 men. Banks organized his men into an infantry corps (the XIX) and four infantry divisions, numbered 1st through 4th, and commanded by Major General Christopher C. Augur;

Brigadier General Thomas W. Sherman; Brigadier General William H. Emory; and Brigadier General Cuvier Glover, respectively. In August 1863, Banks was reinforced with Major General Cadwalader C. Washburn's XIII Corps from Vicksburg.[47] When it arrived in New Orleans, Banks gave up command of the XIX, which was taken over by Major General William B. Franklin. Banks (now commander of the Army of the Gulf) had more than 50,000 men. There were only 21,000 Confederate soldiers west of the Mississippi, and they were scattered over thousands of square miles in Texas, Louisiana, Arkansas, and Indian Territory.

Meanwhile, Butler's plan to invade Texas never really died. The New England textile and financial interests were constantly lobbying for it, and so was the State Department, especially Secretary Seward and Charles Francis Adams, who wanted to disrupt the Confederate trade with Europe via Mexico.[48]

On July 29, 1863, Lincoln wrote to Secretary of War Stanton and asked if they should not renew the effort to invade Texas. Such a move might forestall French intervention in Mexico, Lincoln thought, and also silence the lobby at home.[49] As a result, on July 31 and August 6, 1863, General Henry W. Halleck, the general-in-chief of the Union Army, ordered Banks to invade Texas—even though Halleck did not believe in the operation himself.

"Old Brains" Halleck was born in Westernville, New York, on January 16, 1815, the son of a farmer. He hated farming, however, so he ran away from home and was adopted by his maternal grandfather,

---

47 Washburn replaced Major General John A. McClernand (1812-1890) as commander of the XIII Corps. A political general, McClernand was a Democratic congressman for many years, but his highest military rank was that of private, which he held for three months during the Black Hawk War. Lincoln, however, considered him necessary to help keep the southern Illinois Democrats loyal to the Union cause and made him a major general. Inept and bombastic, Grant relieved him and sent him home in 1863, but he used his political influence to secure reinstatement as commander of the XIII Corps later that year. It was McClernand who commanded Banks' forces on the Texas coast in 1864.

48 O.R., Vol XXVI, Part 1, pp. 656-657.

49 O.R., Vol.XXVI, Part 1, p. 659; Johnson, p. 35.

Henry Wager Halleck, general-in-chief of the U.S. Army, July 23, 1862 to March 9, 1864.

who successively sent him to the Hudson Academy, Union College, and West Point. He graduated third in his class in 1839. He subsequently won a reputation as an outstanding engineer, writer, and military thinker. He studied law in his spare time. Highly gifted intellectually, Halleck participated in the Mexican War and played a major role in writing the California constitution. He left the army in 1854, joined a prestigious California law firm, and was even offered a seat in the United States Senate but declined. He made a fortune as a lawyer and publisher. In 1861, on the recommendation of Winfield Scott, Lincoln appointed Halleck to the rank of major general in the regular army. He was sent to St. Louis, where he commanded the Department of the Mississippi.

Early in the war, Halleck looked good, thanks to the successes of his subordinates. Grant captured Forts Henry and Donelson and repulsed the Rebels at Shiloh; Samuel R. Curtis secured Missouri for the Union by defeating the Confederates at Pea Ridge; and John Pope captured Island No. 10 in the Mississippi River. As a result, Halleck's territory expanded. When he attempted to command an army in the field, however, Halleck's luster dulled considerably. His advance on Corinth, Mississippi, was terribly slow, and the Confederate commander, Pierre G. T. Beauregard, evacuated the town on his own schedule and with few losses, despite being outnumbered more than 2 to 1. Lincoln nevertheless recalled Halleck to Washington as general-in-chief of Union forces.

Although he was a good administrator, Halleck was a poor general-in-chief because he bent with the political winds and did not like to make decisions. He shifted responsibility at every opportunity and was difficult to pin down on any issue. Gideon Welles wrote in his diary that Halleck "is heavy headed; wants sagacity, readiness, courage, and heart."[50] On July 16, 1863, he complained that Halleck "originates nothing, anticipates nothing ... takes no responsibility, plans nothing, suggests nothing, is good for nothing."[51] Clearly over his head in his position, Halleck wanted to carry out Lincoln's orders to invade Texas to the letter—but not to the spirit. He wanted Banks to launch a token invasion of the state, but he wanted his main effort in 1864 to be an offensive up the Red River; furthermore, he wanted it to appear that all this was Banks' idea. He, Halleck, could always take the credit later, if things worked out. Typically, Halleck's orders to Banks did not include any specific plans. Not even objectives were given.[52]

Banks believed that the best way to invade Texas was via the Sabine Pass at the mouth of the Sabine River. From here, he could establish a base, take Houston, and move into the hill country, where German immigrants would join him. On August 31, he ordered General Franklin to load a brigade from the 1st Division, XIX Corps (6,000 men), aboard 16 transports to take the pass. The spearhead consisted of four gunboats. Neither the Union army nor the navy wasted any time in planning the operation.

The Battle of the Sabine Pass was fought on September 8, 1863. The defenders consisted of 46 Confederates from the Jeff Davis Guards (Company F, 1st Texas Heavy Artillery Regiment), commanded by Lieutenant Richard W. "Dick" Dowling, a red-headed Irish tavern owner. He had six smoothbore (i.e., obsolete) guns. Most of his men were Irish immigrants from Houston and Galveston. But

---

50 Gideon Welles, *Diary of Gideon Welles* (Boston: 1911), Vol. I, p. 122 (entry of January 1, 1863) (hereafter referred to as "Welles").

51 Welles, Vol. I, p. 373 (entry of July 16, 1863).

52 Johnson, p. 36; "Red River Expedition: Report of the Joint Committee on the Conduct of the War," 38th Congress, 2nd Session, Vol. II, p. 5.

Major Dick Dowling, January 2, 1865.

they had two major advantages: they were well-drilled and had practiced firing on the very location they were now called upon to defend. Blasting away from behind the walls of a mud earthwork, ambitiously dubbed Fort Griffin, the Rebels brought an accurate and devastating fire on the Union vessels. The first rounds hit the gunboat *Sachen* and cut its main steam pipe, knocking it out of action. Next, Dowling's gunners blasted the gunboat *Clifton* and pierced her boilers. Like the *Sachen*, she ran aground. The rest of the flotilla retired and limped back to New Orleans without landing a single infantryman. Both abandoned gunboats were forced to surrender. The Federals lost 28 men killed, 78 wounded and captured, and 315 captured, including the naval commander of the expedition, Captain Frederick Crocker. The entire operation was a minor disaster. The Confederates suffered no casualties. When Major General John B. Magruder, the commander of the District of Texas, learned what Dowling had done, he promoted him to major on the spot. Dowling bypassed the rank of captain altogether.[53]

---

53 Dick Dowling was born in Ireland in 1837. His family was evicted from their home in 1845, the first year of the Great Potato Famine. Dick and an older sister immigrated to New Orleans, where she ran a successful coffee shop. As a teenager, Dick owned and operated a successful saloon in the French Quarter but moved to Houston in 1857 because of growing anti-Irish sentiment in New Orleans. By 1861, he owned a number of saloons and several pieces of property. Dowling was commissioned first lieutenant of Texas State Troops (militia). He saw action at Galveston in 1863. Sabine Pass was only his second battle. Dowling was honored the rest of his life, and more than a dozen memorials were dedicated in his honor. A born entrepreneur, he became one of the leading businessmen in Houston post-war. Sadly, he died in the Yellow Fever epidemic in 1867 at age 30.

Banks, who used politicians' tactics, officially blamed the "ignorance" of the navy for the fiasco. The rift between the general and Admiral Porter began here and only widened with time.[54]

Incidentally, Banks, Lincoln *et al* were quite wrong in their beliefs that most of the German immigrants were Union sympathizers, as would be proven beyond a shadow of a doubt during the Red River campaign. It is true that some of them were conscientious objectors, but they did not want to shoot anybody—and that included Rebels. Others simply did not want to fight in what they regarded as a "foreign war." Many, however, joined the Confederate Army, where they fought more effectively than Union Germans. "When these people [the conscientious objectors] are set against the actual service records of the Germans as a whole, any criticism of the Germans as a group becomes mere carping nonsense," the historian of the 32nd Texas Cavalry Regiment wrote later. He recalled that many of them spoke German and were completely European in their ideas. Anyone entering their camp, he said, might think that he was entering an encampment of the Prussian Guards.[55]

*

Smarting over the defeat at Sabine Pass, Banks launched a series of amphibious landings along the Texas coast in late 1863. The Confederates did not have enough forces to defeat them or even to contest some of them, so the operations were successful. Footholds and beachheads were established at Brazos Island near Brownsville, on Matagorda Bay, at Arkansas Pass, and at Rio Grande City.[56] Banks' dispatches and the newspaper reports made them sound like great successes, but they really did not amount to much. The only real Union victory was the capture of Brownsville, which fell on November 5. Governor Andrew Jackson Hamilton set up his capitol and a pro-Union government there a few days later.

---

54   O.R., Vol. XXVI, Part 1, pp. 287-292.

55   Carl L. Duaine, *The Dead Men Wore Boots: An Account of the 32nd Texas Volunteer Cavalry, C.S.A.* (Austin, Texas: 1966), p. 23 (hereafter cited as "Duaine").

56   O.R., Vol. XXVI, Part 1, pp. 20-21, 26, 397.

Back in Washington, Old Brains was displeased by the landings, which Banks undertook without telling him. On January 4, 1864, he wrote Banks and informed him that William Tecumseh Sherman and Frederick Steele, the commander of the VII Corps in Little Rock, both agreed with him (Halleck) that the Red River route was the shortest and best way to invade Texas. Halleck did not mention that the most important Union general of them all, Ulysses S. Grant, opposed the Red River operation. As Grant saw it (quite correctly, as events later proved), even if it were successful, the Red River campaign would do little to help the Union war effort, because there were no vital objectives west of the Mississippi River. Even if Banks captured Shreveport, the Trans-Mississippi Department would still be intact and tens of thousands of Union troops would be strung out over a long and tenuous supply line. Grant felt that the proper objective for Banks' army was Mobile. He understood that the war would be won or lost in 1864, and it would be won or lost east of the Mississippi. Here, General George Meade's Army of the Potomac (73,000 men) faced Robert E. Lee's Army of Northern Virginia (38,000 men) north of Richmond.[57] North of Atlanta, Grant's armies faced the Army of Tennessee (General Joseph E. Johnston) with slightly better odds.[58] If Banks' Army of the Gulf drove on Mobile, the worse-case scenario would be that the Rebel garrison (almost 20,000 men under Lieutenant General Leonidas Polk) would be tied down. If he was not engaged by Banks, Grant foresaw, Polk would not remain idle: he would reinforce Joseph E. Johnston, who was defending Atlanta. On the other hand, if Banks advanced on Mobile, the Rebel divisions west of the Mississippi would not be able to do much to interfere with his operations because of the Union inland water navy.

---

57 Douglas Southall Freeman, *R. E. Lee* (New York: 1934-1935), Vol. III, p. 253.

58 Joseph E. Johnston, *Narrative of Military Operations* (New York: 1874), pp. 272-274. In April 1864, Sherman had an estimated 77,000 infantry to Johnston's 34,500, but this was prior to the arrival of Polk. There were, however, another 26,000 Union infantrymen in middle Tennessee, in reserve or guarding supply lines. Thomas L. Connelly, *Autumn of Glory: The Army of Tennessee, 1862-1865* (Baton Rouge: 1971), p. 308 (hereafter cited as "Connelly").

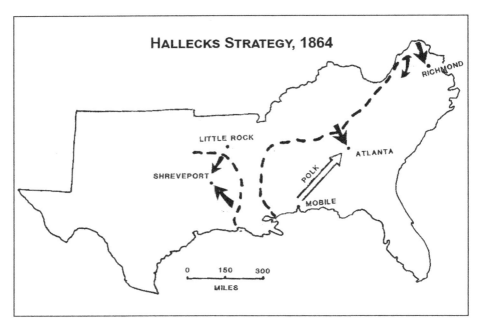

1.1 Halleck's Strategy

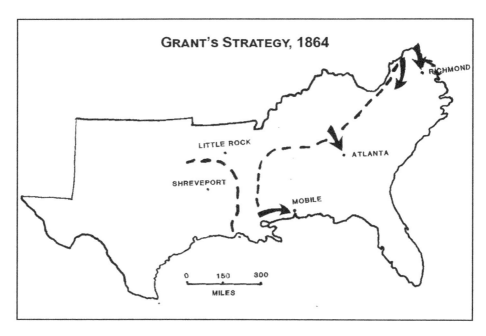

1.2 Grant's Strategy

Events worked out exactly as Grant prophesized. **Map 1.1** shows the strategy advocated by General Halleck. Grant's strategy is shown in **Map 1.2**.

When the war began, in my opinion, the South could have won the war one of three ways: diplomatically, militarily or politically. The diplomatic option was lost when Lincoln issued the Emancipation Proclamation. Prior to that, British and French intervention on the side of the Confederacy was possible. The aristocracy of both countries leaned in that direction, and the common people—even though they strongly opposed slavery—needed the South's cotton. By issuing the Emancipation Proclamation, Lincoln made the abolition of slavery a major Union war objective, second only to preserving the Union. In doing so, he seized the moral high ground. It was no longer possible for Great Britain and France to ally with the Confederacy. Their own populations were too dead set against it.

After Gettysburg and Vicksburg, Southern military victory was no longer a realistic possibility. This left the South with only the political option. If the Republicans lost the 1864 elections and the peace party replaced them, a negotiated settlement was possible—perhaps even likely. Holding Atlanta until after the election was the key to the entire war. Because the Army of the Gulf turned up the Red River instead of driving on Mobile, Leonidas Polk was able to reinforce the defenders of Atlanta with 15,000 men.[59]

Had Jefferson Davis replaced Joe Johnston with an abler army commander than John Bell Hood—perhaps Robert E. Lee, P. G. T. Beauregard, or Richard Taylor—Polk's corps could have made all the difference. The Confederate States of America could very conceivably have survived the war.

---

59 Although he graduated from West Point in 1827, Leonidas Polk resigned his commission six months later to enter the ministry. By 1861, he was Episcopal Bishop of Louisiana. President Davis, a close, personal friend, appointed him major general and later promoted him to lieutenant general in 1862. Despite a demonstrated lack of ability as a field commander, he led a corps for more than two years. He was killed in action at Pine Mountain, near Marietta, Georgia, on June 14, 1864. He was born in Raleigh, North Carolina, in 1806.

*Ulysses S. Grant (1822-1895),
seen here as president of the United States (1869-1877).*

Strangely enough, the only Union general of any statue who agreed with Grant was Nathaniel P. Banks. Banks, however, did not know Grant's opinion. This information was deliberately withheld from him by Halleck. When he received Halleck's dispatch of January 11, 1864, which stated that the best military minds in the Republic agreed that the Red River campaign was the best route to invade Texas and should be implemented, Banks—as he often did—reversed himself 180 degrees. Always anxious to please Halleck and "the powers that be," on January 16, Banks caved completely and committed himself to a campaign up the Red River to Shreveport and into east Texas. To make matters worse, to help induce Banks to commit to this course of action, Halleck had promised to reinforce the Army of the Gulf with an entire 10,000-man corps from Sherman's army. The Red River campaign had thus already shifted the balance of power in the decisive battle for Atlanta by 25,000 men, and it had not even begun. We have seen how Polk was able to provide Johnston, the defender of Atlanta, with 15,000 men he should not have had. Now Sherman would have to attack with 10,000 fewer men than he should have had.

Edmund Kirby Smith

Chapter II

THE REBELS

KIRBY SMITH

The overall commander of the Confederate forces west of the Mississippi River was General Edmund Kirby Smith. A professional soldier, he had a strong military heritage which predated the founding of the United States. His grandfather was Ephraim Kirby, a native of Litchfeld, Connecticut. Ephraim joined the American revolutionary forces at age 18, before the Battle of Bunker Hill. He fought throughout the war, was wounded 18 times, and was left for dead on the battlefield at Germantown. In the process, he rose from the rank of private to colonel.[60]

Ephraim's exemplary military record would fire the imagination of his grandson. The desire for martial glory was deeply ingrained in Edmund Kirby Smith and would animate him throughout his life. This thirst would have a major impact on the Red River campaign of 1864, as we shall see.

---

60 Arthur Howard Noll, *General Kirby-Smith* (Sewanee, Tennessee: 1907), p. 4 (hereafter cited as "Noll").

After the Revolutionary War, Colonel Kirby attended Yale, became a lawyer, spent 13 years in the Connecticut legislature, and was an unsuccessful candidate for governor. President Jefferson appointed him to a judgeship in the newly acquired Louisiana territory, but he died at Ft. Stoddard, Mississippi, on his way to assume his post.

Ephraim married in 1790 and had two sons and a daughter, Francis Marvin Kirby. Around 1807, she married Joseph Lee Smith, the son of a Revolutionary War major, who was also from Connecticut. Joseph Smith was a lawyer too and became major in the 25th Infantry Regiment in 1812. He fought in Canada, was promoted to lieutenant colonel around 1813, and to colonel in 1818. He left the army that same year. President Monroe named him judge of the Superior Court of Florida in 1821.

Edmund Kirby Smith, the future Confederate general, was born in St. Augustine, Florida, on May 16, 1824. He had a passion to be a soldier from childhood. His father sent him to Alexandria Boarding School, a West Point preparatory school in northern Virginia, where he excelled in math and the natural sciences, especially botany and mineralogy. He entered the United States Military Academy in 1841 and graduated four years later, ranking 25th in a class of 41. His classmates included 20 future Civil War generals (12 Federal, eight Confederate). He also knew Daniel Harvey Hill (Class of 1842), James Longstreet (1842), William Rosecrans (1842), Ulysses S. Grant (1843), William B. Franklin (1843), A. P. Hill (1847), and Frederick Steele (1843), whom he would fight in Arkansas. He was a close friend of Cadet George W. Morgan, whom he later defeated at Cumberland Gap in 1862. When he learned who his opponent was, Morgan sent Kirby Smith presents through the lines.[61]

Kirby Smith was a strong Christian throughout his life. As a cadet, he vowed that he would never drink or play cards, and he never did. He was almost dismissed from the academy due to defective vision but graduated on July 1, 1845. He was commissioned brevet second

---

61   Noll, pp. 7-15.

lieutenant and was assigned to the 5th Infantry in Detroit, Michigan.[62] Incidentally, he graduated as "Smith." He did not start using the name "Kirby Smith" until after the Mexican War. He named all 11 of his children "Kirby-Smith."

Second Lieutenant Kirby Smith fought in the Mexican War with Taylor and Scott. His brother, Captain Ephraim Kirby Smith of the 5th Infantry, died of wounds received in the Battle of Molino del Rey, Mexico, while leading a battalion in an attack on an enemy battery.[63] Edmund was brevetted first lieutenant for bravery at Cerro Gordo and to captain for his actions at Contreras and Churubusco.[64] After a year at Jefferson Barracks, Missouri, he became a professor of mathematics at West Point in 1849. During this period, he considered quitting the army and joining the ministry. Three years later, however, he joined his 2nd Cavalry Regiment on the Texas frontier and became an Indian fighter. In the Regular Army, he was known as "Seminole" because he was from Florida and had a swarthy complexion, and the nickname followed him. After a visit to Europe in 1858, he was posted to Camp Radziminski, New Mexico, and on one patrol in 1859 was shot through the upper thigh by a hostile Indian.

A major of the 2nd Cavalry in 1861, he was commanding Fort Colorado, Texas, when he was confronted by state troops under Colonel Ben McCulloch, who demanded that he surrender the post. Kirby Smith refused to do so, stating that he would fight to keep

---

[62] Eicher, *High Commands*, pp. 493-494. In those days, West Point cadets were frequently commissioned brevet second lieutenants, which was equal to the rank of "third lieutenant." Kirby Smith was promoted to second lieutenant on August 22, 1846.

[63] Ephraim Kirby Smith (West Point Class of 1826) was mortally wounded on September 8, 1847, and died on September 11. One of his sons, Joseph Lee Kirby Smith, served on Nathaniel Banks's staff in 1861. He led a regiment in northern Mississippi and was killed in action during the Second Battle of Corinth on October 4, 1862. He was 26 years old.

[64] In those days, the U.S. Army did not pass out medals. Courage, gallant conduct, and sometimes meritorious service was rewarded by a brevet (honorary) promotion.

it, if necessary.⁶⁵ The Texans did not press the issue; however, after Florida seceded, Kirby Smith resigned his commission on April 6. He was immediately offered a lieutenant colonelcy in the Confederate Army and on June 17 was promoted to brigadier general and was given a brigade.⁶⁶

Kirby Smith's command arrived on the field at Manassas at 3 p.m. on July 21, 1861, and quickly entered the fray. Almost immediately, Kirby Smith was seriously wounded by the Brooklyn Zouaves. A Minie ball struck him just back of the collar bone on the right shoulder, narrowly missed the artery and the spine, and came out his left shoulder. He was lucky in two ways. He was fortunate to be alive and lucky in the manner of his recovery. Sent to the home of Colonel McDaniel in Lynchburg to convalesce, he met Cassie Selden. They married on September 24, 1861.

Kirby Smith returned to duty in October and found that his Old Army reputation preceded him. He was quickly promoted to major general and named commander of the Department of Florida. Before he could assume his duties, however, his orders were revoked, and he was given command of a division in Joseph E. Johnston's Army of the Potomac, which Robert E. Lee (who served with Kirby Smith in the 2nd Cavalry) later renamed the Army of Northern Virginia.

In late February 1862, Kirby Smith was transferred to the command of the Department of Eastern Tennessee, Northern Georgia, and Northwestern Carolina. He distinguished himself in the Confederate invasion of Kentucky where, with 6,500 men, he thoroughly defeated a superior Union in the Battle of Richmond. He led the last charge in person. Kirby Smith's "Army of Kentucky" inflicted 5,353 casualties on the Northerners, including more than

---

65 McCulloch already compelled Major General David E. Twiggs to surrender to U.S. forces at San Antonio. Later a Confederate general, Ben McCulloch was killed in action at Pea Ridge on March 7, 1862. Legend has it that he was shot by Wild Bill Hickock, but this is doubtful.

66 Warner, *Generals in Gray*, p. 280. Samuel W. Mitcham, Jr, Encyclopedia of Confederate Generals (Washington, D.C.: 2022), pp. 593-594.

4,300 captured, while losing fewer than 500 men.[67] He then overran much of the state and threatened Cincinnati. He refused to cooperate with or subordinate himself to Braxton Bragg, however, which contributed to the defeat of the Army of Tennessee in the Battle of Perryville. Kirby Smith was nevertheless promoted to lieutenant general in October 1862 at the very early age of 37.

The general looked older than his years. He was tall, had sightly graying hair, a receding forehead, a thick, black beard, and wore spectacles, which made him look scholarly. He was a man of immense energy and was described as an "earnest Christian and a gentleman, [from whom] pleasant manners flow naturally ..."[68] Although affable and courteous, he possessed no "remarkable intellectual endowements," as one of his aides noted.[69]

On January 14, 1863, Kirby Smith was named commander of the Trans-Mississippi Department.[70] He was not at all pleased by the appointment and even asked Jefferson Davis if he were being sent into exile. It is true that many of Robert E. Lee's rejects were sent to the west, including John Bankhead Magruder and Major General Theophilus Holmes, whom Kirby Smith replaced.[71] It is likely that Kirby Smith's failure to work effectively with Braxton

---

67 David J. Eicher, *The Longest Night: A Military History of the Civil War* (New York: 2001), p. 316 (hereafter cited as "Eicher, *Longest Night*").

68 Noll, p. 225.

69 Jeff Kinard, *Lafayette of the South: Prince Camille de Polignac and the American Civil War* (College Station, Texas: 2001), p. 53.

70 John Eicher and David J. Eicher, *Civil War High Commands*, (Stanford, California: 2001), p. 494 (hereafter cited as "Eicher, *High Commands*").

71 Theophilus H. Holmes (1804-1880) was a brave and unpretentious gentleman but lacked energy and was generally considered incompetent as head of the Trans-Mississippi Department. His partial deafness did not help. He commanded a division under Robert E. Lee during the Seven Days Campaign of 1862, where his performance was considered unsatisfactory. Kicked upstairs, he refused to cooperate with John C. Pemberton and thus contributed to the disaster at Vicksburg. Kirby Smith made him commander of the District of Arkansas, where he was again judged a failure. His jealously of Sterling Price detracted from his administration of his department and district. After Kirby Smith relieved him of his command, he was placed in charge of reserve forces in North Carolina. A West Point graduate (1829), he was a major in the 8th Infantry when the South seceded.

Bragg contributed to his posting. In any case, he assumed command of the department at Alexandria, Louisiana, on March 7, 1863. He would be promoted to full general on February 19, 1864.

In 1863, the Confederate Trans-Mississippi Department included Indian Territory (now Oklahoma), Arkansas, Missouri, Texas and Louisiana west of the Mississippi River.[72] Headquartered in Shreveport, Louisiana, from May 1863, it included three major commands: the districts of Texas, Arkansas, and Western Louisiana.

Major General John Magruder commanded the District of Texas. Headquartered in Matagorda, he faced Banks' Texas bridgeheads. Major General Sterling Price assumed command of the District of Arkansas after Holmes departed on March 11, 1864.[73] All but the southwest quarter of the state was overrun by the Yankees. Headquartered in Washington, Arkansas, Price's main opponent was U.S. Major General Frederick Steele's VII Corps, which centered in Little Rock. Facing Banks' main force was Richard Taylor's District of Western Louisiana. Because he faced several Northern threats, Taylor was forced to scatter his men all over the state. They included Brigadier General Alfred Mouton's Louisiana brigade at Monroe in northeast Louisiana; Brigadier General Prince Camille de Polignac's Texas brigade at Harrisonburg, on the Ouachita River south of Monroe; Brigadier General St. John R. Liddell's Sub-District of North Louisiana, which was scattered throughout the subdistrict but with the largest concentration in Monroe; and Major General John Walker's Texas Division, located southeast of Alexandria, near the confluence of the Red, Mississippi, and Atchafalaya Rivers.

After Vicksburg fell on July 4, 1863, Kirby Smith's department was completely cut off from the rest of the Confederacy and faced mammoth problems, including the need to procure arms, ammunition, and supplies of every description.

---

72 It theoretically included the Confederate Territories of Arizona and New Mexico, but they had already been overrun by the enemy.

73 Eicher, *High Commands*, pp. 301-302, 440. Price earlier served as acting district commander when Holmes was on furlough or was ill.

Kirby Smith ordered an economic survey of the department and organized the Trans-Mississippi to make it as self-sufficient as possible. The main focus of his activities was cotton. He was able to buy it cheap, transport it to Europe by way of Mexico, and sell it high. Typically, his Cotton Bureau would purchase cotton at $.03 to $.04 per pound and sell it for $.50 in gold. With the money they received, Kirby Smith's agents purchased machinery, which was shipped back to the Trans-Mississippi via Mexico, where he set up factories and machine shops. It was estimated that Kirby Smith's agents sent half a million bales of cotton to Europe in this manner.[74] A typical bale weighed 450 pounds. He also purchased machinery to exploit Louisiana's salt deposits and exported grains and cattle from Texas. With proper organization, these commodities could be purchased and transported to feed the rest of the department.[75]

General Kirby Smith created a bureaucracy that was too large but which did generally function effectively. His organizations included a Cotton Bureau, a Conscription Bureau, a Medical Bureau, and a Clothing Bureau. He used the latter to set up a shoe factory in Shreveport, one in Arkansas, and four in Texas. They supplied 10,000 shoes a month to the department and to needy civilians. His hat factories were located in the same towns and produced 13,000 caps and hats each month. His Ordnance Bureau set up foundries and shops in Shreveport and Marshal, Texas, to manufacture ammunition. They could produce 10,000 rounds per day, as well as shot and shell for the artillery.[76] He also established a cannon factory near Anderson, Texas.

---

74 Noll, p. 229.

75 O.R., Vol. XXII, Part 2, pp. 799, 854, 872, 969, 1134, 1139; Vol. XXVI, Part 2, pp. 20, 136, 277, 304, 365, 545, 579; Winters, p. 305; Noll, pp. 226-230; William R. Boggs, *Military Reminiscences of General William R. Boggs, C.S.A.* (Durham, North Carolina: 1913), pp. 61-62 (hereafter cited as "Boggs").

76 Jefferson Davis Bragg, *Louisiana in the Confederacy* (Baton Rouge: 1914), p. 165; Joseph H. Parks, *General Edmund Kirby Smith, C.S.A.* (Baton Rouge: 1954), pp. 350-351 (hereafter cited as "Parks"); Winters, p. 321; Albert N. Garland, "E. Kirby Smith and the Trans-Mississippi Confederacy," (Baton Rouge: Unpublished M.A. Thesis, Louisiana State University, 1947), pp. 56-58.

"Seminole" Smith was ably assisted in his efforts by Henry Watkins Allen, the governor of Louisiana. A native of Virginia,[77] he grew up in Missouri, where he was educated at Marion College, and at Harvard, where he studied law. A brilliant entrepreneur, he left home at age 17 to become a private tutor. When he returned ten years later, he was the richest man in the state. Noted for his abundant energy and adventuresome nature, he became a planter and a lawyer in Mississippi and Louisiana, traveled in Europe, founded the Louisiana Historical Society, and served two terms in the Louisiana legislature.[78] When the Civil War began, he was one of wealthiest men in the former United States. He nevertheless enlisted as a private in the 4th Louisiana Infantry, but was soon elected its lieutenant colonel and then colonel. He was wounded at Shiloh, fought in the first Siege of Vicksburg (1862), and his legs were so badly shattered in the Battle of Baton Rouge on August 5, 1862, that he had to walk on crutches for the rest of his life. Even so, he was promoted to brigadier general on August 19, 1863, and was elected governor in November. Here he proved to be an extremely effective CEO—arguably the best to emerge from the Civil War.

Despite his wounds and impediments, Governor Allen remained very energetic and was an extremely capable executive. Pulitzer Prize winning historian Dr. Douglas Southall Freeman wrote: "Allen was the single great administrator produced by the Confederacy. His success in Louisiana indicates that he might have changed history ... if his talents could have been utilized by the Confederate government on a larger scale."[79]

The governor established a system of state stores, factories and foundries, which provided both goods to refugees at little or no charge while simultaneously helping the Trans-Mississippi Department

---

77 Allen was born in Farmville, Virginia, on April 29, 1820.

78 For a more complete summary of Allen's early life, see my essay in the *Abbeville Institute*, "Louisiana's Warrior Governor," August 26, 2019. The cite is free and packed full of information on Southern history and heritage.

79 William Arceneaux, *Acadian General: Alfred Mouton and the Civil War* (Lafayette, Louisiana: 1981), p. 120 (hereafter cited as "Arceneaux"); Charles L. Dufour, *Ten Flags in the Wind: The Story of Louisiana* (New York: 1967), p. 171.

supply the army. He also set up state labs to manufacture turpentine, castor oil, medicinal alcohol, carbonate of soda, and other medicines. He set up a state medical lab under Dr. Bartholomew Egan at Mount Lebanon, and arranged with Kirby Smith to transfer a large amount of Confederate cotton and sugar to the state of Louisiana, in exchange for canceling part of the huge national debt. He sent wagon trains from Louisiana to Mexico and brought back "dry goods, pins, coffee, tobacco, flour, cotton cards, paper, medicine, and other necessities" which the state could not produce.[80] Again, the state gave away these items to refugees who could not pay for them. Allen even ordered a mineral survey of the state be conducted. When it was determined that the resources of Confederate Louisiana were poor, he purchased a major share in the iron works in Davis County, Texas.

Despite the war, he published school books and distributed them to the children through the police juries—free to those whose families could not pay for them. He set up small factories for the manufacturing of clothing, hats, and shoes. He set up several relief committees, sold food, blankets and clothing at low prices or gave them away to those who could not purchase them. He instructed these committees not to ask the political sentiments of those they helped—be they Rebels, Unionists, or Jayhawkers. He helped blacks and whites alike and proposed arming African Americans, who would be given their freedom if they fought for the South or for Louisiana. Men and women from Arkansas and Texas came to Louisiana for aid that they could not get at home and were never turned away by the incredibly efficient state government. The Missouri soldiers in Louisiana went so far as to claim Allen as their governor.[81] Meanwhile, Allen established an iron foundry, a tannery, a woolen factory, and a pharmaceutical plant for the manufacture of medicines.

---

80   Winters, p. 319.
81   Vincent H. Cassidy and Amos E. Simpson, *Henry Watkins Allen of Louisiana* (Baton Rouge: 1964), pp. 106-115. Also see Samuel W. Mitcham, Jr., *Abbeville Institute*, https://www.abbevilleinstitute.org/louisianas-warrior-governor/August 26, 2019. This Internet site is free and is a tremendous asset to anyone studying Southern history.

Henry Watkins Allen, seen here as a Confederate brigadier.

The governor was also a frugal man. In contrast to today's governor's mansion in Baton Rouge, which has more than 100 bathrooms, Allen's "mansion" had three bedrooms: one for himself, one for his staff, and one for guests. Common people visited frequently because Governor Allen put the interests of old women, children, widows, orphans, and soldiers' families above those of the rich and famous. Formerly one of the richest men in the state, he indulged himself in only one luxury: he drank one cup of real coffee, once a day. He was also a paradox in that he was in poor health and constant pain because of his wounds, but he showed indefatigable energy and was totally selfless in his devotion to his citizens. Why, one newspaper asked, was Governor Allen so honored by the people? "Simply because he makes their good his highest objective. He protects the weak, he relieves the needy, he rewards the faithful, he, in short, exercises his every constitutional power with justice, reason and humility ... "[82] He even managed to get along with everybody, including Taylor and Kirby Smith.

RICHARD TAYLOR

Although both Kirby Smith and Allen did their part in preparing Louisiana for defense, the man most directly concerned was Richard Taylor, the commander of the District of Western Louisiana, who called his headquarters the Army of Western Louisiana—even though it had about the strength of a 1861 division.

Richard Taylor was born on his family's plantation in West Feliciana Parish, Louisiana, on January 27, 1826, the only son of Zachary Taylor. He was the sixth generation of a prominent line of wealthy Virginia planters, and his mother was a relative of Robert E. Lee. One of his ancestors (Richard Lee Taylor) was a lieutenant colonel in the American Revolution and was a full colonel when he was crippled during a battle with Indians in 1792.

In 1828, Zachary Taylor was transferred, and Richard spent nine years of his childhood at Fort Snelling, Minnesota, and at Fort Crawford, in what is now Wisconsin. Here he became close to his father's adjutant, Lieutenant Jefferson Davis, who eloped with Richard's sister. In 1836, Dick was sent to Louisville to attend a private school and live with relatives. Later, he attended an exclusive preparatory school in Massachusetts before entering Harvard. He did not like this school, so he transferred to Yale, from which he graduated in 1845. He had a 2.8 grade point average.[83]

Dick Taylor was 5' 8 ½" tall with dark, hazel eyes, a deep tan complexion and a thick, black beard. He smoked, drank, chewed tobacco, and enjoyed good food and fine wine. He grew quite fat before the war but lost the excess weight via active campaigning.

---

82 Sarah A. Dorsey, *Recollections of Henry Watkins Allen, Brigadier General Confederate States' Army, Ex-Governor of Louisiana* (New York: 1866), p. 255.
83 Parrish, pp. 17-18.

He also possessed an aristocratic air, a magnetic personality, and was highly cultured. General Dabney Maury recalled that Taylor was noted for his "keen sarcasm and ready wit."[84] He was very intelligent, possessed a fine memory and was very well read. He made friends easily, and they included Jefferson Davis, William T. Sherman, Pierre Beauregard, Braxton Bragg, and Ulysses S. Grant.[85] He could quote long passages from literature or the Bible but could out curse anyone when aroused—and he was frequently and easily aroused. His own father, President Zachary Taylor, described him as very affectionate but somewhat quick tempered.[86] His men would certainly have agreed with that statement. Historian Ludwell Johnson described him as "High-strung, irritable and extremely self-confident."[87] Of him, one of his friends declared that he had "a total irreverence for any man's opinion."[88] He was, in fact, supremely self-confident, calm in combat, a firm disciplinarian, and not at all afraid to take a risk. Whatever other disadvantages the Army of Western Louisiana had to endure during the Red River campaign, it would never suffer from timid or vacillating leadership.

Richard Taylor also suffered from chronic rheumatoid arthritis all his life and was a poor patient. Few people wanted to be around him when his arthritis acted up. He also had a reputation for treating his slaves well but his superiors poorly. During the Civil War, he got along with Braxton Bragg and Richard S. Ewell, but that pretty well exhausts the list. He did not, however, wish to serve under Bragg again and considered Ewell to be an oddball. Initially, he did not like T. J. Jackson, but the brilliant Stonewall eventually won him over, at least to some degree, despite his West Point background.

---

84 Dabney Maury, Reminiscences of General Taylor," *Appleton's Journal*, Vol. 6 (June 1879), p. 568; Also see Maury, "Sketch of General Richard Taylor," Southern Historical Society *Papers*, Vol. VII (July 1879), pp. 343-345 (hereafter cited as "Maury").

85 Taylor and Grant had a falling out over the president's Reconstruction policies and never reconciled. Dick Taylor was never an easy forgiver.

86 Holman Hamilton, *Zachary Taylor, Soldier in the White House* (Indianapolis: 1951), p. 27.

87 Johnson, p. 88.

88 Maury, pp. 343-345.

Richard Taylor, commander of the Army of Western Louisiana.

In 1846, during the Mexican War, Dick joined his father at Matamoros, where he served as the general's private secretary until his rheumatoid arthritis flared up, and Zachary sent him back to New Orleans. After staying there several weeks, he took over Cypress Grove, the Taylor plantation 30 miles north of Natchez, on a wide bend of the Mississippi River. Initially, it had 81 slaves, but Taylor expanded the number to 127. He proved to be an excellent plantation manager and also established a successful sawmill. He bought his own plantation in St. Charles Parish, 30 miles north of New Orleans. It was more than 1,200 acres in size and was worked by 64 slaves. Eventually, Taylor would own 147 slaves. Taylor named his plantation "Fashion."

In early February 1851, Taylor married Myrthe "Mimi" Bringer, the "vivacious" daughter of a prominent Creole family in New Orleans.[89] They were to have five children: Louise Margaret (1852), Elizabeth "Betty" (1854), Zachary (1857), Richard "Dixie" (1860), and Myrthe Bianca (1864).

Already rich and growing more prosperous, Richard Taylor approached public service (and later military service) out of a sense of obligation, rather than out of ego or of any desire for public acclaim or recognition. It was just something a man of his social rank and standing was expected to do, so he did it. Initially a Whig (like his father), he favored leadership at all levels by the educated and the property holder, rather than the less educated common man. After the Whigs self-destructed, he became a member of the "Know-Nothing" Party and eventually the Democratic Party. He was easily elected to the Louisiana Senate from St. Charles Parish in 1855, even though he refused to campaign and never made a single speech.

Unlike many people in his position in life, Taylor honestly did not care what other people thought of him. He never made a speech in the legislature and did not take part in any of the debates, but nevertheless developed a reputation for honesty, integrity, and forthrightness. (Even then this was unusual for a Louisiana

---

89   Parrish, p. 42.

The Rebels

*President Jefferson Davis
(1808-1889)*

legislator.) If anyone wished to learn his opinion on any issue, all they had to do was ask. If they did not care for Taylor's answers, well ... then they should not have asked. He was reelected by a wide margin, and his peers chose him to head the Federal Relations Committee and later the Military and Naval Affairs Committee.

Like Thomas Jefferson and many others, Richard Taylor considered slavery a necessary evil which would eventually die of natural causes. Although he thought the institution was "the curse of the South" and despised Vice President Alexander Stephens because he allegedly called slavery the cornerstone of the Confederacy,[90] Taylor could not tolerate the moral ravings of the Northern Abolitionists, whom he considered hypocrites. (Most of them did not like African Americans and wanted them kept out of their states. As late as 1862, Abraham Lincoln, for example, supported Amendment XVIII to the Illinois State Constitution which forbade blacks and mulattos from settling in the state. It passed overwhelmingly. They had not protested slavery until the slave trade was declared illegal and the Northern flesh peddlers could no longer make money from it. Then they wanted the Southern slave owners to free their chatels without compensation.) Taylor also despised the Northern Abolitionists because he thought they pandered to the common man—something he never did.

By the standards of the day, Taylor treated his slaves well. As soon as he took over Fashion, Taylor had the dirt floor slave cabins burned and replaced by much larger cabins with wooden floors and broad verandas. Taylor's slaves were fed better than their peers, and after a successful sugar cane season, he would even pay them—not much, to be sure but even a few dollars was 100% more than any other slaves in the area received. They were allowed to grow their own gardens and eat or sell the produce—whichever they chose. He also would not let the Cajuns or white trash bully or abuse them. The Englishman Frederick Law Olmsted visited Fashion from February

---

90 Parrish, p. 55. After the war, Stephens averred that he had been misquoted.

23 to 25, 1853, and interviewed Taylor and his slaves. Even though they would have preferred to be free, the slaves "... regarded him with affection, respect, and pride," Olmsted recorded.[91]

Left to his own devices, Taylor would have spent the rest of his life managing and enjoying Fashion. On March 21, 1861, however, when the Louisiana Convention voted 101 to 7 to secede, Taylor voted with the majority but with a deep sense of foreboding. He retired to Fashion and decided not to serve the new country unless he was called, even though his ex-brother-in-law was the president.[92] His friend, Braxton Bragg, the Confederate commander in Pensacola, contacted him almost immediately. Bragg was in charge of training thousands of raw volunteers, and he asked Taylor to join his staff. Although Bragg recommended he be promoted to brigadier general, Taylor remained a civilian advisor and was happy in this role.

Probably no other civilian in North America was as well read in military history as was Taylor. He studied Napoleon, Julius Caesar, Frederick the Great, Henri Jomini and dozens of others—and in considerable depth. The troops coming out of Pensacola were among the best trained in the South.

In early July 1861, Taylor received a telegram from Louisiana Governor Thomas Moore. It abruptly appointed him to the rank of colonel and announced that he was elected commander of the 9th Louisiana Infantry Regiment. He was ordered to report to Virginia immediately.

Taylor and his regiment missed the 1st Battle of Bull Run by a few hours, arriving shortly after the Yankees hastily departed. The 9th Louisiana remained in Virginia, although their colonel spent most of September bedridden due to rheumatoid arthritis. David F. Boyd, his commissary officer, described Taylor as "genial, full of humor and very witty ... and with his rich melodious voice, he was the most brilliant and fascinating talker that I remember in the Southern

---

91 Olmsted *Journal*, February 23-25, 1853.
92 Taylor's sister, Sarah Knox "Knoxie" Taylor, died of malaria on September 15, 1835, three months after her wedding. She was 21 years old.

army." Another soldier, while conceding that he was a "splendid officer," added that he was "as proud as Lucifer" and was therefore unpopular with the troops.[93]

At the end of October, he was named commander of the Louisiana Brigade and was promoted to brigadier general, even though he had never seen combat. This caused problems for some Louisiana newspaper editors. Taylor even went to Richmond and asked Jefferson Davis to cancel the promotion. Davis refused. He did, however, take what was for him an unprecedented step: he wrote to the three regimental commanders who had been passed over, explained himself to them, and asked them to give Taylor their full support. All three did so.

Taylor's brigade was sent to the Shenandoah Valley, where he worked with Stonewall Jackson for the first time. Initially, both he and his divisional commander, Major General Richard S. Ewell, were perplexed by the secrecy and eccentricities of the former Virginia Military Institute professor, and Ewell even expressed the view that Jackson was insane. Ewell sent Taylor to Richmond, to meet with his (Taylor's) friend, Secretary of War Judah Benjamin, to have Jackson superceded as commander in the Valley by James Longstreet.[94] Benjamin agreed, and the two Louisianans met with Jefferson Davis and convinced him to replace Jackson. Taylor returned happily to the Shenandoah—but nothing happened. After Taylor and Benjamin departed, Davis spoke with his senior military advisor, General Robert E. Lee, who persuaded him to retain Jackson. The results, of course, turned out very positively for the South.

Richard Taylor performed so well as a brigade commander in the Valley Campaign of 1862 that, on the recommendation of Stonewall Jackson, he was promoted to major general on July 28 and was

---

93 Parrish, pp. 138, 151.

94 Richard S. Ewell (1817-1872) was born in Georgetown, D.C., the son of a doctor and the grandson of the first secretary of the navy. He graduated from West Point in 1840 and was assigned to the 1st Dragoons. He fought in Mexico and later served in Texas, New Mexico, and Arizona. He was wounded by Apaches in 1859. A pro-Unionist, he nevertheless went with Virginia when it seceded, and progressively commanded a brigade, division, and corps. He lost a leg in the Second Battle of Manassas (Bull Run).

ordered to return to Louisiana to defend his native state. At age 36, he was the youngest of the 30 major generals in Confederate service at that time. He was also an excellent student and learned a great many lessons from the famous Jackson—lessons he was soon to apply in Louisiana.

Taylor crossed the Mississippi River into Louisiana on August 19, 1862, and traveled all night to Washington, Louisiana, where his family was staying with friends. He had not seen them for 14 months.[95] In the meantime, Fashion was captured and plundered by the Yankees. "Nothing is respected," a Vermont soldier observed. The Federals took, among other things, 130 horses, 200 head of sheep, several hogsheads of sugar, and 175 slaves, which they called "contrabands."[96]

When Taylor learned of this and similar outrages on other plantations, he could barely contain his wrath. He sent General Butler a letter, threatening to shoot 10 Union prisoners per outrage. Butler responded to Taylor's threats by promising to deal harshly with any Federal soldier caught destroying private property, and indeed, the deprivations stopped—for the time being.[97]

After only a few hours, Taylor proceeded to Opelousas, a short distance to the south, where the state capitol was located since the fall of Baton Rouge. There, he met with Governor Moore and learned that he was pretty much on his own.[98] Moore could provide him with only a few hundred poorly equipped militiamen. General

---

95   Taylor officially assumed command of the District of Western Louisiana on August 21, 1862 (O.R., Vol. XV, p. 2).

96   Parrish, p. 247. Southerners used the term "slave" when referring to black people but called them "servants" more frequently. Out of respect, older slaves were called "aunt" or "uncle." Southerners never used the term "Contraband," which is roughly equivalent to the German term "Untermenschen" or sub-human.

97   O.R., Vol. XV, p. 565.

98   Thomas O. Moore (1804-1876) was governor of Louisiana from January 23, 1860 to January 25, 1864. A prosperous cotton planter, he was elected to the state House of Representatives in 1848 and the state Senate in 1856. He played a major role in selecting William Tecumseh Sherman superintendent of the newly formed Louisiana Military Academy at Pineville. Moore fled to Cuba after the war and applied for pardon via Sherman. The general personally carried the application to President Johnson and

Theophilius H. "Granny" Holmes, the commander of the Trans-Mississippi Department, which was then headquartered in Little Rock, refused to help, on the grounds that he needed all his regiments for the defense of Arkansas.

Taylor's first step was to establish his district headquarters at Alexandria. Next, he introduced conscription, in accordance with Confederate laws. North Louisiana had volunteered heavily in 1861 and 1862, but south Louisiana had not, especially in the Cajun areas. Taylor sent out detachments to draft them and by October had almost 6,000 men. He classified another 8,000 as deserters or draft dodgers. His only outside reinforcements were a single battalion of Texas cavalry and the understrength 18th Louisiana Infantry Regiment, which had fought at Shiloh.

By mid-October 1862, Taylor's commander in the Bayou Lafourche region, Brigadier General Alfred Mouton, had 2,500 men—1,000 of whom were inexperienced conscripts or militia. On October 27, U.S. Brigadier General Godfrey Weitzel began an advance up both sides of the Bayou Lafourche with 5,000 men (**Map 2.1**). Most of Mouton's units retreated without firing a shot. Many of the men, who were not far from their cabins, deserted. The general made a stand at Labadieville and was soundly defeated.

Fortunately for the Rebels, Weitzel stopped at Berwick's Bay. He established his headquarters at Thibodaux and began to implement a Butler plan of using slave labor to operate abandoned or confiscated plantations. (White Gold was more important than pursuing defeated Confederates.) Had Weitzel known how weak Taylor and Mouton were, he could have overrun most of Louisiana.

---

asked him to approve it. He did. Moore spent the rest of his life working to rebuild his plantation in Rapides Parish. Because Sherman was looking out for his old benefactor, the Louisiana Carpetbaggers did not harass him.

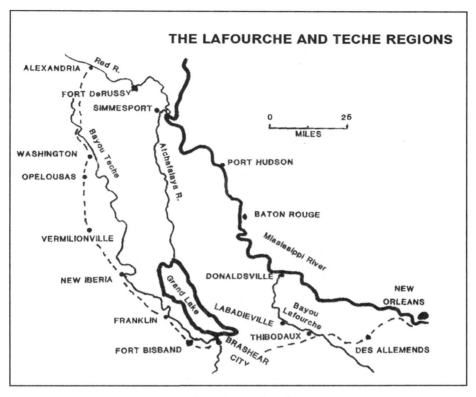

2.1 The Lafourche and Teche Regions

The Butler plan, and a similar plan instituted later by Banks, failed. The efforts were not well organized and Rebel cavalry and irregulars were too prone to raid outlying farms and plantations. Even when cotton was picked, it was often burned by Taylor's men. Once again, production lagged.

While the Yankees looked for ways to solve their cotton problem, Taylor set up a salt mining operation on Avery Island (in Vermilion Bay, south of New Iberia), which had huge deposits of rock salt. Using slave labor, he also established a meat packing plant for curing beef on the island. Meanwhile, he organized the rest of Louisiana for defense. With Kirby Smith's engineers, his men built forts to guard the rivers against Union gunboats. They included Forts DeRussy on the Red, Beauregard on the Ouachita, and Burton

General Henry H. Sibley.

on the Atchafalaya at Butte a la Rose. Kirby Smith and his chief of staff, Brigadier General William R. Boggs, had much more faith in these defensive works than Taylor, who did not have enough men to properly garrison them. Each fort had less than 100 men—barely enough to man the guns. Boggs also constructed some impressive fortifications around Shreveport.

In February 1863, Jefferson Davis assigned Henry Hopkins Sibley's Texas Cavalry Brigade to Taylor, giving him almost 4,000 men. Taylor was pleased to receive the men, although he did not appreciate their lack of discipline or their general, who was an alcoholic and was called the "Walking Whiskey Keg" by his men. It was not an affectionate nickname. Theophilus Noel, a reporter for the Richmond *Inquirer* and the New Orleans *Picayune*, stated that Sibley "had never been sober in the New Mexico campaign" and his "love of liquor exceeded that for home, country or God."[99]

Unlike many non-professional officers on both sides, Dick Taylor was not afraid to sack a Regular Army officer—even a general. He quickly fired Sibley, brought him up on court-martial charges, and replaced him with Colonel (later Brigadier General) Thomas Green, a man more to his liking. Taylor "overcharged" Sibley when he charged him with cowardice (Sibley was clearly not a coward), and the former commander was acquitted, but his military career was ruined just the same.

On April 10, General Banks moved out of Brashear City with three divisions—16,000 men. Their objective was Fort Bisland, 15 miles to the north. Meanwhile, in naval transports, General Glover moved up

---

99 Theophilus Noel *Autobiography and Reminiscences* (Chicago: 1904), pp. 61-62 (hereafter cited as "Noel"). Henry Hopkins Sibley was born in Natchitoches in 1816 but grew up in Missouri. He graduated from West Point in 1838 and fought in the Seminole War, in Mexico, and against Indians in Texas. He directed the unsuccessful Confederate invasion of Arizona and New Mexico. An alcoholic, he was court-martialed for cowardice at Taylor's insistence in 1863. Sibley was not convicted, but he was censured and his career was effectively over. He ended the war without a command. Sibley later served in the Egyptian Army and died in poverty in Fredericksburg, Virginia, in 1886. He invented the Sibley Tent, which was used by both sides early in the Civil War, and the Sibley Stove, which was used until World War II. He was a distant cousin of Henry Hastings Sibley, a Union general and the first governor of Minnesota.

the western side of Grand Lake with 4,000 men. His objective was to land above the fort, cutting off Taylor and his men. The fractious rebel was up to the challenge, however, and he conducted a brilliant operation, inflicting the maximum possible number of casualties on the enemy while managing to escape at the last possible moment.

Taylor conducted a skillful retreat, but outnumbered 5 to 1, he was only able to slow Banks, not stop him. The Federals overran the Bayou Teche country, and Opelousas fell on April 20. Much of the countryside was looted or plundered. By the last week in April, it was obvious that Banks intended to take Alexandria, a Red River town in the center of the state. On April 25, Taylor kissed his family goodbye and put them, including his two sons, Zach and Dixie, on a steamboat, to travel upriver to Shreveport. He never saw either of them again. Six-year-old Zach died of scarlet fever on April 27. Dixie died on May 20. Had he lived another month, he would have celebrated his third birthday. They were the only sons Dick Taylor would ever have.

Acting in their father's absence, General Kirby Smith arranged for the funerals of both boys. Taylor's daughters also contracted the fever but survived. Mrs. Taylor also fell ill and never completely recovered her health, although she lived until after the war.

Richard Taylor suppressed his grief and would not allow himself to think about his sons. He buried himself in his work, which was going badly. He evacuated as much government property as he could from Alexandria, which fell on May 7.[100] Taylor, meanwhile, fell back to Natchitoches. He retreated 150 miles.

---

100   Hollandsworth gives the date for the fall of Alexandria as May 7. Parrish places it as May 8. Long cited May 6. E. B. Long, *The Civil War Day by Day* (Garden City, New York: 1971), p. 350 (hereafter cited as "Long").

As soon as they reached Alexandria, the Federals continued to do what they were doing since April 10: they seized all the cotton they could. During the drive from Brashear City to Alexandria, they seized an estimated $10,000,000 worth of cotton and 6,000 "contrabands."[101]

A delegation of civilian leaders from Rapides Parish visited Banks and called upon him to show mercy and to restrain his men. "Believe it, gentlemen, as if you heard God himself speak it, I will lay waste your country," Banks snapped, "... so that you will never organize and maintain another army in your department."[102]

Banks was only in Alexandria for a week. He evacuated it on May 14 and turned back to the east, toward a more important goal: Port Hudson on the Mississippi River. He did not burn Alexandria, however, because he intended to come back later.

Still angling to be elected president in 1864, Banks planned to capture Port Hudson quickly. He would then drive north to Vicksburg, where he would link up with Ulysses S. Grant. He would then assume command of both armies (he was still senior in rank to Grant) and capture Vicksburg, clearing the Mississippi of Rebel forces. These huge victories would, Banks believed, help propel him toward the White House. The Confederates at Port Hudson, however, threw a monkey wrench into his plans.

On May 21, Banks cut the last road out of Port Hudson. The Confederate bastion was defended by fewer than 7,000 men, well commanded by Major General Franklin Gardner, a native of New York City.[103] Gardner had 4.5 miles of trenches and breastworks,

---

101   Johnson, p. 56. Hollandsworth (p. 121) placed the total at $10,000,000, which was worth $213,421,879.71 in 2020, according to the Morgan Friedman Inflation Calculator, https://westegg.com/inflation/infl.cgi?money=10000000&first=1863&final=2020.

102   Henry Watkins Allen, *The Conduct of Federal Troops in Louisiana During the Invasions of 1863 and 1864* (Shreveport, Louisiana: 1865), p. 145.

103   Franklin Gardner (1823-1873) graduated from West Point in 1843, four places above Ulysses S. Grant. He fought in Mexico, where he earned two brevets. Gardner married into the Mouton family of Louisiana. He resigned from the army in 1861 and joined the Confederate Army as a lieutenant colonel. Promoted to colonel, he led a brigade of cavalry, served in Mississippi and Tennessee, and fought at Shiloh. Promoted

which were designed to be held by 21,000 men.[104] Banks attacked the fortress on May 27. He sent his units in piecemeal, rather than launching one, overwhelming attack, and was repulsed. Banks lost 2,000 men. Gardner suffered only 235 casualties.

Banks attacked again on June 14 with the same lack of coordination and with even poorer results. He lost 400 killed and missing and 1,400 wounded. Rebel losses were very light: 22 killed and 25 wounded. Port Hudson did not surrender until July 9—five days after Vicksburg. Banks captured 6,300 prisoners and 51 guns. He lost 4,000 men in combat and another 7,000 to illness. The Rebels lost 750 dead; several hundred of these perished due to disease.[105]

When Banks turned east in May, Taylor wanted to drive southeast to recapture New Orleans. This, he believed, would force Banks to abandon the Siege of Port Hudson, free Gardner's men, and would perhaps allow Joseph E. Johnston to break the Siege of Vicksburg. Kirby Smith, however, ordered Taylor to move directly against Vicksburg, which he did under protest. For this operation, he was given Major General John Walker's Texas Division, which was then in north Louisiana. On June 7, 1863, he attacked Grant's screening force on the west bank, in the Battle of Milliken's Bend, where he won a minor, indecisive victory. The Union forces fell back to the protection of their gunboats in disorder. They lost 652 men. Walker's assault forces lost 185 men.[106] Grant's Siege of Vicksburg was never threatened.

*

---

to brigadier general on April 11, 1862, he took part in Bragg's invasion of Kentucky. Advanced to major general in late 1862, he was placed in command of Port Hudson, which he defended very well. After being exchanged, he worked for Richard Taylor in Mississippi in late 1864 and 1865.

104 Banks and Farragut attempted to take Port Hudson in March 1863 but failed. Gardner had 21,000 men at that time.

105 See Lawrence L. Hewitt, *Port Hudson: Confederate Bastion on the Mississippi* (Baton Rouge: 1994). Sources differ slightly as to the number of Union casualties suffered in this battle.

106 Long, p. 363.

Having obeyed his orders, Taylor hurried back to the south to execute his own strategy. He was followed by General Walker's hard-marching regiments. On June 23, he attacked Brashear City (now Morgan City). The Union garrison was taken completely by surprise. A thousand men surrendered, a dozen guns were captured, and $2,000,000 worth of Union supplies and property were seized.[107] Taylor lost three men killed and 18 wounded. He immediately pushed on to Thibodaux and by July 1, was only 20 miles from the Crescent City. There was great excitement in New Orleans, but on July 11, Taylor learned that Vicksburg and Port Hudson had fallen. He was now only 16 miles from the city but, with Banks' army now freed, he had no choice but to retreat and again abandon the Lafourche region. He was pursued by General William Franklin.

Franklin slowly retook the Bayou Lafourche and Bayou Teche regions, but this time, Taylor had enough men to put up a more stubborn defense. Unwilling to be pinned down in a battle he could not win, General Taylor denied Franklin a decisive engagement but did turn on him and attack when an opportunity presented itself. On September 29, for example, his forces fell upon a Union outpost of less than a thousand men at Morgan's Ferry and routed it. The Rebels took 450 prisoners.

General Franklin took New Iberia on October 3, without opposition. He then advanced slowly on Vermilionville (now Lafayette) and occupied Opelousas on October 21. At this point, Taylor was unsure whether the Yankee general planned to drive up the Red River or head across country to Texas. He did neither. Correctly believing that there was not enough forage this late in the season to support his regiments, Franklin stopped. His supply lines were vulnerable to guerrillas and Confederate cavalry, and Banks' men already stripped the country of provisions, so Franklin had difficulty feeding his men.

---

107   Equal to $42,684,375.94 in 2020 dollars, according to the Morgan Friedman Inflation Calculator.

On November 3, Taylor's cavalry commander, General Green, took his horsemen, along with three of Walker's regiments (the 11th, 15th, and 18th Texas Infantry) and three artillery batteries and fell on U.S. Brigadier General Stephen G. Burbridge's brigade near Bayou Bourbeau, seven miles south of Opelousas, in yet another surprise attack. Burbridge's brigade was routed. The Yankees lost 154 killed and wounded and 500 captured, including 30 officers. The Rebels suffered 125 casualties.[108] Shortly after, seeing that nothing would be accomplished in Louisiana until the spring, Franklin withdrew down the Teche to New Iberia and went into winter quarters. He did not stay there, however. As Banks withdrew XIII Corps units for his Texas adventure, Franklin was left with just over 5,000 men from the XIX Corps and Brigadier General Alfred Lee's cavalry division. Then smallpox hit the Union camp, so Franklin retreated again, this time to Franklin, Louisiana, from where he would begin the campaign of 1864.

CONFEDERATE STRATEGY

Confederate strategy can be described briefly because it was largely reactive in nature. The demographics were clearly against her. The North had every advantage. The population of the United States in 1860 was 31,443,321. Of this, 9,000,000 people resided in the Southern states. This included 3,500,000 slaves, giving the South 5,500,000 white people from which to field their armies. According to John H. and David J. Eicher, the "Military Population" of the North (white males aged 18 through 45) was 3,954,776, as opposed to 1,064,193 for the South.[109] Another roughly 191,000 black men served in the Union Army, as opposed to 80,000 to 96,000 in the Confederate Army.[110] At their maximum extent, the Northern armies

---

108   Parrish, p. 312.

109   Eicher, *High Commands*, p. 6. These figures exclude 516,085 from the border states of Missouri, Kentucky, and Maryland and 89,011 from the territories and the District of Columbia, most of whom adhered to the Union.

110   Many Southern African-Americans were conscripted into the Union Army against their will. See James Ronald Kennedy and Walter Donald Kennedy, *The South Was Right!*, 3rd ed. (Columbia, South Carolina, 2021). Also see the Report of U.S. Brigadier General Rufus Saxton to Secretary of War Edwin M. Stanton, December 30, 1864, in *The War of the Rebellion: A Compilation of the Official Records of the Union and*

fielded more than 1,000,000 men. During the 1861 to 1865 period, 2,898,304 men served in the Union Army.[111] That was 1,812,121 more troops than served in all of America's other wars combined up until that point. We do not know exactly how many men served in the Confederate Army because many Southern records were lost or destroyed at the end of the conflict. Estimates vary between 600,000 to over a million, with 800,000 to 850,000 being commonly cited figures. General Cooper and Thornton H. Bowman, however, put the number at 600,000.[112] It is unlikely that President Davis and his generals ever fielded more than 300,000 men at any one time.[113]

The North also recruited mercenaries on a grand scale. Some 489,920 foreign soldiers of fortune were recruited from 15 different countries, mostly from Germany (210,000) and Ireland (150,000). This led one Rebel to ask: "Do we have to whip the world?"[114] The South depended largely on its own resources.

*

With its white population base of 5,500,000, against a Northern population base of 22,500,000, the South was at a clear demographic disadvantage of 4 to 1, even if the Union's foreign mercenaries are excluded. It is therefore not surprising that the Confederacy lost the war; what is amazing, however, is that it lasted as long as it did. Years later, Sam Watkins declared that the Southern cause was lost

---

Confederate Armies, Fred C. Ainsworth and Joseph W. Kirkley, comp. (Washington, D.C.: 1900), Series 3, Vol. IV, Sec. 2, pp. 1022-1042, for an eye-opening account of conditions among black people in South Carolina.

111   Thomas L. Livermore, *Numbers and Losses in the Civil War in America* (Boston and New York: 1900), p. 1 (after cited as "Livermore").

112   Joseph Jones and Samuel Cooper, "Confederate Losses During the War: Correspondence between Dr. Joseph Jones and Gen. Cooper," Southern Historical Society *Papers*, Vol. VII (1879), p. 290; Thornton H. Bowman, *Reminiscences of an Ex-Confederate Soldier or Forty Years on Crutches* (Austin, Texas: 1904). A lieutenant during the war, Bowman was later Texas secretary of state.

113   All the figures cited above include state and militia units.

114   David E. Johnston, *Confederate Boy in the Civil War* (Portland, Oregon: 1914), n.p. Johnston enlisted in the Confederate Army at age 16. He became sergeant major of the 7th Virginia Infantry Regiment in 1863 and was a judge in Oregon in 1914.

from the beginning.[115] I respectfully disagree. In my opinion, when the war began, the South could have won the war one of three ways: diplomatically, militarily, or politically.

Diplomatically, the South could have won the war if it secured a military alliance with Great Britain and France. This almost occurred when the Union Navy foolishly seized a British packet ship, the *Trent*, and removed two Confederate diplomats, who were under the protection of the British flag. War was only averted when the Lincoln regime backed down, issued an embarrassing apology, and released its captives. The diplomatic threat was one of the major reasons Lincoln issued the Emancipation Proclamation. The British lower classes might have accepted a war against the United States (which many of the King's subjects did not like), but the Emancipation Proclamation reframed the debate. The simple and unsophisticated Englishman, Frenchman, and Irishman now believed that the war was about slavery, and there was no way they were going to fight for that. Their ruling classes realized this, so there was now no way they were going to ally with the South. The Confederacy had lost the diplomatic option.

Because of the ineptitude of the Northern military and political leaders, and the brilliance of certain Rebel generals, the South came much closer to winning the war militarily than it ever should have. But after the fall of Vicksburg and the defeats at Gettysburg and Chattanooga, military victory was no longer a realistic possibility. The military option was now gone, but the political option remained. If the South could fight on until November 1864, Abraham Lincoln might be defeated for re-election, and there were a great many peace Democrats. A negotiated settlement of the conflict, including the recognition of the Confederate States of America, was a realistic possibility. Such was the situation when 1864 dawned.

*

Since the fall of Vicksburg, both Kirby Smith and Taylor expected the Yankees to move up the Red River. The danger seemed to lessen on February 3, 1864, when Sherman left Vicksburg with more than

---

115 Samuel R. (Sam) Watkins, *Co. Aytch* (Chattanooga, Tennessee: 1900), p. 220.

26,000 men and drove on Meridian in eastern Mississippi. His opponent, Leonidas Polk, had 20,000 men, but they were scattered throughout the entire state of Mississippi. He was unable to prevent Sherman from recapturing Jackson on February 5 and taking Meridian on February 14. Sherman's men remained in Meridian until February 20, when they returned to Vicksburg. In the meantime, they thoroughly demolished the Confederate infrastructure in the region, destroying 115 miles of railroads and 61 bridges as well as arsenals, supply depots, hospitals, and anything else of military value.

The Sherman drive to Meridian momentarily deceived the Rebel generals in the Trans-Mississippi, who thought that Mobile, not Shreveport, might be the objective after all. They were surprised when he returned to Vicksburg. Taylor was especially baffled. He simply could not believe that Grant would allow any of Sherman's troops to be used in an invasion up the Red. It was too illogical.

Illogical or not, that was exactly what the Yankees were planning to do. It must be pointed out that Grant was not officially given command of all Union armies until March 10, 1864. Until then, Halleck was general-in-chief. Even after that date, Grant retained Halleck as his chief of staff in Washington. More than anyone else, except for certain cotton speculators, Halleck wanted Banks to launch a Red River campaign. He got his wish.

Neither Taylor nor Kirby Smith saw any logic in making Shreveport and not Mobile the strategic objective of Banks' 1864 campaign. Kirby Smith wrote Taylor in early February 1864: "I still think that the enemy cannot be so infatuated as to occupy a large force in this department when every man should be employed east of the river, where the result of the campaign this summer must be decisive to our future for our weal or woe."[116]

The Rebel generals may have been baffled by the illogic of a Red River campaign, but the warning signs were too clear to be ignored. Although (to our regret) historians have never been able to learn much about the highly effective Confederate Secret Service and/or

---

116   O.R., Vol. XXXIV, Part 1, p. 494.

Dick Taylor's spy network in New Orleans, they were both extensive and very good, and Northern security measures were non-existent. Yankee troops were being withdrawn from Texas and sent to south Louisiana, and new units were arriving in New Orleans. Halleck sent Banks (and Franklin) four new infantry regiments: the 29th and 30th Maine, the 153rd New York, and the 14th New Hampshire. The War Department also sent the "Fighting Politician" seven new cavalry regiments and mounted seven veteran infantry regiments, giving Brigadier General Albert L. Lee, Banks' cavalry commander, 19 regiments. Franklin's XIX Corps was reinforced to a strength of 19 regiments in two divisions: the 1st (Weitzel) and the 2nd (Glover).

Meanwhile, all U.S. Army operations in Texas were suspended, and the 3rd and 4th Divisions of the XIII Corps were transferred to Brashear City (now Morgan City) and were placed under the command of Brigadier General Thomas E. G. Ransom, an officer who was held in high esteem by Ulysses S. Grant.[117] Large Federal infantry and artillery units were also transported from New Orleans to Franklin and a huge wagon train formed in the region. It was far too large for Banks' army, but the intended use of the excess wagons was obvious to the Confederates: they were planning to haul off captured plunder, especially cotton, which grew in abundance in the rich Red River Valley. This also ruled out southwestern Louisiana as a target for the invasion because, except for low quality longhorn cattle, its prairies were largely barren, and wagons would not be required to haul cattle in any case. By early March, General Franklin was reinforced to a strength of about 19,000 men. Their intentions were obvious. To block a possible Union drive to the west, from Vicksburg to Shreveport via Monroe, Taylor concentrated Walker's Texas Division between Marksville and Simmesport, near the confluence of the Red, Atchafalaya, and Mississippi Rivers.[118]

---

117   The 1st and 2nd Divisions of the XIII Corps remained in Texas but did not engage in any more offensive operations.
118   O.R., Vol. XXXIV, Part 1, p. 479.

As early as January 28, 1864, Taylor began to clear out the Atchafalaya region of wagons, horses, mules, and slaves—anything that could be used by the invader. The owners were given Confederate vouchers, which were basically useless. They protested, of course, but it did them no good. Taylor ordered that nothing be left for the Yankees and little was.

Meanwhile, Dick Taylor dealt with the Jayhawkers.

In Louisiana, the term "jayhawkers" referred to outlaws, criminals, and anyone else who was considered disloyal to the Confederacy.[119] Taylor ordered his men to "scour ... the country thoroughly" and to shoot "every man found with arms in his hands, against whom reasonable suspicion exists of a determination to resist the laws ... ." He emphasized that "Such men are not to be arrested" but were to be shot out of hand; only suspicion, not proof of guilt, was required. Furthermore, any unarmed man "capable of bearing arms, of whatever age, who [could not] give substantial proof of his loyalty to the Government" was to be arrested and carted off to Taylor's Headquarters. Colonel William J. Vincent's 2nd Louisiana Cavalry became particularly adept at flushing out jayhawkers. Its men captured 18 in a single day, and they executed them all the same day. One company under Captain Whittington captured 19 on the Mermenton River. They shot 12 and sent the other seven to General Taylor's headquarters. They were placed on trial and "will doubtless be executed," Taylor reported on March 6.[120] It is a pretty safe bet that he saw to it.

Taylor further ordered that all draft dodgers be impressed into the army. He also gathered up parolees who surrendered when Vicksburg and Port Hudson fell and sent them to special training camps. Some considered this an illegal act. Dick Taylor did not care.

---

119 Rickey Pittman, "Louisiana Jayhawkers," presentation to the Major Thomas McGuire Camp 1714, Sons of Confederate Veterans, January 10, 2023.
120 O.R., Vol. XXXIV, Part 1, p. 489.

Finally, in early 1864, Taylor established a series of supply depots from just south of Shreveport to Alexandria. If he had to retreat, his men, horses, and mules would be fed, armed, and supplied with ammunition. If the retreat did not prove necessary, Taylor reasoned, that was fine; it was better to have one too many supply depots than one too few.

By the second week in March, there was little for Taylor to do, except await the arrival of reinforcements from Texas and for the Union invasion to begin.

Chapter III

Opening Moves

Northern Preparations

As New Years' Day 1864 dawned, the North was very optimistic about having a quick end to the war. Lee had only 38,000 men present for duty in Virginia to oppose Major General George G. Meade's 78,000.[121] Sherman's armies in Georgia also badly outnumbered Joseph E. Johnston's Army of Tennessee. On April 15, Johnston and his cavalry commander, Joseph Wheeler, estimated that there were 103,000 Northern troops (77,000 of them infantry) in the Chattanooga area, but Johnston could field only 34,500 infantrymen to oppose them.[122] Surely, the Northern newspaper editors thought, the end was near. The Rebels were on their last legs, the editors declared; one more offensive would finish them off.

They were wrong. The more astute Union officers understood this. Lieutenant Colonel Theodore Lyman of General Meade's staff, for example, wrote: to his wife: "The newspapers would be comic in their comments, were not the whole thing so tragic ... These Rebels

---

121   Douglas Southall Freeman, *R. E. Lee* (New York: 1934-1936), Vol. III, p. 253.
122   Connelly, p. 308.

are not half-starved and ready to give up—a more sinewy, tawny, formidable-looking set of men could not be. In education they are certainly inferior to our native-born people; but they are usually very quick-witted within their own sphere of comprehension; and they know enough to handle weapons with terrible effect. Their great characteristic is their stoical manliess; they never beg, or whimper, or complain; but look you straight in the face, with as little animosity as if they had never heard a gun."[123]

"The South was clearly declining in power," Johnson wrote later, "but it still possessed, unknown to many, astonishing reserves of vitality."[124] The Northern people, however, believed the Confederacy was on its last legs militarily. Halleck, Grant and some of the more astute Union generals realized that this was not true. On January 17, 1864, Halleck wrote to Grant: "The rebels seem to be making the most desperate efforts for the next campaign. Almost every man, of whatever age, capable of bearing arms, is being pressed into their ranks ... Our people, on the contrary. are acting in the mistaken supposition that the war is nearly ended, and that we shall hereafter have to contend only with fragments of broken and demoralized rebel armies. Such is the tone of the public press and of the debates in Congress."[125] This incorrect attitude largely explains the Northern public's reaction to the huge numbers of casualties their armies suffered in the summer of 1864. The fact that this overly optimistic view infected at least part of the Union military leadership also goes a long way toward explaining the disaster which befell their army in Louisiana in 1864.

*

---

[123] Theodore Lyman, *Meade's Headquarters, 1863-1865*, George R. Agassiz, ed. (Boston: 1922), p. 100. Lyman (1833-1897) was a scientist and the descendent of a wealthy Massachusetts shipping family. Part of his job during the war was to carry a flag of truce into Southern lines when General Meade felt it necessary or appropriate, so he had a unique opportunity to observe the Confederate soldiers. Later he served in the U.S. House of Representatives.

[124] Johnson, p. 80.

[125] O.R., Vol. XXXII, Part 2, p. 122.

One of Ulysses S. Grant's greatest fears at the beginning of 1864 was that a Red River expedition would tie up troops greatly needed for a spring campaign east of the river. Grant, however, was not yet general-in-chief of the Union armies, so he could not dictate strategy. He, nevertheless, did try to influence it. He even got two of his staff officers to write Charles A. Dana, a former Greeley editor who was now assistant secretary of war, asking him to intervene via Stanton, to make sure Banks' army was diverted from the Red River toward its proper goal, which was Mobile. Nothing came of this indirect approach, however; Grant was finally forced to defer to the general-in-chief and accept Halleck's flawed strategy.

As we have seen, Banks was gradually won over to Halleck's concept of operations but not for military reasons. He wanted cotton. In January 1864, he received several reports from spies stating that there was now a huge amount of cotton in the Red River country as well as tens of thousands of bales in southern Arkansas. Some of these spies were his own staff officers. There were also at least two Confederate officers who were willing to see to it that the cotton was not burned as the Northern troops approached—for a price.[126] Banks stood to gain a great deal of favorable publicity for capturing this cotton—not to mention campaign contributions from the New England textile mill and financial interests. Promises, in fact, were already made, and Banks still had his sights set on the presidency in 1864. On January 23, even though he had stated earlier that Mobile should be the main objective of the Army of the Gulf in 1864, Banks wrote Halleck and completely accepted his strategy. He did so for three reasons: cotton, politics, and a desire to please Halleck. Military considerations did not enter into his thinking.

Halleck, Banks, *et al* realized the need for the Department of Arkansas and the Gulf to be under a single commander. "The difficulty," Halleck wrote Sherman, "is to get a suitable commander. General Banks is not competent, and there are so many political objections to superseding him by Steele that it would be useless to ask the President to do it. Moreover, I fear the command would be too

---

126 Johnson, p. 47.

large for Steele"[127] His solution to the problem was to ignore it and not appoint an overall commander. The entire Union effort west of the Mississippi would suffer from a serious lack of unity of command.

On February 16, Grant received a telegram from Halleck, informing him for the first time that troops from the east would be used for a Red River Expedition. Two days later, Grant wrote to Sherman and declared that, unless he (Sherman) went with them, any troops he detached to the Army of the Gulf would be permanently lost to him. Go with them, however, is exactly what William Tecumseh Sherman wanted to do. Strangely enough, General Sherman, the commander of the XV Corps at Vicksburg, not only agreed with Halleck's strategy—he wanted to direct the Red River campaign himself. From 1859 to 1861, he was superintendent of the Louisiana State Seminary of Learning and Military Academy at Pineville (now L.S.U. in Baton Rouge), which was just across the river from Alexandria. He was very ambitious to command an army in central Louisiana and fight his old friend, Richard Taylor. In early 1864, however, he was (like Grant) junior in rank to Banks. On March 1, he traveled by steamboat from Vicksburg to New Orleans to confer with Banks and ask for the command. When they met the next day, he promised Banks 10,000 of his best troops and Admiral Porter's Mississippi River Squadron. He would meet Franklin's XIX Corps at Alexandria on March 17, he declared, and then drive on Shreveport. Meanwhile, Major General Frederick Steele's VII Corps would advance from Little Rock to Monroe, Louisiana, and then push 105 miles due west, joining with the main body at Shreveport. Banks, however, told a disappointed Sherman that he would personally command the expedition. Although Banks expressed himself diplomatically, he let Sherman know that he was not welcome to join in. He also invited Sherman to stay in New Orleans for the inauguration of Michael Hahn, the new Republican chief executive of the Free State of Louisiana and the state's first Reconstruction governor.

---

127   O.R., Vol. XXXII, Part 3, p. 289.

Sherman and his generals. Standing left to right: Oliver Howard, William Hazen, Jefferson C. Davis and Joseph A. Mower, who distinguished himself in the Red River campaign. Seated are John A. Logan, Sherman, and Henry W. Slocum.

The inauguration was scheduled for March 4. A disgusted Sherman returned to Vicksburg that same day—but not before he stipulated to Banks that he must have his 10,000 men back by April 15.[128]

Sherman left New Orleans with a sense of foreboding. It was obvious that Banks was more interested in politics than in military affairs and put more effort into planning inaugural festivities and balls than into the Red River Expedition, which was scheduled to begin on March 7.

General Steele, meanwhile, was given a considerable amount of discretion in planning his phase of the advance. Instead of driving on Monroe, he opted to take the shorter, direct route from Little Rock to Shreveport. **Map 3.1** (pg. 78) shows the final Union plan for the Red River campaign.

*

---

128   O.R., Vol. XXXIV, Part 2, pp. 494, 496-497.

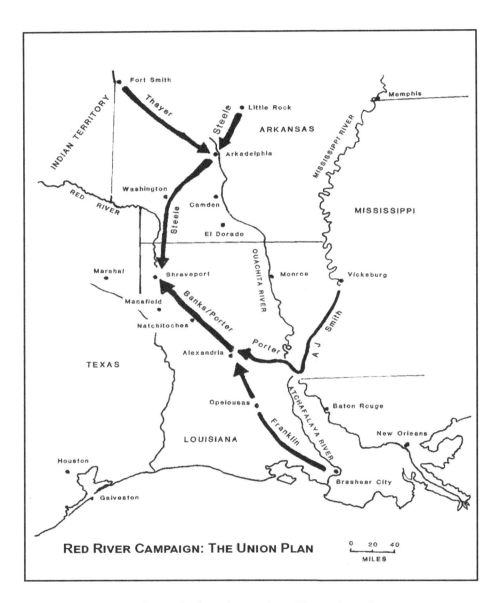

3.1 The Red River Campaign: The Union Plan

For the Red River campaign, Nathaniel P. Banks' Army of the Gulf controlled the XIX Corps and the 3rd and 4th Divisions of the XIII Corps—about 17,000 men. He specified that "No negroes shall accompany the command, except authorized officers' servants or employees of the quartermaster's and commissary departments."[129] It also directed Brigadier General Albert Lee's cavalry division (5,000 men), 1,000 Marines, and Colonel William H. Duckey's *Corps d'Afrique* (2,500 men). It also included 10,000 men from the XVI Corps, which were loaned to Banks by Sherman.

Andrew Jackson Smith, the commander of the XVI Corps, was born in Bucks County, Pennsylvania, in 1815. He graduated from West Point in 1838 and was commissioned in the 1st Dragoons. A. J. Smith spent the next 23 years in the West and was not promoted to major until 1861. Since then, he commanded the 2nd California Cavalry (1861), Halleck's cavalry in the Corinth campaign (1862), a division in Sherman's corps in the disastrous attack on Chickasaw Bluffs (late 1862), and a division in the XIII Corps at Arkansas Post and in the Vicksburg campaign. A drunkard, he was nicknamed "Whiskey" Smith, and he was a short, unimpressive man with a sloppy beard and wire-rimmed glasses. Highly vulgar, profane, gloomy, and cruel by nature, he was not a particular success in life before 1861. Perhaps as a result, he was jealous of Banks and had more than his share of the Regular Army officers' contempt for the political soldier. Decidedly unprofessional but a good fighter, A. J. Smith was highly critical of Banks and encouraged his officers and men to follow his example. Very often, he was on the border of being insubordinate and, at least once, fermented a mutiny against General Banks. Richard Taylor would have put him in his place in a heartbeat because he knew how to handle disloyal subordinates, but Nathaniel Banks did not. A. J. Smith often acted as if he were not under Banks' command at all.

*

---

[129] O.R., Vol. XXXIV, Part 2, p. 491.

A. J. "Whiskey" Smith

The USS Mound City, a heavy, city-class ironclad.

All totaled, Banks' army had about 33,600 men and 90 guns when the campaign began. It was supported by the most impressive force of all: David D. Porter's Mississippi River Squadron.

Admiral Porter's flotilla totaled 104 vessels—the largest concentration of inland naval power seen in the Civil War. It included the large ironclads *Benton, Essex, Choctaw, Eastport, Lafayette, Carondelet, Louisville, Mound City, Pittsburg,* and *Chillicothe*; the river monitors[130] *Neosho, Osage* and *Ozark*; the large tinclads *Black Hawk* and *Ouachita*; the tinclads[131] *Covington, Fort Hindman, Gazelle, Cricket, Juliet, Forest Rose, Signal, St. Clair,* and *Tallahatchie*; the timberclad *Lexington*; and the captured ram *General Sterling Price*. In all, they boasted an incredible total of 210 guns.[132] The fleet also included an impressive array of support vessels, including supply boats, tugs, tenders, and dispatch vessels. In addition, the army's Quartermaster Corps followed it with its own transports and supply vessels—enough to carry 10,000 men.

The most impressive weapon in Porter's arsenal was the *Eastport*. This ironclad was 280 feet long, 43 feet wide at the beam, and drew six feet three inches of water. It was armed with two huge 100-pounder rifled cannons, four 9-inch smoothbores, and two 50-pounder rifled cannons. The twin 100-pounders were located in the front, facing forward.[133]

Porter decided that the *Eastport*, his heaviest vessel, would lead his fleet in this campaign. This was because he heard that the Confederate Navy was building huge ironclads (possibly rams)

---

[130] Monitors were ironclads with rotating turrets, and their decks barely cleared the water.

[131] A tinclad was a boat partially covered with ¼ to ½ inches of armored plating. An ironclad was covered with at least 2 ¼ inches of armored plating.

[132] Joiner, pp. 39-41. Gary D. Joiner, *Through the Howling Wilderness: The 1864 Red River Campaign and the Union Failure in the West* (Knoxville, Tennessee: 2006), p. 53 (hereafter cited as "Joiner, *Howling Wilderness*").

[133] Paul H. Silverstone, *Warships of the Civil War Navies* (Annapolis, Maryland: 1989), p. 156.

Admiral David D. Porter

William Buel Franklin (1823-1903), commander of the XVI Corps.

and even submarines at Shreveport. The reports were grossly exaggerated, and there were no submarines at Shreveport, but they did influence his thinking.

Admiral David Porter was one of the most interesting characters to emerge from the War Between the States. He was born near Philadelphia in 1813, the son of Commodore David D. Porter, who captained the USS frigate *Essex* during the War of 1812. David, Senior, took his son to sea as a cabin boy when he was 10, and young David saw action against the West Indies pirates from 1823 to 1825. Later, the elder Porter was court-martialed for exceeding his authority. Suspended for six months, he resigned in disgust and moved to Mexico, where he served as commander-in-chief of the Mexican Navy from 1825 to 1829. Young David began his career as a cadet in the Mexican Navy but joined the U.S. Navy as a midshipman in 1829. He fought in the Mexican War, moved steadily up in rank, and was named captain of the USS *Powhatan* when the Civil War began.

He took part in the capture of New Orleans under the command of his foster brother, Admiral David Farragut. Named commander of the Mississippi River Squadron in 1862, he supported Grant's army in the operations against Vicksburg and was wounded in the head while directing amphibious operations at Grand Gulf, Mississippi, in April 1863. He was promoted to rear admiral on July 4, 1863—the day Vicksburg fell. Somehow, over the years, he managed to secure enough shore leave to marry and father 10 children. Later, he would be one of only seven naval officers to officially remain on active duty for life—the others being Farragut, George Dewey, William Leahy (F.D.R.'s chief of staff), Ernest King, Chester Nimitz, and William Halsey. Admiral Porter was also a gifted writer and authored several novels as well as his Civil War memoirs, which read like an exciting novel—as indeed they are in several places. On the other hand, David D. Porter was undoubtedly a fine sailor and a war hero of the first order—and he knew it. He was also an accomplished cotton thief. Historian Gary D. Joiner described him as "… intelligent, witty, brash … and prone to self-aggrandizement. His ego was legendary, and he exuded self-confidence."[134] He was also short-tempered, excitable, and difficult to work with.[135] He shared A. J. Smith's contempt for the political soldier, Banks.

Banks left most of the detailed military planning to his deputy commander, Major General William Buel Franklin, the commander of the XIX Corps. Although he was a professional soldier, Franklin was under a cloud since the Battle of Fredericksburg. Born in York, Pennsylvania, on February 27, 1823, the 41-year-old Franklin graduated from West Point in 1843 at the top of his class. Commissioned in the engineers, he participated in the Great Lakes survey (1843-45) and in the exploration of the Rocky Mountains. He won a brevet for gallantry at Buena Vista in the Mexican War, where he served under General Zachary Taylor. When the Civil War broke out, he was in charge of constructing the new Capitol Dome and the huge Treasury Department addition in Washington, D.C. He was

---

134   Joiner, p. 47.
135   Hollandsworth, p. 176.

commissioned colonel of the 12th U.S. Infantry Regiment on May 14, 1861, but was promoted to brigadier general of volunteers three days later. He led his brigade, which included two Massachusetts regiments and the 1st Minnesota, in the 1st Battle of Bull Run, where he did well by the standard of the day. He was given a division in September and distinguished himself in the Peninsula Campaign of 1862. After fighting at Sharpsburg (Antietam), where he led the VI Corps, Franklin commanded the Left Grand Division (the I and VI Corps) during the Fredericksburg disaster. After this battle, the commander of the Army of the Potomac, Ambrose E. Burnside, needed a scapegoat, so he charged Franklin with disobeying orders. He declared that Franklin was largely responsible for the debacle which resulted in the slaughter of 13,500 Federal soldiers by Robert E. Lee's army and demanded that he be discharged from the service. Lincoln refused to take this action and relieved Burnside instead, but Franklin's career was badly damaged nevertheless. He was relieved of duty and was unemployed for several months. Finally, he was exiled to Louisiana as commander of the XIX Corps. His first operation here was the Saline Pass disaster (Chapter II). Although he was given another chance, William Franklin was clearly out of favor with the administration and was on probation in the spring of 1864.

SOUTHERN PREPARATIONS

"This is Gen'l Taylor's Country," Captain Elijah Petty of Walker's Texas Division wrote to his wife in January 1864. "He has set his heart to defend it."[136]

Kirby Smith also recognized the danger. In early 1864, he wrote to Jeff Davis: "The only true line of operations by which the enemy can penetrate the department is the valley of the Red River, rich

---

136 Norman D. Brown, ed., *Journey to Pleasant Hill: The Civil War Letters of Captain Elijah P. Petty, Walker's Texas Division, C.S.A.* (San Antonio, Texas: 1982), p. 304 (hereafter cited as "Petty").

in supplies; with steam-boat navigation for six months of the year, it offers facilities for the co-operation of the army and navy, and enables them to shift their base as they advance into the interior."[137]

Despite the fact that the route of advance of the Northern invaders was obvious to all the Rebel generals (except for John Magruder in Texas, who thought the target might be Texas), Kirby-Smith did little to reinforce the Army of Western Louisiana. " ... it was a 'far cry' to Shreveport," Taylor recalled, "and the emergency seemed less pressing in the rear than at the front."[138]

From December 1863 to early March 1864, Taylor's repeated requests for reinforcements were basically ignored. All Taylor received was Colonel William G. Vincent's rather mediocre 2nd Louisiana Cavalry Regiment. Increasingly frustrated, Taylor pled ill health and asked for a leave of absence on March 4. Knowing that he could not spare his best commander on the eve of the Yankee invasion, Kirby Smith caved completely. On March 5, he ordered Magruder to send Green's cavalry division back to Louisiana at once.[139] (Intelligence reports that Sherman visiting Banks in New Orleans contributed to this decision. Kirby Smith suspected that Sherman might be planning to advance on Shreveport via Monroe, in a coordinate offensive with Banks.) This move left Magruder with less than 3,000 men (exclusive of state troops and the coastal garrisons), and Kirby Smith ordered them to be near the Red River, as a reserve, in case the Federals from Fort Smith advanced behind Taylor.[140] The next day, Taylor ordered Prince de Polignac to march his brigade to Alexandria without delay, leaving the defense of northeast Louisiana to Liddell's tiny fourth-class brigade. Sherman's troops at Vicksburg could have easily overrun the Ouachita River country, but Taylor correctly guessed that they would not. The commander of the Army of Western Louisiana, however, did not foresee two developments:

---

137   O.R., Vol. XXIV, Part 2, pp. 895-896.

138   Richard Taylor, *Destruction and Reconstruction* (New York: 1879), p. 154 (hereafter cited as "Taylor").

139   O.R., Vol. XXXIV, Part 2, p. 1027.

140   O.R., Vol..XXXIV, Part 2, p. 1028.

that General Sherman would send significant forces from Vicksburg against his deep left flank, and Magruder would take his time in sending the cavalry to Louisiana.[141] "Prince John" did not dispatch Green's vanguard, Colonel Xavier R. Debray's 26th Texas Cavalry Regiment, until March 15. He was followed immediately by elements of Brigadier General James Patrick Major's cavalry Division. **Map 3.2** shows the Red River Valley.

The Red River Expedition began with a false start. On March 7, 5,000 Yankee cavalrymen, commanded by Brigadier General Albert L. Lee and spearheaded by Colonel Nathan A. M. "Gold Lace" Dudley, left Franklin, Louisiana, and headed north for Alexandria. The next day, the heavens opened up, and the column was swamped by one of the infamous Louisiana rainstorms, which last for days. One author stated that it "removed the bottoms from the roads," which were all made of dirt and were mostly "buckshot" clay, which sticks to shoes, boots, and wheels like glue—maybe worse.[142] The infantry, which was supposed to start north on March 8, could not move until March 15 and then only with difficulty because the roads were still muddy.

On March 10—three days later than originally planned—A. J. Smith steamed out of Vicksburg with 15 infantry regiments in 21 transports.

The Ouachita/Black River joins the Red near its mouth. The Atchafalaya River is a distributary and exits the Mississippi at the mouth of the Red at Turnbull Island, a huge sandbar. Some of the Red flows into the Mississippi, but most of it empties into the

---

141   John Bankhead "Prince John" Magruder (1807-1871) was born in Port Royal, Virginia, and graduated from West Point in 1830. An artillery officer and an amateur actor, he won three brevets for courage and gallantry in Mexico—an unusually large number. He resigned in 1861 and was commissioned brigadier general, C.S.A., in June and was promoted to major general on October 7, 1861. He distinguished himself by deceiving General McClellan as to the size of his forces in the Peninsula Campaign and significantly delayed the Union advance on Richmond. His performance in the Seven Days Campaign, however, left much to be desired. One of Lee's rejects, he was named commander of the District of Texas, New Mexico, and Arizona in the summer of 1862. He scored a brilliant victory at Galveston on New Year's Day, 1863, and gobbled up the entire Union garrison.

142   Johnson, p. 98.

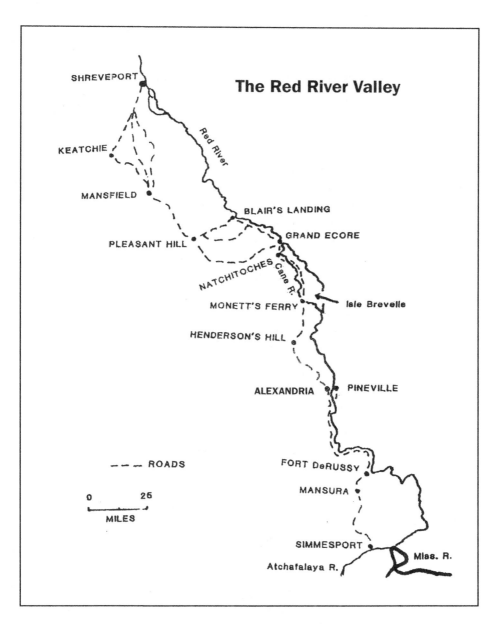

3.2 The Red River Valley

Atchafalaya. Escorted by Porter's ironclads, Smith was able to enter the Red River through the Mississippi. He landed unopposed at Simmesport and began to off-load troops.

Major General John G. Walker was in charge of the Confederate defenses in this area. Born in Cole County, Missouri, in 1822, his father was state treasurer for many years. He was educated at Jesuit College in St. Louis and was commissioned directly into the U.S. Army in 1846–a highly unusual honor at that time. He saw action in Mexico and served in Arizona, New Mexico, California, and Oregon after the war. A captain in 1861, he joined the Regular Army of the Confederacy as a major and was soon promoted to lieutenant colonel in the 8th Texas Cavalry. He was given command of the 2nd Virginia Infantry later that year and distinguished himself in several battles on the Eastern Front, rising to the rank of brigadier general (January 9, 1862) and major general (November 8, 1862). Meanwhile, he played a prominent role in the capture of Harpers Ferry, where the Union lost 12,600 men. His timely arrival on the field at Sharpsburg probably saved the Army of Northern Virginia on September 17. About that same time, Jefferson Davis learned that the Texas Division in Little Rock, then commanded by Brigadier General Henry E. McCulloch, was a mess from the Confederate point of view.[143] He dispatched John G. Walker to Arkansas to straighten it out.

President Davis could not have made a better choice. Walker was one of the best division commanders in the Rebel army, and his long years of service in the West gave him a deep understanding of the Texas frontier mentality. He soon whipped the division into shape, and it became known as "the Greyhounds," because it marched so rapidly. The general was also extremely popular with his troops. When he appeared, the men in the ranks often placed their hats on their

---

143 Blessington, pp. 72-73. Henry McCulloch (1816-1895) was the elder brother of Brigadier General Ben McCulloch, who was killed at Pea Ridge. A native of Tennessee, he and his brother were on their way to the Alamo in 1836 to join their former neighbor, Davy Crockett, but Ben fell ill with the measles (a more serious disease then than now). Henry variously served as a sheriff, captain in the Texas Rangers, and U.S. marshal for east Texas. His Civil War career was less distinguished and was spent mainly in Texas. Described as "gentle and unassuming," he spent the last 10 years of his life farming in Guadlupe County, Texas. He was survived by seven children.

bayonets and cheered him loudly. "No commander could surpass him," one private wrote. "Devoid of ambition, incapable of envy, he was brave, gallant and just."[144] Brigadier General Camille de Polignac, who was not afraid to criticize his peers, called General Walker "a man of sound judgement ... quiet and modest ... always perfectly self-possessed."[145] In late 1863, General Taylor selected Walker to command the lower Red River area, his most endangered sector.

In March 1864, Walker's division was small by the standards of 1862. It included 3,800 men and 12 guns.[146] They were divided into three brigades: Brigadier General Thomas N. Waul's 1st, Colonel Horace Randal's 2nd, and Brigadier General Richard Scurry's 3rd. Neither Walker nor any of his brigade commanders would be left standing at the conclusion of this campaign. Table 3.1 shows the Order of Battle of the Texas Division at the beginning of the Red River Expedition.

The Greyhounds recrossed into the Atchafalaya country at Morgan's Ferry on December 11, 1863, and went into winter quarters near Marksville. Here, the men of Waul's and Randal's brigades were forced to build their own huts. Scurry's men were more fortunate. They camped on the Norwood Plantation, about a mile north of Bayou de Glaize, and were able to use vacated slave cabins. On days of good weather, the Greyhounds built a fortification called Fort Humbug on Yellow Bayou.

The men grew restless as the time for active campaigning neared. They knew all about the Union buildup at Brashear City (now Morgan City) and were concerned that a rapid advance by Banks might cut them off from Alexandria. Men who were AWOL (away without leave) returned to the ranks, and on March 6, all the

---

144 Blessington, p. 73.

145 Kinard, p. 103.

146 See O.R., Vol. XXXIV, Part 1, p. 598-601 for General Walker's report on the Yellow Bayou operation.

division's sick and infirmed were ordered to board steamboats. They were transported to Alexandria and then to Shreveport. Scurry's brigade was put on alert on March 7.

THE BATTLE OF FORT DERUSSY

The northern anchor of Walker's defenses was Fort DeRussy on the Red River. It was planned by Brigadier General William R. Boggs, Kirby Smith's chief of staff, and was built by Colonel Lewis G. DeRussy, after whom it was named.[147] Map 3.3 shows the Simmesport-Fort DeRussy sector.

Boggs was a brilliant engineer. Born in Augusta, Georgia, in 1829, he attended the Augusta Academy and West Point, where he studied under the legendary Professor of Engineering Dennis Hart Mahan. Boggs graduated fourth in his class (1853) and became an engineer and ordnance officer. He served on General Beauregard's staff at Charleston (1861) and on Bragg's staff at Pensacola (1861), where he was chief of engineers and artillery. He was the chief of engineers for the state of Georgia in 1862 and was promoted to brigadier general on November 4. Named chief of staff to General Kirby Smith for the Perryville Campaign, he accompanied the general to the Trans-Mississippi in March 1863.

Boggs also had an excellent working relationship with Dick Taylor, even though the army commander was from the Stonewall Jackson school of thought. Taylor believed in speed and outmaneuvering the enemy and had no faith in fixed fortifications. (Boggs' relationship with Kirby Smith grew less cordial over time.) On the other hand,

---

[147] Lewis Gustave DeRussy (1795-1864) was reportedly the oldest West Point graduate to fight for the South in the Civil War. His father, Thomas, was a French naval officer recruited for the U.S. Navy by Benjamin Franklin. He served under John Paul Jones in the American Revolution and was aboard the *Bonhomme Richard* until just before it sank. Lewis graduated from West Point in 1814, fought in the War of 1812, and survived three wars. He was named major general in the Louisiana Militia in 1848 and briefly commanded the 2nd Louisiana Infantry Regiment in Virginia. His brother Rene was a Union general, as was one of his nephews. Steven M. Mayeux, "The Life and Times of Lewis DeRussy," A Paper Presented before the First Annual History Symposium, Fort Jessup, Louisiana, March 1, 2002.

Order Of Battle, Walker's Texas Division, March 12, 1864

Commander: Major General John G. Walker

1st Brigade: Brigadier General Thomas N. Waul

    8th Texas Infantry Regiment: Colonel Overton Young

    18th Texas Infantry Regiment: Colonel W. H. King

    22nd Texas Infantry Regiment: Colonel R. B. Hubbard

    13th Texas Cavalry Regiment (Dismounted): Colonel A. F. Crawford

2nd Brigade: Colonel Horace Randal

    11th Texas Infantry Regiment: Colonel O. M. Roberts

    14th Texas Infantry Regiment: Colonel Edward Clark

    28th Texas Cavalry Regiment (Dismounted): Colonel Eli H. Baxter

    23rd Texas Cavalry (Dismounted): Colonel Nicholas C. Gould

3rd Brigade: Brigadier General Richard Scurry

    16th Texas Infantry Regiment: Colonel George Flournoy

    17th Texas Infantry Regiment: Colonel G. W. Jones

    16th Texas Cavalry Regiment (Dismounted): Colonel William Fitzhugh

    19th Texas Infantry Regiment: Colonel Richard Waterhouse

    Fort DeRussy: Lieutenant Colonel William Byrd

Table 3.1 Order Of Battle, Walker's Texas Division, March 12, 1864

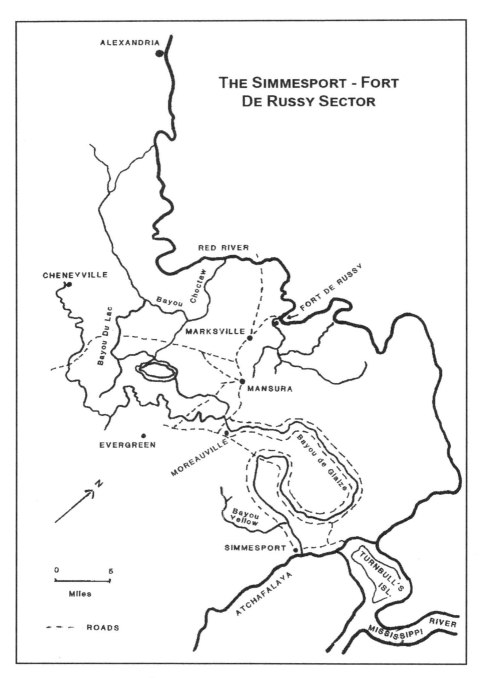

3.3 The Simmesport-Fort DeRussy Sector

Taylor and Major Henry T. Douglas, the chief engineer of the Trans-Mississippi Department, despised each other.[148] Taylor, therefore, worked directly with Boggs but not Douglas.

In Fort DeRussy, Boggs designed a very impressive fort. Well placed on a sharp curve in the river, it featured 40-foot thick walls that were 12 feet high and protected by a ditch. Its eight siege guns and two field pieces effectively controlled the Red River. Fort DeRussy was garrisoned by three companies from Walker's division (which were rotated periodically) and was commanded by Lieutenant Colonel William Byrd of the 14th Texas.

Fort DeRussy had only one flaw, but it was a major one—it was vulnerable to attack from the land side. For this reason, General Taylor initially opposed constructing it and derisively called it "the Gibraltar of the South." Kirby Smith, however, enthusiastically supported the concept of constructing forts, and Taylor eventually gave it tepid support. He used every slave he could lay his hands on as laborers, although many of them ran away.

On March 12, A. J. Smith's transports appeared opposite Simmesport and began disembarking infantry by the thousands. The men of the Confederate outposts watched in shock and horror. They did not risk firing on the landing parties because they knew it would provoke a reaction by an overwhelming force; instead, they sent messages to General Scurry, who informed Walker. He, in turn, ordered Scurry to occupy Fort Humbug and sent dispatches to Richard Taylor, who was taken by surprise. He guarded against them, true enough, but he did not expect the Yankees to make the mistake of committing an entire corps of Sherman's troops west of the Mississippi. Now his deep left flank was in serious danger.

Fort Humbug was built for one purpose only: to protect the rear of Fort DeRussy. It was, however, only half finished and if it were lost, would place its defenders in grave danger of being trapped with their backs to the Red River. In addition, it could be easily

---

148   Joiner, *Howling Wilderness*, p. 28.

outflanked because it was a dry winter, and the swamps on its left and right did not offer the protection they would have afforded in normal years. As the day wore on, estimates of the number of Union soldiers landing at Simmesport increased, and Walker was without his "eyes." He had only three companies of cavalry attached to his division, and they were east of the Atchafalaya, where they were cut off by the Union landings. (They ultimately escaped and rejoined the division.) Eventually, the Rebel outposts reported that the entire area was crawling with Yankees and the Federals had landed 15,000 to 17,000 men and 30 to 40 guns. This number was high by more than a third, but even given the overestimations, Walker knew that he was in deep trouble. He had only 3,800 men and 12 guns. He sent word to Taylor that his position was "extremely hazardous" anyway, since he was basically on an island formed by the Red River, Bayou de Glaize, Bayou Du Lac, and Bayou Choctaw. His only route of escape was over the Bayou Du Lac Bridge, eight miles to the south.

Meanwhile, a woman on horseback arrived at Fort Humbug, breathless after a wild gallop through the woods. She informed General Scurry that the Yankees were advancing on his positions. Unfortunately, history does not record the name of this Southern "Paula Revere," but she convinced Scurry that he was in danger of being outflanked. Shortly after, the Confederate pickets and outposts came in across the Yellow Bayou bridge. They were also breathless because they had been running. They had lost all their kitchen equipment and excitedly declared that they would have been lost also, except for the fact that they could run faster than the Yankees. That was enough for General Scurry, who ordered the Yellow Bayou bridge burned. It was also enough for General John Walker, who ordered Scurry to retreat to the south to join the rest of the division near Marksville, about three miles south of Fort Humbug. They would then continue to march south, Walker decided, to see if they could avoid being trapped between A. J. Smith and Banks' main body, coming up from Franklin. They abandoned Fort Humbug at 10 p.m. By now, Rebel scouts and outposts reported that the Yankees had landed 15,000 infantry, 2,000 cavalry, and 1,000 artillerymen—18,000 men in all.[149] This number almost doubled the Federals' actual strength, but even if the correct number was reported, Walker was still outnumbered nearly 3 to 1.[150]

Richard Taylor wanted to protect Louisiana as far forward as practical, so he encouraged Walker to defend the Marksville area, if he deemed it feasible. "Close, sharp, quick fighting is our game where there is any reasonable chance of success ..." Taylor wrote to Walker. "Any severe check to the head of their column would probably break up this expedition." He instructed Walker to "take more than ordinary hazards" and reminded him that "the loss of our [guns] at Fort DeRussy and the occupation of Alexandria by the Federals would be a great disaster."[151] Walker, however, considered his position untenable, and he was not about to risk his entire division, so he retreated. (He did, however, send a dispatch to Taylor, stating that he would attack the Union flank if an opportunity presented itself.) Prince de Polignac, whose brigade was nearing Alexandria from the north, considered this a mistake and labeled Walker's withdrawal "hasty;"[152] however, it seems obvious to this author that Walker did the right thing.

On March 13, A. J. Smith sent a reconnaissance force to Fort Humbug and found it undefended. After capturing a few stragglers, he headed for Mansura and Fort DeRussy with most of his command. Later that day, the Union soldiers crossed Bayou de Glaize and entered the Avoyelles prairie. U.S. Brigadier General Thomas Kilby Smith, the commander of the Provisional Division of the XVII Corps, wrote to his wife and described it as "one of the most beautiful prairies

---

149 Blessington, p. 169. The actual number was 11,000, if the Marine Brigade is included. Its men did leave the transports but were too busy looting nearby plantations to count as effective combat troops. They should in no way be confused with modern U.S. Marines.

150 These figures exclude sailors.

151 O.R., Vol. XXXIV, Part 1, pp. 492-493.

152 Kinard, p. 131.

imaginable."[153] At 3 a.m. the following day, A. J. Smith was at Mansura when he learned that Scurry's brigade had joined the rest of Walker's division, which was now five miles west of the town and was apparently expecting him to try to cross the Bayou de Glaize at that point because they burned the bridge there. A. J. Smith, however, was not about to accommodate Walker by walking into an ambush. Instead, he tore up a cotton gin and used the lumber to construct a bridge at Mansura. He crossed the bayou and thus outflanked Walker, who was on his left, and headed for Fort DeRussy with his entire corps.[154] Early that afternoon, the XVI Corps entered the Creole town of Marksville and by late afternoon was about a mile and a half south of Fort DeRussy. A. J. Smith positioned Kilby Smith's division to his left rear, to guard against Walker, and ordered Brigadier General Joseph A. Mower, the commander of the 3rd Division, XVI Corps, to attack the fort.

Joseph Mower always wanted a military career. Born in Vermont in 1827, he grew up in Lowell, Massachusetts, and was educated at the famous Norwich Academy in Vermont. He was working as a carpenter when the Mexican War began in 1846, so he enlisted as a private and served until 1848. In 1855, he finally obtained an appointment as a second lieutenant in the 1st U.S. Infantry Regiment. He took part in the early actions in Missouri in 1861, and was elected commander of the 12th Missouri (Union) Infantry Regiment in May 1862. He fought at Iuka and Corinth, where he was wounded and captured. Mower escaped from prison but was captured again before he reached Union lines. Finally exchanged, he was promoted to brigadier general on March 16, 1863, and commanded a brigade in Sherman's XV Corps during the Vicksburg campaign. Sherman

---

153 Walter G. Smith, *The Life and Letters of Thomas Kilby Smith, Brevet Major General, U.S. Volunteers, 1820-1887* (New York: 1898), p. 357 (hereafter cited as "Kilby Smith"). The general's name was "Smith," but he will be referred to as "Kilby Smith" throughout this book to avoid confusion. He was born in Massachusetts but grew up in Ohio. He studied law under Salmon P. Chase, Lincoln's secretary of the treasury and later chief justice of the U.S. Supreme Court. A lawyer, he joined the army in 1861 as lieutenant colonel of the 54th Ohio and served under Grant and Sherman. He was promoted to brigadier general on August 13, 1863.

154 Winters, p. 328.

called him "the boldest young soldier we have."[155] An outstanding commander by any measurement (as we shall see), he was only 36 years old when he prepared to attack the Confederate Gibraltar.

Mower deployed his 1st and 2nd Brigades in line, followed closely by the 3rd Brigade. His plan was to attack the fort and overwhelm it in one rush, while part of his men kept the heads of the Southern artillerymen down with rifle fire. (They were already busy exchanging shots with Porter's ironclads in any case.) Mower thus hoped to avoid suffering serious casualties. The plan worked perfectly. The Confederates were overcome in a matter of minutes, and Mower lost only three men killed and 35 wounded. The Rebels lost five killed, four wounded, and 319 captured.[156] They also lost 10 guns, including two huge 32-pounder Parrott guns, which took a dozen oxen each to transport. Only Captain Adams of the 28th Texas Cavalry (Dismounted) escaped with 22 of his greyhounds.[157] Admiral Porter later compared the Confederate defense to "the antics of Chinamen, who build canvas forts, paint hideous dragons on their shields, turn somersets ... and run away at the first sign of an engagement."[158]

Meanwhile, Walker's division was nearly surrounded. Harassed by Union cavalry, it marched all day and all night on March 14, passed through Evergreen (30 miles south of Alexandria), and continued marching until 2 p.m. on March 15. After a three-hour break, it started marching again at 5 p.m. and continued until 10 p.m., when it at last camped on Bayou Du Lac. Here, its men were finally fed. The Texans received only one meal a day during the entire march. During one of the halts, Captain Elijah Petty wrote to his wife: "The men are weary

---

155   O.R., Vol. XXXII, Part 3, p. 325.
156   O.R., Vol. XXXIV, Part 1, p. 305.
157   O.R., Vol. XXXIV, Part 1, p. 600-601.
158   James L. Nichols, *Confederate Engineers* (Wilmington, North Carolina: 2000), pp. 61-62.

and foot sore, broken down and jaded. Even the horses have fagged under it."[159] Another of Walker's men wrote: "Our men have suffered very much, but marched like heroes ..."[160]

On March 16/17, they made a night march of 28 miles to Lloyd's bridge on Bayou Boeuf, about 25 miles south of Alexandria, and after marching on the 18th were finally out of danger of being trapped between Banks' main body and A. J. Smith. On March 19, they marched another 20 miles and finally joined up with the rest of Taylor's infantry and the 2nd Louisiana Cavalry Regiment at Carroll Jones' plantation, which was owned by a wealthy free African American.[161]

Meanwhile, back at Fort DeRussy, Mower's men reembarked on the transports on the morning of March 15 and steamed toward Alexandria, which was 30 miles away. A. J. and Kilby Smith stayed behind to destroy Fort DeRussy. This involved tearing down and burning wooden beams, leveling the earthworks, and destroying the magazine. A. J. Smith personally supervised this operation, and he botched it. For some reason, he got the hair-brained idea of blowing up the magazine in the middle of the night, after most of the troops were sleep. Two Union regiments were camped too close, and no one thought to inform them what Smith was up to until the Confederate gunpowder erupted in a series of huge explosions. The result was panic. Hundreds of unarmed, half-naked Yankees—who had never run from the Rebels and never would—fled into the woods in terror as huge chunks of Fort DeRussy fell all around them. Two men were killed by falling debris and dozens were injured, several of them seriously.[162] Afterward, Whiskey Smith was booed and hooted at by his own men every time he appeared until he threatened them with repercussions unless they stopped.

---

159 Petty, p. 379.
160 Parrish, pp. 328-329, citing Theophilus Perry to Harriet Perry, March 17, 1864, in the Person Family Papers.
161 Blessington, p. 175.
162 Johnson, p. 94; Kilby Smith, p. 358.

Back in Shreveport, as soon as he learned that Porter and A. J. Smith entered the Red River, General Kirby Smith ordered Major General Sterling Price, his senior commander in Arkansas, to send all his infantry to Shreveport. He also ordered Brigadier General Samuel Bell Maxey, his commander in the Indian Territory, to join Price with all available forces, including his Indians. He simultaneously commanded Magruder to dispatch all his available infantry to Marshall, Texas, near the Louisiana border. He was to leave the "absolute minimum" infantry for the defense of the Texas coast. Finally, he directed Brigadier General St. John R. Liddell, his commander in the Ouachita River Valley (i.e., the Monroe, Louisiana, area) to send to his entire command to Natchitoches, except a small mounted force at Monroe.[163] These moves came too late for Alexandria, however; it had already fallen.

THE FALL AND OCCUPATION OF ALEXANDRIA

On March 15, the day after the fall of Fort DeRussy, Porter's inland fleet moved slowly up the Red to find that Taylor and Boggs blocked the river with a huge raft of logs secured by large piles driven into the river bed. He did not have any men to defend it, however. Unmolested by Confederate snipers, Porter fastened hawers over the piles and pulled them up with his huge ironclads. He broke the log ram in two hours.

Porter selected the heavy monitor *Osage* to lead the final advance to Alexandria. It would be followed by General Mower and 5,000 men. As naval commander, Porter selected his best man: Lieutenant Commander Thomas O. Selfridge, Jr.

Although only in his late 20s, Selfridge already had a colorful career. He was aboard the U.S.S. *Cumberland* when the first ironclad, the C.S.S. *Virginia* (formerly the *Merrimac*) sank it. He was commander of the U.S.S. *Conestogs* when he was accidentally sunk by a "friendly" vessel. He also commanded the U.S.S. *Cairo*,

---

163 Taylor, who did not like Liddell, kept him north of the Red. Liddell's strength dropped from 2,500 to 800 fourth class cavalrymen.

USS Osage, a single-turreted river monitor. It was sunk by a Confederate mine near Mobile, Alabama, on March 29, 1865.

which was sunk while on patrol in the Yazoo River, north of Vicksburg, when the Rebels detonated the first electrically fired mine underneath it.[164] He was a little nervous as he steamed up to Alexandria because he did not know what to expect.

Meanwhile, General Taylor personally supervised the evacuation of Alexandria. All public property was loaded into steamers and was sent above the Red River rapids. One boat did run aground and had to be burned because there was no time to free it. Through an oversight, three field pieces were left behind and were captured by the Yankees. Private property, including a huge cache of cotton, was not harmed. The Confederate rearguard was just pulling out when the Federals arrived.

---

164 Born in Charleston, Massachusetts, in 1836, Selfridge graduated from the U.S. Naval Academy in 1854. He later played a major role in the capture of Wilmington, North Carolina, in 1865. He retired as a rear admiral in 1898 and died in 1924. His father was also a rear adminral.

Opening Moves

To Captain Selfridge's surprise and relief, Alexandria surrendered without firing a shot. Polignac's brigade of Taylor's army just departed, however, and Tom Selfridge felt nervous and isolated until the transports caught up the following morning. Then the party began.

Second Lieutenant Lawrence Van Alystyne of the 90th U.S. Colored Infantry wrote of Alexandria: "It is a pretty place, not quite so large as Baton Rouge, but in every way a much better place to live in ... . Alexandria is rather a big village than a city. The streets are wide, and the houses are not crowded up against each other. Nearly every house has a yard and one or more shade trees ... . Altogether it is the finest place to live in I have seen in Louisiana."[165]

A. J. Smith's men began plundering the town as soon as their feet hit solid ground. Admiral Porter recalled that Smith's men "made an indiscriminate onslaught upon every private residence, appropriating to themselves everything of value."[166] Porter himself never looted private residences. He had bigger fish to fry.

Admiral David D. Porter was not only an incredibly brave and brilliant naval officer; he was also perhaps the most accomplished cotton thief of all time. As soon as he arrived on March 16, his sailors began to plunder cotton in and around Alexandria, if it belonged to the Confederate government, Confederate sympathizers, or "loyal" citizens. (When the gunboats arrived, the number of "loyal" citizens in Alexandria increased remarkably, although most of the citizenry was and remained solidly pro-Confederate.) Operating under the prize laws of the navy, Porter's men took 300 bales from one warehouse along the Alexandria waterfront and immediately started looking for more. His sailors quickly appropriated wagons and mules, which they branded "USN" (United States Navy) and by March 24 were operating up to 10 miles from Alexandria, systematically seizing every pound of "White Gold" they could lay their hands on. They

---

165 Lawrence Van Alystyne, *Diaries of an Enlisted Man* (New Haven, Connecticut: 1910), p. 292. Van Alystyne was formerly a member of the 129th New York Infantry.

166 David D. Porter, *The Naval History of the Civil War* (New York: 1885), p. 497 (hereafter cited as "Porter, *Naval History*").

even stole U.S. Army wagons and teams so they could haul more cotton. Porter's friend William Halliday, a noted cotton speculator, traveled on the admiral's flagship and also made himself rich.[167]

Theoretically, the navy was only supposed to seize cotton owned by the Confederate government, but this technicality posed only a minor challenge to Porter's uniformed entrepreneurs. Confederate cotton was marked "CSA." In their wagons, the sailors of the Mississippi River Squadron carried stencils with "CSA" and "USN" on them. If they wanted a bale of cotton (and they wanted them all), they simply marked it "CSA." Then they stenciled over it "USN." The cotton bales were then carried back to Alexandria, where they were put on naval transports for shipment to Cairo, Illinois. There they were sold by the admiralty court. All the sailors in the squadron reaped a share of the proceeds, but as commander, Porter received by far the largest share. He even confiscated empty coal barges and attached them to his gunboats, which he sent up to 30 miles downriver, to be loaded with cotton. The gunboats were also loaded with cotton. There is only one extant photograph of the Union fleet at Alexandria. It shows the gunboat *Neosho* with its deck loaded with bales of cotton because they were too large to fit in the hold.[168]

So many cotton bales were marked "CSA USN" that a joke made its way across central Louisiana. "CSA USN," it was said, stood for "Cotton Stealing Association of the United States Navy." When someone had the audacity to tell the joke to Admiral Porter, he laughed heartily. He could afford to. Dick Taylor, however, was not amused. Until now, his men were reluctant to burn privately owned cotton, and the general had not pressed the issue. Now, however, he reiterated his orders, and this time, his men carried them out with ardor. They did not want the Yankees to get the cotton either.

Admiral Porter was very angry when he learned that Taylor was now burning private property. In a state of righteous indignation, he wrote to Secretary Welles: "The Rebels are retreating before the

---

167   Johnson, p. 287.
168   Winters, p. 331.

army, and, as usual, are destroying everything that can fall into our hands, treating public and private property alike. This is the last hold they will have in this country, and they seem determined to wreak their vengeance on the unoffending inhabitants who have some little cotton to dispose of ... General Dick Taylor has left a name behind him to be execrated when the Rebellion is long past."[169]

Porter had a right to be indignant. If Taylor's men continued to burn privately owned cotton, they could put the CSA of the USN out of business.

David Porter was checked only once. As he was riding his horse down a street in Alexandria, a Southern lady suddenly blocked his path and demanded to know how he liked his horse. Taken aback, the sailor declared that it was a fine horse. She was delighted to hear that, the woman replied in a voice wreaking with sarcasm, since it was her horse before Porter's men stole it from her and gave it to the admiral; furthermore, she expected it to be returned to her when he was through with it. The sailor sheepishly promised to do so. To the lady's surprise, he personally returned the horse the very next day. Confessing that she did not expect to ever see him or the horse again, she invited him inside and served him what he later described as the best piece of pie he ever ate. (Even today, Southern women are still the best cooks in the world, in my humble but accurate opinion. Jewish mothers are second. The French are third.) Porter returned to the house on at least two other occasions. Admiral David D. Porter liked pie.

*

While Porter's cotton procurers ranged far and wide, Banks' main force (Franklin's XIX Corps, two divisions of the XIII Corps, and Lee's cavalry division) left the Bayou Teche region on March 13 and marched toward Alexandria. The column stretched out for 20 miles. Although Franklin's men were occasionally fired upon by a guerrilla and were shadowed part of the way by the 2nd Louisiana

---

169 Hollandsworth, p. 178, citing a dispatch from Porter to Secretary Welles, March 29, 1864.

Cavalry, there was virtually no opposition. There was some arson and some destruction of private property—and a great many broken windows—but the XIX Corps did not leave the path of wanton destruction which characterized the marches of A. J. Smith's corps.

Banks' vanguard, about 100 men from Lee's cavalry division, arrived in Alexandria on March 19, but the main body was still strung out for miles. Franklin did not arrive until March 25, and the rearguard did not reach the town until the following day. General Banks left Major General Joseph J. Reynolds in charge of the New Orleans, Baton Rouge, and Lafourche regions and proceeded by steamer to Alexandria, arriving on March 24.[170]

Banks insulted Porter before he reached dry land. He arrived aboard the army transport *Black Hawk*. Porter's previous flagship was the *Black Hawk*—implying that Banks was equal to Porter as a naval commander. This implication may seem petty or trivial to some readers, but it was certainly not trivial to Admiral Porter, who was furious.

Banks was not happy, either. His *Black Hawk* was crowded with cotton speculators, but Admiral Porter already seized much of the cotton. Captain Deming N. Welch, the departmental assistant quartermaster in Alexandria, wrote to his boss, Colonel Holabird: "Every gunboat is loaded with cotton, and the officers are taking it without regard to the loyalty of the owners. It looks to me like a big steal."[171] Banks demanded that the admiral give up the confiscated cotton, but the naval officer coldly refused. (As a flag officer, he would receive 5% of the prize money when the admiralty court sold it. By any estimate, his share would make him a wealthy man.) Since Halleck distrusted Banks' abilities, he failed to appoint an overall commander of the Red River Expedition, so Banks lacked the authority to give

---

170   The appointment of J. J. Reynolds was probably a political move on Banks' part, and it was an astute one. Reynolds and Grant were personal friends and graduated from West Point together in 1843. Grant was appointed general-in-chief less than two weeks before Banks made the appointment. Reynolds previously commanded a division at Chickamauga and was George Thomas' chief of staff at Chattanooga.

171   O.R., Vol. XXXIV, Part 2, p. 655.

Major General John G. Walker

Porter an enforceable order. (Lack of unity of command plagued the Northerners throughout the campaign, with Banks, Steele, and Porter—and to a lesser degree, A. J. Smith—all acting more or less as they pleased.) There was only one course of action left to Banks: seize as much of the remaining Red River Valley cotton as he could before Porter did. A weird, three-way race developed between the U.S. Army, U.S. Navy, and the Rebels. The Union army vied with the navy to confiscate as much cotton as possible, while the Confederates tried to burn it before either could get their hands on it. Each side had advantages and disadvantages in this race. Banks had the wagons, but his men, who were not governed by the naval prize laws, were not driven by the profit motive, which energized the sailors. On the other side, Magruder was slow in dispatching cavalry units to Louisiana, so most of Taylor's horsemen were still in Texas; he was therefore physically unable to burn all the cotton. Who won the cotton race is a matter of conjecture, but the Southern private citizen, plantation owner and small farmer alike, clearly lost.

*

If there was friction between the Union army and navy, there was also friction between the XIX Corps and the rest of Banks' army. The XIX Corps was composed of men from the Midwest, who, according to U.S. Major Elias P. Pellet, bore an "unremitted hatred toward Eastern troops."[172] The feeling was reciprocated by the Easterners. Even General Banks publicly called the Westerners "gorillas"—a nickname that stuck. The Midwesterners, who had seen more action than the New Yorkers and New Englanders of the XVI Corps, derisively called them "paper collar soldiers" because, they alleged, the purpose of Banks' huge wagon train was to carry their feather beds and paper collars. It wasn't, of course. The purpose of the wagon train was to haul off Red River cotton.

---

172   Pellet, p. 183.

Chapter IV

Taylor Reorganizes

While Banks and Porter were busy in and around Alexandria, Richard Taylor withdrew to Carroll Jones' Plantation, a two-day march from the town, on the road to Natchitoches. Jones was a wealthy, African American slave owner and loyal Confederate, and Taylor established a supply depot on his property, no doubt because of his large barns and outbuildings. The Jones Plantation was about 12 miles from Cane River and Bayou Rapides, where two other depots were located. Taylor ordered General Walker and Colonel Vincent, the commander of the 2nd Louisiana Cavalry, to join him at Jones', where he decided to concentrate his army. Vincent arrived on March 19, and the Greyhounds came up on the 22nd and 23rd. The Polignac and Mouton brigades were already there.

At Jones', Taylor organized his infantry into two divisions. Walker's Texas Division was already established. He created the second division and placed it under the command of Brigadier General Jean-Jacques Alexandre Alfred Mouton, who was succeeded as brigade commander by Colonel Henry Gray, the former commander of the 28th Louisiana Infantry Regiment. His other brigade was a Texas unit, commanded by Camille Armand Jules Marie, Prince de Polignac.

Alfred Mouton was the son of former Governor Alexandre Mouton, a Louisiana secessionist leader.[173] Alfred was born in Opelousas on February 18, 1829. His mother died when he was eight, so his father placed him in a boarding school, St. Charles College of Grand Coteau. He returned home in 1842, when his father (then a U.S. senator) married Anne Emma Gardner, who would give Alexandre seven children. Blended families sometimes have problems, but Alfred loved his stepmother until the day he died.[174]

Alfred received a good classical education, but it was in French, the language of south Louisiana and the language he grew up speaking. Because his father was governor, getting an appointment to West Point was no problem, but surviving the Military Academy was a challenge for Mouton. His English was poor, and West Point emphasized the sciences and engineering, rather than the classics. He nevertheless graduated in 1850, 38th in the class of 44. He was commissioned second lieutenant in the infantry and resigned from the army almost immediately. He returned to New Orleans, where he ran (or helped run) "Ile Copal," his father's huge plantation. It had 200 slaves, and Alfred proved to be a successful manager.

In early 1854, he married Philomene Zelia Mouton, his second cousin. He purchased more than 300 acres from his father and started his own plantation on the banks of the Bayou Vermilionville. By 1860, he owned 13 slaves and was worth $12,000 ($432,797.85 in 2022 money).[175] He also fathered a son and four daughters.

Mouton remained interested in military affairs. In 1856, he was commissioned brigadier general in the Louisiana Militia. He commanded the 1st Brigade, which had 2,762 men on its roles. This was a paper organization only, since there were never any drills.

---

173 Alexandre Mouton, who admired Andrew Jackson, was the first Democrat to be elected governor of Louisiana. He served from 1843 to 1847. Before that, he was a legislator and U.S. senator (1837-1842).

174 For the best biography of Mouton, see William Arceneaux, *Acadian General: Alfred Mouton and the Civil War* (Lafayette, Louisiana: 1981), from which much of the information presented in this part of the book is extracted.

175 Inflation Calculator, westegg.com/inflation/ accessed 2023.

Alfred Mouton

Mouton nevertheless managed to get himself demoted in 1859 to the command of the 2nd Brigade, which had only 1,053 men. The reason was a disagreement with Governor Robert C. Wickliffe.[176] The governor opposed vigilantes. Mouton led them.

The close ties between the Southern culture and the Western culture is not appreciated by most Americans, but they were really strong, especially before 1865. The colonial records of South Carolina, for example, speak of brandings, roundups, chaps, and cattle drives. Everything was the same as it would later be in the American West,

---

[176] Robert Charles Wickliffe (1819-1895) was governor from 1856 to 1860. He was a planter by profession and advocated annexing Cuba as a slave state. During the war, he unsuccessfully tried to act as an intermediary between Union and Rebel factions. He was not an effective governor.

except for the Spanish saddle horn, which the Southern cowboys did not have.[177] It is no accident that one of the major battles in the American Revolution was the Battle of the Cowpens.

The culture of the American frontier did not begin in the west: it moved west. As cotton became profitable in the South, it displaced cattle, which were much less profitable. The plantation then replaced the ranch, and the Southern culture replaced the frontier culture. In some parts of the South where cotton could not be produced profitably, the cattle culture persisted. Southwestern Louisiana, for example, was still cattle country until the mid-1880s, when Seaman A. Knapp proved that rice could be grown there commercially.

Nathan Bedford Forrest is another good example of the tie between the two cultures. Although correctly seen today as a Southerner, he grew up on the Western frontier, which was then in western Tennessee. He killed at least 34 men in his legendary career, but the first men he shot were gunfighters. Four gunfighters were planning to kill his uncle. Forrest met them on the main street of Hernando, Mississippi, and demanded that they go away. They drew on him. Forrest also made a quick draw, shot one of them dead, and crippled a second. He slashed a third with a knife, and the other man ran away. Ironically, when he heard the shooting, Forrest's uncle stepped outside his business establishment to see what was going on. One of the fleeing gunfighters fired a parting shot at Nathan and mortally wounded the uncle.[178]

The two surviving gunfighters were later tried for murder. The jury acquitted them on the grounds that it was a fair fight. Forrest apparently accepted this verdict.

---

[177] Dr. Charles Aiken, University of Tennessee lecture delivered in 1981.

[178] See Brian Steele Wills, *A Battle from the Start: The Life of Nathan Bedford Forrest* (New York: 1992), for an excellent biography. You might also enjoy *Bust Hell Wide Open: The Life of Nathan Bedford Forrest* (Washington, D.C.: 2016) by the present author.

Another characteristic the Southern and Western cultures have in common is the vigilante. In 1856, a small outlaw gang began operating in Acadia. At first, they only engaged in small-scale rustling and petty theft, but by 1857, they graduated to stealing entire herds, robbing banks, and committing murders. Even when they were arrested, the prosecution could not get convictions because the outlaws hired excellent attorneys, threatened jurors, tampered with juries, and engaged in other extralegal activities. As a result, "Major" Aurelian Saint-Julien, a prominent citizen of Vermilionville (now Lafayette) established a *comites de vigilance* in Lafayette Parish. Soon, six more parishes established similar committees, all of which merged as a single organization with Saint-Julien as the commander. Alfred Mouton was named "drillmaster" and second-in-command.

In Acadiana, Saint-Julien was a highly respected man, but he was old, his military rank was honorary, and his position was nominal. Mouton, who drilled the men regularly and actually prepared them to meet the outlaws in battle, was looked upon as the real leader.

Governor Wickliffe feared the collapse of law and order in the region and called upon the vigilantes to disband. They ignored him. He then threatened them with prosecution. Again, he was ignored. He did nothing to suppress the outlaws.

Thinking that the government was on their side and that no one else would oppose them, the outlaw gang became bolder and more violent in 1859. "Emboldened by constant success and encouraged by the governor's proclamation, the outlaws openly began to make plans for a complete takeover of the area," Arceneaux wrote later.[179] They began holding regular meetings and stockpiling arms and ammunition near Vermilionville, which they bragged that they were going to attack, loot, and burn.

Knowing the date, place, and time of the outlaws' next meeting, Mouton secretly assembled 500 men. On September 3, 1859, he and his men attacked and quickly surrounded the outlaws. The bandits

---

[179] Arceneaux, p. 31.

planned to resist and even fired on the vigilantes, but when they saw how many men Mouton had, they quickly surrendered. Fortunately for the outlaws, no vigilantes were killed or wounded.

Mouton's men captured nearly 1,000 small arms. They threatened 80 of the outlaws and frightened them but released them after they promised never to disturb the peace again. The remaining 15 or so, the leaders and the worst of the lot, they severely beat with bullwhips. Each was then taken to a different location on the Attakapas country border and released, on the promise that they would leave the state and never return. Apparently, none of them ever did.

Mouton and his men also "corrected" the crooked lawyers, who were henceforth more careful in choosing their clients. With law and order restored, the vigilante committee dissolved itself. Mouton, now a local hero, was promptly elected to the police jury, the governing body of the parish. When the jury met, he was elected its president.

Albert Mouton was physically big and impressive, especially for an Acadian, who are typically small men. Prince de Polignac said that Mouton looked "like a lion—dark, tall and handsome."[180] Over six feet tall, Mouton weighed 210 pounds. He was hairy, had a dark, full beard, and looked like a tough and competent officer, which he was.

He joined the Confederate Army in 1861 and was promptly elected colonel of the 18th Louisiana Infantry (731 men), which was sent to the Western Front. On March 1, 1862, he was the officer-in-charge of Pittsburg Landing when the Union inland fleet, which was commanded by Flag Officer Andrew H. Foote, attacked. It was a battle of gunboats against muskets and field artillery. The 18th Louisiana lost nine men killed and 22 wounded, but the Yankees lost 70 men. They were unable to get close enough to the shore to off-load their infantry and had to retire. That night, Mouton returned to his headquarters at Shiloh Church.

---

180   Kinard, p. 103.

For his victory, Mouton was named acting commander of the 4th Brigade of Brigadier General Daniel Ruggles' Division. General Grant, meanwhile, landed 18,000 men at Crump's Landing, five miles above Pittsburg Landing, on March 12. In the face of overwhelming ground forces, Mouton retreated toward Corinth.

Mouton fought in the Battle of Shiloh on April 6, where his horse was shot out from under him. The next day, he was severely wounded in the face and forced to leave the field. His regiment lost 211 men killed, wounded, captured, or missing. Only 10 officers were still fit for duty on April 8. Mouton was in a hospital in New Orleans on April 17 when Jefferson Davis announced his promotion to brigadier general. Shortly before the city fell, he returned home to recover but could not return to active duty until October. At that time, he assumed command of a brigade at Thibodaux.

Mouton fought in the Lafourche and Teche campaigns of 1862 and 1863. When Taylor left for northeast Louisiana in the summer of 1863, he left Mouton in charge of all the forces south of the Red River. When he returned to Alexandria in June, he wrote that Mouton's reports as an independent commander were "exceedingly unsatisfactory, and indicate that no movements commensurate with the forces under his command have been made, and that little activity has been displayed by that officer ... he is, I fear, unequal to the task of handling and disposing of any large body of troops ..." Taylor did, however, express the view that Mouton was "an excellent officer in the field, of great gallantry and fair qualifications ... "[181] He obviously concluded that Mouton was a decent enough leader when properly supervised, so he retained him as a brigade commander, although he never recommended him for promotion to major general. Operating under Tom Green's command, Mouton played a credible role in the Battle of Stirling's Plantation (aka the Battle of Morganza) on September 29, 1863, where U.S. Brigadier General Frank S. Herran's brigade was routed. The Northerners lost 515 men (mostly captured) to 121 for Green and Mouton.

---

181 O.R., Vol. XXIV, Part 2, p. 462.

In early October, General Franklin finally began to move up the Teche. He captured Ile Copal, Governor Mouton's plantation, which served as a headquarters for Grover, Weitzel, and finally Franklin. It was plundered and later burned, as was Alfred's plantation nearby. A pregnant Zelia Mouton was forced to take up residence in the basement of a local school with her four small children.

Shortly after, the Union advance halted, and in November, the Yankees fell back to New Iberia and then Franklin. That same month, Mouton was ordered to move to Monroe, Louisiana, to protect the Ouachita region from a possible advance by General Sherman. It was a tough winter. "It would not be an exaggeration to compare the winter hardships endured by Mouton and his command on the banks of the Ouachita with those endured by George Washington's army at Valley Forge," Arceneaux wrote later. Each man had one blanket and had to sleep on frozen ground. Not even the general had a tent. Many soldiers had no shoes, the food supply was inadequate, and it was too cold for Cajuns.[182] He and his men were happy to return to Alexandria in March 1864. Like Taylor, Mouton had some scores to settle in the spring of 1864.

*

Mouton's senior brigade commander was one of the most interesting and colorful men ever to don Confederate gray. Camille Armand Julie Marie, Prince de Polignac was born in Millemont, France, on February 16, 1832. His mother, Charlotte Parkyns, was an English aristocrat, and his father, Jules Armand August Marie, Prince de Polignac, former prime minister of France and ambassador to London, was in prison in the Fortress of Hamm in the Somme Valley at the time for his part in a failed royalist coup in 1830.

Jules was a bit of a religious fanatic. A fervent champion of the restoration of the monarchy, he claimed he received personal visits from the Virgin Mary. His passionate defense of the Catholic Church after the French Revolution led Pope Pius VII to grant him and his descendants the title "prince" in 1822.

---

182   Arceneaux, p. 115.

Prince de Polignac

The entire family had a colorful history. Camille's grandmother, Comtesse Gabrielle Jules de Polignac, was the best friend and most trusted confidant of Queen Marie Antoinette. A beautiful woman, it was rumored that the two were lovers. In any case, the Comtesse acquired the title duke for her husband in 1780 and became governess to the queen's children. She fled to Italy during the French Revolution. After Marie's execution, she fell ill with grief and died in December 1793.

The duke and his family, meanwhile, became exiles, and he moved to Russia, where he served in the Czar's army. He moved to England in 1800, where he became an aide to Count d'Artois (later King Charles X of France). Later captured by Napoleon's forces, Jules spent 10 years in prison but was released during the Bourbon Restoration.

Charles X became king in 1824. He took Polignac's bad advice and attempted to suppress the democratic spirit in France. As a result, he was forced to abdicate to Louis Philippe, the Duke of Orleans, in 1830, and Jules de Polignac was arrested and sentenced to life imprisonment. He was released in 1836 and banished from France. After living in England and Bavaria, he was finally allowed to return home, where he died in 1847.

From childhood, Prince Camille de Polignac wanted to be a soldier. His father was a close friend of the Swiss military philosopher, Henri Jomini, who was a frequent visitor to the Polignac estate. Camille later credited him with playing a major role in his life.[183]

The young prince attended College Stanislaus and graduated with honors in mathematics in 1852. He applied for the French military academy, *l'Ecole Polytechnique*, but was rejected. Devastated, he enlisted in the army as a private in the 3rd Chasseurs in 1853. He believed in his destiny absolutely and felt that he could rise through the ranks—which he did. Soon promoted to sergeant of artillery, he fought in the Crimean War (1854-56) and was commissioned in the 4th *Chasseurs d'Afrique* in 1855. Later stationed in Paris, he was bored with garrison duty and resigned from the army in 1859. Shortly after, he sailed for Nicaragua, where he boldly presented himself as a military engineer. After he was hired, he met a valuable contact: U.S. Ambassador Alexander Dimitri, a native of Louisiana.[184] Dimitri arranged for him to go to New York City and meet U.S. Senator John Slidell, the former ambassador to Mexico, and his law partner, Senator Judah P. Benjamin. Both were from Louisiana. They introduced him to Major Pierre G. T. Beauregard, an up-and-coming officer. Polignac was very sympathetic to the Southern cause and corresponded with them for months. He was back in France in the spring of 1861, but almost as soon as the war began, he sailed for North America.

"Camille de Polignac came from that breed of men who could not be satisfied with the formal and leisurely life of most people of noble birth. He belonged to that group who would stubbornly suffer

---

183 Kinard, p. 5. This is the best book available on Polignac and the principle source for much of the information on this section of the book.
184 Dimitri was simultaneously U.S. ambassador to Nicaragua and Costa Rica.

many hardships while fighting for a cause," Hatton wrote later.[185] In any case, after the formation of the Confederacy, Polignac joined Beauregard's staff as a lieutenant colonel on July 6, 1861.

The prince was slim and of average height, had auburn hair, deep blue eyes, was a meticulous dresser, and had beautiful, Old World manners. One Southern belle described him as a "fiery little man; erect in figure with keen blue eyes, white teeth that showed brilliantly when he smiled, and a dark waxed mustache which lent a fierceness to his expression ... "[186] He spoke proper British English and initially suffered from a total lack of grasp of Southern vernacular. On the other hand, as Kinard wrote, " ... raised in the traditions of the ancient regime, he had been prepared from birth to navigate such intrigues as those of the evolving Davis court."[187] In 1861 and early 1862, he successfully courted the favor of Mary Boykin Chesnut, the wife of James Chesnut, a Confederate congressman and aide to Jefferson Davis, and then Varina Howell Davis, the first lady of the Confederacy. He became a frequent visitor to the Brockenbrough mansion, the Confederate White House.

Well connected, Polignac followed Beauregard to the Western Front but arrived in Corinth 10 days after the Battle of Shiloh. He soon befriended Braxton Bragg. Beauregard gave him command of the 18th Louisiana Infantry Regiment on or about April 22, but to Polignac's surprise, the Louisiana boys refused to accept him. The former regimental commander, Colonel Preston Pond, Jr., resumed command on April 29.

Prince de Polignac was going through culture shock. It never would have occurred to European soldiers to refuse to accept a commander, but the Confederate Army worked very differently than any other army Camille de Polignac had ever seen. After he attended a fire-and-brimstone sermon by a Southern preacher, he staggered away, even

---

[185] Roy O. Hatton, "Prince Camille de Polignac and the American Civil War, 1863-1865," *Louisiana Studies*, Vol. III (Summer 1964), pp. 163-164 (hereafter cited as "Hatton").

[186] Mrs. D. Giraud Wright, *A Southern Girl in '61* (New York: 1905), p. 92.

[187] Kinard, p. 25.

more shocked. The bishops and cardinals at the Royal Court never spoke like that! Polignac, however, determined to learn Southern. He befriended Colonel John Pegram, a 30-year-old Virginian who was Bragg's chief of staff. (Beauregard fell ill, and Bragg now commanded the army in the west but retained Polignac as an assistant adjutant general.) The two men were complete opposites in certain respects. Pegram was very religious, did not chase women, and never drank, which Polignac noted, was "strange for an American."[188] In any case, the two officers played chess, discussed Southern culture and military strategy, and even read to each other.[189]

During the Kentucky campaign, Polignac impressed and befriended General Kirby Smith, who assigned him to the 5th Tennessee Infantry Regiment as second-in-command. He was greeted "with hostility and derision."[190]

Part of Polignac's problem was that Confederate regiments were recruited from the same locality. Most of the men were from rural areas, and they tended to distrust authority. Also, the prince too often retired to his tent in the evenings (often to study English), which increased his isolation. He became lonely and morose, but he was nevertheless determined to become accepted and to advance in rank.

Polignac also faced hostility in Kirby Smith's headquarters because not everyone there liked him. Captain Paul E. Hammond, the general's aide, detested him. He called the Frenchman "undeniably ugly" and a cross between a "buffoon and [an] Italian organ-grinder."[191]

Polignac was acting commander of the 5th Tennessee in August and September 1862 and led it during the Battle of Richmond, Kentucky. He wrote later: "All day long I had endeavored to observe

---

188 Kinard, p. 47.

189 Pegram was a brigadier general commanding a division in the Army of Northern Virginia when he was killed in action on February 6, 1865. He was married only three weeks before.

190 Kinard, p.68.

191 Paul E. Hammond, "General Kirby Smith's Campaign in Kentucky in 1862," Southern Historical Society *Papers*, Vol. IX (1881), pp. 251-252.

[show] more coolness and experience than their old officers, by standing upright under fire, not dodging ... knowing the effect of personal valour on soldiers, I worked myself up to a degree which I did not think myself capable of, took the colors of the Regiment over the fence, waved my handkerchief from the top of a tombstone as we entered the cemetery, urged the men [on and] stood constantly by them."[192] Colonel Bejamin J. Hill, his brigade commander, wrote in his official report: "I feel it obligatory to mention the gallantry of Lieutenant Colonel Polignac, who, in the last fight before Richmond seized the colors of the Fifth Tennessee, bearing them triumphantly through the thickest of the fight and encouraged the men to withstand the terrible fire."[193] As a result of his courage and gallantry, Polignac was finally accepted by the enlisted men of the 5th Tennessee. The officers, however, did not accept him and pressured the brigade commander into calling new elections. (Confederate units elected their officers.) As a result, Polignac ended up back in a staff assignment, this time working for Kirby Smith.

In November 1862, Polignac went to Richmond, Virginia, to lobby for promotion. By nature a connoisseur, he enjoyed fine wines, fine cuisine, and fine women. A noted *bon vivant*, he had a romance in the Confederate capital and at least one tryst. He, in fact, took Richmond by storm and secured a promotion to brigadier general on January 10, 1863. He was assigned to the Trans-Mississippi Department (which he later called "Kirby Smithdom") that spring.

For reasons not made clear by the records, Kirby Smith gave Polignac command of the 2nd Texas Brigade in Dick Taylor's army. It fielded about 800 men and consisted of the 22nd Texas Cavalry, the 34th Texas Cavalry, and the 17th Texas Consolidated Cavalry—all recently dismounted.[194] Kirby Smith considered the brigade "an

---

192   Kinard, p. 68.

193   O.R., Vol. XVI, Part 1, p. 952. Hill commanded the 2nd Brigade, 4th Division of the Army of Kentucky.

194   The 17th Consolidiated consisted of elements of three regiments which were destroyed at Arkansas Post. The men of the new regiment were exchanged prisoners of war.

undisciplined mob, the officers as worthless as the men."[195] They were very unhappy about losing their horses and were certainly not happy about having a "frog eater" as their commander.

Polignac was fortunate in that Colonel William R. Trader, Kirby Smith's aide, took the brigade to a camp four miles west of Shreveport the following month and turned them into a recognizable military unit. Polignac stayed out of Trader's way and seemed more interested in Shreveport society than in training the regiments, which were sent to Grand Ecore in July. When Polignac arrived on July 20 and actually tried to assume command, there was a near revolt. The men could hardly understand him and could not pronounce his name, and he was clearly not a Texan. His name sounded a little like "Polecat," which is Southern for skunk, so the men would hold their noses when he walked by. Polignac pretended not to notice. At the time, however, the brigade was part of Walker's Texas Division, and he supported the Frenchman, as did Colonel Almerine M. Alexander, commander of the 34th Texas Cavalry; Colonel James R. Taylor, commander of the 17th Consolidated; and Lieutenant Colonel James E. Harrison, the leader of the 15th Texas Cavalry. More to the point, Dick Taylor supported him, also, probably because he did not like the alternative, Colonel Joseph W. Speight. An uneasy situation ensued until October 14, 1863, when Polignac's brigade was transferred to a temporary division under Mouton and was ordered to absorb Colonel Speight's small brigade, a temporary formation which consisted of the 15th Texas Infantry and 8th Texas Cavalry (Dismounted) Regiments.

As a regimental commander, the hard-drinking Speight encouraged his men to rebel against Polignac, and now Speight wanted command of the consolidated brigade. The result was a bit of a mutiny, and Dick Taylor was called in to settle the situation. Even the Confederate Patton, however, felt compelled to negotiate with the wild Texans. They would temporarily accept Polignac as their commander, Taylor said; otherwise, there would be serious consequences for them personally. (Clearly, this was a threat, and

---

195   Kinard, p. 62.

Taylor hanged enough men for his threats to be taken seriously.) He expected them to let Polignac command them in one engagement. If, after one battle, they felt the same way and wanted to be rid of Polignac, he would relieve the prince of his command. This deal sounded fair to the Texans, who accepted it.

In the past year and a half, Prince de Polignac became more aware of what it took to command a Confederate unit. In Europe, officers hardly talked to enlisted men, except to give orders, which were never questioned. Things were completely different in Texas and Louisiana. Polignac became much less aloof and was cognizant of the need to talk to the men in the ranks, even to the point of sitting down, listening to them, and learning their names. He became very solicitous of their welfare, and they responded positively. They also respected him for his gallantry and his bravery under fire. After his first engagement, a skirmish near Vidalia, Louisiana, on February 7, 1864, few wanted to replace him, and Colonel Speight was sent back to Texas.

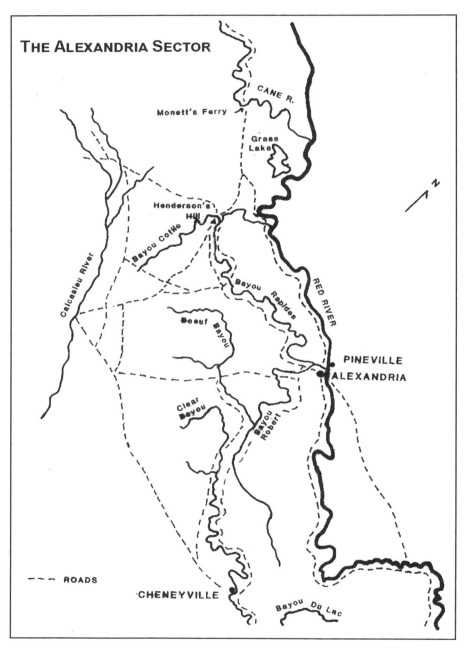

5.1 The Alexandria Sector

Chapter V

Up The River And Through The Woods: The Battle Of Henderson Hill

In spite of the need for speed, General Banks delayed in Alexandria to dabble in politics. He called for elections on April 1 in that city, Opelousas, Marksville, and Harrisonburg, in the belief that they would strengthen the Free State of Louisiana. Voters would select delegates for a Constitutional Convention, which would be held in July. The new constitution would replace the old (slavery) constitution, and the inclusion of delegates from central and north-central Louisiana would at least create the impression of widespread support for the new (Republican) state government, or so Banks hoped. Alexandria, which is called "Alec" by the locals, was always a Confederate town, however, and the behavior of A. J. Smith and his gorillas did nothing to change that. Voter turnout was disappointingly light. Only 300 people cast ballots, and Admiral Porter denounced the entire election as a farce.

Meanwhile, from his base at Jones' Plantation, General Taylor sent Colonel William Vincent's 2nd Louisiana Cavalry Regiment toward Alexandria with orders to get as close to the town as possible.

He skirmished with A. J. Smith's scouts on March 20 and 21.[196] The regiment was nearly exhausted because it was almost constantly in the saddle since March 7. March 21 a was cold, rainy day. Most of the 2nd Louisiana Cavalry camped for the night at Henderson Hill, near the confluence of the Bayous Cotiles and Rapides, 23 miles northwest of Alexandria (Map 5.1). The position seemed safe. The constant rain of the past few days turned the woods at the base of the hill into a swamp. Most of the men grouped around campfires, and the few sentries they posted were not vigilant.

On the night of March 21/22, central Louisiana was pelleted by heavy rainstorms and hail. The cold and wet Southern cavalrymen had no idea that U.S. Brigadier General James Mower, the man who captured Fort DeRussy, was advancing on their positions.

Mower's force consisted of his own 1st Division, XVI Corps; a regiment from the 3rd Division; and the 1st Division of Lee's Cavalry Corps, led by Colonel Dudley. In all, Mower had about 6,000 men. After marching 23 miles, Mower had Vincent's regiment practically surrounded. He captured a couple of dispatch riders, so he knew Vincent's strength, which was about 300 men, and Captain William Edgar's light artillery battery (four guns). Jayhawkers supplied Mower with the exact location of Vincent's squadrons and with his password. Through the rain and hail, with mud up his horses' bellies, Mower attacked Vincent's front with three infantry regiments and most of the cavalry; simultaneously, he struck the rear of the hill with two infantry regiments and the 16th Indiana Mounted Infantry.

---

196 William G. Vincent was born in Norfolk, Virginia, in 1829 but grew up in Louisiana. He was a second lieutenant in the 2nd New York during the Mexican War. From 1848 to 1861 he was a businessman in New Orleans. He organized the Light Guards, a militia company, in 1861, and was elected its captain. His was the first Louisiana unit to offer itself to Jefferson Davis after the Confederacy was established. Later, the Light Guards became part of the 1st Louisiana Volunteers, and Vincent became its colonel. After serving in Virginia, he returned to Louisiana in 1862 and organized the 2nd Louisiana Cavalry in north Louisiana. He distinguished himself in the defeat at Labadieville (October 27, 1862) and in the Teche Campaign and was severely wounded in the neck while leading a charge at Irish Bend (near Franklin) after the fall of Fort Bisland. Richard Taylor thought highly of him and exonerated him from blame after Henderson's Hill. John Dimitry, *Louisiana*, in Clement A. Evans, ed., *Confederate Military History*, Vol. X (Atlanta: 1899), pp. 111, 127 (hereafter cited as "Dimitry").

It was over in minutes. Mower captured 252 Rebels and all four guns and hardly fired a shot in the process. Colonel Vincent escaped (reportedly in his slippers), along with a handful of men.[197]

Mower's brilliant little operation effectively deprived Dick Taylor of almost all his cavalry in one blow. Not only was he vastly outnumbered—now he was blind as well. If Banks advanced again, he would have no choice except to retreat until fresh cavalry arrived from Texas. Anticipating this course of action, he withdrew Mouton's division and his wagon trains to Beasley's Plantation, from which he could cover the Natchitoches-Many Road.

Richard Taylor was an astute observer and learned a great deal while serving with Stonewall Jackson in the Shenandoah Valley. Among other things, he learned to get his wagon trains out of harm's way well before a battle. Using this tactic, they did not get in the way or slow him down. It is true that his men were not as well supplied as they otherwise would be, but that was what hardtack was for.

If one has never had it, hardtack is difficult to imagine. It was the 19th-Century equivalent of C-Rations or MREs, but much worse. It was a small, rectangular, bread-like substance which if heated long enough in water (about two hours) could actually be eaten. Before simmering, it is impossible to chew and is even difficult to break by a man of ordinary strength. Hardtack, however, is easy to carry and never spoils.[198]

The Drive To Grand Ecore

Back in Alexandria, Banks was preparing to advance again. There was a need to hurry. On March 26, he received a dispatch from Ulysses S. Grant. Dated March 15, it read: "the success of your present move is of great importance in reducing the number of troops necessary for protecting the navigation of the Mississippi River. It is also

---

197 Hollandsworth, p. 178; Johnson, p. 97; Taylor, p. 157.
198 The last I heard, a chapter of the Sons of Confederate Veterans makes hardtack and sells it at the Camp Moore, Louisiana, historic site.

important that Shreveport should be taken if possible." However, if it appeared that the capital of the Trans-Mississippi Department could not be taken by the end of April, he was to return A. J. Smith's corps to Sherman by the middle of that month, "even if it leads to the abandonment of the main object of your expedition." If he did capture Shreveport, Banks was to garrison it and the Red River line, return to New Orleans, and be prepared to move against Mobile.[199]

General Albert Lee's cavalry vanguard moved out of Alexandria and headed for Natchitoches and Grand Ecore (Natchitoches' river port, located four miles above the town) that same day. Taylor retreated, burning the bridges and cotton as he went. One Yankee wrote: " From the day we started on the Red River expedition, we were like the Israelites of old, accompanied by a cloud by day, and a pillar of fire by night.[200]

Lee was followed on March 27 by Smith's XVI Corps, which marched to Cotile Landing, 21 miles north of Alexandria, where it was to embark on steamers and head up the Red. That same day, Brigadier General William H. Emory's division began the march to Natchitoches. It was followed on March 28 by the rest of the XIX Corps and the two divisions of the XIII Corps, which was commanded by Brigadier General Thomas E. G. Ransom.[201] Brigadier General Cuvier Grover's 4th Division, XIX Corps (3,000 men) remained behind as an occupation force in Alexandria.

On March 28, Lee's cavalry reached Monett's Ferry, about 40 miles upriver from Alexandria, near the confluence of the Red and Cane Rivers. Here, he encountered light resistance from the remnants of the 2nd Louisiana Cavalry but had no problem driving them off. As the Yankees advanced, Taylor's ragged infantry retreated without engaging the enemy. The Federals crossed the Cane River at Monett's Ferry and advanced across the rich Isle de Breville, an island formed

---

[199] O.R., Vol. XXXIV, Part 2, pp. 610-611.

[200] Kinard, p. 133.

[201] For the sake of convenience and clarity, Ransom's command will occasionally be referred to hereafter as the XIII Corps Detachment, even though it did not officially bare this designation.

by the two rivers. They were amazed to find that the large plantations here were owned by wealthy black slaveholders. Otherwise, except for an occasional incident of sniper fire, the march was uneventful. They captured Cloutierville on March 29. The Union vanguard exited the Isle Breville just south of Natchitoches on March 31 and occupied the town the same day. The head of Franklin's infantry column arrived the next day, having covered 80 miles in four days.

Natchitoches was (and is) a beautiful, prosperous old town with rich Spanish architecture. It was the first permanent settlement built in Louisiana.[202] Its residents were strongly pro-Confederate—even those whose cotton was burned by Taylor. They greeted the invaders with closed doors and drawn drapes.

Confederate Strategy

As the Army of the Gulf advanced up the Red, Kirby Smith's strategy kept changing. As of March 20, he intended to defeat Banks first, then turn to face Steele in Arkansas with the combined forces of Price and Taylor. By March 23, however, it became obvious that Steele had the much smaller force, and he became uncertain as to what to do. On April 3, he tentatively decided to strike Steele first, despite the fact that Banks was much nearer to Shreveport.

Meanwhile, Price's infantry arrived in Shreveport on March 24. It consisted of two small divisions under the command of Brigadier Generals Thomas J. Churchill and Mosby M. Parsons. Unsure of what he wanted to do, Kirby Smith held them in reserve, allegedly because of defective ammunition.

---

202 Natchitoches, the oldest town in the Louisiana Purchase, was founded in 1714. New Orleans was founded in 1718. Because of a huge natural logjam, which clogged the Red River for two miles, Natchitoches was the headwater of navigation at that time. Captain Henry M. Shreve, for whom Shreveport is named, cleared the Great Raft, as this obstruction was called. The operation took more than a year.

On March 27 or 28, Taylor was visited by his brother-in-law, Confederate Congressman Duncan Kenner.[203] He told the general that the Arkansas infantry arrived in Shreveport and that Kirby Smith detained them there. According to Kenner, Kirby Smith interpreted Taylor's repeated vows to fight Banks as soon as Green's cavalry arrived to mean that he did not want additional reinforcements. Taylor immediately dispatched a heated note to Kirby Smith and reminded him that Green was already 11 days late. He commented upon his determination to fight Banks as soon as Green arrived, but he could "scarcely conceive how this could be interpreted into a declaration that I did not want reinforcements."[204]

Kirby Smith replied that the infantry was originally held at Shreveport because they needed ammunition. Now, however, Steele's movement seemed more serious, so he would have to wait three or four days before deciding whether to send them to Taylor or not.[205]

The exact words General Taylor uttered when he received this dispatch was not recorded. They probably could not be printed in any case. Kirby Smith's excuse seems thin today and must have seemed incredibly flimsy to Taylor in 1864.

Shortly after, another dispatch arrived from Kirby Smith, informing Taylor that Steele left Little Rock with 10,000 men and 24 guns and was driving on Washington, the Confederate capital of Arkansas. The commander of the Trans-Mississippi Department

---

203   Duncan F. Kenner (1813-1887) was a wealthy sugar planter and the Louisiana delegate to the Confederate Provisional Congress (1861-1862). By 1864, he was the chief Confederate diplomat to Europe. He lost his wealth during the war but successfully rebuilt this fortunes. Kenner created the Louisiana Sugar Producers' Association in 1877. He served in both houses of the Louisiana legislature before the war. He was married to Anne Guillelmine "Nanine" Bringier, the sister of Louise Marie Myrthe Bringier Taylor, General Taylor's wife. Another Bringier sister, Ann, married Confederate Brigadier General Allen Thomas, Jr., (1830-1907), who succeeded Prince de Polignac as division commander in early 1865.

204   O.R., XXXIV, Part 1, p. 513.

205   O.R., Vol. XXXIV, Part 1, p. 513.

estimated that Banks had more than 50,000 men. He thought it might be better to return Price's infantry to Arkansas and defeat Steele; then he could reinforce Taylor with 13,000 men, instead of 5,000.

Taylor was furious. He saw the best part of Louisiana devastated and he was spoiling for a fight. He simply could not understand why Kirby Smith would not send him Price's infantry. Now on the border of insubordination, he answered Kirby Smith, saying: "… the only possible way to defeat Steele is to whip the enemy now in the heart of the Red River Valley. Price's command could have been here on the 28th, and I could have fought a battle for the department today. To decline concentration when we have the means, and when the enemy is already in the vitals of the department, is a policy I am too obtuse to understand."[206]

The next day, Taylor wrote his commander: "Had I conceived for an instant that such astonishing delay would ensue before re-enforcements reached me I would have fought a battle even against the heavy odds. It would have been better to lose the State after a defeat than to surrender it without a fight. The fairest and richest portion of the Confederacy is now a waste. Louisiana may well know her destiny. Her children are exiles; her labor system is destroyed. Expecting every hour to receive the promised re-enforcements, I did not feel justified in hazarding a general engagement with my little army. I shall never cease to regret my error."[207]

The fact that Kirby Smith's chief surgeon and close friend, Colonel Dr. Sol Smith, was telling people that Taylor refused reinforcements from Kirby Smith did nothing to improve the relationship between the two generals.

---

206   O.R., Vol. XXXIV, Part 1, pp. 514-515.
207   O.R., Vol. XXXIV, Part 1, p. 515..

UP THE RIVER

Before the war, the Red River normally began to rise in December or January. In 1864, for the first time in 10 years, it did not. What rise there was (and there was not much) took place at the end of February and early March. By mid-March, there was not enough water to safely float the ironclads above the Alexandria Falls, just upriver from the city.

The Alexandria Falls were not waterfalls at all; they were rapids caused by huge sandstone boulders which were not visible in periods of high water. They were a danger to navigation even then, but an experienced pilot could determine their location by observing the swirls and eddies in the river and thus avoid them. They were more dangerous when they were visible and caused rapids in the swallow water. In 1864, they were visible and extended for about a mile upriver from Alexandria. Admiral Porter was reluctant to try to go above the falls but was convinced to do so by the eloquent General Banks and by the lure of more cotton.

Against the advice of his chief pilot, Wellington W. Withenbury, who had spent 18 years on the Red, Porter decided to take his heaviest gunboat, the *Eastport*, upriver first. Porter had heard rumors that the Rebels were building up to five ironclads—possibly rams—and even submarines at Shreveport, and he wanted his fleet protected by the two huge, forward-facing 100 pounder guns of the *Eastport*. On March 23, with a full head of steam, the *Eastport* attempted to negotiate the falls, ran aground, and stuck fast. It took Porter three days to drag the ship over the rapids and only then with the help of Union soldiers.

The next ship to try to cross the shoal waters was the *Woodford*, a hospital ship. It ran aground, wrecked itself, and had to be destroyed.

Between March 26 and April 3, a dozen gunboats and 30 transports steamed or were dragged across the falls. They included the ironclads *Mound City, Chillicothe, Carondelet, Pittsburg,*

Ozark, Neosho, Louisville, and *Osage*; the tinclads *Cricket* and *Fort Hindman*; and the wooden gunboat *Lexington*. The rest of the fleet either remained in Alexandria or returned to the Mississippi.

Porter's problems were just beginning. "The Red River is mostly crooks," Lieutenant Van Alystune wrote later, and apparently there was not a single ironclad or tinclad which did not run aground at least once. "Oh, the snags and sand-bars we ran upon!" Admiral Porter lamented later.

"We had no pilots of any account ... If one got on a bank, another would haul him off, and there was not a vessel there that did not haul the others off three or four times before we got to Loggy Bayou—the name is significant ...

"The people all along were kind to us as we went up, and gave us information cheerfully whenever we asked it. Only it was curious that their information led us into all kinds of difficulties. Where they told us the deep water was, we found shoals and snags, and where we were told to go through a cut-off we found it a blind...

"The good people who met us on the way up, at the different landings, seemed so sorry to see us going back; they got their guns out and saluted us, but, unfortunately, the guns were shotted. They killed a number of our men, and they kept up such a continuous salute that at last we began to suspect their sincerity.

"At first the balls came like single drops of rain, then more of them, then they came in showers, and we were absolutely obliged to land and take on cotton-bales for protection [!] ...

"Of course we fired back; but what harm could that do to people who were in deep rifle-pits, screened by trees or in a canebrake? The affair reminded me very much of the retreat of the French from Moscow ..."[208]

---

208   Porter, *Anecdotes,* p. 231.

On April 2, Second Lieutenant Van Alystyne was sent to Grand Ecore on a recruitment mission for the 90th U.S. Colored Troops (USCT) Regiment. He boarded the transport *Jennie Rogers* along with some of A. J. Smith's gorillas. His transport promptly collided with another ship, which punched a hole in the hull below the water line. Van Alystyne wrote: "... by the time she struck there, there was such a panic among the Vicksburg heroes as I don't believe eastern men ever thought of... . They rushed for the side and began jumping from the upper and lower deck at the same time, landing on each other and some of them in the water, and then began quarreling and fighting over the hurts they got... . The whole thing was amusing from our point of view ... "[209]

The leak was stopped and the *Jennie* resumed its place in the line early the following morning. Meanwhile, Van Alystyne recorded: "The western men are all right on a chicken raid, for I don't think one escaped them."[210]

Porter's vessels bounced along the bottom of the Red River for days. The first of them did not reach Grand Ecore until April 3. Meanwhile, Dick Taylor's long delayed reinforcements began to arrive.

THE CAVALRY ARRIVES

The first unit to arrive from Texas was the 5th Texas Cavalry Regiment, which joined Taylor on March 30. Formerly commanded by Tom Green, it was now led by Colonel Henry C. McNeill.[211] It had

---

209 Van Alystyne, p. 298.

210 Van Alystyne, p. 298.

211 Henry C. McNeill (1833-1876) was born in Natchez but is family moved to Texas when he was a toddler. He attended the Kentucky Military Institute and the Western Military Institute (Nashville, Tennessee) before he graduated from West Point in 1857. He was appointed first lieutenant in the Confederate Regular Army in March 1861 and became lieutenant colonel of the 5th Texas Cavalry in August. He distinguished himself by capturing a Union regiment in Sibley's New Mexico Campaign. He was promoted to colonel in 1863. McNeill served with the 5th Texas Cavalry in the Trans-Mississippi throughout the war, despite the fact that General Green recommended him for a brigade command. He was a farmer in the Eagle Lake area after the war. Bruce S. Allardice, *Confederate Colonels* (Columbia, Missouri: 2008), p. 270 (hereafter cited as "Allardice, *Colonels*").

a strength of 250 men, 50 of whom were unarmed.[212] The next day, Lieutenant Colonel P. T. Herbert's 7th Texas Cavalry joined the Army of Western Louisiana at Natchitoches with 350 men—half of whom had weapons.[213] Taylor ordered the 5th Texas to join Liddell on the north bank of the Red, where he was harassing the Union fleet with the vastly understrength 3rd, 4th, 5th, and 6th Louisiana Cavalry Regiments. The 5th Texas, however, was already busy skirmishing with the Federal cavalry in the vicinity of Many, west of Natchitoches, so apparently these orders were cancelled. Taylor, meanwhile, received word that more Texas cavalry was on the way.[214]

The Texas horsemen who were riding to General Taylor's assistance served under him in the Lafourche and Teche campaigns of 1863 and were delighted to be back. "We were ... overjoyed at the prospect of returning to Louisiana with our favorite chieftain [Green] to our favorite General—Taylor," one of them wrote later.[215]

The cavalrymen who were arriving from Texas were veteran warriors and some of the best equestrians in the world. Many of them were former Texas Rangers who had fought outlaws, Mexicans, and Indians. A good example of these regiments was the 32nd Texas Cavalry, which was formed in the spring of 1862. It was led by Colonel Peter C. Woods, a medical doctor. A native of Tennessee, he practiced in Water Valley, Mississippi, before moving to Texas in 1851. He became a wealthy planter and slave owner, although he

---

212 John W. Spencer, *Terrell's Texas Cavalry* (Austin, Texas: 1982), p. 86 (hereafter cited as "Spencer"); Alonzo H. Plummer, *Confederate Victory at Mansfield* (Mansfield, Louisiana: 1969), p. 8.

213 Philemon Thomas Herbert was born in Alabama in 1825. He attended the University of Louisiana but was suspended for stabbing another student. He fought in the Mexican War and moved to Texas and then California, where he was elected to Congress in 1854. He ruined his political career when he killed a waiter during a brawl in a D.C. restaurant. He was a strong secessionist and was Texas's commissioner to Arizona in 1861. He was on General Sibley's staff and raised a cavalry battalion in 1862. He was promoted to colonel in 1864 (probably on March 17) but was mortally wounded at Mansfield. He died on July 23, 1864 (Allardice, *Colonels*, pp. 193-194).

214 Spencer, p. 172.

215 Carl L. Duaine, *The Dead Men Wore Boots: An Account of the 32nd Texas Volunteer Cavalry, C.S.A., 1862-1865* (Austin, Texas), p. 26 (hereafter cited as "Duaine").

did not carry a single servant to the field with him.[216] His men came primarily from the San Marcos/Hays County area, although some came from Caldwell, Comal, and Guadalupe counties. Quite a few were Germans.

When the regiment was formed, Woods was elected colonel, Ned Benton (the runner up) became lieutenant colonel, and W. O. Hutchinson was elected major. It was a good slate of officers.[217] Private John Franklin of Company E recalled: "It might seem that the necessity to be elected by the men could give rise to a group of officers who would be subservient to the men, but this was not the case. The men elected the officers to lead them, and any officer who failed to lead would have been deposed." He added: "I never wanted any man over me, but if I had to have one, I wanted the hair on his chest as thick as pencil lead."[218]

The 32nd Texas Cavalry elected all of its officers and even elected its sergeants and corporals.

The men were paid $11 per month. (The colonel was paid $300 a month.) They were expected to provide their own horses, equipment, guns, and ammunition. A horse cost $60 to $100 in 1862. Arms cost $12 to $100, depending upon style and quality, and other equipment cost $10 to $40. Tents, clothing, blankets, cooking equipment, utensils, and playing cards were optional. The army

---

216   Dr. Woods was born on December 31, 1820, in Franklin County, Tennessee, and died in San Marcos on January 27, 1898. He graduated from the Louisville Medical Institute in 1842 and married Georgia Lawshe of South Carolina in 1846. She died in 1872. He married Ella Rives Ogletree the following year. Dr. Woods had at least eight children by his first marriage and four by his second. After his slaves were freed, Colonel Woods gave them tracts of land. The survivability rate of people Dr. Woods operated on was said to be extremely high.

217   Woods briefly commanded a brigade but was not selected as its permanent commander. His sole weakness as an officer was that he cared too much for his men's welfare. This made him too slow on the march.

218   Duaine, p. 26.

would replace horses killed in battle but not otherwise lost. "... the Confederacy asked that a man pay for the privilege of dying for her," Private James Foster added sarcastically.[219]

As in all Confederate regiments, discipline in the 32nd Texas Cavalry was loose. Enlisted men called officers by their first names but obeyed their orders. AWOLs were frequent when times were quiet, but most of these men returned to the ranks when action appeared to be imminent. In their spare time, the men sat under trees and played cards, foraged for pecans, ran horse races, had fist fights for fun, gambled, drank, and brawled. "They were the gamblingist, most profane group of men I ever met," Trooper Foster, whose father was a Methodist minister, recalled. "They would bet on the way a bird would fly." They also had their own code of manners. No one abused anyone else or called another man a liar or a bastard. They all had six shooters, but no one wanted to use them against a comrade.[220]

Most of the men of the regiment were given nicknames by their friends. A man with an olive complexion became "Pedro." Another, whose initials were P. C., became P-6. A Louisiana native became "Opelousas." Others included "Bugler," "Captain's Cook," "Corn," "Nublin'," and "Slim." Very young men were called "Jaybird," and very old men were "Grandpa." During training, one sergeant woke up the men yelling: "Off your ass and on your feet, out of the shade and into the heat!" Predictably, he became "Sergeant Ass."[221]

Each regiment also had a deeply religious group that refused to drink or gamble. Their beliefs were respected as well; in fact, religious revivals were common during nights leading up to a major campaign. Walker's division, for example, had a "big tent" religious service every night it was practical during the Red River campaign.

---

219 Duaine, p. 25. Private James M. Foster was born in Pascagoula, Mississippi, in 1846. His family moved to Hardin County, Texas, in 1848. After the war, he married and became a prosperous farmer, businessman, and rancher. He died in Alice, Texas, in 1908.

220 Duaine, pp. 28-29.

221 Duaine, p. 30.

The 32nd Texas Cavalry trained at Salado and Camp Clark, Texas. In August 1862, it was sent to the Rio Grande to patrol the border. Here it saw action against Mexican bandits and Comanches. From the summer of 1863 until early 1864, it fought against Banks' troops near Corpus Christi and along the Texas coast. It was ordered to Louisiana on March 12.

Woods' regiment moved slower than some of the others. A medical doctor, Woods kept his wagon train with him because it carried his sick. Other colonels, such as Xavier Debray, headed east as rapidly as possible. Their wagoneers were ordered to catch up when they could.

In 1863, General Taylor made an inspection trip and was quite miffed when he inspected his first Texas cavalry regiment. When he arrived, he was greeted casually. No one bothered to come to attention. He asked where to find the colonel and was directed to a big tree, where the hard-drinking Joseph W. Speight was sitting with a group of men in a circle. The general found that they were not discussing tactics or any other military subject; they were playing Monte, a Mexican card game, on a blanket, and the colonel was dealing. When Taylor approached the circle, Speight saw no reason to move, but he did instruct his men to scoot over and make room for the general, so that he could take part in the betting. Taylor coldly refused. The colonel, he recalled later, was somewhat put out by what he considered Taylor's unfriendliness.[222]

Taylor was none too happy to see Colonel Xavier B. Debray on April 3, when he arrived with the 26th Texas Cavalry, after skirmishing with Lee's Union horsemen on the Old Fort Jessup Road the day before. The general coldly informed him that, had his men not performed so well in yesterday's action, he would have court-martialed him. When the surprised colonel asked why, Taylor responded that his regiment was 10 days late. Now insulted, Debray explained that the 26th Texas marched more than 250 miles and was slowed by the additional duty of escorting a wagon train,

---

222 Taylor, p. 126.

which was full of vital supplies for Taylor. This explanation seemed to have a calming effect on the general. "I see that you are no politician," he replied in French and extended his hand. Delighted at being answered in his native language, the colonel shook his hand heartily.[223]

A day or two later, when Colonel Walter P. Lane's cavalry brigade arrived at Mansfield with the 1st and 2nd Texas Partisan Ranger Battalions and the 2nd and 3rd Arizona Cavalry Regiments, Taylor was in a better mood. "Boys, I am glad to see you," he called to his newest reinforcements.[224] The Texans and Arizonians cheered.

Other reinforcements also arrived which were of much lower quality than the Texas cavalrymen. On April 2, Louisiana Governor Henry Watkins Allen issued a proclamation, appealing to the patriotism of his citizens and calling out his militia. Since the Confederacy was drafting all males between the ages of 17 and 50, Allen's militia consisted almost entirely of old men and a few boys. Militarily speaking, the governor's battalions were next to useless. All totaled, they numbered just a few hundred old men. They did, however, have a major positive impact on the morale of the regular Confederate units. "Old men shouldered their muskets and came to our assistance, to help drive back the invader," a Texas soldier recalled. The fact that they were being led by the governor, a former Confederate general and war hero who was so badly wounded that he could not walk without crutches, so he led from horseback, touched the heart of the toughest veteran. "No nobler men ever shouldered a musket!" one of them declared.[225]

Realizing that Allen's Louisiana State Militia would be ineffective against regular Federal troops, Taylor kept them in the rear, as sort of a reserve of the last resort. Even though he was outnumbered more

---

[223] Parrish, p. 336; Xavier B. Debray, "A Sketch of Debray's Twenty-Sixth Regiment of Texas Cavalry," *Southern Historical Society Papers*, Vol. XII (1884), pp. 15-16.

[224] Mamie Yeary, *Reminiscences of the Boys in Gray* (Dallas: 1912), Vol. II, p. 781 (hereafter cited as "Yeary II"); Parrish, p. 337.

[225] Blessington, p. 179; Parrish, p. 336; Vincent H. Cassidy and Amos E. Simpson, *Henry Watkins Allen of Louisiana* (Baton Rouge: 1964), p. 123.

than 3 to 1, he rarely used them in battle and then only reluctantly. They did, however, form part of the Army of Western Louisiana and marched with it, insofar as they were able. When an individual old man could no longer keep up, he discharged himself from the army and went home. He was neither questioned nor molested.

*

The main body of Banks' Army of the Gulf went into camp in and around Natchitoches and Grand Ecore on April 2. The general left Alexandria that day on his headquarters boat, the *Black Hawk*. Just before he left, he sent General Halleck a most optimistic letter, stating that he was worried lest the Rebels abandon Shreveport without a major battle. He expected to be in the northwest Louisiana city by April 10; then he would pursue the remnants of Taylor's army into east Texas until time expired and he had to return A. J. Smith's corps to Sherman. **Map 5.2** shows the Natchitoches-Shreveport sector.

When Abraham Lincoln read the letter, he became apprehensive. "I am sorry to see this tone of confidence," he declared "The next news we shall hear from there will be of a defeat."[226]

Prophetic words indeed.

*

On the way to Grand Ecore, Banks was delayed in the Red River because the *Eastport* ran aground again and blocked the channel. He docked on April 3, the same day Porter arrived in his flagship, the *Cricket*. A. J. Smith and his men would not arrive until the next day. That same evening, Banks and Brigadier General Charles P. Stone, his chief of staff, met with Withenbury, Porter's chief river pilot, to discuss which route to take to Shreveport. It was the decisive conference of the campaign.

In his drive to Shreveport, Banks had three possible options: 1) the Campti-Fort Towson Road, on the eastern (northern) side of the Red; 2) the inland route, via Pleasant Hill and Mansfield; or 3) the

---

226   Johnson, p. 111, citing Nicolay and Hay, *Lincoln*, Vol. VIII, p. 291.

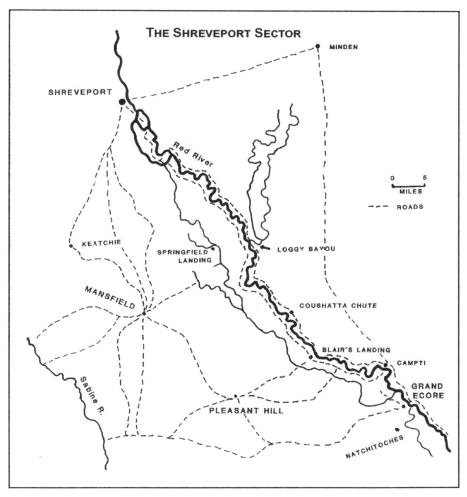

5.2 The Shreveport Sector

road which closely followed the west bank of the Red. Banks chose option Number 2. Option number 1 had the advantage of being nearer to Steele's column but was rejected because it was on the wrong side of the river and would require an assault over the Red once Banks reached a position opposite Shreveport. Option number 2 placed the army and fleet out of supporting range of each other, but this did not concern Banks because, having learned little from the

Valley campaign, he did not expect Taylor to fight before he reached Shreveport, if then. He therefore did not worry about the dangers of that route. One question remains: "Did Banks know about the third alternative, and if so, why didn't he choose it?"

There was, in fact, an excellent road along the west bank of the Red, and Withenbury had to know about it. Did Withenbury present it as an alternative? Historian Ludwell Johnson believed that he did not because he owned cotton in the area and did not want it burned by Taylor or confiscated by Banks or Porter.[227] This is entirely possible. Even so, Banks should have learned about the third route. A great many local African-Americans sought freedom behind Union lines. They would have eagerly pointed out the better route to Banks, but he chose not to question them or have his staff question them. He also failed to order a reconnaissance along the river.

General Franklin did not like the idea of traveling inland through the Louisiana piney woods, so he asked Banks' permission to conduct a reconnaissance along the west bank of the river. Banks refused. His mind was made up.

The possibility exists that the river route was mentioned in the conference of April 3, but Banks chose not to drive along the river because so many small streams and bayous emptied into the Red that Taylor could have delayed him too long. Sherman's April 15 deadline for the return of XVI Corps was rapidly approaching. Banks needed to be at least on the verge of capturing Shreveport by then. If he were to push into eastern Texas, he would have to advance rapidly, so he gave the order—advance inland!

It was a fatal mistake.

---

227 Johnson, pp. 113-116.

Taylor Concentrates At Mansfield

While Banks concentrated at Natchitoches and Grand Ecore, Taylor seemingly created an army from thin air at Mansfield, as one small regiment after another joined the Army of Western Louisiana.

The Texas cavalry which was en route to Louisiana was reorganized on March 17, 1864, by Special Order 76. Alexander W. Terrell's 34th, James B. Likens' 35th, and Buchel's 1st Texas Cavalry Regiments were brigaded under the command of Colonel Augustus C. Buchel. Buchel was succeeded as commander of the 1st Texas Cavalry by Lieutenant Colonel William O. Yager. A second brigade was formed under Debray and included the 23rd Texas Cavalry (Colonel Nicholas C. Gould), the 26th Texas Cavalry (Lieutenant Colonel John J. Meyers, replacing Debray, who still traveled with the regiment), and the 32nd Texas Cavalry Regiment (Colonel Woods). Both brigades were part of Brigadier General Hamilton P. Bee's cavalry division. A second cavalry division was formed under Brigadier General James P. Major. It included the brigades of Colonels Walter P. Lane, Arthur P. Bagby, and William G. Vincent. Vincent's new brigade was very small and consisted of Colonel Louis Bush's 7th Louisiana Cavalry and the remnants of his own 2nd, which was now commanded by Major Winter O. Breazeale.

Terrell's 34th Regiment (360 men) crossed the Sabine River, which formed the Texas-Louisiana border, on April 1 and headed toward Pleasant Hill. A courier intercepted it, however, and ordered the former judge to go to Mansfield by way of Logansport (**Map 5.3**).[228]

---

228 Alexander Watkins Terrell was another highly esteemed Texas cavalry leader. Born in Virginia in 1827, he moved to Missouri after his father died when he was five. He and his brothers did the farm work after school and on Saturdays. They frequently plowed by moonlight. Terrill briefly attended the University of Missouri, studied law, and was admitted to the bar in 1849. He moved to Texas in 1852. He was considered one of the finest legal minds in the state and was elected district judge in 1857.

Like his close friend Sam Houston, Terrill opposed secession but joined the Confederate Army after his term expired in June 1862 and rose rapidly. He served on Henry McCulloch's staff before becoming a battalion commander at Bonham in early 1863. His battalion was expanded into the 34th Texas Cavalry Regiment on June 8 with Terrill as colonel. This unit should not be confused with the 34th Texas Cavalry Regiment (Dismounted).

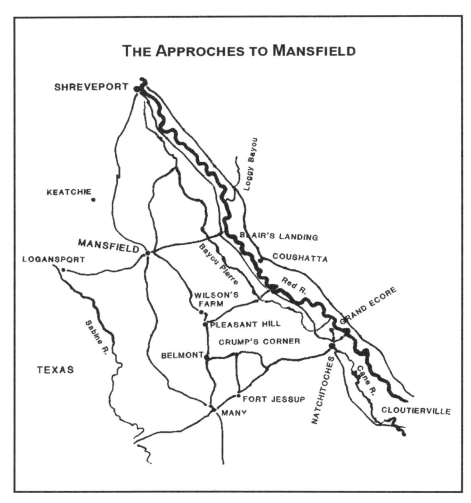

5.3 The Approaches to Mansfield

Late that evening, Brigadier General Thomas Green arrived at Taylor's Headquarters and informed him that Colonel Debray and the 26th Texas Cavalry Regiment were moving up from Many to Pleasant Hill. Taylor worked with Green before and already selected him to command his Cavalry Corps.

Tom Green was another legendary Texas cavalry commander. He was born in Buckingham County, Virginia, on July 8, 1814, the son of a lawyer who became a Tennessee state supreme court judge (1832 to 1852) and head of the Cumberland University Law School from 1852 until his death in 1866.[229] His father saw to it that Tom received a fine education at Jackson College, Tennessee, Princeton College, Kentucky, and the University of Tennessee, from which he graduated in 1834, at the age of 20. A prolific reader of military history, young Green also studied law but apparently never stood for the bar; instead, he heeded the call of adventure. In late 1835, he migrated to Texas, joined Sam Houston's army, and won a battlefield promotion at San Jacinto. He was discharged as a major in 1836 but returned to Texas, drawn by the lure of free land.

He acquired more than 2,000 acres in south-central Texas and served as a county surveyor; clerk of the Texas House of Representatives; member of the Texas Congress; secretary of the Texas Senate; and clerk of the Texas Supreme Court. In his spare time, he served in military campaigns against the Indians and in the war against Mexico (1846-48), where he commanded a company of Texas Rangers. He also married and had five daughters and a son, and raised six other children, whom he and his wife adopted after their mother's death.

After the secession of Texas (which he supported), Tom Green was elected colonel of the 5th Texas Cavalry and played the major role in the Confederate victory at Valverde, New Mexico, on February 21,

---

Kirby Smith wanted to place Terrill in charge of his Cotton Bureau in September 1863, but the judge refused the appointment.

229 See Odie Faulk, *General Tom Green* (Waco, Texas: 1963) (hereafter cited as "Faulk") for a somewhat unreliable biography of Green.

Brigadier Generals Tom Green and James P. Major

1862.[230] He also played a prominent role in keeping the army together during the retreat from Albuquerque. He later distinguished himself in the capture of Galveston and its garrison on January 1, 1863.

Green and his regiment were sent to Louisiana in early 1863. Taylor soon replaced "Whiskey Keg" Sibley with Colonel James Reily, who was killed in action at Fort Bisland on April 12.[231] Green succeeded him as brigade commander and was promoted to brigadier general on May 20. For the next six months, he led his cavalry in a series of quick, hard-hitting raids which plagued the Federals, who were unable to catch him because he never appeared where they expected him. At Brashear City on June 23, for example, he surprised the garrison and captured 1,800 prisoners, a dozen guns, and $3,000,000 worth of property ($64,026,563 in 2020

---

230 Green was acting commander of all Confederate forces. The permanent commander, General Sibley, was ill and probably inebriated. The Union commander in this action was Colonel Edward R. S. Cauby.

231 Faulk, pp. 52-53.

money), along with more than 2,000 black laborers. He lost three killed and 21 wounded.[232] He won similar victories at Morgan's Ferry (Morganza) on September 29 and at Burbeaux on November 3. In the process, his brigade was expanded into a division.

Banks' landings on the Texas coast compelled Kirby Smith to send Green's command back home in December 1863. He was recommended for advancement to major general on February 18, 1864, but President Davis never nominated him for this promotion.

Tom Green was described as "a firm friend and a bitter enemy." He was, as Duaine wrote later, "brave and untiring, and had dash and imagination. He hated the enemy with a passion which had experienced much practice in hating enemies."[233] He was a simple man and a bold, daring warrior. To his fellow Southerners, he was a gentleman who treated everyone with kindness and courtesy—when he was sober. This was not very often. Despite his taste for the bottle, a bond quickly developed between this tough, audacious frontiersman and the aristocratic Taylor, cemented no doubt when they determined that they were distantly related via their Virginia ancestors. Green's only weakness as a military commander was an excessive fondness for adult beverages, which characterized a great many Civil War generals and no doubt got a great many men on both sides killed.

When Green arrived back in Louisiana, Taylor placed him in charge of all the Confederate cavalry. "Green's Cavalry Corps" included Bee's, Major's, and Brigadier General William B. Steele's divisions. Its composition is shown in Table 5.1.

On April 2, Union General Albert Lee sent out a strong reconnaissance in force from Natchitoches in the direction of Pleasant Hill. At that moment, Colonel Debray and the 26th Texas Cavalry were moving down the Old Fort Jessup Road to join Colonel Bagby's brigade on the Confederate forward outpost line. Debray collided

---

232   Faulk, pp. 56-57.
233   Duaine, p. 59.

The Cavalry Corps, Army Of Western Louisiana

Cavalry Corps: Brigadier General Thomas Green (killed, April 12); Brigadier General Hamilton P. Bee (relieved May 14); Major General John Wharton

Bee's Division: Bee; Brigadier General Arthur P. Bagby (May 14)

Debray's Brigade: Colonel Xavier B. Debray (1)

    23rd Texas Cavalry: Colonel Nicholas C. Gould

    26th Texas Cavalry: Lieutenant Colonel John J. Meyers

    32nd Texas Cavalry: Colonel Peter C. Woods

Buchel's Brigade: Colonel Augustus C. Buchel (mortally wounded, April 9); Bagby (1); Colonel Alexander W. Terrell

    1st Texas Cavalry: Lieutenant Colonel William O. Yager

    35th Texas Cavalry (2): Colonel James B. Likens

    37th (34th) Texas Cavalry: Colonel Terrell

Major's Division: Brigadier General James P. Major

Lane's Brigade: Colonel Walter P. Lane (wounded, April 8); Colonel George W. Baylor

    1st Texas Partisan Ranger Battalion: Lieutenant Colonel Richard P. Crump

2nd Texas Partisan Ranger Battalion: Colonel Isham Chisum

2nd Arizona Cavalry: Colonel Baylor; Lieutenant Colonel John W. Mullen

3rd Arizona Cavalry: Lieutenant Colonel George T. Madison

Bagby's Brigade: Bagby; Colonel William P. Hardeman

4th Texas Cavalry: Hardeman; Lieutenant Colonel George J.Hampton

5th Texas Cavalry: Major Hugh A. McPhaill

7th Texas Cavalry: Lieutenant Colonel Philemon T. Herbert, Jr. (mortally wounded, April 8); Lieutenant Colonel Gustave Hoffman

13th Texas Cavalry Battalion: Lieutenant Colonel Edward Waller

Vincent's Brigade: Colonel William G. Vincent

2nd Louisiana Cavalry: Vincent; Major Winter O. Breazeale

7th Louisiana Cavalry: Colonel Louis Bush

NOTES:

(1) "Assigned to duty" as a brigadier general by Edmund Kirby Smith, April 13, 1864.

(2) Detached to the Sub-District of North Louisiana, April 1864.

Table 5.1 The Cavalry Corps, Army Of Western Louisiana

with the rear of Lee's cavalry and mounted infantry units and some heavy fighting ensued. Before the Yankees could bring their superior numbers to bear, however, Debray retired in perfect order.[234]

*

While Banks thought that there would be no major engagement before Shreveport, General Taylor was spoiling for a fight. On April 4, he sent Kirby Smith a dispatch, stating that he received information that the rest of Green's cavalry division would arrive within the next 36 to 48 hours. He then intended to move against Banks' vanguard and Natchitoches.[235]

On April 5, Colonel Terrell's regiment, up from Logansport, joined Taylor at Mansfield. That same day, Colonel Augustus Buchel and the 1st Texas Cavalry Regiment joined the concentration with 500 men.[236]

Meanwhile, on April 5, A. J. Smith probed northwest of Grand Ecore but ran into the Louisiana cavalry, hidden in the dense growths of cottonwoods north of the hill mass. The fighting was heavy and the Northerners took several prisoners. "But it was plain that General A. J. Smith ran afoul of something that was a match for him," Lieutenant Van Alystyne of New York recalled. Smith's men advanced through the woods to a clearing, which they attempted to cross, only to run into a Southern ambush, and "panic was the result." The narrow road was full and reinforcements could not easily be brought up, and the fresh infantrymen "could not stop the retreat." They had to get out of the way "or get run over by crazy men and horses that filled the narrow road."[237] This small battle was a precursor of future events. This time, however, the Confederates did not pursue.

---

[234] Spencer, pp. 11-12.
[235] O.R., Vol. XXXIV, Part 1, pp. 522-523.
[236] Spencer, p. 9.
[237] Van Alystyne, p. 301.

Among the Southern prisoners was a Captain Todd, who claimed to be a cousin of Abraham Lincoln's wife, Mary Todd Lincoln. Todd was subdued, quiet, civil, and polite to his captors, and hoped aloud that he would receive a clerkship in the government after the war. The word "polite" did not apply to another captured captain, whose name was Faulkner. He was "as full of venom as a rattlesnake," Lieutenant Van Alystyne recalled, "... If he carries out his present intentions we had better skip for the north before he gets loose." Faulkner claimed to be the officer in charge of the Rebels that riddled the *Black Hawk* with bullets at Morgan's Bend, and indeed he and the captain knew each other by sight. "I had four shots at you at Morgan's Bend," Faulkner told Captain Frayer, "and all I ask for is one more."[238]

*

It was obvious to everyone that Banks would soon leave Natchitoches and launch his drive on Shreveport. On April 4, Taylor wrote to General Boggs (Kirby Smith's chief of staff) and said: "While we are deliberating the enemy is marching. King James lost three kingdoms for a mass. We may lose three states without a battle."[239] He also made it clear that he thought he could defeat Banks. Taylor, of course, had commanded a brigade in Stonewall Jackson's Army of the Shenandoah when it crushed Banks' army in 1862. "Action, prompt, vigorous action is required," Taylor declared. "... We may lose three states without a battle. Banks is cold, timid, easily foiled ... Steele is bold, ardent, vigorous ..." Taylor made it plain that, if Kirby Smith insisted upon dealing with Steele first, he was prepared to march to Arkansas, crushing the U.S. VII Corps, and then double back to deal with Banks.[240]

---

238 Van Alystyne, p. 301.

239 O.R., XXXIV, Part 1, p. 522. Taylor was referring to King James II of England, who lost his throne to William of Orange in 1688 because of his Catholicism.

240 O.R., Vol. XXXIV, Part 1, pp. 484, 513-519, 522-523.

The result was another conference. Kirby Smith met with Taylor in Mansfield at noon on April 6. Taylor escorted him to his assembly areas four miles north of the town to inspect his troops. Including the men still shadowing or delaying Banks to the south, he now had 8,800 men and 40 guns.

Kirby Smith expressed his inclination to move against Steele with the bulk of his forces, but no firm decision was reached as of yet. He saw no need to engage Banks' forces. The Army of Western Louisiana was performing a valuable enough duty, Kirby Smith said, just tying them down, so that they could not be used east of the Mississippi. He also brought up the possibility of a siege of Shreveport or a retreat into eastern Texas. Taylor emphatically rejected both options. He believed that a Confederate army in the interior of Texas could provide Robert E. Lee *et al* no more aid than if they were on the Sandwich Islands. Not persuaded by Taylor's arguments, Kirby Smith ordered him not to engage the enemy without written orders. He then returned to Shreveport, where a ball was being held in his honor that evening.[241]

From Taylor's point of view, the only positive news from the conference was that Kirby Smith moved Churchill's and Parson's divisions to Keatchie, about 20 miles closer to Mansfield and within supporting distance of both Taylor and Shreveport.[242]

Also on April 6, Banks resumed his offensive on Shreveport. He failed to conduct a reconnaissance along the west bank of the Red to find an existing road which would have allowed him to advance with the protection of the gunboats. There was, in fact, an excellent road—much better than the one he took. It was also a shorter route to Shreveport, offered plenty of drinking water for his men and horses, and even contained an abundant supply of cotton. It would

---

241 Thomas Ayres, *Dark and Bloody Ground: The Battle of Mansfield and the Forgotten Civil War in Louisiana* (Lanham, Maryland: 2001), pp.219-220; Edmund Kirby Smith, "The Defense of the Red River," B & L, Vol. IV, p. 371; Taylor, p. 59;

242 B & L, Vol. IV, p. 371; Taylor, p. 159.

also offer him the support of Porter's heavy naval artillery. Banks felt secure, however, because he did not expect Taylor to make a stand, much less launch a counteroffensive.

Lee's cavalry led the way out of Natchitoches and into the piney woods. It was followed by more than 300 wagons; then two divisions of the XIII Corps; the XIX Corps; and 700 more wagons, which were escorted by a brigade of the Corps d'Afrique under Colonel William H. Dickey. Two divisions of A. J. Smith's XVI Corps (which did not depart Natchitoches until April 7) were next in the line of march, while Colonel Oliver P. Gooding's cavalry brigade screened the left flank and covered the rear. Banks and Porter agreed to link up again at Springfield Landing on April 10. This landing was on Bayou Pierre, four miles from the Red, and 60 miles by road from Grand Ecore. Due to the meandering of the river, however, the gunboats would have to travel 100 miles to get there. Because of the constantly decreasing level of the river, Porter left the *Eastport* at Grand Ecore.

As Banks' column moved west, the nature of the terrain changed completely. Gone was the rich alluvial soil, prosperous farms, and lush plantations. They were now in what a Massachusetts cavalryman called "a howling wilderness."[243] The dirt road became just a sunken cart path, which one survivor said resembled a deep ditch. By now, the roads were dry and the deep dust made breathing difficult. The tall pine trees blocked the breeze and ventilation was poor. The troops were soon short of water, but there was none to be found in the piney woods, except when it rained. The floor of the forest was covered in thickets which resembled the walls of a corridor. The thick forest "shrouded the road in deep gloom, cutting off the air ... "[244]

On April 6, General Lee's vanguard pushed through the rolling red clay hills west of Natchitoches, passed the ruins of Los Adaes, the old Spanish capital of Texas, and then north to the store at Crump's

---

[243] James K. Ewer, *The Third Massachusetts Cavalry in the War for the Union.* Maplewood, Massachusetts: 1903), p. 142 (hereafter cited as "Ewer").
[244] Winters, p. 335.

Corners, where it spent the night.[245] The next day, April 7, the column was struck by a heavy rain. The road turned into gummy red mud. The dust became a muddy red paste which was simultaneously sticky and slippery. The column slid along and soon stretched out more than 20 miles. Eventually, it neared the village of Pleasant Hill. By now, General Lee felt a sense of foreboding, and it was not solely due to the gloomy pine forest, the rain, the ominous clouds and the changing terrain. He was now skirmishing against Brigadier General James P. Major's cavalry division, and this was different. His "amateur equestrians" were no longer fighting the mediocre 2nd Louisiana Cavalry Regiment. These Texas boys grew up on the frontier and rode horses almost since they were able to walk. By the time they were eight, they were able to perform circus tricks on horseback. Many of them were former Texas Rangers. Quite a few fought outlaws, bandits, Mexicans, Comancheros, Apaches, and other Indians. Although Lee probably did not know it, General Major himself personally killed three "hostiles" in a single engagement when he was a lieutenant in the famous 2nd Cavalry.[246] For the first time in the campaign, the Union horsemen were facing opponents who were clearly superior to them. (Obviously, it takes a certain level of skill to ride a horse down the streets of Boston; however, when fighting people like Geronimo on the Western plains, an entirely different skill level is required.) Now the Rebels forced them to deploy into line of battle formation much more frequently. Even more alarmingly, the Rebels did not dismount or melt away. They remained on the backs of their horses and rode through the brush and thickets just as if they were on the open prairie, which the Yankee cavalrymen could not do. Driving them off was much more difficult. It was noon before the

---

245 Joiner, *Howling Wilderness*, p. 81.

246 James Patrick Major (1836-1877) was a native of Missouri. He graduated from West Point in 1856 and was posted to the Texas frontier in 1857. He married a sister-in-law of Tom Green and was thoroughly westernized. He resigned his commission in 1861 and joined the staff of Earl Van Dorn, eventually becoming his chief of artillery. He played a major role in repulsing the Federal fleet at Vicksburg in 1862. Sent to Louisiana, he impressed Dick Taylor, who recommended he be promoted. A brigadier general as of July 21, 1863, he led a cavalry brigade in the Bayou Teche and Lafourche regions and then in south Texas. He was severely wounded at Donaldsonville on June 28, 1863.

Union horsemen could take Pleasant Hill, and still the Texans were nipping at their flanks. Although he was all alone at the moment, General Albert Lee was growing concerned.

He would have been even more concerned if he had known that General Major was being reinforced. On the morning of April 7, he had only Colonel Bagby's small brigade (the 5th and 7th Texas Cavalry Regiments, led by Major Hugh McPhaill and Lieutenant Colonel Philemon T. Herbert, Jr., respectively). Shortly after 9 a.m., however, he was joined by another entire brigade, led by another famous Texas cavalry commander: Colonel Walter P. Lane.

Lane was born in Ireland in 1817 but came to America with his parents in 1821. He lived in Ohio for a time but was in Texas when the Revolution began in 1835. He won a battlefield commission at the age of 18 during the Battle of San Jacinto, where he was wounded by a Mexican lancer. Later, he joined the crew of a Texas privateer and raided Mexican commerce in the Gulf of Mexico. On another occasion, he and 24 other frontiersmen were surrounded in an open field by hundreds of Indians. They held them off for hours and shot a great many. When the battle was over, Lane was one of the four whites left alive, and he was wounded.[247]

During the Mexican War, Lane was a captain and company commander in the 1st Texas Cavalry Regiment. He distinguished himself at Monterrey, where his horse was shot from under him. Later in the war, he was shot through the leg. Discharged as a major in 1848, he spent much of the next 13 years as a prospector and miner in California, Nevada, Arizona, and Peru, where he made and lost several small fortunes. He was engaged in the mercantile business in Marshall in 1861, when he was elected lieutenant colonel in the 3rd Texas Cavalry without opposition. He fought Indians until early 1862, when he led the 3rd in the Battle of Pea Ridge. Here, he again showed his trademark reckless courage by charging and capturing a six-gun Union battery. He later served with Taylor in 1863, where he commanded a brigade in Green's cavalry division. In late 1863, he

---

247 Walter P. Lane, *Adventures and Recollections of General Walter P. Lane* (Austin, Texas: 1970), pp. 115-16 (hereafter cited as "Lane").

served with Magruder on the Texas coast. His courage was legendary, and he had eight horses shot out from under him in various wars. In 1864, his brigade consisted of the 1st and 2nd Texas Partisan Ranger Battalions and the 2nd and 3rd Arizona Cavalry Regiments. Major George A. Warford of the 1st Texas Partisan Rangers recalled riding through the streets of Mansfield and passing Richard Taylor, who was delighted to see them.[248]

Although Lee's forces at Pleasant Hill were still almost twice as large as Major's, the odds definitely changed. Of Lee's 10 available regiments, five were mounted infantry. As Brigadier General William Dwight later testified, these men "were not good riders, and did not understand how to take care of their horses properly. They were infantry soldiers who had been put on horseback ..."[249]

As the odds changed, so did the behavior of the Rebels. At Wilson's Farm, three miles beyond Pleasant Hill, the bluecoats met the Southern cavalry again. This afternoon, they were facing the 200 men of Lieutenant Colonel George T. Madison's 3rd Arizona Cavalry Regiment. The Confederates fought for half an hour and then fled in apparent confusion, pursued by the Federals. This time, however, the bluecoats rode straight into an ambush. Colonel Lane was waiting in the woods at the end of the field with the rest of his brigade, which was now fighting dismounted. The ensuing volley was delivered at less than 100 yards and staggered the Northerners, who fell back for cover into the woods on the other side of the field.

Not wanting to attack across open ground, the Yankees dismounted and extended their line to their left and right, to outflank the former pirate. When the Union line was about a mile long, the Rebel cavalry mounted up and pulled back again. Thinking the Rebels were retreating, the Federals mounted up again and

---

248   Yeary II, pp. 780-781.

249   Thirty-Eighth Congress of the United States, *Report of the Joint Committee on the Conduct of the War: Red River Expedition, Fort Fisher Expedition, Heavy Ordnance* (Washington, D.C.: 1865), p. 58 (hereafter cited as "JCCW"); O.R., Vol. XXXIV, Part 1, pp. 450, 616-617. Lee's Division had four brigades. The 1st, 3rd, and 4th went forward with him. The 5th Cavalry Brigade was in the rear, guarding the wagon train.

pursued, "yelling and whooping." It was another ambush. Lane posted three companies under the brow of a hill. They opened up at a range of 30 yards and "emptied a good many saddles."[250]

Lane fell back to Ten Mile Bayou, where he was joined by Colonel William P. Hardeman's 4th Texas Cavalry, the last regiment of Bagby's brigade to reach the field after a long march from coastal Texas.

Meanwhile, a strong wind from the south carried the sound of gunfire to the headquarters of the Army of Western Louisiana. General Taylor promptly mounted his horse and headed for the sound of the guns. On route, he ran into 50 Texas cavalrymen, who were headed the other way. Knowing what was about to happen, the Texas leader shouted: "General! If you won't curse us, general, we will go back with you!" Taylor smiled, bowed slightly, and kept his mouth shut. When he met General Green a short time later, he brought 50 reinforcements.[251]

The Northerners advanced on Green's latest position on foot because of the rough terrain. Green's men remained on their horses' backs, ducked in and out of the woods, hit the Yankees where they were most vulnerable, and then fell back before they could be decisively engaged. Taylor recalled that he "enjoyed his [Green's] method of handling his wild horsemen."[252]

Green made a stand at Ten Mile Bayou. He placed Bagby's Brigade (4th, 5th, and 7th Texas Cavalry Regiments) on his right and Lane on his left, with the Valverde Battery (whose guns he personally captured in New Mexico in 1862) in the center. In spite of grape and canister, the Yankees pushed across the bayou, but the fire from the 7th Texas was so heavy that they had to withdraw. A second attempt met the same fate. The vanguards of two other Texas cavalry brigades—Buchel's and Debray's—were reaching the field as evening approached, but Green—acting on orders from Taylor—avoided a general engagement.

---

250 Lane, pp. 108-109.
251 Taylor, p. 192.
252 Taylor, p. 160.

As more Northern regiments were committed to the battle, Green gradually fell back about five miles to Carroll's Mill, where he staged yet another ambush and shot down several more Yankees. By the time Lee advanced with his main body, however, Green was gone. It was here that the Yankee cavalrymen stopped for the night.

"We haven't had much show yet, Colonel," General Green exclaimed to Augustus Buchel, "but we will give them hell tomorrow!"[253]

The Confederacy also had its prophets.

*

Meanwhile, the Confederate wounded were hauled back to Mansfield. Among them was Captain Stephen Webb, a company commander in Lane's brigade. He was shot through the body and was not expected to live. Webb, however, not only made a full recovery, he also married his nurse—much to the delight of his brigade commander.[254]

*

In the meantime, Brigadier General Hamilton Bee's cavalry brigade arrived in Mansfield from southern Texas. It included the 23rd, 35th, and 36th Texas Cavalry Regiments. Taylor immediately sent it to the front.

After the Battle of Wilson's Farm, General Lee was alarmed. The Rebels had not put up such spirited resistance since the campaign began. He begged General Franklin for a brigade of infantry because his cavalry was not effective in this wooded, rolling terrain. Franklin refused on the grounds that his infantry was tired and could not be expected to keep up with Lee's cavalry.

That night, Colonel John S. Clark of Banks' staff visited Lee at Carroll's Mill and found him depressed about the resistance he met. Lee asked Clark to carry back a request to Franklin, who was spending

---

253 Ayres, p. 221.
254 Lane, p. 109.

the night at Pleasant Hill. He still wanted an infantry brigade. He also wanted the line of march changed to place his wagons behind the infantry, not between his cavalry and the foot soldiers. Clark agreed to run this important errand. When Franklin rejected both requests, Clark took the matter to Banks, who turned up at Franklin's headquarters late that evening. The commanding general overruled Franklin and ordered him to send Lee an infantry brigade. (This is probably why Lee asked Clark to carry the message in the first place. Lee could not go over Franklin's head without violating military protocol. As a member of Banks' staff, Clark could and did.) Banks did not approve changing the order of march, however. Apparently, he agreed with Franklin when he said Lee should look after his own wagons. Neither Banks nor Franklin thought there was much to worry about. Neither expected a major battle before they reached Shreveport.

Lee was still worried. He was marching down a hilly, dirt road which only provided enough room for one wagon or four soldiers to march abreast, and the impenetrable pine forest and the rain would make turning them around difficult, if not impossible. Bringing up additional artillery would be out of the question.

Meanwhile, as ordered, General Franklin sent a message to Brigadier General Thomas E. G. Ransom, the commander of the XIII Corps Detachment, and instructed him to reinforce Lee with a brigade or a division at daybreak—preferably a division, since his brigades were small. Ransom sent him only Colonel William J. Landram's 4th Brigade of the 1st Division, which contained only 1,200 combat effective soldiers.[255]

*

---

[255] Thomas E. G. Ransom was born in Norwich, Vermont, in 1834, the son of a university president. Ransom earned a degree in civil engineering in 1851 and was working in Illinois when the war began. He joined the 11th Illinois as a captain and was successively promoted to colonel—and was wounded in the battles of Charleston, Missouri, Fort Donelson, and Shiloh in the process. He served as chief of staff to General McClernand in the summer of 1862 and later commanded a brigade in the XIII Corps and another in XVII Corps. He distinguished himself at Vicksburg and Grant already earmarked him to command his cavalry in Tennessee and Georgia (Warner, *Generals in Blue*, pp. 389-390).

On the other side of the lines, Richard Taylor attended a ball thrown in his honor by the ladies of Mansfield. By every account, these women were beautiful, both inside and out. They were also worried, and several of them asked Taylor not to let the Federals destroy their town or burn their homes. "To do that, ladies, Banks would first have to pass over my [dead] body," the general replied.[256] This was more than a gallant response on Taylor's part: he meant it. Since March 12, Dick Taylor retreated 200 miles. He was determined to retreat no further.

Taylor left the party around 9 p.m. and returned to his quarters. There, he sent a written order to General Churchill at Keatchie, instructing him to march to Mansfield at first light. He also wrote a carefully worded letter to Kirby Smith, asking if he should "hazard a general engagement" the next day. He implied that if he did not receive an answer before sunrise, he would act on this own initiative.[257]

Taylor was covering himself here. He knew that there was no way this dispatch would reach Kirby Smith in Shreveport in time for him to respond and get an answer back to Taylor at Mansfield by dawn. Even so, he waited another hour before he sent the message. He then instructed Tom Strother, his slave, to wake him up at first light, and he went to bed. Tomorrow would be a long day.

Even the choice of the courier was a calculated move on Taylor's part. The message was carried by Captain Wilbur F. Blackman, Colonel Gray's adjutant. Blackman knew what was going on at army headquarters, he knew that Taylor did not want the dispatch to reach Kirby Smith in time for him to forbid the attack, and he was in full agreement with Taylor's strategy. Like Taylor, the captain was itching for a chance to turn on and defeat the invader.[258] When Blackman finally got around to leaving Mansfield, he was in a slow hurry to get to Shreveport.

---

256   Ayres, p. 221.

257   O.R.,Vol. XXXIV, Part 1, p 526.

258   J. E. Sliger, "How General Taylor Fought the Battle of Mansfield, Louisiana," *Confederate Veteran*, Vol. XXXI (1923), p. 457 (hereafter cited as "Sliger").

Chapter VI

The Battle Of Mansfield

About 2 a.m. on April 8, 1864, the clouds finally broke, the stars came out, and the sky was crystal clear. Many of the men who watched were struck by the beauty of it all. They wondered—would this be the last time they saw the stars?

The Confederates were especially edgy and anticipated a major battle. There was only one road going into Mansfield but three going out. Banks could take any of the three to Shreveport. This meant that, if Taylor was going to defend Shreveport, he would have to do it here.

Four miles north of Mansfield, Lieutenant Colonel William Walker began waking up the men of his 28th Louisiana Infantry Regiment at 6 a.m. and ordered his company commanders to prepare to march.

The 28th Louisiana had enjoyed the previous four days. They were fed by the ladies of Mansfield, who brought home-cooked meals to their camp and mended their uniforms. The girls from the town's female academy even gave them a music recital.[259]

---

259 Ayres, p. 222.

Colonel Henry Gray.

Around 7 a.m., Colonel Gray's Louisiana brigade moved out. It was led by the 28th Louisiana, followed by the 18th Louisiana and the Louisiana Consolidated Crescent Regiment. In all, Colonel Gray had 1,100 men.

Behind Gray, the four dismounted Texas cavalry regiments and one infantry regiment of Brigadier General Camille de Polignac's brigade fell in. The prince had only 1,200 men. With Gray and Polignac together, Mouton's division had 2,300 combat effectives.

The men were watching General Taylor and his staff. They knew that if this group turned north, they were going to retreat to Shreveport. If it turned south, there was going to be a battle. The suspense was terrible. Then Dick Taylor turned his massive black horse south, and his officers followed him. At that exact moment, the soldiers knew they were going to fight.

The boys in butternut and gray marched south for Mansfield, followed by the 3,800 men of Walker's Texas Division. On the road, they passed the army's wagon trains which were heading north, out of harm's way. In the pretty town of Mansfield, they were cheered by the citizens while a band played "Dixie." They saw ambulances waiting in rows. The men of the provost marshal were on hand to keep order if necessary. The town's women were carrying bundles of sheets, which would be stripped into bandages. The medical staff and civilian volunteers (mostly old men) were carrying cots and blankets to the churches and large buildings, which were being set up as hospitals. By this time tomorrow, virtually every building in Mansfield would be a hospital.

"As we passed through the streets of the beautiful town," Colonel T. R. Bonner of the 18th Texas Infantry recalled, "they were thronged with fair ladies—misses and matrons—who threw their bright garlands at our feet, and bade us, in God's name, to drive back the Yankees and save their cherished homes. As their cheerful songs of the Sunny South fell in accents of sweetest melody upon our ears, we felt that we were indeed 'thrice armed,' and though greatly outnumbered, would drive back the foe."[260]

Beyond Mansfield, they were met by General Taylor, who was wearing his trademark black greatcoat, and by Colonel Gray, atop his huge charger, Caesar. They were directed off the Pleasant Hill Road and were led to a rail fence on the edge of the pine forest. A field was situated on their right, and it extended downhill to a ravine and then uphill to a small, tree-lined ridge half a mile away. Beyond that lay the skirmish line, the Confederate cavalry, and the Yankees.

---

260 Thomas R. Bonner, "Sketches of the Campaign of 1864," *The Land We Love*, Vol. V (1868), p. 464.

The men did not know it, but the field was selected days before. On April 5, riding alone in the cool, gray dawn, without even an aide in attendance, even before Banks left Natchitoches for his final push on Shreveport, Richard Taylor chose this place as the battlefield. It was about two and a half miles southeast of the town of Mansfield. He decided to deploy his men along the north side of a fence facing a cleared wheat field on the Moss Plantation. The field was not planted this year because its owner fled the Northern invasion. Taylor deployed his men in the woods facing south, where they would meet the Yankee who would be advancing to the north.

The field was 800 yards wide (north to south) and 1,200 yards long (east to west), with a small, tree-lined ridge called Honeycutt Hill on the southern (Union) end. A thick pine forest lay on the northern (Confederate) side, while the Mansfield-Pleasant Hill Road ran perpendicular to the Rebel line, right through the middle of the battleground. A moderately deep ravine lay about 300 yards in front of the ridge, which the Federals would no doubt occupy. If the Yankees (or Rebels) charged, they would have to go downhill and then uphill to reach the enemy's lines.

The Union generals were also up early on April 8. Franklin's plan for the day called for a short march to a point 10 miles northwest of Pleasant Hill for the infantry and wagon trains of the XIII and XIX Corps. This would give the animals a rest and allow the column, which was now more than 20 miles long, a chance to close up. A. J. Smith's XVI Corps would bring up the rear and camp at Pleasant Hill, where Franklin's men were this morning. Banks approved the plan.

At 5 a.m., on the orders of Colonel William J. Landram, the commander of the 4th Division, XIII Corps,[261] Colonel Frank Emerson arrived in the cavalry camp with his brigade and reported to General Lee. His men already made a two-hour march. A few minutes later,

---

261   Colonel William J. Landrum (1828-1895) was born in Lancaster, Kentucky. He enlisted in the 1st Kentucky Cavalry and fought under Zachary Taylor at Buena Vista, where he was severely wounded. Later he became a lawyer and newspaper editor. He led the 19th Kentucky Infantry in several actions and was given command of the 2nd Brigade of the 4th Division in 1862. He later commanded the District of Baton Rouge and was a

the cavalry moved out and immediately met serious resistance from Tom Green's Texans. The Union cavalry fought dismounted in the thick undergrowth, supported by the infantry. They slowly pushed the Rebels back toward Mansfield.

By now, Albert Lee was thoroughly alarmed. More astute than the average Union general, he survived a Richard Taylor trap before in the Bayou Teche country, although just barely. In November 1863, as he and his men advanced across Vermilion Bayou, toward Washington, Louisiana, north of Opelousas, he wondered why Taylor had not burned certain bridges. Later, as he and his men fled for their lives, he knew why. Taylor had channelized them into an ambush. It did not escape his attention that the bridges on the Pleasant Hill Road had not been burned.[262]

Sensing a trap, General Lee called for a dispatch rider, who carried another message to General Franklin, asking for another infantry brigade to replace the one which had been fighting all morning.

About 11 a.m., Franklin's infantry reached Carroll's Mill on Ten Mile Bayou, about 10 miles northwest of Pleasant Hill. The men of the XIII Corps were beginning to make camp when Lee's dispatch rider galloped up, just after General Banks arrived. Franklin decided to give Lee Colonel Jones W. Vance's command, the other brigade of Landram's division. He also ordered Brigadier General Thomas E. G. Ransom, the commander of the XIII Corps Detachment, to accompany it to the front. Franklin wanted to make sure that Vance actually relieved Emerson. He was afraid that Lee intended to put Vance in the line beside Emerson, giving himself two infantry brigades. This seems to be exactly what Lee had in mind.

---

collector of internal revenue in Kentucky for 20 years after the war. Married with nine children, he is buried within sight of his old home. *Report of the Proceedings of the Society of the Army of the Tennessee*, Vol. 28 (1896) (Cincinnati: 1897), pp. 204-205.

262 The Union forces in this battle were under the overall command of General Franklin. They were driven back to Bayou Bourbeau (Ayres, p. 219).

Brigadier Generals Albert L. Lee and Thomas E. G. Ransom

Ransom, who left Pleasant Hill at 5 a.m., had just stopped to bivouac for the day. No matter. He packed up again and, along with Vance, resumed his march on Mansfield shortly before noon.

About 11:30 a.m., Banks decided to go to the front himself. He assured Franklin that, if there was no heavy fighting, he would return soon. "There will be no heavy fighting," Franklin assured him as he rode off.[263]

Albert Lee, meanwhile, was battling Confederate cavalry (mainly Bee's fresh brigade) since 5 a.m. Bee's tactics were excellent. He formed his three regiments into three different lines of battle, about 500 yards apart. Fighting dismounted, the forward regiment held its line as long as possible and then mounted up and retreated behind the third line, while the second line opened fire on the Yankees. The process was repeated again and again. Union casualties mounted. The dead included Lieutenant Colonel Lysander R. Webb of the 77th

---

263   JCCW, p. 10.

Illinois, who was killed while speaking to General Lee.[264] At 11:45 a.m., Lee sent back a report that the Rebels were disputing his progress at every favorable position.[265]

The drive forward continued until about 12:30 p.m., when Lee ordered Colonel Landram to move forward against General Green with the 19th Kentucky in the lead and the rest of his brigade in close support. He drove in the Rebel skirmish line, but it required three regiments to do it (two infantry and one dismounted cavalry regiment). Lee even probed the Confederate left but was sharply repulsed by the Louisianans. Around 1 p.m., he captured Sabine Crossroads. The road heading east led to the Red River, and the one going west ended up in Texas. Lee, however, continued north for three-quarters of a mile, where he came to a large clearing. Taylor was waiting for him on the other side with his entire army, but Lee declined this opportunity to get his division slaughtered. He simply halted and deployed his men. No one knew it yet, but the Union advance had reached its high water mark.

*

As we have seen, General Taylor had two divisions of infantry: Brigadier General Alfred Mouton's and Major General John G. Walker's. He initially deployed Mouton's division on the left side of the Pleasant Hill Road and Walker's on the right. Mouton's left flank was covered by Tom Green's cavalry, while Walker's right was protected by Bee's brigade of Texas horsemen, who were fighting dismounted. The far Confederate left was screened by a thick pine forest, while its right flank ended where a swamp began. These deployments were faultless. Appendix 1 shows the Order of Battle of the Army of Western Louisiana, and Appendix 2 gives the same information for the Army of the Gulf on April 8, 1864.

---

264   Webb was called "a singularly handsome man, with brown hair and eyes, and an engaging manner that few could resist." He was a popular officer known for his bravery. W. H. Bentley, *History of the 77th Illinois Volunteer Infantry* (Peoria, Illinois: 1883), p. 33.
265   Spencer, p. 14.

Lee's first patrol arrived at the Moss Plantation shortly after noon, when 30 of Green's cavalrymen topped the rise, pursued by approximately 50 Union cavalrymen, who were calling "Soooee, Soooee," as if they were running hogs. The Rebels headed straight for the tree line, where the Louisiana Brigade lay hidden, deliberately leading the Federals into an ambush. General Mouton was the first of the defenders to realize what was happening. He let the Texans pass and then ordered the first rank of the 18th Louisiana Infantry to rise up, much to the consternation of the pursuers, who were by now only a few yards away. The Yankee cavalrymen reigned up just before Mouton unleashed his volley. The horses then returned to Union lines, but most of their saddles were empty. The forward Rebel infantry then rounded up at least 10 wounded prisoners. They were unable to escape because their horses were killed by Mouton's volley. General Taylor, who was so close to the action that a Yankee bullet struck his saddle, was delighted. The morale of Mouton's men soared, and they gave three cheers for Louisiana.

Mouton's ambush was the first of several nasty surprises in store for Banks' Army of the Gulf that day. The slaughter would have been much greater had it not been for Alfred Lee, the commander of the Union cavalry division. Like Banks, Lee had no qualifications for his post. He was a lawyer and an associate justice on the Kansas Supreme Court, and except for briefly commanding an infantry brigade in the last Vicksburg campaign (where he was wounded) and some experience chasing bushwackers, he had no military credentials of any kind. He did, however, have good military instincts. Of all the senior Union commanders on the field at Mansfield on April 8, he alone made no mistakes. Lee, in fact, already suspected what Taylor was up to.

Sometime after 1:30 p.m., one of Banks' staff officers arrived and told Lee that the commanding general expected him to charge across the field to his front and advance on Mansfield immediately. Lee was shocked. There must be some mistake! But there wasn't. He rode over to see Banks, who repeated the order. Lee protested. If we advance, he said, there will be a general engagement within 10 minutes, "in which we should be most gloriously flogged," and he did not want to do it. A startled Banks argued briefly but agreed to postpone the attack. (He had been "gloriously flogged" before.) He sent another staff officer off to bring up more infantry.[266]

Although Banks and his second-in-command laughed at Lee's alleged timidity behind his back, he had, in fact, saved the Union cavalry and possibly the entire army. A cavalry charge across Mr. Moss' wheatfield and into Taylor's hidden positions would have made the charge of the Light Brigade look like a sensible military exercise.

Alexandre Alfred Mouton, meanwhile, deployed his 1st (Louisiana) Brigade on his left and his 2nd (Texas) on his right, with nothing in reserve. The Louisiana Brigade was commanded by Colonel Henry Gray, who had recruited the 28th Louisiana Infantry Regiment at the request of his close personal friend, Jefferson Davis. His command included the 28th, now commanded by Lieutenant Colonel William Walker; the 18th Louisiana, led by Colonel Leopold L. Armant; and the Consolidated Crescent Regiment, which was directed by Colonel James Beard.

Theoretically, the Louisiana Brigade had 1,100 men and Taylor's Army of Western Louisiana had 8,800. These were actually more because, as if by magic, the ranks of many companies suddenly filled—especially in Gray's brigade. The new volunteers were mysterious, shadowy, ghost-like men. They did not talk much, they did not smile, they generally did not have last names, and no one from Dick Taylor down asked them any questions. When you are outnumbered more than 3 to 1 and someone offers to help you, you do not ask questions, particularly if those people are willing to obey orders. And these mysterious figures were willing—especially if those orders involved closing with and killing the enemy.

Although they did not discuss it, everyone knew they were veterans. They fought at Shiloh, Corinth, Baton Rouge, Chickasaw Bluff, Port Gibson, Champion Hill, and Big Black River. They were not ghosts, however; after months of fighting and sieges, they surrendered at Vicksburg and Port Hudson in July 1863. They were

---

266   JCCW, p. 61.

parole violators, which is why no one asked them any questions. What they were doing was highly illegal, and the punishment for their crime was death. These men, however, were not looked upon as criminals by their officers or their comrades in gray. Instead, they were treated with deference and respect.

According to the law and terms of their parole, these men should have been at home and should have remained there until they were properly exchanged for Union prisoners-of-war. Most of them, however, had no homes. Their houses and cabins were burned by A. J. Smith's gorillas, and even their corn cribs and outhouses were torched. Their wives and children were fugitives—homeless refugees in Shreveport or somewhere in Texas—they did not know where exactly.

The "Total War" methods of warfare as practiced by Sherman, A. J. Smith, et al., were about to pay monstrous negative dividends to their practitioners. These homeless Rebels gave up their rifles and muskets when they surrendered and were now generally armed with shotguns, which was about all they had left, other than the ragged, homespun clothes or uniforms on their backs. They were solemn, tight-lipped, grim-faced men with hard, deep-set eyes and determined looks upon their faces. They meant business.

How many parole violators were there in Richard Taylor's army? Obviously, we do not know precisely. Estimates vary from three or four hundred to more than a thousand. Their impact on the Battle of Mansfield is also impossible to measure precisely, but we do know that it was significant because these men were highly motivated. They had scores to settle with the men in blue, and they were about to settle them with a vengeance.

*

Initially, Major Watford of the 1st Texas Partisan Rangers recalled, "We were sent as pickets in front of the enemy and when we got in sight of them we were ordered to tie our horses in the brush and advance as infantry. We beat them back about half a mile, when we saw that we were about to run into Banks' Army.

The Battle Of Mansfield

We were ordered to retreat to our infantry line. We had to retreat through a field and slightly up hill. We were ordered to dismount and take our places on the left of our infantry. My position on the left was in the timber ..."[267]

*

It finally dawned on Banks that he might be in trouble. Shortly before 2 p.m., he told Lee to hold his positions and sent another dispatch to Franklin, ordering him to bring up his men as quickly as possible. This was easier said than done, because they were strung out over 20-odd miles of bad Louisiana roads, and there was a wagon train between them and the Union vanguard. Franklin nevertheless ordered Brigadier General Robert A. Cameron, the commander of the 3rd Division of the XIII Corps, to march toward Mansfield.

General Franklin galloped ahead of his reinforcements and arrived at the front shortly before 4 p.m. At about the same time, Taylor made a minor adjustment to his line on the left. Banks and Franklin mistook this as an indication that Taylor intended to concentrate most of his strength here. Franklin immediately moved several of his units to his right. Watching from atop his horse, Taylor assumed that Banks was preparing to launch a turning movement against his left. He, therefore, ordered Terrell's cavalry regiment to reinforce Major on his far left and sent Randal's brigade of Walker's division north of the Pleasant Hill Road, to strengthen Mouton's right. Although still part of the Texas Division, it would fight under Mouton's command on April 8. Taylor, meanwhile, posted Debray's brigade in his center, on both sides of the road. When the battle began, however, he shifted Debray to his far right. Map 6.1 shows the dispositions of both sides at 4 p.m., when the Battle of Mansfield began.

---

[267] Yeary, Vol. II, pp. 780-781. Watford was a native of North Carolina. In 1861, he was a 29-year-old school teacher in Tyler, Texas. His boys wanted to join the fray and, "as I could not hold them, I decided to go along." He was elected captain and company commander. He survived the war and was still alive in 1900.

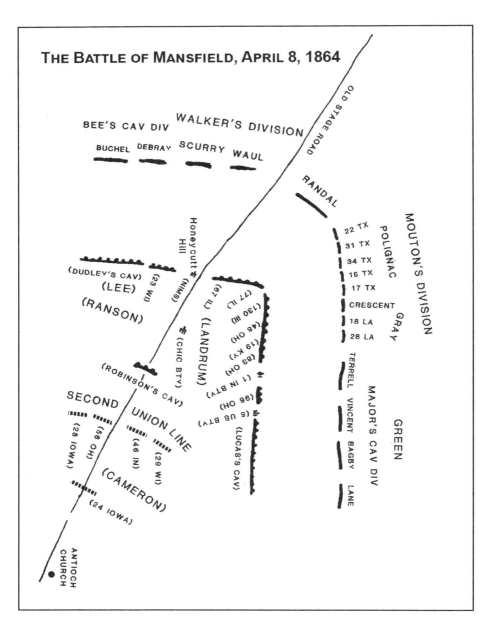

6.1 *The Battle of Mansfield*

Lieutenant J. E. Sliger of the 28th Louisiana Infantry was also in trouble. He normally commanded B Company, but on April 8, he was ordered to take Companies A and B forward of the main Rebel battle line and form a skirmish line.

Sliger was extremely well dressed for a Confederate in 1864, with a fine gray uniform, complete with a cape. He was too well dressed, in fact, because he attracted the attention of a Federal sharpshooter who carried an excellent Sharps sniper's rifle. Fortunately for Sliger, the Yankee missed with the first shot, and the young lieutenant dove behind a stump. The Confederate skimishers immediately saw what was happening and wanted to save their company commander, so they opened up on the sniper. They also narrowly missed, but their bullets compelled the Northerner to go to ground behind a log. Neither the Yankee nor the lieutenant could get off a clean shot, and both were pinned down for what seemed like forever.

After two and a half hours of skirmishing and ineffective exchanges of artillery fire, Dick Taylor's always limited supply of patience was exhausted. He had retreated 200 miles and had abandoned some of the most prosperous sections of his native state to the enemy without a fight, and was as frustrated as he was furious. He told Polignac: "Little Frenchmen, I am going to fight Banks here if he has a million men!" By 4 p.m., he realized that Banks declined his invitation to attack and had reinforced his cavalry with a second infantry brigade (Colonel Joseph W. Vance's 2nd Brigade of Landrum's Division). Taylor also knew from Green's reconnaissance reports that Banks' army was strung out for 20 miles and that he had the advantage *at the moment*. But time was not on his side. He also knew that, if he waited any longer, more Union reinforcements would arrive and the balance of power would change. (We know now that Banks already had 7,900 men at the front at 4 p.m.)

Meanwhile, Taylor heard Gray's field officers pumping up their men.

"Shall we abandon Louisiana?" they cried.

"No!" the enlisted men roared in unison. They were almost as frustrated as Dick Taylor.

"Will we fight for Louisiana?" the officers cried.

"Yes!" the Rebels screamed. They were ready.

"It appears your Louisianans are anxious for a fight, Mr. Mouton," Taylor observed, dryly.

The darkly handsome Creole general drew his sword and stood up in his stirrups. "They are, sir!" he replied. The time was a few minutes after 4 p.m.

"Then they may advance and engage the enemy," he replied. The excited Mouton immediately wheeled away to issue the necessary orders and move his division forward.

General Mouton's "customary reserve evaporated," one author recalled. With his sword drawn, he roared at Polignac: "Let us charge them right in the face and throw them into the valley!"[268]

Having set events in motion, General Taylor retired to a slightly higher piece of real estate, hooked his right leg over his saddle horn, and lit a cigar. He assumed the calm demeanor of a detached observer and would remain so until it was time to send in another brigade. One witness declared that he "looked almost serene" as he watched the attack.[269] He would direct this battle just like his father did when he defeated Santa Anna at Buena Vista, 28 years before.

"Colors to the front!" the regimental commanders cried. "By the right of companies, to the front, forward march! By companies, into line!"

---

[268] Kinard, p. 139; Parrish, p. 344; Rebecca W. Smith and Marion Mullins, ed. "The Diary of H. C. Medford, Confederate Soldier, 1864 (Part 2)." *Southwestern Historical Quarterly*. Vol. XXXIV (1930-31): pp. 203-30 (hereafter referred to as "Medford"); Edwin C. Bearss, ed., *A Louisiana Confederate: Diary of Felix Pierre Poche*, Eugenie Watson Smith, trans. (Natchitoches, Louisiana: 1972), pp. 106-107.

[269] Kinard, p. 139.

With a cheer, the Louisianans tore down the fence that bordered the northern face of the battlefield and surged forward—but they did not strictly obey General Taylor's orders.

In military terminology, an advance and a charge are two different things. Advances are slower, better organized, and more orderly. A charge is a wild, unrestrained run, directly at the enemy. The men of the 28th Louisiana, however, did not understand this distinction—would never understand it. When they enlisted in the spring of 1862, most of these men were north Louisiana farmers who used shotguns for hunting and recreation, and they carried them with them when they joined the Confederate Army. Since then, most—but by no means all—of the shotguns were traded for rifles, rifled muskets, and muskets. Now the ranks of the regiment were filled by parole violators, who were carrying shotguns. The shotgun is a very short-range weapon which is useless at long range. It is ironic, but to the men of the 28th Louisiana, safety lay in getting as close to the enemy as possible, *before* opening fire. Even the men who now carried muskets retained the shotgun mentality. As soon as the fence came down, they broke into a wild charge and screaming their Rebel yells, headed straight for the enemy.

The Confederate officers were initially startled by this mad charge. They quickly recovered, however, and put their spurs to their horses to keep up with their men.

Enthusiasm is contagious. When they saw the 28th Louisiana rushing the enemy, the 18th Louisiana followed suit. Not about to be left behind, the men of the Crescent Regiment also broke into a run.

Prince de Polignac was momentarily taken aback by the behavior of his Louisiana comrades, but he was also determined not to lag behind. He ordered his five regiments to charge. Eight Confederate regiments were now barreling pall mall toward the enemy.

Five Union regiments and four batteries of artillery immediately opened up on the charging Southerners. "The crossing of that field was awful," Major Watford recalled. "The bullets were flying like hail and the shells were bursting, yet the infantry were marching bravely right into the jaws of certain death."[270] Lieutenant Colonel Franklin Clack of the Crescent Regiment did not advance 200 yards when a cannon ball exploded right next to him. Rider and horse went down, and the mutilated colonel bled to death before medical help could reach him.

Carried away by their own enthusiasm, the field grade officers of the Louisiana Brigade decided to direct their men from horseback.[271] It was a terrible decision which cost several of them their lives. Lieutenant Colonel William Walker, the commander of the 28th Louisiana, was the next to go. He was struck by a Minie ball, fell off his horse, and lay on the wheatfield in great pain. Realizing that his wound was fatal, the former sheriff of Winn Parish nevertheless pushed himself up on one elbow to watch the battle. He was later carried to Mansfield, where he died in the home of a friend the next day. His men, however, pushed on.[272]

"Our troops advance pale with excitement, compressed lips and blazing eyes [showing] the spirit of their determination," one ex-Confederate wrote later. "Casting your eyes along the column, you behold the flags of the various regiments floating on the breeze, and each regiment trying to be the first to scale the fence."

"Nearer our troops advance," he continued. "The color-sergeants flaunt their flags at the enemy, and fall; others grasp them and fall, and they are borne by the corporals."[273]

"Masses of Rebels, no less than four lines in depth, emerged from the woods and charged with impetuous force, while yelling like crazed demons," Union gunner William H. Eastman wrote to his mother after the battle. "Our guns were filled to the muzzles with grape, canister and bags of bullets, making wide gaps in the Rebel ranks at every discharge ... but the rebs kept a full front &

---

270   Yeary, Vol. II, pp. 780-781.
271   Field grade officers are majors, lieutenant colonels, and colonels. "Company grade" officers are captains and lieutenants.
272   Kinard, p. 139.
273   Blessington, p. 188.

as fast as they fell other filled their places."[274] "Shots plow gaps through them, shells burst in their midst and form caverns in the mass of living men. [But] ... others taking the place of their dead comrades march rapidly on," John M. Stanyan on the 8th New Hampshire Volunteers recalled.[275]

As the 28th Louisiana surged forward, its advanced skirmishers fell in wherever they could, and Companies A and B temporarily ceased to exist, leaving Lieutenant Sliger free to pursue his own agenda. He ran directly toward the log behind which the Yankee sniper who tried to kill him took cover. He jumped the log, thrust his pistol in the Federal's face and demanded his surrender. The startled Northerner promptly did so. Sliger sent him to the rear but not before he relieved him of his Sharps rifle and his cartridge box.

To reach the Union line, the Louisiana Brigade charged across an open field a quarter of a mile long before it descended into a gully. From there, it was another 300 yards to the main Union line on the ridge. While in the gully (or small ravine), the Rebels were safe from enemy fire, unless they stood up. Naturally, the men of the 28th Louisiana stopped in the ravine to catch their breath. As was often the case in the Civil War, much of the Union fire was high, and the 28th suffered only moderate casualties. The slower 18th Louisiana and Crescent Regiments suffered more serious losses.

The Union artillery, including the Chicago Mercentile Battery, the 5th U.S. Artillery Battery and the 6th Missouri Battery, all concentrated their fire on the Crescent Regiment, which halted in the open field. This was the worst thing it could have done. Seeing the graycoats stop, the Union infantry turned on it as well. "Hissing Minie balls filled the air and the smoke from the muskets and cannons darkened

---

274 Parrish, p. 346.

275 John M. Stanyan, *A History of the Eighth Regiment of New Hampshire Volunteers* (Concord, New Hampshire: 1892), pp. 402-403.

the sky," Spencer wrote later. "Bullets and grapeshot ripped through Confederate lines, thudding into chests, tearing at arms and legs, and popping Rebel heads back in instant death."[276]

Realizing that the regiment would be destroyed if it remained still, Colonel James Beard seized the regimental battle flag from the color bearer and called for his men to rise and advance. Almost immediately, he was struck by a Union bullet and fell from his horse. His horrified and nearly hysterical brother, Ned, raced to his aid and dragged him behind a log a few yards away. Although Ned shook him and begged him to speak, the colonel died. His last thoughts were probably of his wife and their four-month-old son. Mercifully, the colonel never knew that his baby boy died, a homeless refugee, six days before.

Seeing Colonel Beard fall, Major Mercer Canfield grabbed the battle flag and urged the men forward. He only advanced a few feet, however, before he was also cut down. He commanded the regiment for less than five minutes.

Private Louis Hall was near Canfield when he was killed. Almost instantly, he was shot through the knee. He crawled behind a log where he found Ned Beard, who was clinging to the body of his brother and begging him to speak. But the colonel was already dead.[277]

Colonel Gray saw that the Crescent Regiment was pinned down, so he sent his assistant adjutant general, Lieutenant Arthur Martin, to rally it and get it out of the open field. Martin picked up the battle flag but fell almost immediately, mortally wounded.

The next man to seize the standard was Captain Seth Field, the commander of Company A. A resident of Mansfield, Captain Field was quite literally fighting for his home that afternoon. Earlier that day, he broke ranks as his regiment marched through the town, stopped long enough to hold his baby one last time, and kiss his

---

276 Spencer, p. 17.
277 Ayres, p. 229.

wife, assuring her that there was no Yankee bullet made for him. He was wrong. When he fell dead a few moments later, his body was riddled with Northern bullets.[278]

At least seven of the color bearers of the Crescent Regiment were killed in action or seriously wounded on April 8.[279] The last man to pick up the colors was Captain William C. C. Claiborne, Jr., a highly respected company commander and grandson of Louisiana's first governor. Young Claiborne took charge of the stalled regiment and got it moving again. When they reached the safety of the gully, the survivors of the Crescent were horrified to see Claiborne standing upright. They shouted at him to get down, and some even risked their lives to pull at his coattails, but the captain would have none of it. "Leave me be, boys!" he cried. "If I am going to die, I prefer to do it standing up." Minie balls buzzed around him like angry hornets, but young Claiborne was not even nicked. From then on, the Crescent was *his* regiment, almost by attrition. It lost all three of its field grade officers and nine captains that day.[280]

Meanwhile, the men of the 28th Louisiana caught their breath. Astride his massive black charger, Caesar, Colonel Gray galloped down into the ravine and ordered them forward. They responded instantly, led by Major W. F. Blackmon, who grabbed the regimental battle flag and urged his men forward. "Follow the colors, boys!" he cried. Astride his horse, the major was an easy target, and one Union soldier later estimated that more than 200 rounds were fired at him. They ripped through his coat and wounded his horse twice, but the major was miraculously not hit.[281]

The Southerners pushed to within 200 yards of the Union line, and the Union artillery could no longer depress their guns enough to bring them under fire. With the infantry advancing below them and

---

278 J. E. Hewitt, "The Battle of Mansfield, Louisiana," *Confederate Veteran*, Vol. XXXIII (1925). p. 173 (hereafter cited as "Hewitt").
279 O.R., Vol. XXXIV, Part 1, p. 564.
280 Ayres, p. 229. The typical Confederate regiment had ten captains.
281 Ayres, p. 230.

Green's Texas cavalrymen in their rear, many of the Union gunners were ready to fall back to safer parts, but their captain refused to allow it. He was on a horse, waving his sword. He was spotted by Lieutenant Sliger of the 28th Louisiana, who was armed with a Sharps rifle he took from the captured Union sharpshooter. Sliger fell to one knee, aimed, and fired. The captain toppled off his horse. His battery, Sliger recalled, did not fire another round "... but left in a hurry. That was all the fighting I did in the battle of Mansfield," he wrote later.[282] But it was enough.[283]

They were 200 feet from the Union line when the 19th Kentucky and the 48th Ohio halted them with a devastating volley. At the same time, laughing and cheering, General Mouton—who seemed to be everywhere—led the 18th Louisiana and Crescent Regiments up the ridge, where they were met by volleys from the 130th Illinois and 48th Ohio. Two hundred Rebels went down in moments—about 50 of them killed. Colonel Leopold L. Armant, the commander of the Creole 18th Louisiana, hit the ground when his horse was slain. Popping up instantly, he continued to lead his men forward, sword in hand, until a bullet broke his right arm. He picked up the saber with his left hand and continued forward, even though bullets struck him in both thighs, until he was almost on top of the Union line. There he was killed by a minie ball in the chest.[284]

Until this point, the battle was going all the Yankees' way. Hardly a Southerner even fired a shot. Now, however, the 28th Louisiana was exactly where it wanted to be: practically in the face of the enemy. Here, it delivered a truly devastating volley at point blank range. The muskets were more effective at this distance because it is obviously easier to hit a target at 30 feet than at 400 yards. More significantly, however, was the fact that the Rebels were now within easy shotgun range. The north Louisiana farmers and the parole

---

282   Sliger, p. 458.

283   Sliger's statement is not exactly correct. He also took a Union captain prisoner near the end of the battle.

284   Marie Louise Benton Bankston, *Camp-Fore Stories of the Mississippi Valley Campaign* (New Orleans: 1914), p. 131 (hereafter cited as "Bankston").

violators fired one barrel, then the other. The bear balls left huge holes in their victims, and the buckshot was especially effective—and especially messy. And so the veterans who lost their homes had their opportunity to extract a full measure of revenge, and they did not miss. In an instant, the entire complexion of the battle changed completely. Federals dropped by the dozen, blown back by the pure force of the Rebel volley. Very few units in the annals of military history could withstand this kind of punishment, and certainly Landrum's infantry and Lee's dismounted cavalry could not. Shocked by the volley, the Union line staggered, wavered, and broke. Here and there, brave Yankees made a stand, but they were finished off in hand-to-hand combat. Some were bayoneted; most, however, were simply bludgeoned by Rebels, who were now using their guns as clubs. Leaving behind scores of dead and wounded, the men in blue moved briskly to the rear, followed rapidly by the riflemen and shotgunners of the 28th Louisiana, who were now flushed with victory. Panic broke out in Union ranks, and some of the bluecoats dropped their rifles, so they would be able to run faster.

The 130th Illinois, however, did not behave that way. One Rebel survivor later recalled that it was "a typical regiment of American farmers who did not shoot and run away, but stood up manly."[285] The men of the 130th stayed behind to "smell the patching." This 19th Century expression meant to be in big trouble. All of the men who carried muzzle loaders (i.e., the vast majority of the soldiers on both sides) also carried gun patching: a bunch of square-cut, greasy cloth patches. A charge of powder was first poured into the muzzle of the gun; then a bullet was fitted into the fold of the cloth and driven in on top of the powder with a ramrod. The patching helped clean the fouled musket barrel and kept the bullet in place until the soldier pulled the trigger. In heavy fighting involving musketry, the ground became littered with small, burning rags, and the troops could "smell the patching." Only the soldiers who stood their ground in heavy fighting could smell it.[286] As the Rebels closed in on the men

---

285 Hewitt, p. 173.
286 Duaine, pp. 29-30.

of the 130th Illinois, the surviving intact companies of the 48th Ohio delivered another volley into the ranks of the 18th Louisiana and Crescent Regiments. It was their last organized volley, but it killed General Mouton. He pushed too far forward and riding his charger, made an easy target. He was struck by five bullets, three of them in his chest. He slid from his horse and died without saying a word.[287] General Taylor later described Mouton's charge as "magnificent."[288]

Although he was a harsh disciplinarian and a bit of a martinet, the men of the Louisiana Brigade loved their former commander. "Mouton!" would be their battle cry for the rest of the campaign. Furious, they threw themselves at the 130th Illinois. Meanwhile, strong elements of General de Polignac's brigade looped behind the 130th, to encircle and destroy it, while Randal's brigade surged forward and protected Polignac's right and rear. Seeing what was happening, U.S. Brigadier General Thomas E. G. Ransom, the commander of the XIII Corps Detachment, sent Captain Cyrus Dickey, his adjutant, to order Major John A. Bering (the acting commander of the 48th Ohio) and Major John B. Reid (the commander of the 130th Illinois) to withdraw. He never made it. Exactly who shot him is unknown, since there were Rebels all over the place, but the bullet struck him right in the head, and he was dead before he hit the ground.

In dangerous situations, generals of this era frequently sent two dispatch riders with important messages via different routes, in case one did not make it to the intended recipient. General Ransom, however, did not exercise this option. (Although he was no doubt one the best Union generals, Ransom did not perform up to his usual

---

[287] Almost immediately after his death, the rumor spread that General Mouton was murdered by five Yankees who had surrendered, but when they saw the general, they retrieved the weapons they had just dropped and shot the Creole. The Rebels who witnessed this cowardly act, according to the rumor, promptly killed the five Yankees, along with 30 other prisoners. I consider this story implausible because the killers had to know that they would be shown no mercy if they murdered Mouton. I could understand it if one man momentarily lost his head and shot the general, but five? This is very unlikely, in my view.

[288] O.R., Vol. XXXIV, Part 1, p. 564.

standard at Mansfield.) As a result, neither major received the order, and Gray and Polignac soon surrounded both regiments. Ransom later commented that his men were caught in a nutcracker.

Major Reid tried to form a defense and somehow hold out long enough to escape, but a Southern infantryman quickly cut him down. The bullet entered his chest, passed through the upper lobe of his right lung, and came out his back. Remarkably, he survived and showed incredible powers of recuperation. Captured, he was taken to a private home in Mansfield, where he was well enough to be exchanged 10 weeks later. He died in bed in 1904.

The heroic 130th Illinois was finished off by Lieutenant Colonel John H. Caudle's 34th (Dismounted) Texas Cavalry Regiment of Polignac's old brigade. The 34th was left in reserve with the artillery when Mouton began his charge, but Caudle soon followed his comrades and decided that now was the moment to launch a bayonet charge.[289] He was right. The fighting was soon hand-to-hand and was obvious to everyone that the surrounded Northerners had only two options left: drop their weapons and raise their hands or die. The 130th Illinois surrendered, along with the remnants of the 48th Ohio. Captain G. W. Mosgrove, the commander of Company D, 48th Ohio, somehow punched his way through Rebel lines and made good his escape. He was the only officer in his regiment who was not killed or captured during the battle.

Lieutenant Colonel Joseph W. Lindsey was the permanent commander of the 48th Ohio, but he was serving as acting deputy commander of Vance's brigade on April 8. When he saw his regiment was about to be swamped, he tried to join it. He was quickly shot through the right arm and captured. He was taken to Mansfield, where Confederate surgeons were able to save his arm.

---

289   Spencer, pp. 17-18. John H. Caudle (1835-1895) was born in Alabama but moved to Texas in 1850. He was a merchant when the war began and, in early 1862, became a captain and company commander in the 34th Texas (2nd Partisan Ranger) Regiment. He was promoted to lieutenant colonel in August 1863 and was later promoted to colonel. He was a merchant and farmer after the war.

Both of the Union infantry brigade commanders, Colonels Frank Emerson and Joseph W. Vance, also tried to rally their commands. Both were promptly shot down by the insurgents, shouting "Mouton!" Although both lived, they did so due to efforts of the Confederate Medical Service Corps and the care of the ladies of Mansfield, almost all of whom were now serving as volunteer nurses for the Confederacy. Even Yankee prisoners who detested everything Southern later had nothing but praise for these women, whose homes they once intended to burn. Every house in Mansfield became a hospital, and they treated Northerners and Southerners exactly the same. Both Emerson and Vance soon recovered and were exchanged, but their men were sent to Camp Ford, a Confederate prisoner-of-war compound near Tyler, Texas. There they would not be shown the same compassionate and humane treatment as their wounded commanders received in Mansfield.

Meanwhile, Colonel Landram tried unsuccessfully to rally his division, which had lost half of its men. This was a hopeless effort. They fell back rapidly to the rear, where General Cameron arrived with his fresh division. Behind it, the Yankees made their second stand of the day. They were pursued closely by Gray, Randal, and the Polignac Brigade, which was commanded by Colonel James R. Taylor since the prince assumed command of the division after Mouton's death.[290] Colonel Taylor was succeeded as commander of the 17th (Dismounted) Texas Cavalry by Lieutenant Colonel Sebron M. Noble, who was killed moments later. Major Thomas F. Tucker then took charge of the regiment. The Mouton (now Polignac) Division had, by now, lost almost a third of its men, and the casualties among its senior officers was even higher.

---

290   Kirby Smith intended that Colonel Wilburn H. King (1839-1910), the commander of the 18th Texas Infantry, succeed Polignac as permanent commander of the brigade, but he was so badly wounded in the Battle of Pleasant Grove that he was incapacitated for months. Kirby Smith nevertheless assigned him to duty as a brigadier general on April 16. King distinguished himself in the Battle of Bayou Bourbeau on November 3, 1863. He was later adjutant general of Texas (1881-1891).

The Battle Of Mansfield

Like the Louisianans, Polignac's Texas Brigade did not let the loss of their officers phase them. They captured three guns of a Union battery. "Within minutes they had turned the pieces around and were merrily reissuing Federal ordnance to its former owners in ten – and twelve – pound parcels," Kinard recalled.[291]

On the left of the Mouton Division, Brigadier General James P. Major's Cavalry Division also moved forward against the Union right, accompanied by General Tom Green. Major's command included Lane's Brigade, Bagby's Brigade, and Vincent's small Louisiana cavalry brigade. All but Lane's men were fighting dismounted, and some of them were advancing on foot as well. Major Watford of the 1st Texas Partisan Rangers recalled: "… the bullets came pretty thick. One ball struck the tree and glanced onto my knee. This did not hurt, and it was the only ball that hit me during the war … In a few minutes our men raised the [Rebel] yell and charged the fence."[292]

The Union right was protected by Colonel Thomas J. Lucas' Cavalry Brigade (14th New York Cavalry, 16th Indiana Mounted Infantry, and the 2nd Louisiana Mounted Infantry, an unreliable "Jayhawker" unit, which was reinforced by two of Vance's infantry regiments. In a brilliant move, Tom Green attacked the exposed end of Lucas' line and doubled it up. Lucas tried to counterattack but was checked by Lane's mounted horsemen. His men now had two options: flee or be destroyed. They joined the stampede. The entire Union right flank disintegrated. Major Watford laconically noted: "… the Yankees left in a hurry."[293]

J. E. Sliger described Green as "a general of no mean ability and his courage, dash and bulldog hang-on-a-tiveness was unsurpassed …" A bulldog he certainly was. "With the genius of a Murat" he

---

291 Kinard, p. 143.
292 Yeary, Vol. II, pp. 780-781.
293 Yeary, Vol. II, pp. 780-781.

pursued the Federals immediately and almost captured General Banks and his staff, which left the Antioch Church just minutes before Green arrived."[294]

Meanwhile, the Rebels lost another of their best officers. Colonel Walter P. Lane's coat was pierced by six bullets during the Battle of Mansfield. Two of them drew blood, and the last wound was serious. He was carried back to Mansfield and eventually returned to Marshall, Texas, in an ambulance.[295]

By now, the Union artillery was trying to escape with their guns, but they never really had a chance to accomplish this. The forest was too thick. Artillerymen abandoned their pieces, hopped onto the backs of their horses, and headed for the rear. Even the few guns that got out of the forest found escape impossible because the cavalry wagon train blocked the only road.

General Taylor, still perched on his horse, watched all this and calmly sucked on his cigar. Seeing that the Union line was coming unraveled, he summoned his dispatch riders and initiated phase two of his plan. He ordered the Texas Division on his right to drive forward in echelon to the left to hit the Yankee line like rapidly breaking waves.

John Walker was certainly ready. Like Dick Taylor, the Texas commander was a picture of serenity. One of his men recalled: "... about 600 yards from the enemy's position, we beheld General Walker, mounted on his iron-gray horse, with his field-glass to his eye, taking observations of the enemy's position. His actions and features were a study for the closest scrutinizer of physiognomy. Not a quiver on his face—not the movement of a muscle, to betray anxiety or emotion, notwithstanding the shower of balls whizzing around him."[296]

---

294   Lane, p. 110.
295   Blessington, pp. 188-189.
296   Blessington, pp. 188-189.

Walker's men were also ready. Of Mouton's charge, Colonel T. R. Bonner of the 18th Texas Infantry wrote: *"This was the turning point of the entire campaign"* (his italics). "Just at the critical period defeat would have been ruinous. But now our division, animated with the reckless exuberance of feeling produced by unexpected success, was now anxious to be led into action ... every man moved quickly off with confident and determined step."[297]

The Union left was successively hit by the brigades of Thomas N. Waul and William R. "Dirty Neck Bill" Scurry. (Randal's brigade on Walker's left flank had joined the battle shortly after Mouton.) On the right of the Texas Division (on Taylor's far right flank), Brigadier General Hamilton P. Bee attacked with Debray's and Buchel's cavalry brigades.[298] Taylor intended for Bee to outflank the Union left, but because of the thick woods, this maneuver did not work initially. The Texas infantry, on the other hand, faced an open field. They were wildly excited after Mouton's success and seemed irresistible, especially after Colonel Scurry ordered a bayonet charge. The Federals "greeted our coming with a perfect shower of leaden hail," Colonel Bonner recalled.[299] There were few casualties, however, because the Yankees fired too high and most of their "iron pills" flew over the Rebels' heads. "Nothing could withstand the impetuosity of our charge," Private Blessington recalled.[300]

Meanwhile, Colonel Landram reinforced Captain Ormand F. Nims's 2nd Massachusetts Light Artillery Battery with the Chicago Mercantile Battery (Lieutenant Pickney S. Cone) and the 1st Indiana Artillery Battery (Captain Martin Klauss), and posted them in the center of the ridge, so they could fire against Walker or Mouton. They cut holes in the Southern ranks, but the Greyhounds kept coming. "Close up! Close up!" the Rebel officers cried, and their men

---

297 T. R. Bonner, "Sketches of the Campaign of 1864," *The Land We Love*, Vol. V (1868), p. 464.

298 Buchel's Brigade included his own 1st Texas Cavalry Regiment (now under Lieutenant Colonel William O. Yager), Liken's 35th Texas Cavalry Regiment, and Terrell's 34th Texas Cavalry Regiment.

299 Bonner, p. 464.

300 Blessington, pp. 188-189.

promptly did so. "'Twas a sublime, yet appalling spectacle to see those noble men of Waul's brigade, while their comrades were falling mangled, bleeding, dying, press on, and still on ... and fill up their broken ranks," one officer recalled. Of the Texas infantry, Colonel Bonner recalled that "their determined resolution to conquer gave an irresistible power to their advance and the astonished and amazed Federals fled in confusion."[301] Soon Cone's and Klauss' batteries were under such heavy musket fire that General Ransom ordered them to withdraw. Their fate, however, was already sealed.

"Mouton!" The cry was picked up by virtually every Rebel unit and reverberated throughout the battlefield, like "Remember the Alamo!" at San Jacinto.

The Texans came forward "like a cyclone," one Northerner recalled. "Yelling like infuriated demons," Walker's men pushed back the 3rd Massachusetts Cavalry and surged up Honeycutt Hill, forcing back the 67th Indiana, 23rd Wisconsin, and the 8th New Hampshire Mounted Infantry.[302] They now had to deal with Captain Ormand F. Nims' 2nd Massachusetts Light Artillery Battery.[303]

Nims' battery was considered by many to be the finest in the entire Union army.[304] Recruited in Boston in April 1861, its commander, a major, accepted a demotion to command it. He drilled it constantly, until it functioned like a well-oiled machine. It spent the winter of 1861/62 in Maryland and Virginia, and first saw action against the ironclad *Merrimac* in March 1862. It was sent to Ship Island,

---

301   Bonner, p. 464

302   Frank M. Flinn, *Campaigning with Banks in Louisiana, '63 and '64 and with Sheridian in the Shenandoah in '64 and '65*, 2nd ed. (Boston: 1889), p. 108; R. B. Scott, *The History of the 67th Regiment, Indiana Infantry* (Bedford, Indiana: 1892), pp. 71-72

303   Ormand F. Nims was born in Sullivan, New Hampshire, in 1819, the son of a farmer. His maternal grandfather was a colonel and commanded a Massachusetts regiment in the Revolutionary War. Nims moved to Boston in 1854, where he operated a drug store and joined the state militia as an artillery officer.

304   See Caroline E. Whitcomb, *History of the Second Massachusetts Battery (Nims' Battery) of Light Artillery, 1861-1865* (Concord, New Hampshire: 1912) (hereafter cited as "Whitcomb").

The Battle Of Mansfield

Mississippi, and then to Louisiana in the spring of 1862. It took part in the initial attempts to capture Vicksburg with Admiral Farragut in July 1862. On August 5, it saved the Union army at Baton Rouge in a fierce five-hour battle. It fought so hard that, at one point, the guns were so hot that it was impossible to use them. Among those cut down by Nims' guns was Colonel Henry W. Allen, the future governor of Louisiana, who survived his horrible wounds but would never walk again without crutches.

Since Baton Rouge, the 2nd Massachusetts Light Artillery had distinguished itself in every major battle fought by the Army of the Gulf. It was in 17 major engagements. Now, at Mansfield, it also met its doom. Captain Nims ordered his men to fire double-shot canister, and, as the Rebels got very close, they loaded bags of minie balls into their guns. Each bag contained 300 balls. But even this desperate measure did not work. Nims and his men fired their cannons until the last possible moment and then, with the Rebels only 60 yards away, tried to hitch up their teams to escape. The Confederates, however, shot down most of their horses, and Nims abandoned four of his six guns to the Greyhounds. (Shooting the horses was standing operating procedure for both sides in situations of this nature, when artillery was trying to escape. Horses are easier to hit than men and are harder to move when they fall.) The other two guns the men pushed back by hand, but without horses, they did not get very far. Lieutenant Snow, Nims' second-in-command, tried to spike one of the lost guns before the Texans arrived but was promptly shot down.

In desperation, General Ransom ordered the 83rd Ohio Infantry to move from the extreme right of the Union line to the far left. The regimental commander objected because the Rebels already turned his right, but Ransom insisted. General Stone, Banks' chief of staff, personally led the Ohioans to their new position, but when he got there, he found that the Union line had dissolved.[305] He sent a dispatch to Ransom, stating "There is no left flank."[306]

---

305   T. B. Marshall, *History of the Eighty-Third Ohio Volunteer Infantry* (Cincinnati: 1912), p. 134.
306   Ayres, p. 231.

Outflanked on both ends of the line, Ransom ordered Landram to pull back into the dense pine forest behind Henderson Hill. Things were coming apart too quickly, however, and Ransom was not able to execute the orderly withdrawal he envisioned. Then, at the worst possible moment, the "Phantom General" went down with a bullet in the knee. Seeing their best and most trusted leader being carried to an ambulance did nothing to help the morale of the bluecoats' left flank, which was finished as an organized combat force.

"Cheer after cheer burst forth from our lines, as the enemy is seen fleeing ... " Blessington recalled. "Through the woods and along the road, our cavalry and artillery completely slaughter them ... the road is red with their blood."[307]

General Banks kept his head and tried to rally the men, taking off his hat so everybody could see who he was. He "rode through the storm of lead as coolly as if at a holiday review," one reporter wrote, "encouraging the men to stand up to the work of death." Banks shouted: "My brave men of the XIX Corps, stand your ground, and we shall win the day!"[308]

But it was too late. The Union line snapped. "It was every man for himself, and 'Dick' Taylor take the hindmost," one survivor recalled.[309] Private Harris Beecher of the 114th New York recalled seeing "Men without guns or accoutrements, cavalrymen without horses, and artillerymen without cannon, wounded men bleeding and crying at every step ... all in a state of fear and frenzy."[310]

Landram, meanwhile, fell back to a second wooded ridge, where he rallied some of his men. He was joined here by Cameron's 3rd Division, XIII Corps (almost 1,300 men), all under the command of General Franklin. Realizing that he would not be able to hold out indefinitely, Franklin ordered Brigadier General William H. Emory,

---

307 Blessington, p. 189.
308 Hollandsworth, p. 188; Andrews, p. 312.
309 Parrish, p. 349, citing Byam, *Swapping Stories in Texas*, p. 314.
310 Harris H. Beecher, *Record of the 114th Regiment, New York State Volunteers: Where It Went, What It Saw and What It Did* (New York: 1866), pp. 312-313.

the commander of the 1st Division, XIX Corps, to establish a third defensive line in the first adequate clearing. Franklin then returned to the front, where his horse was immediately shot. The general injured his left tibia and suffered a broken left arm in the fall, and was carried off the battlefield.[311]

Polignac and Walker now struck the second Union line, which began to buckle. The attack was spearheaded by Randal's brigade, which "crushed" Cameron's line and took 500 prisoners. "In vigor, energy and daring Randal surpassed my expectations, high as they were of him and his fine brigade," Richard Taylor reported later.[312] Five days later, Kirby Smith assigned him to duty as a brigadier general because of his success at Mansfield.[313]

"Gold Lace" Dudley and Thomas Lucas made a stand with what was left of their cavalry brigades and succeeded in slowing Taylor briefly, but the Yankee infantry was routed. Before long, the foot soldiers and the entire forward echelon of the Army of the Gulf were streaming to the rear. General Cameron's stand only lasted 20 minutes. Five more Union regiments as well as elements of the Corps d'Afrique, which were guarding the cavalry wagon train, joined the rout.

---

311   Joiner, p. 102.

312   Randal was born in McNairy County, Tennessee, in 1833, the son of a doctor. The family moved to the St. Augustine area of Texas in 1838. His father was later elected to Congress. Randal attended West Point and graduated in 1855, finishing 45th in a class of 46. Initially in the infantry, he transferred to the 1st Dragoons and won a brevet fighting Apaches. Winfield Scott thought highly of him and offered him a promotion to major to remain "loyal," but he resigned in February 1861. He served on the staffs of Braxton Bragg at Pensacola and with Major General G. W. Smith (his brother-in-law) in Virginia, and was a favorite of Joseph E. Johnston. He was sent to Texas in late 1861, raised the 28th Texas Cavalry, and became its colonel in February 1862. He was commander of an infantry brigade in the Texas Division by the end of the year. Kirby Smith recommended him for promotion to brigadier general in 1863, but his brigade was considered too small to justify it. Bruce S. Allardice, *More Generals in Gray* (Baton Rouge: 1995), pp. 192-193 (hereafter cited as "Allardice, *Generals*").

313   Because he was cut off from Richmond, Edmund Kirby Smith took the liberty of promoting general officers without the consent of Jefferson Davis or the Confederate Senate. He used the formula of assigning them to duty at the higher rank, while submitting their names to the president for nomination or confirmation later. The procedure was highly irregular and of dubious legality.

About a mile from Henderson Hill, the cavalry's wagons attempted to turn around so they could head for the rear, but they only succeeded in blocking the road. As a result, all the Union artillery forward of the blocked road was abandoned. "The terror of the fleeing infantrymen was magnified when they came upon the roadblock; like scared rabbits, they detoured through the woods, tossing aside blanket rolls, canteens, rifles and all other items that encumbered their flight ..." John D. Winters wrote later. "All semblance of order had disappeared."[314]

Lieutenant Colonel Henry M. Favrot's 2nd Louisiana Cavalry Battalion and Colonel Hardeman's 4th Texas Cavalry Regiment were the first units to plunge into the Federal rear, and they captured most of the cavalry wagon train. Nearly all the teamsters were already gone, however. Unable to turn around, they cut loose their teams and headed to the rear on the backs of their mules, leaving the road completely blocked behind them. (In the Civil War, teamsters had the reputation of always being the first to panic.[315]) When the Confederate cavalry arrived, they were amused to see that the Yankees had labeled their wagons "Houston," "San Antonio," "Galveston," etc., in anticipation of their future conquests.

Through this mass of running men and terrified animals, the men of Emory's 1st Division, XIX Corps, came up from the south. It was a large division—more than 5,000 fresh men—with eight regiments of New York infantry, four regiments from Maine, and the 47th Pennsylvania, as well as three batteries of artillery. The guns, however, could not negotiate the fleeing mob and were of no help to General Emory on April 8. (The third phase of the Battle of Mansfield was a strange one in that neither side had any artillery. Banks lost his, Taylor outran his, and Emory could not get his up.) Emory's infantry worked its way to Chapman's Bayou, three miles behind the original Union lines, where it quickly deployed in line of battle on a ridge just above the stream. It just finished its deployment when the first Louisianans and Texans arrived.

---

314 Winters, p. 344.
315 Johnson, p. 137.

U.S. Brigadier General William H. Emory

"Men, you must hold this position at all hazards," Emory shouted. "Before the enemy gets past here they must ride over me and my little gray mare!"[316] They certainly tried to do so. "On they came, flushed with victory ... ." one of Emory's soldiers recalled. Now it was the Rebels' turn to be surprised. In the twilight, Brigadier General James W. McMillan's 2nd Brigade delivered a concentrated volley into Polignac's division as it appeared to scale the ridge. The Southerners were briefly staggered, but they soon rallied and delivered volley for volley.

---

316   Beecher, *114th New York*, pp. 312-313.

The next 20 minutes reminded the veterans of the Battle of Shiloh. "The very air seemed dark and hot with balls, and on every side was heard their dull, crushing sound, as they struck that swaying mass, tearing through flesh, bone and sinew," one survivor wrote later.[317]

Among those killed here was Colonel James R. Taylor, the commander of the Polignac Brigade. He was succeeded by Lieutenant Colonel Robert D. Stone, the commander of the 22nd (Dismounted) Texas Cavalry, who was killed a few minutes later. Command devolved on Lieutenant Colonel James E. Harrison, the erstwhile commander of the 15th Texas Infantry. He was the fourth commander the brigade had in the past two hours.[318]

In what became known as the Battle of Pleasant Grove, the victorious Rebels quickly formed a battle line. Green, Polignac, and Randal attacked the Union right, while Walker and Bee struck the Union left.[319] They pushed Emory's men back 400 yards, but this Union division did not break, and night fell before Taylor could organize a well-coordinated attack.

During the early part of the night, the Yankees could hear the Rebels calling roll and celebrating their victory. Two Union lines were routed. The third was not decisively defeated, but it lost the all-important Chapman Bayou. There was no other source of water for miles, and without water, Emory knew that he would not be able to hold the next day.

April 8/9 was a horrible night for all concerned, especially for the Yankees, because they were cold, hungry, and without food or water. They were also ordered not to light fires because the enemy

---

317   Bonner, p. 465; Kinard, p. 146.

318   James Edward Harrison (1815-1875) was born in South Carolina but grew up in Alabama and Mississippi. He served two terms in Mississippi Senate before moving to Texas in 1857. He settled near Waco and joined the Confederate Army as a major in Colonel Joseph W. Speight's 1st Texas Infantry Battalion (later the 15th Texas Infantry Regiment) in 1861. Harrison was promoted (i.e., assigned to duty) as a brigadier general on December 22, 1864. He was a trustee of Baylor University from 1861 to 1874, and was fluent in Choctaw and Creek.

319   Spencer, p. 20.

The Battle Of Mansfield

was too close. Doctors and chaplains spent the night going over the battlefield, caring for both Northern and Southern wounded. The chaplains also administered a great many last rites.

*

Historian T. Michael Parrish called the Battle of Mansfield "one of the most humiliating Union defeats of the war."[320] Of the 32,000 men in the Army of the Gulf, they only managed to commit about 14,000 to the decisive battle, and Taylor outnumbered them at every major point of contact. The North officially lost 240 men killed, 671 wounded, and 1,541 captured or missing, or 2,452 total casualties. These figures exclude the teamsters, who were civilians. Civilian laborers and assorted camp followers were also taken prisoner. Banks' report, however, was only for the action at Sabine Crossroads. His figures do not include the losses Cameron suffered when his five regiments were crushed, nor do they include Emory's casualties in the Plum Orchard (Pleasant Grove). All totaled, his losses easily exceeded 3,000 men.[321] But Banks, as historian Thomas Ayres records, "never lost a battle in a report."[322] Taylor claimed to have captured 2,500 prisoners. Banks also admitted to losing 20 guns, 156 government-owned wagons, and about 1,000 horses and mules in addition to a plethora of small arms, supplies, blankets, ammunition, and other equipment.[323] Taylor also captured 90 to 100 civilian-owned wagons, which was contracted out to the Union army.

Confederate casualty reports are, as usual for this stage of the war, very incomplete. Taylor lost about 1,000 men. About 80% of these were from Mouton's division. He lost no artillery and very little in the way of equipment.

---

320 Parrish, p. 352.
321 Ayres, pp. 233-234.
322 Ayres, p. 235.
323 Dorsey, p. 263; Joiner, p. 103.

Meanwhile, Kirby Smith received Dick Taylor's dispatch of April 7. He sent him an ambiguous letter, instructing him to retreat toward Shreveport but offering to send him reinforcements if a general engagement appeared to be imminent. He also instructed Taylor to inform him if a major battle appeared likely, so he could come to the front.[324]

According to General Boggs, chief of staff of the Trans-Mississippi Department, Kirby Smith wanted Taylor to avoid a battle with Banks, but if one seemed likely, he wished to arrive before it began. This strategy, Boggs said, was the brainchild of Dr. Sol Smith, who did not like Taylor. Boggs wrote: "Taylor was to harass Banks up to the last moment and then General Smith was to move down with additional troops, take command, and carry off the glory of a pitched battle."[325] But Taylor would not play this game, and as historian Ludwell Johnson wrote later, "Smith was not to be allowed to play Bluecher to Taylor's Wellington."[326] By the time Kirby Smith's dispatch arrived, Mouton already launched his famous charge. "Too late, sir," Taylor gleefully replied to the courier who brought the message, "the battle is won!" He then added: "It is not the first [battle] I have fought with a rope round my neck."[327]

*

Nathaniel P. Banks was no Robert E. Lee, but he was no coward either. As night fell on April 8, he wanted to resume the Battle of Pleasant Grove the next day. He did, in fact, have a considerable reserve. A. J. Smith's XIX Corps alone had more men than Taylor had at Mansfield, and Banks' army had more unengaged soldiers than Taylor had in his entire army. General Franklin, however, pointed out that Banks' plan was not practical. He averred that A. J. Smith's men were at Pleasant Hill, 14 miles away. Even if they marched all night, they might not make it in time for a dawn battle. Even if they

---

324 O.R., Vol. XXXIV, Part 1, p. 528.
325 Boggs, pp. 75-76.
326 Johnson, p. 124.
327 Debray, p. 17.

did arrive in time, they would be in no shape to fight after such a march. Emory agreed with Franklin and, more importantly, so did William Dwight.

Brigadier General William Dwight was born in Springfield, Massachusetts, in 1831. He flunked out of West Point in 1853 and engaged in the manufacturing business until the war began. Commissioned lieutenant colonel in the 70th New York, he fought bravely in the Peninsula Campaign, where his regiment suffered 50% casualties at the hands of Robert E. Lee. Dwight was left for dead on the battlefield. He recovered in a Confederate hospital, was soon exchanged, and was promoted to brigadier general on November 29, 1862. He was then sent to Louisiana, where he fought in all the major battles of the Army of the Gulf. As Emory's senior brigade commander, he seemed more interested in confiscating Rebel cotton for the New England textile interests than in anything else.[328] He, however, became close personal friends with his fellow New Englander, Banks, and probably had greater influence over him than anyone else. When Dwight agreed with Franklin and Emory, Banks reluctantly gave in and, at 10 p.m., ordered the retreat. It was to begin at midnight.

---

328 Warner, *Generals in Blue*, pp. 134-135; Johnson, pp. 57-59.

Chapter VII

THE BATTLE OF PLEASANT HILL

The Yankees' retreat began at midnight. It was led by the XIII Corps Detachment, which was now commanded by General Cameron. The decimated cavalry division followed. Then came the XIX Corps, with Dwight's brigade of Emory's division forming the rear guard. The men knew they had to retreat 14 miles to Pleasant Hill, and they had to make that distance by dawn or shortly after; otherwise, they would likely be gobbled up by Walker's rapidly marching Greyhounds or Tom Green's cavalry. To accomplish this, they would have to march all night. This is exactly what most of them did.

They carried as many of their wounded back with them as they could. They lost many of their ambulances and wagons, and the rest were heading to the rear as rapidly as possible, so they used appropriated local carts and a few surviving artillery caissons. It was not enough. Most of the wounded were left to the clemency of the enemy.

During the night of April 8, Taylor ordered Walker to pursue Banks vigorously, while he tried to get Churchill's and Parsons' divisions moving toward Pleasant Hill. "There was nothing to our front but the troops we beat today," Taylor observed, "and the XIX

Corps—all Yankees whom we have always whipped."[329] He wanted to send Polignac's decimated division back to Mansfield, where it could lick its wounds and where drinking water was available but was overruled by Kirby Smith.

At dawn, Dick Taylor accompanied Green's cavalry in pursuit of Banks. Behind him came Churchill's infantry, followed by Walker. Polignac brought up the rear. They left behind a scene of desolation. Dead men and horses seemed to be everywhere over a nine-square-mile area. "Hundreds of negroes and straggling soldiers are plundering the battlefield," H. C. Medford recorded in his diary, "robbing the pockets of the dead. Here a dead negro in the road, in a Yankee uniform, over whom a hundred wagons have rolled. He is mangled until he has scarcely any resemblance to human shape."[330]

Back at Mansfield, the Rebels first buried their dead where they fell. The officers were buried in the town cemetery. The Yankees killed in the battle were buried in mass graves. Those who later died of their wounds were buried in individual graves near the city cemetery. Along with the Confederate Medical Corps, the women of Mansfield worked day and night to prevent that from happening. The unwounded Union prisoners were sent to Camp Ford, near Tyler, Texas, where most of them spent the rest of the war. It was not Boca Raton, but it was not Andersonville, either. Very well designed for its time, Camp Ford had one of the lowest mortality rates of any prison on either side in the Civil War.

In northwestern Louisiana, April 9, 1864, was a beautiful spring day. Captain Clark of the 116th New York recalled that "it hardly seemed possible that so much beauty in nature was soon to see the fierce passions of men engaged in bitter strife."[331]

---

[329] Taylor, pp. 198-199; Hollandsworth, pp. 190-191; OR XXXIV, Part 1, p. 194ff (General Banks' report of operations to Secretary of War Stanton); Richard B. Irwin, *History of the Nineteenth Army Corps* (New York and London: 1892), p. 314.

[330] Medford Diary, April 9, 1864; Kinard, p. 148.

[331] Hollandsworth, p. 191; Orton S. Clark, *The One Hundred and Sixteenth Regiment of New York State Volunteers* (Buffalo: 1868), p. 160.

While the Yankees marched all night, most of the Rebels slept the sleep of exhaustion on the battlefield at Pleasant Grove. Churchill's Division, which camped four miles north of Mansfield, was marching by 3 a.m. and followed Green's horsemen. Brigadier General Mosby M. Parsons' division came next, followed by Walker and Polignac.

As the Confederates moved forward, they found a scene of further devastation. As they retreated, Banks' men fouled every well and burned every building they passed—including the Negro cabins, free or slave. Women and children stood or sat by the side of the road, lost, crying, and not knowing what to do. Quite a few of the Bluecoats could not keep up. These stragglers were captured by Green and Taylor and spent the rest of the war at Camp Ford. The road was littered with discarded Yankee equipment.

Meanwhile, Green and Taylor caught up with the 165th New York and captured a number of prisoners. The 165th was a Zouave unit, dressed like the French North African troops in blue vests, bright red fezzes, and scarlet pants which resembled bloomers. The Texans thought they looked like women and made fun of them. One declared that if he had to fight women, he was going home. Others joked that Lincoln must be getting desperate if he was sending women into battle.[332]

Pleasant Hill, the objective of both armies, was a picturesque, one square mile plateau on the Mansfield and Fort Jessup Road. The village was a summer resort community before the war and consisted of about two dozen buildings, including a Methodist church, a post office, a hotel, a school for girls, and the Pearce Payne Methodist College for Boys, which consisted of two large, unfinished buildings.

The head of Banks' columns reached Pleasant Hill at 8:30 a.m., where the men were fed a hot meal and were at least partially organized into lines of battle. Most of them promptly fell asleep.

---

332   Kinard, pp. 148-149.

Among the units that rallied at Pleasant Hill was the 2nd Massachusetts Light Artillery—the Nims Battery. Formerly considered by many as the best battery in the army, it had lost all six of its guns, 82 horses, two men killed, 13 men wounded, five men wounded and captured, and seven missing or captured. "It was a sorry looking company of men that gathered at Pleasant Hill the next morning—the remnant of the finest battery in the army!" Colonel Whitcomb wrote later. "Guns, caissons, wagons and supplies lost—nothing left but the clothes the men wore ... one rubber and one woolen blanket had to do for five men ... "[333]

Mansfield was the last action for the 2nd Massachusetts Artillery. It was sent to the rear with the wagon train and then back to Boston, where it was disbanded.

Pleasant Hill was essentially a partially cleared knoll which provided the Federals with a good defensive position—except for the fact that it lacked water and was too far from the supply depots at Alexandria. It also offered Banks the opportunity to communicate with Porter's fleet. Even though he knew he could not remain here indefinitely, Banks decided to make a stand. He even entertained the idea of rallying his army and resuming his advance on Shreveport. In the meantime, he sent his wagons back to Grand Ecore and dispatched messages to Porter and Kilby Smith, informing them that he defeated Taylor at Mansfield (!) but was retreating due to a lack of water. He asked them to rendezvous with him at Grand Ecore.

Cameron's XIII Corps Detachment, which could barely muster 2,000 men, only stopped briefly at Pleasant Hill before continuing its withdrawal to Grand Ecore. (Banks intended for Cameron to cover the extreme Union left flank at Pleasant Hill, but due to a misunderstanding in the orders, Cameron abandoned his position and fell back toward Grand Ecore with the wagon train. He was miles away when the battle began.)

---

333   Whitcob, p. 70.

At the same time, Albert Lee selected 1,000 men from his 1st and 5th Cavalry Brigades to remain with the army and sent the rest back to Grand Ecore with Cameron. He placed Colonel Lucas in charge of this battle group and ordered him to watch all possible Rebel approach routes.

As Banks' first fugitives staggered in, A. J. Smith ordered Colonel William Shaw, the commander of the 2nd Brigade of Mowers' 3rd Division, to take up positions on the road northwest of the village, blocking the road to Mansfield. Due to the chaos and the routed column on the road, Shaw's men were forced to go through the woods to reach their assigned positions. When they arrived, they relieved Brigadier General James McMillan's brigade, which fell back into reserve behind them.

Shaw ordered the 14th Iowa to straddle the road, with the 24th Missouri on a small ridge to the right and the 27th Iowa and 32nd Iowa on the left. They were backed by elements of the 25th New York Artillery.

Colonel Shaw was in an exposed position and he knew it. He was more than a mile in front of Whiskey Smith's main body, and the nearest friendly forces were a quarter of a mile to his left. This was Colonel Lewis Benedict's New York brigade, which was positioned astride the Logansport Road to the west.

Later that morning, A. J. Smith arrived to inspect Shaw's dispositions. He generally approved of them (even though they were weird) but shifted the entire brigade to the right, increasing the already significant gap between Shaw and Benedict. Dwight placed his brigade in reserve behind Shaw's right rear but at a right angle to him, doing nothing to cover his exposed flank. A. J. Smith chose not to alter this arrangement.

Early that afternoon, Colonel Benedict (who was in position since April 7) pulled his brigade back from the edge of the woods to a dry ditch south of it, exposing Shaw's left even further. Mower's command, meanwhile, took positions behind Benedict and covered the roads to Fort Jessup, Natchitoches, and Blair's Landing.

The Yankee dispositions were unusual, to say the least, and seemed to indicate that no one had assumed overall control of their forces—as was indeed the case. Shaw was in an exposed and poorly supported forward position. The reserves behind him (Dwight and McMillan) were not intelligently placed. Benedict was in a good position but again was vulnerable to a flanking attack on either side. (The undergrowth protected him somewhat but not enough, as we shall see.) The entire Union deployment was a haphazard affair. The Northern generals and colonels positioned their units wherever they felt like it, with little or no guidance from above. This is why two-thirds of the Union army was in reserve. Map 7.1 shows the dispositions of both sides in the initial phase of the Battle of Pleasant Hill.

Banks, meanwhile, set up his headquarters at the Childers' House, the largest residence in Pleasant Hill and 50 yards from the 89th Indiana. He and his staff spent most of the morning and early afternoon doing nothing. One witness commented that he saw General Stone, the chief of staff of the Army of the Gulf, practicing blowing smoke rings. Banks did not believe that there was any reason to worry. There was no way Richard Taylor would be bold enough to attack again.[334]

But he was.

Writing five hundred years before the birth of Christ, the great Chinese military philosopher Sun Tzu declared that, if a commander knew his opponent, he had won half the battle. It is therefore remarkable that Nathaniel P. Banks still did not have the slightest understanding of the fertile and aggressive mind of Richard Taylor, despite having fought him in the Shenandoah (1862), in the Lafourche and Teche campaigns (1863), and at Mansfield (1864). Taylor's objective was always the same: attack the enemy and destroy him. Even when he was forced to go on the defensive, Taylor's overall strategy changed little. Defense, to him, was a temporary expedient, designed to check the enemy and damage him as much as possible,

---

334 Parrish, p. 356.

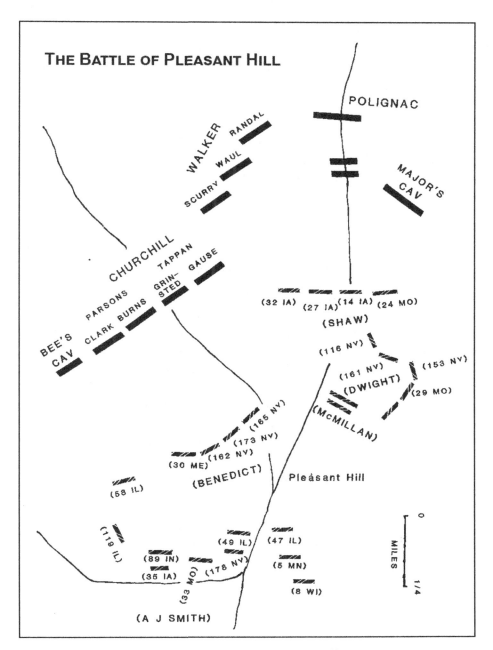

7.1 The Battle of Pleasant Hill

until he could go over to the offensive, attack the enemy, and destroy him. On the morning of April 9, Dick Taylor made his plan. He intended to attack the enemy and destroy him. Why this surprised Banks on April 9 is difficult to understand.

*

As early as 9 a.m., the Texas cavalry clashed with McMillan's pickets, just as they were being relieved by Shaw. Dick Taylor himself was within two miles of Pleasant Hill at 10:40 a.m., when he sent Kirby Smith a message, stating that the enemy "has retreated rapidly ... The burning wagons, abandoned arms, knapsacks, and other property along the road furnish ample evidence of the haste with which he is endeavoring to get away. He is now making something of a stand for the purpose of gaining time."[335]

Brigadier General Thomas J. Churchill arrived at Taylor's improvised command post two miles west of Pleasant Hill at noon and found the general sitting on a pine log, whittling on a stick. It was a long march. His Arkansas infantry division and Parsons' Missouri Infantry (4,400 men in all) left Keatchie at dawn on April 8 and marched 18 miles to the Confederate camp four miles north of Mansfield, which they reached at 3 a.m. on April 9. Here, they were issued two days' rations and marched out again immediately, passing through the Mansfield battlefield at dawn. They continued marching until between 1 p.m. and 2 p.m., when they finally joined the main body of the Army of Western Louisiana. They marched 42 miles in less than two days.

General Churchill galloped ahead of the main body and met with his army commander at noon. Taylor organized Churchill's and Parsons' commands into a temporary corps, with Churchill in command and Brigadier General James C. Tappan assuming temporary command of Churchill's division.

---

335 O.R., Vol. XXXIV, Part 1, p. 528.

Thomas J. Churchill

Taylor deployed Major's cavalry division on the far left. Major's division consisted of Lane's brigade (now under Colonel George W. Baylor) and Bagby's brigade, both fighting dismounted. To Major's right lay General Bee's cavalry division, with Debray's and Buchel's brigades. General Green commanded all the cavalry and directed the Confederate left wing.

To Bee's right (west of the Mansfield Road) lay Walker's Texas Division, which formed the Rebel center. Churchill's corps formed the Confederate right wing. His far right was covered by William P. Hardeman's 4th Texas Cavalry and Colonel Henry C. McNeill's 5th Texas Cavalry, acting under Hardeman's command.[336]

---

336 William Polk "Old Gotch" Hardeman (1816-1898) was a native of Tennessee and a cousin of President James K. Polk. He migrated to Texas in 1835, fought in the Texas Revolution, and took part in an unsuccessful attempt to reach the Alamo. He was a Texas Ranger after the war, fought the Comanches, and was present at the Battle of Buena

Polignac's depleted division was posted behind Green's cavalry. It suffered so many casualties at Mansfield that Taylor did not intend to use it unless it was absolutely necessary. It would be.

*

The Union forces at Pleasant Hill included A. J. Smith's XVI Corps (about 8,500 fresh infantry), the battered XIX Corps (6,000 men), and Lee's 1,000 cavalrymen—about 15,500 men in all. Taylor estimated that Banks had 20,000 men. He had 12,500 men, most of whom were nearly exhausted. He decided to attack anyway. Unlike the Army of the Gulf, his troops were well deployed.

Because of the jaded state of Churchill's corps, Taylor gave them a two-hour break until 3 p.m. He then set his plan into motion.

Taylor's battle plan called for Churchill to move to his right, get behind the Union left flank and turn it. Simultaneously, Walker and Bee would attack the Union front, preventing a retreat and diverting their attention from the right, while Hardeman and McNeill cut the Union escape route. At the same time, Major's and Bagby's cavalry, fighting dismounted, were to move around the Union right flank and cut the Pleasant Hill-Blair's Landing Road, thus severing Banks' connection with Porter's fleet, which Taylor intended to destroy after he smashed Banks. Taylor ordered his men to "... rely on the bayonet, as we had neither time nor ammunition to waste." He noted: "These orders were well carried out, as many ghastly wounds among the Federals testify."[337]

Vista. Thereafter, he established a plantation in Guadalupe County and owned about 30 slaves. He voted for secession in the 1861 Convention, commanded a company in the 4th Texas Cavalry in New Mexico, and was wounded twice at Valverde. He successfully defended Albuquerque against General Canby in April 1862 and fought with Taylor in Louisiana in 1863. He would be assigned to duty as a brigadier general after the Red River Campaign. After the war, he was a battalion commander in Maximilian's army, inspector of railroads, and later superintendent of public buildings and grounds for the state of Texas, and one of the founders of Texas A & M. He was married twice and had seven children. He died of Bright's disease and is buried in the State Cemetery in Austin.

337   O.R., Vol. XXXIV, Part 1, p. 567.

Churchill ordered his men to fall in at 3 p.m. and started through the woods. After two miles, he reached the Sabine Road and formed a line of battle. Left to right were Parsons' Division (Brigadier General John B. Clark, Jr.'s and Colonel Simon P. Burns' brigades) and Tappan's division (Colonel H. L. Grinsted's and Colonel Lucien Gause's brigades). He pushed forward another 3/4ths of a mile toward Pleasant Hill and then realized that he had not gone far enough to his right. He turned his entire command to the right and marched south, until Parsons' entire division was on the south side of the road. He then left-faced the column into a line of battle again and moved toward the Yankees.[338]

General Churchill made a terrible mistake. Due to the thick undergrowth, he still had not gone far enough to the right. Instead of turning the Union left, he was driving into it—and right in front of the U.S. reserves.

Back on the Mansfield Road, at 4:30 p.m., Taylor began the battle by starting an artillery duel. He had a brilliant gunner, Major Joseph Brent, bring up a dozen guns and opened on a battery of the 25th New York Artillery, which was 200 yards in front of the 24th Missouri.[339] Taylor had two purposes in this maneuver: eliminate the Union guns and divert attention from Churchill's impending attack. The Union guns were neutralized in less than 30 minutes and the New Yorkers fled, leaving two of their pieces on the field. Brent then shifted his fire onto Shaw's infantry.

---

338 O.R., Vol. XXXIV, Part 1, p. 602; Taylor, p. 167.

339 Joseph L. Brent (1826-1905) was born in Maryland, but his family moved to Louisiana, where his father was elected to Congress. Brent was educated at Georgetown, briefly practiced law in St. Martinsville, and moved to Los Angeles, California, in 1849. There, he specialized in litigating land claims for Mexican-Americans. He served two terms in the California legislature. He returned to the South in early 1862 as a captain on John Magruder's staff and was promoted to major and chief of ordnance in his command. Brent returned to Louisiana after the Seven Days Campaign. Richard Taylor, a close personal friend, named him chief of artillery for the District of Western Louisiana. Kirby Smith promoted him to colonel on April 17, 1864, and, on October 15, assigned him to duty as a brigadier general and gave him a brigade in north Louisiana. After the war, he practiced law in Baltimore and Louisiana and represented Ascension Parish in the legislature. He married a daughter of Congressman Duncan Kenner and became a nephew-in-law to Generals Richard Taylor and Allen Thomas. Allardice, *Generals*, pp. 42-43.

As the Yankees withdrew their cannons, an excited General Green and a few of his horsemen advanced to within 200 yards of the abandoned guns but were driven off by the Union infantry. Shortly after, Churchill's attack went forward into Benedict's 3rd Brigade. The Rebels delivered a powerful volley and charged without reloading, attacking Benedict's men with their rifle butts and bayonets. After a brief hand-to-hand struggle, Benedict's line broke, and three New York regiments took flight in disorder to the hill above the ditch. The hill was defended by Colonel Francis Fessenden's 30th Maine, which successfully held its position until both of its flanks were turned. It then fell back under heavy fire but was rallied by Fessenden, along with elements of the 3rd Brigade. The Rebels were delayed by the heavy undergrowth, but when they attacked again, Benedict's men broke and ran "in great confusion."[340] They carried with them the body of their brigade commander.[341] He was shot five times: once through each arm, once through a leg, once in the foot, and once in the head. The historian of the 162nd New York Volunteers wrote: "conspicuous bravery made him a mark for the enemy and, according to their tactics, he must have been the target for a volley."[342]

As soon as he heard the fire from Churchill's attack, General Walker unleashed his Greyhounds. One Northerner recalled that they let out "a most hideous yell, such as Texans and Border ruffians alone can make."[343] They were soon exchanging musket fire at close range with Shaw's Iowans.

---

340 Winters, p. 351.

341 Henry M. Benedict, *A Memorial of Brevet Brigadier General Lewis Benedict* (Albany, New York: 1866), p. 102 (hereafter cited as "Benedict"). Benedict was born in Albany in 1817 and graduated from Williams College in 1837. He studied law and became city attorney for Albay in 1845. He was elected to the New York Assembly in 1860 and volunteered for the Union Army immediately after Fort Sumter. He was commissioned lieutenant colonel of the 73rd New York and was wounded and captured at Williamsburg. After several months in prison, he was exchanged and in September 1862, became colonel of the 162nd (3rd) Metropolitan) Regiment, which was sent to Louisiana in October.

342 Anonymous, *An Historical Sketch of the 162nd Regiment, New York Volunteer Infantry* (Albany: 1867), p. 26-27 (hereafter cited as "*162nd New York*").

343 Benedict, pp. 79-82.

The Battle Of Pleasant Hill

Colonel Lewis Benedict

The roar of Churchill's guns, the withdrawal of the Union artillery, and the advance of Walker's division convinced Thomas Green that the Northerners were demoralized and defeated, so he ordered General Bee to attack. Polignac later said that Green was intoxicated when he ordered this assault.[344] With Debray's and Buchel's brigades, General Bee advanced in columns of fours, right between the 24th (Union) Missouri and the 14th and 27th Iowa—and right into an ambush. Colonel Buchel spotted it in time and sent a courier to Green, warning him of the trap, but Green ignored

---

[344] Kinard, p. 152. Polignac also blamed Green for much of the confusion at Pleasant Hill.

him. Buchel reigned up before the Yankees could snare him in their crossfire, but Debray plowed right on in. The Yankees let loose a devastating volley, and the cavalry went down in a horrible heap.[345]

Buchel, meanwhile, veered right and pushed back Shaw's front line but was mortally wounded when three musket balls hit him in the chest.[346] Debray, meanwhile, lost a third of his brigade killed or wounded. The colonel was pinned down near the Union line when his horse was killed and fell on his right leg, trapping him. After a considerable effort, he extricated himself by pulling his foot out of his boot and limped back to Confederate lines, using his sword as a cane. He was met by General Taylor, who asked if he was wounded.

"I am slightly hurt," Debray replied, "but, as you can see, I was sent on a bootless errand."

"Never mind your boot," Taylor answered. "You have won your spurs."[347] Kirby Smith must have agreed. Four days later, Debray was "assigned to duty" as a brigadier general.[348]

---

345 August Carl Buchel was born in Guntersblum, Germany, on the west bank of the Rhine, in 1813. Educated in the old school military tradition, he was commissioned second lieutenant in the Hesse-Darmstadt 1st Infantry Regiment at age 18. A restless adventurer in his youth, he joined the French Foreign Legion, fought in Spain, and was knighted by the queen. After serving as an instructor in the Turkish Army, he returned to Germany, where he killed a man in a duel. As the surviving duelist, he was, by German law, exiled for life. He moved to Texas, established a home in Indianola, and served as an aide to Zachary Taylor in the Mexican War. He joined the Confederate Army in late 1861 as a lieutenant colonel in the 3rd Texas Infantry Regiment. He became colonel of the 1st Texas Cavalry in 1863. Robert W. Stephens, *August Buchel, Texas Soldier of Fortune* (privately published: 1970).

346 The exact date of Buchel's death is unclear. General Bee said he died at his headquarters on April 11. Other sources (including Buchel's tombstone) say April 15.

347 Debray, pp. 158-159.

348 Xavier Blanchard Debray was born in Epinal, France, on January 25, 1818. In later life, he would not talk about his early years, so most of the details are sketchy and mostly untrue. He arrived in New York City in September 1848, a refugee from the revolution of that year, and eventually settled in San Antonio, where he edited a Spanish language newspaper. He founded an academy in 1858, and it flourished until the war broke out. He joined Tom Green's 4th Texas Cavalry as a first lieutenant in 1861 and, in August, was promoted to major; simultaneously, he became drillmaster of the 2nd Texas Infantry Regiment. He became a lieutenant colonel of the 26th Texas Cavalry in late 1861 and was promoted to colonel on March 17, 1862. He was highly

Colonels August Carl Buchel and Xavier DeBray

Hamilton Bee, who had two horses shot out from under him, called the charge "disastrous." Taylor defended Green, as usual, by saying the charge had a morale effect, even if it was premature.[349]

Meanwhile, General Major's dismounted Texas cavalrymen launched an attack against Shaw's right flank, while Taylor pulled Polignac's division out of reserve and inserted it into the battle between Major and Walker, whose men were still exchanging volleys with the Union center. One of the bullets caught General Walker in the groin. Although he was in great pain, the general ignored his wound until his chief of staff, Major Robert P. McClay, saw him

---

praised for his part in the capture of Galveston on January 1, 1863, and for a time was commandant of the island. Kirby Smith considered Debray a "superior cavalry officer" (Allardice, *Generals*, pp. 74-77).

349   Parrish, p. 361.

momentarily faint. He summoned a litter team and persuaded the general to lie down.[350] Walker would not go to the rear, however, until Dick Taylor arrived and made him do so.

As Walker went down, the old Mouton division went forward. Standing up in his stirrups, Prince de Polignac pointed his sword toward the Yankees and cried "My boys, follow your Polignac!" Screaming "Mouton!" and shouting their Rebel yells, Polignac's men crashed into the U.S. line, where the fighting was hand-to-hand.[351]

With Major attacking his right, Polignac pounding his center, and Walker pushing his left, Shaw was in deep trouble. Seeing this, A. J. Smith ordered him to disengage. He did so, but not before Scurry's brigade cut the 32nd Iowa to pieces. With Rebels pouring into Shaw's and his own rear, Dwight committed two of his regiments against the Texans. The Union situation was now desperate because their center and right flank were crushed. At the same time, Churchill's men swept forward, overran a Union battery, and "with more courage than discretion" (as General Polignac recalled), pursued Benedict's remnants into the village of Pleasant Hill.[352] In doing so, they failed to see the bulk of A. J. Smith's XVI Corps in the woods to their right. The 58th Illinois emerged from their hidden positions in the trees and attacked Churchill's exposed right flank. The Rebel line was rolled back upon itself. Seeing this obvious opportunity to turn the tide of the fight, A. J. Smith ordered his entire corps to charge. This was the turning point of the battle. Parsons' brigade was quickly driven back, which exposed Tappan's right flank, and it was also forced to retreat. Meanwhile, Emory ordered McMillan to

---

350 A native of Pennsylvania, Robert P. Maclay (1820-1903) was the grandson and grandnephew of U.S. senators. He graduated from West Point in 1840 and fought in the Seminole and Mexican Wars. He was stationed in Texas from 1849 to 1860 and married into a wealthy Point Coupee, Louisiana, family. He served in the Louisiana Militia before joining the Confederate Army as a major of artillery. He was a strong Episcopalian and was considered a very nice man.

351 Kinard, p. 151.

352 Kinard, p. 151.

charge Churchill's left (Gause's and Grinsted's brigades). The result was heavy fighting. "The air seemed alive with the sounds of various projectiles ..." one survivor recalled.[353]

Churchill's men put up a stiff resistance initially, but outnumbered 2 to 1, they were steadily pushed back in heavy fighting. Then Colonel William F. Lynch's brigade attacked Churchill's right flank, along with McMillan's brigade and what was left of Benedict's. The Union attacks resembled a general offensive, and soon, Churchill's corps was nearly surrounded. "Churchill's men, seeing the hopelessness of their situation, threw down their arms and ran to the rear," Spencer recalled. "No one could stop them."[354] Some of them even reached the places where the cavalry tied their horses. They stole them and dashed for the rear.

As Churchill's corps withdrew, it doubled back on Scurry's brigade (on Walker's right flank), which was in a very constricted space between McMillan, Dwight, and Shaw and had nowhere to go. The Texans also broke ranks and fell back in disorder. For a brief few minutes it appeared that Scurry's entire brigade would be captured, but Richard Taylor sent Randal and Waul to its rescue.[355] "Thank God!" General Scurry cried. "My brigade is saved!"[356]

The entire Union advance, Johnson wrote later, "now resembled a grand right wheel, pivoting on the village."[357] "The army was swaying all along the lines," one Rebel recalled.[358] A Confederate captain later remembered that he "ran up near the enemy and found Generals Green, Taylor, and Major right up in the thickest of the fight, encouraging the men."[359] As night fell, the Yankees pushed

---

353 Edwin B. Lufkin, *History of the Thirteenth Maine Regiment* (Bridgton, Maine: 1898), p. 85.
354 Spencer, p. 38.
355 Johnson, pp. 160-161; Taylor, pp. 168-169.
356 Blessington, p. 196.
357 Johnson, p. 161.
358 Parrish, p. 364, citing *Reminiscences of Levi Lamons Wight*, p. 32.
359 Parrish, p. 364.

Churchill back into the woods from whence he came. Nightfall, the tough, wooded terrain, and their own heavy losses put an end to their advance. "God bless you, general!" Banks said to A. J. Smith. "You have saved the army."[360]

As darkness descended on northwestern Louisiana, both sides were badly hurt and neither wanted to continue the carnage. "The enemy was badly cut up and was willing to let our men go without following them," one Yankee observed.[361]

Losses were heavy for the number of troops engaged. The Rebels lost about 1,200 killed and wounded, along with 426 captured or about 1,626 total. The Yankees lost 289 killed, 773 wounded and 1,062 captured or missing, or a total of 2,124 men.[362] Predictably, both sides claimed victory. The truth is that both sides lost. After Pleasant Hill, Banks gave up all hope of capturing Shreveport and bringing the campaign to a successful conclusion. On the other side, Taylor failed to destroy the Army of the Gulf. But Dick Taylor was nothing if not persistant. He would try again later.

Tactically, the Battle of Pleasant Hill was a draw, but the Union withdrawal made it appear to be a defeat. (In this sense, it was Antietam in reverse.)

Given their poor dispositions at the beginning of the battle, the accomplishments of the Army of the Gulf were truly remarkable. There was little in the way of command and control on the Union side. Banks was on the field but did very little, exercised no control, and did not even offer anything in the way of reaction. The Confederate plan, on the other hand, was excellent, although its execution was faulty. It failed only because General Churchill did not move far enough to the right; instead of rolling up the Union left, he crossed right in front of it and was himself rolled up. Had he positioned himself as Taylor intended, the South might have won

---

360 O.R., Vol. XXXIV, Part 1, p. 309.
361 Parrish, pp. 364-365.
362 Joiner, p. 116.

a major victory. Churchill later admitted his mistake, although he placed part of the blame on his civilian guide, who was assigned to him by Taylor.

Dick Taylor blamed himself for the Confederate failure. "Instead of intrusting the important attack by my right to a subordinate," he wrote later, "I should have conducted it myself and taken Polignac's division to sustain it ... All this flashed upon me the instant I learned of the disorder of my right. Herein lies the vast difference between genius and commonplace: one anticipates errors, the other discovers them too late"[363]

*

"It was my misfortune to stand picket on the battle field that night," Corporal J. M. Thompson of the 1st Texas Cavalry recalled, "and of all the duties of the war this was the most heartrending."[364] Old men later remembered April 9/10 as the worst night of their lives. The firing continued all along the front as night fell but gradually petered out. Then the horror set in. The night was very cold and the wounded were without attention. "The wails and cries of agony ... are still ringing in my ears," one Northerner wrote years later. "There is scarcely a soldier that would not prefer the hottest engagement rather than spend such a night [again] ..."[365] "The air was filled with groans and shrieks and delirious yells," a New Yorker recalled.[366] There were wounded men everywhere, crying out for water.

Bee picketed the battlefield with four companies of cavalry from Debray's and Buchel's brigades. (Buchel's Brigade was now commanded by Colonel Terrell.) General Taylor, meanwhile, sent most of the infantry and cavalry back to Mansfield or Ten Mile Bayou, where there was water.

---

[363] Taylor, p. 171.

[364] Yeary, Vol. II, pp. 746-747. Thompson hailed from Nashville, Texas, which no longer exists. He enlisted in 1861 and served throughout the war in the Trans-Mississippi Department.

[365] Pellet, pp. 212-213.

[366] Johnson, p. 164.

Shortly after the fighting died down, Banks called a meeting of his top generals. A. J. Smith did not bother to attend, but Dwight, Franklin, and Emory did. Banks asked their opinions as to what to do next. Not one suggested continuing the drive on Shreveport. Franklin and Emory thought it would be best to take the road to Blair's Landing and link up with Admiral Porter, who had plenty of supplies. Dwight, however, thought it would be best to retreat to Grand Ecore. He correctly pointed out that no one had heard from the fleet in days; for all they knew, Taylor might have already destroyed it. Predictably, Banks agreed with Dwight. I probably would have as well. Certainly, this was the safer play.

When he received the order to retreat, A. J. Smith almost begged Banks to reconsider. Later, Smith met with Emory and Franklin and threw a temper tantrum. He denounced Banks with such venom that one staff officer left the room. Almost out of control, A. J. Smith asked Franklin to arrest Banks, take charge of the army, and resume the drive on Shreveport. This was too much for General Emory, who stood up and declared: "Gentlemen, this is mutiny!" He then left the room. Whiskey Smith, for once realizing that he had gone too far, quickly dropped the subject.[367]

*

"We did not run from Pleasant Hill," one Yankee later remarked, "but you will have to agree that we struck a gait that didn't have a bit of lost motion to it."[368]

Because they had very little transportation available, the Federals left 400 critically wounded soldiers behind because they could not be moved. A. J. Smith was so upset over leaving his wounded veterans behind that he cried. A number of surgeons and medical personnel

---

[367] Wickman Hoffman, *Camp, Court and Siege: A Narrative of Personal Adventure and Observation During Two Wars, 1861-1865, 1870-1871* (New York: 1877), pp. 96-97. This is not the most reliable source.

[368] Parrish, p. 369.

remained behind to take care of them. The gallant General Bee refused to take these people prisoner. Later, with the full backing of General Taylor, they were returned to Union lines.

Southern doctors also did what they could to help the wounded, regardless of the color of their uniform. Union survivors "never tired of telling of the kind and considerate treatment they received at the hands of the Confederate surgeons."[369]

A few days later, several wagons were sent through Confederate lines to the Union wounded, carrying food and medicine. (The food was necessary. Southerners had lived for months on only tough beef, corn meal, and water, but the wounded Yankees were not accustomed to this inferior diet. They needed better nutrition in their fragile medical conditions.) The Rebels promised that the supplies would be used only for the Union wounded, and this promise was kept.

About half the wounded prisoners died. Most of them were buried in mass graves. The gravediggers took bayonets and bent the tips so that they became hooks. They then hooked the collars of the dead and dragged them to their graves. The war now converted the beautiful little village of Pleasant Hill into a ghoulish place. Buzzards swarmed by the dozens and gorged themselves on dead horses and mules, of which there were hundreds, and probably on human flesh as well. A few weeks later, during the high temperatures of a Louisiana summer, both the mass graves and the shallow graves swelled up and cracked open. The smell was sickening, but not to the flies. There were nasty green flies everywhere.

*

That night, Dick Taylor lay down with his men on the battlefield. Despite his victory, he was depressed by the loss of so many good men, especially among his officers. "Above all, the death of the gallant Mouton affected me ..." he recalled later. "Modest, unselfish, and

---

[369] Charles B. Johnson, *Muskets and Medicine or Army Life in the Sixties* (Philadelphia: 1917), p. 177.

patriotic, he showed best in action, always leading ... "[370] Eventually, however, exhaustion won out over ghosts, and the general nodded off. He was awakened from a deep sleep at 10 p.m. by an excited and somewhat angry General Kirby Smith, whose dreams of martial glory were frustrated. He was not informed of Taylor's victory at Mansfield until 4 a.m. on April 9 but initially did not believe it. He was convinced only when a dispatch from Governor Allen arrived. (Allen witnessed the battle.) He saddled up at dawn and rode 65 miles to confront Taylor He immediately assumed command of Taylor's forces and ordered Polignac's division to remain on the battlefield, in support of Bee, as a precaution. (Taylor ordered it to return to Mansfield, where there was water.) Listening nearby, Lieutenant J. E. Sliger of the 28th Louisiana overheard the conversation, which was held over coffee at General Bee's campfire.

"Bad business, bad business, General," Kirby Smith moaned.

"I don't know, General," Taylor replied. "What is the trouble?"

"Banks will be upon you at daylight tomorrow with his whole army," Kirby Smith declared.

"Well, General," Taylor answered, "if you will listen, you will hear Banks's artillery moving out now on their retreat."[371]

Kirby Smith later commented that he was relieved because Banks "covert[ed] a victory which he might have claimed into a defeat."[372] Few men on either side would have agreed with him, however.

*

On the morning of April 10, to their surprise, the Confederate cavalry did not see any Union pickets to their front. Emboldened, they pushed forward and still met no opposition. They then entered Pleasant Hill and found that the Union army was gone. General

---

370 Taylor, p. 165.
371 Sliger, p. 458.
372 Kirby Smith, "Defense of the Red River," *B & L*, IV, p. 372.

Hamilton Bee joined them shortly after, offered what help he could to the Union surgeons, and began the pursuit. He advanced 20 miles without opposition and took a number of stragglers prisoner.

Later that evening, the first detachments of Banks' defeated army limped into Grand Ecore (a good defensive position) and dug in. Most of the army staggered in on the 11th.

Behind them, Taylor and his generals correctly agreed that Banks' Red River Expedition was defeated. On April 11, Kirby Smith wrote Taylor and stated that Steele now clearly represented a greater threat to Shreveport than did Banks. He wanted to destroy Steele, save Arkansas for the Confederacy, reoccupy the fertile Arkansas Valley, and invade Missouri. He pointed out that Taylor's ultimate strategic objective—the recapture of New Orleans—was impossible, due to the U.S. Navy.[373] Taylor did not agree and called Kirby Smith's strategy and his Arkansas adventure a "wild goose chase."[374] Taylor nevertheless marched the three infantry divisions (Walker, Churchill [Tappan], and Parsons) to Shreveport as ordered. He planned to lead them to Arkansas, defeat Steele, and return to Louisiana to finish off Banks. Taylor's plans were not Kirby Smith's plans, however.

The two generals met in Shreveport on April 15. Even though Steele was now retreating and represented no danger to Shreveport, Kirby Smith announced that he was nevertheless going to keep the infantry and advance into Arkansas.. Taylor, he declared, was not invited to accompany him. He could remain in Shreveport as deputy commander of the department or return to the Army of Western Louisiana. "All of this with a curt manner of a superior to a subordinate, as if fearing remonstrance," Taylor recalled.[375] He clearly felt that he was betrayed.

The next day, April 16, Kirby Smith unofficially promoted Richard Taylor to lieutenant general as something of a consolation prize. He wrote to Jefferson Davis: "Of the three district commanders, Major

---

373 O.R., Vol. XXXIV, Part 1, pp. 530-531.
374 Taylor, p. 218.
375 Taylor, p. 180.

Generals Magruder, Price and Taylor, the latter is junior and the only one of the three I consider suited to take charge of the affairs of the department."[376] He decreed that, if he were killed in Arkansas, Taylor would succeed him in charge of the Trans-Mississippi. Now that it was too late, he also gave Taylor a pontoon bridge. Dick Taylor, however, was not about to be placated by a promotion and a bridge. "Doubtless General Kirby Smith thought that a pontoon train would supply the place of seven thousand infantry and six batteries," he wrote later.[377]

---

376 O.R., Vol. XXXIV, Part 1, p. 476.
377 Taylor, p. 218.

Chapter VIII

BOUNCING DOWN THE RIVER

And what was happening to the Union inland water fleet while Taylor and the Yankee army slugged it out at Mansfield and Pleasant Hill?

Porter's Mississippi River Squadron left Grand Ecore on the morning of April 7 and headed for Shreveport, the strategic objective of the campaign. The bottoms of their boats bounced along the river bed almost immediately and would do so for the next month. Shallow water, snags, and the many curves in the Red plagued the tinclads and transports. They ran aground constantly and had to be pulled clear by the other boats. Rebel snipers on the north (east) bank of the Red also posed a constant threat.

Porter did not reach Campti until 5 p.m. on April 7. An hour later, he arrived at the town of Coushatta and the mouth of the Coushatta Bayou (also known as Coushatta Chute). Here, General Kilby Smith sent Colonel Lyman Ward's brigade ashore to deal with the Confederate snipers, but they only captured two.[378] Fortunately, there were fewer snipers on April 8 and 9.

---
378   Joiner, p. 140.

As Porter passed the hill complex north of Grand Ecore, it was obvious that the water level was dropping. He did not know that he was matching wits with Brigadier General William Robertson Boggs, Kirby Smith's chief of staff and a brilliant military engineer. Since Porter defeated all of his efforts between Fort DeRussy and Grand Ecore, Boggs played his trump card. If he could not defeat the fleet, he would remove the river. That would stop them! The innovative genius blew up the levee and the Tone's Bayou Dam and thus diverted at least half and perhaps as much as three-quarters of the water from the Red into the Bayou Pierre drainage basin. As a result, the level of the river continued to drop for several days, despite the heavy rains. Porter, nevertheless, reached the mouth of Bayou Pierre before nightfall on April 8.

The squadron continued to bounce along on April 9, its spirits buoyed by the rumor that the North won a great victory on the ground. Porter was impressed by the rich farmland, although he was disgusted by the fires. On the orders of Richard Taylor, Brigadier General St. John R. Liddell, the commander of the Sub-District of North Louisiana, burned all the cotton and surplus corps.[379] Porter was also impressed with the quality of the Red River road and wondered why Banks did not use it to advance on Shreveport.

Porter reached his initial objectives, Loggy Bayou and Springfield Landing, at 2 p.m. on April 10. It took him three days to cover 100 miles. It was here that he was supposed to link up with Banks, but the general was nowhere to be found. There was, however, considerable evidence that William Robertson Boggs had been there. A mile above the bayou, Porter found that the river was completely blocked. Boggs took the steamer *New City Falls* (the largest vessel to navigate the Red in peacetime), ran it aground sideways on a sandbar in the channel, and filled it so full of sand and rocks that the hull broke. Porter wrote his friend, General Sherman: "When I arrived at Springfield Landing I found a sight that made me laugh; it was the smartest thing I ever knew the rebels to do. They had gotten that huge steamer, *New Falls City*, across the Red River, one mile above Leggy [sic] Bayou, 15 feet

---

[379] O.R.N., Volume XXVI, Part 1, p, 380.

of her on shore on each side, the boat broken down in the middle, and a sandbar making below her. An invitation in large letters to attend a ball in Shreveport was kindly left stuck up by the rebels, which invitation we were never able to accept."[380]

Removing this obstacle would require a major engineering effort. First, however, the snipers were chased off. Kilby Smith off-loaded several hundred of his men, who began plundering and securing the area. Admiral Porter, who loved to ride and who was concerned about Banks' non-appearance, rode out on a reconnaissance on the west side of the Red with Kilby Smith, a detachment of mounted troops, and half a dozen cotton speculators. Like Porter, Kilby Smith sensed that something was terribly wrong. They found that they were being watched. Porter became really alarmed. These men were not rag-tag militia or annoying snipers in civilian clothes who ran away on the slightest pretext. They were regular Confederate cavalry, and they weren't going anywhere.

"Banks has been defeated," Porter proclaimed to General Kilby Smith, "or we wouldn't see those men here."[381] He verbalized his fear that Taylor might move his entire force against the fleet, turned his horse around, and went back to his boats.

Shortly after, Captain William H. C. Andres of the 14th New York Cavalry rode up with 50 men, delivered a dispatch from Banks, and confirmed Porter's worst fears. Although Banks carefully avoided saying so directly, the Army of the Gulf was defeated. Andres also carried orders to Kilby Smith. He was to return to Grand Ecore at once. Porter ordered his fleet to withdraw as well. The admiral later wrote that he did so "with a heavy heart" but was "anticipating that the rebels, flushed with victory, with our army in full retreat before them, would come in on our flank and cut us to pieces."[382] He knew

---

380   O.R., Vol. XXXIV, Part 3, p. 172.
381   Porter, *Naval History*, p. 502.
382   O.R.N., Vol. XXVI, Part 1, p. 61.

he needed to get back to Grand Ecore as quickly as possible, or the Confederates could bring up their artillery, and he would be in serious trouble.

He was already in serious trouble. And Shreveport was saved.

*

For the Union sailors, retreating down the Red was even more difficult than steaming up it. The channel was so narrow that the larger gunboats could not turn around and had to travel in reverse for miles. The *Chillicothe* had the most trouble. She impaled herself on a submerged tree, and the *Black Hawk* had to pull her off. It took the men two hours to patch her hull.

After the Battle of Pleasant Hill, Dick Taylor gave up on the idea of destroying Nathaniel Banks' army, at least for the moment. He decided to use his cavalry and artillery to destroy Porter's fleet instead.

On the evening of April 9, Dr. Woods' 32nd Texas Cavalry and Colonel Nicholas C. Gould's 23rd Texas Cavalry finally reached Mansfield from Texas. They joined the Army of Western Louisiana the following day. Taylor, at once, assigned them to General Green and ordered him to cut off Porter at Blair's Landing. Colonel William Henry Parsons' 12th Texas Cavalry Regiment marched behind him as a reinforcement. Taylor also sent Bagby's cavalry brigade toward the Red, to attack the fleet at Grand Bayou Landing, north of Blair's Landing. Meanwhile, General Bee (with Buchel's and Debray's brigades) was ordered to pursue Banks to Grand Ecore. Terrell's cavalry regiment was initially held in reserve; then it was sent to follow Green.

The major problem the Rebels faced was Bayou Pierre, which was 300 feet wide and too deep to ford. What they needed was a pontoon bridge, but Dick Taylor did not have any. Two were in Shreveport, and Taylor officially asked for them several days before, but Kirby Smith refused to part with them until it was too late to bring them down in time to cut off Porter. This was another big black mark against Kirby Smith in Taylor's book. Kirby Smith's short-

The tincald USS Fort Hindman

sightedness now mitigated in favor of the Union fleet because by the time Bagby negotiated Bayou Pierre, the inland squadron already passed by. Further south, on the morning of April 12, Green crossed the bayou using only the boats he could find locally. He could get only three artillery pieces across the bayou but nevertheless covered the 16 miles to Blair's Landing in record time.

On April 11, the navy continued its retreat. Most of the opposition was from snipers on the east bank; however, since a great many of the Yankees stayed in the hold, little damage was done until they had to come up on deck. This occurred when a boat got stuck on a stag or ran aground. The *Chillicothe, Emerald*, and several transports got stuck on stumps or snares and had to be pulled off, which exposed the crews to the Southern riflemen. The Union gunboats tried to protect them with their 11-inch guns, which was like hunting quail with cannons. The navy suffered a number of damaged bottoms, rudders, and wheels but was never in serious danger and casualties were light.[383]

April 12, however, was a day filled with more danger. At 9 a.m., near Coushatta, the gunboat *Lexington* collided with the transport *Rob Roy*, staving in her wheel house and damaging her chimneys. She was forced to lay in for repairs.[384] More seriously, Green beat the boats to Blair's Landing (the port for the Pleasant Hill area, about 45 miles north of Grand Ecore) and was waiting for them. He posted his three guns 400 yards from the bank with Woods' and Gould's regiments in front, with Parsons' regiment coming up. Terrell's regiment remained mounted and served as flankers on either side.

In his memoirs, Admiral Porter recalled the Battle of Blair's Landing. General Green, who was drunk on Louisiana rum, charged the gunboats with Woods' Texas cavalry regiment, and a cannon shot tore off his head. Three hundred of the 700 attackers were killed or wounded. When the Union sailors went ashore, they found "Every man we picked up had his canteen half full of whiskey. [They were] well set up with it or they wouldn't have attacked."[385]

Admiral Porter was letting his imagination run wild when he wrote that. For one thing, the entire west bank of the Red was swarming with Rebels. Not one Union soldier or sailor set foot on the shore. To have done so would have been suicide. For another thing, Woods' and Gould's regiments suffered 48 casualties on April 12 (12 killed, 32 wounded, and four missing), while Parsons' 12th Texas Cavalry lost two killed and seven wounded. Terrell's regiment did not suffer any casualties. The total Confederate losses on April 12 were 14 killed, 39 wounded and four missing—57 total.[386]

---

383   O.R.N., Vol. XXVI, Part 1, pp. 778, 781, 789.
384   O.R.N., Vol. XXVI, Part 1, p. 789.
385   Porter, p. 763.
386   Spencer, p. 43.

Southerners can stretch the truth too, of course, and Blair's Landing was a battle that gave both sides the opportunity to give full vent to their imaginations. According to Confederate reports, hundreds of Union servicemen aboard the gunboats and transports were slaughtered by their riflemen, Federal body parts were flying in all directions, and the decks ran red with Yankee blood. In reality, however, most of the Union soldiers who did come on deck took cover behind the cotton bales. In fact, the Federals lost seven men on the gunboats and 50 on the transports—57 total and exactly the same number as the Rebels lost. Taylor wrote later: "No Confederate went aboard the fleet and no Federal came ashore, so there was a fine field of slaughter—which the imagination of both sides could disport itself."[387]

As a historical footnote, the U.S.S. *Osage* employed a periscope during the Battle of Blair's Landing on April 12, 1864. This reportedly marked the first time this innovation was used in combat. It would certainly not be the last.

When the Northern fleet reached Blair's Landing, they were met by what Captain Thomas Selfridge called "the heaviest and most concentrated fire of musketry that I ever witnessed."[388] The fleet answered with its heavy guns, and General Thomas Green was right in the middle of the fray.

One of his men wrote that "Colonel Green was a man who, when out of whiskey, was a mild mannered gentleman, but when in good supply of old burst-head was all fight."[389] In 1864, his drinking problem seems to have worsened; it was definitely affecting his performance as a military commander. He still showed flashes of brilliance, such as he did at Mansfield, but he was not the same wizard on horseback that he was in 1862 and 1863. We saw how he got Debray's Brigade slaughtered and almost Colonel Buchel's as well at Pleasant Hill. On the afternoon of April 12, he got himself killed.

---

387   Taylor, pp. 177-178.
388   O.R.N., Vol. XXVI, Part 1, p. 49.
389   Noel, pp. 100, 143.

Sometime after 4 p.m., Captain Selfridge's *Osage* tried to take a sharp turn in the Red and ran aground. Green thought he saw an opportunity to capture it and ordered Colonel Woods to charge the gunboat. The commander of the 32nd Texas Cavalry, however, considered the order ridiculous and flatly refused to obey it. A medical doctor, he was very solicitous of his men's welfare (perhaps too much so), and he would never throw their lives away—especially on the whim of a drunkard. He declared that he would go himself, but he would not order a single one of his men to do so.

Green was taken aback by Woods' refusal, but he did not try to pressure or threaten him; instead, he decided to call for volunteers.

Meanwhile, the *Black Hawk* was covering the *Osage*, which was working itself free. One of the Union gun crews spotted a cluster of Confederate horsemen and fired at it. The shell burst about 40 yards from the group, and an iron ball about the size of a marble tore off half of General Green's skull. As Green fell forward, his shoulder strap caught on the horn of his saddle, and blood and brains spattered upon his comrades. His horse panicked and had to be chased down before Tom Green's body could be recovered. Another iron ball from the same shell practically tore off Lieutenant Colonel Benton's right arm. It had to be amputated near the shoulder. Private George Maverick of the 32nd Texas Cavalry wrote to his brother after the battle: "Genl Green was killed about 25 steps behind me ... Lawnee Calvert was killed just behind me. Wofford and Russell, all of Co. B, were killed about 20 feet of me; and one of Co. K and Lewis, were wounded just by me, with the explosion of the same shell. Dr. Collier was wounded in the thumb immediately behind me. But still I escaped unhurt. Just before we were ordered to retreat, I received a scratch from a Minnie [sic] ball in the left ear, of which I am very proud ... ."[390]

---

[390] Duaine, p. 118.

Colonel Parsons immediately assumed command of the Confederate cavalry and ordered a retreat at nightfall. Hamilton P. Bee succeeded Green as commander of the Cavalry Corps.[391]

Although they did not suffer heavy casualties, the Union gunboats were badly shot up. Porter later recalled that there was not a spot on the *Black Hawk* six inches square that did not have a bullet hole in it.[392] "Everything that was made of wood on the gunboats ... was riddled with bullets," Spencer recalled.[393] After Blair's Landing, the chimneys on the gunboats and transports resembled Swiss cheese.

The Rebels also suffered collateral damage in that they lost several horses to naval artillery fire. Exact figures are lacking.

Porter continued his retreat during the night of April 12/13 using torches—a very dangerous procedure. Several of his transports ran aground in the darkness, and the admiral finally gave up and ordered the fleet to anchor at 1 a.m.

Things were little better for the Union boats after dawn. The quartermaster ship *John Warner* ran aground and could not be freed. Liddell's snipers opened up from the north (east) bank but were driven off by Captain Selfridge and the 280mm Dahlgreen guns of the river monitor *Osage*. Meanwhile, the *Rob Roy* lost its rudder and was towed by the *Clara Bell*.[394]

When dawn broke on April 14, General Kilby Smith was gripped by the fear that he might be steaming into a Rebel trap if he remained stationery any longer. He ordered the transports and

---

391 William Henry Parsons (1826-1907) was born in New Jersey, but his parents moved to Alabama when he was a small child. He attended Emory College in Georgia but dropped out to fight in the Mexican War, where he served under Zachary Taylor. He settled in Texas, married, had five children, and became an editor, state legislator, and prominent secessionist. He raised the 4th Texas Cavalry Regiment, which was redesigned 12th Texas Cavalry and fought in Arkansas, Missouri, and Louisiana. After the war, he was a state senator and a Republican office holder, living in Washington, D.C., and New York City. He died in Chicago.

392 Porter, *Naval History*, p. 502.

393 Spencer, p. 43.

394 O.R., Vol. XXXIV, Part 1, p. 382.

their gunboat escorts to proceed down river to Campti, leaving the gunboat *Fort Hindman* (commanded by Lieutenant John Pearce) with the *John Warner*.

Meanwhile, at Grand Ecore, A. J. Smith and Colonel Shaw could hear the sounds of gunfire from upriver and became anxious about the safety of the fleet and Kilby Smith's division. Shaw asked Smith's permission to cross the Red and take his brigade north to Campti to clear the east bank of Rebels. A. J. Smith refused, declaring that he lacked the authority to give permission. Shaw would have to ask Banks, but Banks would not allow it. Whiskey Smith then launched into another tirade about Banks' lack of military ability. Smith was now calling him "Napoleon P. Banks" even in front of the enlisted men, who laughed and passed it on. The nickname stuck.

When A. J. Smith finished cursing Banks and the air cleared, Colonel Shaw declared that, unless Smith forbade it, he was going to Campti, with permission or without it. Smith, for once, said nothing, so Shaw began building a pontoon bridge across the river.

On the afternoon of April 13, Admiral Porter arrived at Grand Ecore for the very purpose of asking for infantry support on the north bank. Banks went to the river and only then learned that Shaw built his bridge and was crossing the Red. Ever the political chameleon, he immediately reversed himself completely and ordered A. J. Smith to reinforce Shaw with another brigade.[395]

Shaw reached Campti at nightfall on April 13 and cleared the area of Rebel snipers. Kilby Smith and his transports reached Campti early the next morning and continued on to Grand Ecore unmolested. The next day, April 15, Lieutenant Pearce finally succeeded in pulling the *John Warner* off the sandy bottom of the Red and proceeded downriver, reaching Grand Ecore the same day.

---

395 Johnson, p. 213; John Scott, *The Story of the Thirty Second Iowa Infantry Volunteers* (Bedford, Indiana: 1896), p. 243.

With all the boats of the fleet anchored at Grand Ecore, Shaw burned every building in Campti and returned to base. The fleet was safe, at least for the moment, but it was considerably worse for the wear. One soldier from the 114th New York observed that "the sides of some of the transports are half shot away, and their smoke stacks look like huge pepper boxes."[396]

*

With the Union tide receding in Louisiana, Kirby Smith, who always coveted personal martial glory, cast his eyes northward toward Arkansas. On April 12, he wrote Taylor: "Steele is bold to rashness, will probably push on without thought of circumspection. To win the campaign his column must be destroyed." He assured Taylor that Banks "was so crippled that he cannot soon take the offensive." He also felt that Banks would soon evacuate Alexandria, but since Taylor would have to conduct a pursuit through a country denuded of supplies, trying to cut him off would be useless. He ordered him to send Churchill's command and three additional infantry brigades immediately.[397]

The next day, Kirby Smith came down from Shreveport and met with Taylor at Mansfield. He again pointed out the need to deal with Steele. Taylor tried to convince him that Steele would retreat when he learned that Banks was crushed but without success. After failing to convert Kirby Smith, Taylor offered to personally take the infantry to Sterling Price in Arkansas and to serve under his command (if necessary) to defeat Steele. He could then return to Louisiana to deal with Banks.

---

396   Pellet, p. 222.
397   Winter, p. 361.

Early on the morning of April 14, Taylor divided his forces at Mansfield. He sent Polignac's division toward Natchitoches to reinforce Bee, who was shadowing Banks at Grand Ecore. Then, he personally headed for Shreveport, along with Walker's, Parsons' and Churchill's divisions.[398]

General Taylor met with Kirby Smith in Shreveport on the night of April 15. We saw the results of this meeting. Even though Steele gave up his drive on Shreveport and retreated to Camden, the commander of the Trans-Mississippi Department took three of Taylor's four infantry divisions and plunged into a military adventure in Arkansas. Disgusted, Dick Taylor was left with only one infantry division (the smallest) and his cavalry to deal with Banks and Porter.[399]

---

[398] O.R., Vol. XXXIV, Part 1, pp. 531-534. Prince de Polignac was the acting commander of the Army of Western Louisiana during Taylor's absence. He was promoted to major general on April 15, 1864.

[399] Taylor, p. 180.

Chapter IX

The Camden Expedition

To divert Confederate attention and resources from the Red River Expedition, the Union strategists decided to send Major General Frederick Steele's VII Corps on a drive from Little Rock to Shreveport. It took a direct order from General Grant to secure Steele's participation because he did not want to do it. This is because Frederick Steele knew southwestern and south-central Arkansas much better than did Ulysses S. Grant.

From the invaders' point of view, the military geography of Arkansas was even worse than that of northwestern Louisiana. Except for the Mississippi River on the eastern border of the state, Arkansas had no reliable rivers—unlike most Southern states. To develop the state economically during the antebellum era, longtime Governor Elias Nelson Conway focused on building a transportation infrastructure based upon dirt roads. His attitude was: "they will do for now, because they are all we can afford. Later, as the state prospers, we will be able to afford better roads." He built so many of these roads that he was dubbed "Dirt Roads Conway," and this nickname endures to this day.

Major General Frederick Steele

Conway's scheme was reasonable (and indeed was smart) by the standards of his day and explains why he was the longest-serving governor of Arkansas for more than a century. He retired in 1860.[400] In building his road network, however, Conway unwittingly set a trap into which the Union army fell in 1864. Conway's dirt roads were perfectly adequate for small-scale traffic, such as a few dozen wagons and pedestrians per day, but they could not handle more than 12,000 Union soldiers supported by hundreds of wagons and dozens of artillery pieces.

There is an adage in the higher levels of the military: "Amateurs talk about battles. Professionals talk about logistics." Although this is not entirely true, there is certainly an element of truth in it. Steele knew that, as the Union column struggled south, the roads would deteriorate under its great weight and, for all practical purposes, would cease to exist. Also, because of its poor soil, southwestern Arkansas was largely a wilderness in 1864, and Steele's corps would not be able to live off the land, as Sherman did on his "March to the Sea" in Georgia later that same year. Finally, southwestern Arkansas has many small streams and bayous, and the rudimentary bridges that Conway built were never designed to bear the weight of an army. Soon, Steele suspected, he would not be able to supply his advanced forces with the necessities—most notably food and water. **Map 9.1** shows the Arkansas portion of the campaign and the location of all the major battles.

Steele was a professional soldier. Born in New York on January 14, 1818, he graduated 30th in the West Point class of 1843—nine places behind Ulysses S. Grant. He distinguished himself in the Mexican War and earned two brevets for his gallantry, skill, and courage under fire. He later served in the West and in Minnesota as an infantry officer and was a major stationed at Fort Leavenworth,

---

400   The brother of the first governor of Arkansas, James S. Conway (1796-1855), Elias N. Conway (1812-1892) served as governor from 1852 to 1860—longer than anyone until Orval Faubus arrived on the scene a century later. His record has since been exceeded by Bill Clinton and Mike Huckabee. Conway retired to his cotton plantation in 1860 and lived a nearly reclusive life thereafter. He was a cousin of Henry M. Rector (1816-1899), the first Confederate governor of Arkansas (1860-1862).

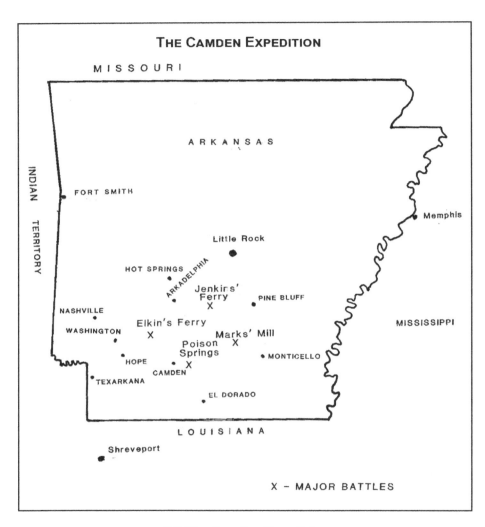

9.1 The Camden Expedition

Kansas, when the Civil War began. He commanded a battalion of Regulars at Wilson's Creek, Missouri, in 1861, before being named colonel of the 8th Iowa in September. Promoted to brigadier general on January 29, 1862, he served in Arkansas and Mississippi, where he took part in Sherman's disastrous attack on Chickasaw Bluffs in December 1862. He subsequently directed a division in Sherman's XV Corps in the Vicksburg campaign and was promoted to major general on March 13, 1863. After Vicksburg surrendered, he was given command of the VII Corps (12,000 men) in August 1863 and was ordered to eliminate any Confederate threat to the Mississippi River, as well as any possibility of Arkansas Rebels joining their brothers east of the river. He accomplished this with great efficiency and, in the process, captured Little Rock on September 10, 1863, with a loss of only 137 men. Despite his solid record of achievement, Steele was not popular with all his men or with the politicians in Washington because they considered him too lenient with Southern civilians. He was even called a Copperhead behind his back.[401]

Banks asked Steele, who now had more than 20,000 men, to commit 15,000 of them to the expedition.[402] Steele decided that 10,000 would be enough—and all he could supply in southwestern Arkansas.

The planning for his part of the operation was left strictly to Steele. He initially decided to advance southwest from Little Rock and cross the Ouachita River between Hot Springs and El Dorado. From there, he would push on to Monroe, Louisiana, which was 105 miles due east of Shreveport. From Monroe, he would follow the unfinished bed of the Southern Pacific Railroad to Shreveport. Later, for reasons he never explained, he decided on a more southwesterly route, from Little Rock to Arkadelphia to Washington, the capital of Confederate Arkansas. From there, it was 70 miles to Shreveport. Steele probably selected the Arkadelphia-Washington route over the

---

401 Warner, *Generals in Blue*, p. 474.
402 Hollandsworth, p. 176.

Monroe route because it allowed him to keep VII Corps between the Confederate Army and Missouri, but this is pure speculation on the author's part.

On March 17, 1864, General Steele ordered Brigadier General John Thayer, the commander of Fort Smith, Arkansas (on the border of Indian Territory), to march 170 miles to Arkadelphia with his Frontier Division. He was ordered to meet Steele there on April 1.[403]

Steele's phase of the expedition began on March 23, 1864, when he left Little Rock with the 3rd Division of his VII Corps and two brigades of cavalry—8,000 men and 16 guns. His Order of Battle is shown in Table 9.1. It was a beautiful spring day, and they left Little Rock to the tune of a band playing Yankee Doodle. They made a leisurely march of nine miles on the first day because many of the troops were accustomed to garrison duty, rather than the rigors of active campaigning.[404] Things were tougher from the second day on, when longer marches were required, and Steele announced that, except for coffee, only half rations would be issued on this march.[405]

The column crossed the Ouachita at Rockport on March 24 and continued its slow pace until March 29, when it entered Arkadelphia. Sick of half rations, the soldiers broke ranks and flooded the town, searching for food. Unlike the Army of the Gulf, they paid for almost all they took. Some of the men did get out of hand and smashed a local girls' school, breaking desks, benches and even the piano, but by and large, the citizens of Arkadelphia were quite pleased with the behavior of the invaders.

---

403   Joiner, p. 124. John Milton Thayer (1820-1906) was a Massachusetts lawyer who moved his family to the Nebraska Territory in 1854, where he became a skilled Indian fighter. He was appointed colonel of the 1st Nebraska Infantry in 1861 and fought at Fort Donelson, Shiloh, and Vicksburg, where he commanded a division. He accompanied Steele to Arkansas and was named commander of the District of the Frontier on February 22, 1864.

404   Johnson, p. 171; O.R., Vol. XXXIV, Part 2, pp. 513-516.

405   A. F. Sperry, *History of the 33rd Iowa Infantry Volunteer Regiment* (Des Moines: 1886), p. 61.

Major Generals Sterling Price and John S. Marmaduke.

From March 29 to April 1, Steele sat in Arkadelphia, waiting for Thayer and consuming supplies. On April Fools' Day, however, he decided he could wait no longer.

He took the Old Military Road to Washington and ran into Confederate cavalry for the first time in the campaign.

*

The Confederate Department of Arkansas was commanded by Major General Sterling Price, who had no infantry and five brigades of cavalry. Two of the five (Colonel William A. Crawford's and Brigadier General Thomas P. Dockery's brigades of James F. Fagan's division) were east of the Saline River, near Monticello and Mount Elba in southeastern Arkansas. The other three belonged to Brigadier General John S. Marmaduke's division and were commanded by Brigadier General Joseph E. "Jo" Shelby, Colonel Colton Greene, and Brigadier General William L. Cabell. On March 25, Cabell was on the Red, 16 miles west of Washington. Shelby and Greene were with Marmaduke at Camden. All totaled, Marmaduke had 3,200 men.

Order Of Battle, Union VII Corps And The Department Of Arkansas April 5, 1864

Commander: Major General Frederick Steele

3rd Division: Brigadier General Frederick Salomon

    1st Brigade: Brigadier General Samuel A. Rice

        50th Illinois

        29th Iowa

        33rd Iowa

        9th Wisconsin

    2nd Brigade: Colonel William McLean

        43rd Indiana

        36th Iowa

        77th Ohio

    3rd Brigade: Colonel Adolf Engelmann

        43rd Illinois

        40th Iowa

        27th Wisconsin

Frontier Division: Brigadier General John M. Thayer

    1st Brigade: Colonel John M. Edwards

        1st Arkansas

        2nd Arkansas

        18th Iowa

2nd Brigade: Colonel Charles W. Adams
- 1st Kansas Colored
- 2nd Kansas Colored
- 12th Kansas

3rd (Cavalry) Brigade: Lieutenant Colonel Owen A. Bassett
- 2nd Kansas Cavalry
- 6th Kansas Cavalry
- 14th Kansas Cavalry

Cavalry Division: Brigadier General Eugene A. Carr
- 3rd Iowa Cavalry
- 1st Missouri Cavalry
- 2nd Missouri Cavalry

3rd Cavalry Brigade: Colonel Daniel Anderson
- 10th Illinois Cavalry
- 1st Iowa Cavalry
- 3rd Missouri Cavalry

Pine Bluff Garrison: Colonel Powell Clayton
- 18th Illinois
- 7th Missouri
- 28th Wisconsin

1st Indiana Cavalry

5th Kansas Cavalry

Table 9.1 Order of Battle, Union Vii Corps and The Department Of Arkansas April 5, 1864

Sterling "Old Pap" Price was a political soldier and not an effective commander, although he did have some military experience and was not totally incompetent. Born in Prince Edward County, Virginia, he was educated at Hampden-Sydney College and studied law. He moved to Missouri and served in the legislature for six years—four of them as speaker. He was elected to the U.S. House of Representatives in 1844 but resigned in 1846 to fight in the Mexican War, where he became colonel of the 2nd Missouri Infantry and brigadier general of volunteers. He also served as military governor of New Mexico. After he returned home, he was governor of Missouri from 1853 to 1857. Although he opposed secession, he commanded the Missouri Militia against the extreme Unionists and accepted a Confederate commission as major general on March 6, 1862. By the spring of 1864, he had fought in Missouri, Arkansas, and Mississippi, without winning any notable successes. He was described as "Tall [and] handsome, with flowing white hair."[406] Price had a forceful personality and the appearance of a fine soldier and was very popular with his men. Despite their personal friendship, and despite the fact that he usually took Price's advice, Kirby Smith had serious misgivings about his military abilities—quite correctly, as it turned out.

The other senior Confederate commanders were more noteworthy. John S. Marmaduke, for example, was educated at Yale, Harvard and West Point, from which he graduated in 1857. He commanded the 1st Arkansas Battalion and the 3rd Confederate Infantry Regiment with distinction at Shiloh and Prairie Grove and was promoted to brigadier general on November 15, 1862. Thereafter, he commanded cavalry in Arkansas and led successful raids into Missouri. He fought a duel with Brigadier General Lucius Marshall Walker and mortally wounded him on September 6, 1863.[407] Marmaduke celebrated his 31st birthday just before Steele left Little Rock.

---

406 Johnson, p. 177.

407 Marmaduke's pistol bullet struck Lucius M. "Marsh" Walker on the left right side. He died the following evening. Walker forgave Marmaduke for killing him shortly before he died. See Samuel W. Mitcham, Jr. *Encyclopedia of Confederate Generals* (Washington, D.C.: 2022), pp. 429-30, 682-83 (hereafter cited as "Mitcham, Encyclopedia").

Brigadier General Jo Shelby

Jo Shelby was also noteworthy. Born in 1830, he was the son of a prominent Kentucky family. Educated at Transylvania University, he moved to Missouri in the 1850s and ran a highly successful rope business. A slaveholder and a "border ruffian" in Bleeding Kansas, he was a natural cavalry commander and was the Nathan Bedford Forrest of the Trans-Mississippi Department. His reputation was enhanced by his adjutant, John Edwards, a former newspaper editor who idolized him and wrote his reports. Edwards also wrote three books about Shelby's exploits and made him a larger-than-life hero. Edwards' exaggerations notwithstanding, Jo Shelby was a superb cavalry commander. He was promoted to brigadier general on December 15, 1863.

As soon as he heard that Steele left Little Rock, Sterling Price sent Marmaduke, Green, Cabell, and Shelby toward Arkadelphia to harass the VII Corps. There was heavy skirmishing on April 1 and 2.

Early on the afternoon of April 2, scouts brought word to Marmaduke that the Yankee column unexpectedly turned off the Old Military Road and were marching toward Elkins' Ferry on the Little Missouri River. Steele's men took the ferry before the Southern cavalry could react. Marmaduke and Shelby tried to disrupt the crossing by launching light attacks on April 3 but without success. The second day of the battle was characterized by lightning, thunder, and a hailstorm that turned the entire landscape white. In the end, the Rebels were driven off when Yankee cannon fire hit some beehives, and the Confederate horsemen fled, chased by the angry insects. Marmaduke lost 18 men killed, about 40 wounded, and several stung. Eight Yankees were killed, and 30 were wounded in the fighting.

Marmaduke withdrew about 16 miles down the Camden-Washington Road on April 5, hoping to lure Steele into an attack. While he threw up earthworks, Steele did not move on April 6. He learned that Thayer's missing Frontier Division (which left Fort Smith on March 21) was between Hot Springs and Arkadelphia, so he decided to wait on it. It began to rain that evening, so Steele had a pontoon bridge built over the Little Missouri.[408] That same evening, Marmaduke was reinforced by Colonel Richard M. Gano's cavalry brigade from Indian Territory.[409]

On April 7, Sterling Price joined Marmaduke with Crawford's and Dockery's brigades of Fagan's division. It was now too late to contest Steele's crossing of the Little Missouri, however, and the South's best chance of defeating Steele on the battlefield was lost. The Rebels could do little except wait for Steele to make the next move.

Frederick Steele was disappointed when Thayer arrived on April 9. True, he brought 4,000 men and 16 guns with him, but their appearance was rag-tag and unimpressive, and they had no supplies. Instead of receiving food from Thayer, as he hoped, Steele was forced to dip into his own diminishing reserves to feed the Frontier Division. He sent back to Little Rock for a supply train with 30 days of half rations for 15,000 men.[410] More significantly

---

408 O.R., Vol. XXXIV, Part 1, 660, 675, 780; Part 3, pp. 77-78.

409 Richard M. Gano (1830-1913) was a Disciples of Christ (now Church of Christ) preacher who was associated with Alexander Campbell and Barton W. Stone in the Restoration Movement. Born in Bourbon County, Kentucky, he was also a medical doctor, having graduated from Louisville Medical University in Kentucky. He and his wife (by whom he had 12 children) moved to Texas by 1858, when Gano distinguished himself as a militia company commander in actions against the Comanches. He was also a rancher, elected to the Texas legislature in 1860, joined the Confederate Army in January 1862, and recruited two companies of cavalry at the request of his friend, Albert Sidney Johnston. He rode with John Hunt Morgan but transferred to the Trans-Mississippi in late 1863, where Kirby Smith gave him command of a brigade of cavalry operating in Indian Territory.

410 O.R., Vol. XXXIV, Part 3, pp. 77-79.

from the military point of view, he decided to abandon his drive on Shreveport at this point. He never really believed in it, was concerned that Kirby Smith might combine Price's forces with Taylor's army and crush him (a very real possibility), and now he was sure that he did not have enough supplies to reach the city.

On April 10, spearheaded by Brigadier General Frederick Saloman's division, Steele began to move across Prairie d'Ane, against Shelby and Dockery, near present day Prescott, Arkansas. The Confederate cavalry retreated to the south, followed by the Union infantry. The next day, the Union advance was even slower and more tentative, and when night fell, the bluecoats returned to their camp of the previous night.

During the night of April 11/12, Sterling Price fell back to positions eight miles east of Washington and prepared to defend the Confederate capital of Arkansas. The next day, Steele executed his strategy. He faked an advance on Washington with his cavalry, and then reversed directions and headed due east for the fortified town of Camden. This move surprised everyone and caught the Rebel commanders flat-footed.

General Steele decided that he could not advance southwest on Shreveport until his supply problems were solved, if then. He intended to make Camden his advanced supply base and await developments. "Our supplies were nearly exhausted and so was the country," he wrote Halleck a few days later. "We were obliged to forage from 5 to 15 miles on either side of the road to keep our stock alive."[411] The soldiers were already on half rations for three weeks, and the horses and mules were also suffering.

On April 13, Confederate Brigadier General Samuel B. Maxey joined Price east of Washington with the rest of his division: Colonel Tandy Walker's 2nd Indian (Choctaw) Brigade.[412] Price moved

---

411 O.R., Vol. XXXIV, Part 1, p. 661.

412 Samuel Bell Maxey was born in Kentucky in 1825, graduated from West Point in 1846, and was brevetted for courage during the Mexican War. He left the army in 1849, became an attorney, and moved to Texas in 1857. He organized the 9th Texas Infantry in

against Steele's rear guard with five brigades (Maxey's and Fagan's divisions) and even captured a section of artillery, but Thayer turned on him with superior numbers and took it back. Table 9.2 shows Price's Order of Battle on April 13.

Steele's main body, meanwhile, struggled through the bottomless roads. Several stretches had to be corduroyed with timber or fallen trees to be passable at all.[413]

On April 14, the Union column passed Cypress Bayou, where the roads were better. Scouts, meanwhile, informed General Steele that the Rebels were trying to cut him off before he reached Camden. He sent Brigadier General Samuel A. Rice's Brigade ahead with orders to secure Camden as quickly as possible. Rice reached White Oak Creek, 18 miles west of Camden, at 8 p.m., and was joined by Brigadier General Eugene A. Carr's cavalry. They spent a cold, uncomfortable night and were marching again by dawn.

The reports were correct: Marmaduke was indeed trying to cut Steele off before he could reach Camden. He left the Washington area on April 13, rode 60 miles around Steele's right flank, and cut the Camden-Washington Road 14 miles west of Camden. Steele now would have to clear the road or surrender his army. Fortunately for the men in blue, they had a numerical superiority over Marmaduke and were well led. Eugene A. Carr was a West Point graduate with many years of service on the frontier.[414] Samuel Rice was a very

---

1861 and as its colonel, fought in Kentucky. Promoted to brigadier general on March 1, 1862, he served in East Tennessee, in the 1st Battle of Port Hudson (a Union debacle) and in the Vicksburg relief expedition under General Joseph E. Johnston. A very good commander, he was placed in charge of the Indian Territory, where he proved to be an effective organizer as well. He was assigned to duty as a major general by Kirby Smith on April 18 but was never appointed to this rank by Jefferson Davis or confirmed by the Senate.

413   O.R., Vol. XXXIV, Part 1, pp. 675, 687.

414   Eugene A. Carr (1830-1910) graduated from West Point in 1850 at the age of 20. A New York native, he spent 43 years serving on the frontier and went down in history as a great Indian fighter. He also fought in the Battle of Pea Ridge (Elktown Tavern), where he was wounded three times and won the Congressional Medal of Honor.

talented amateur.[415] With commanders as gifted as Marmaduke and with many more troops, the Union army was able to break the encirclement and clear the road after a two-hour battle. Marmaduke sent a detachment of cavalry back to Camden to burn the public property and withdrew to positions eight miles southwest of the town. Price joined him here the next day with the rest of his troops and established his headquarters at Woodlawn.

Just before dark on April 15, the vanguard of the Union Army of Arkansas entered Camden. Although it had a population of 2,300 and was the second largest town in Arkansas, Camden appeared to be a ghost town. A strongly Confederate locality, all its men of military age were off with the Rebel army, and the women closed their doors and pulled their window shades. There was no one on the streets.

Exhausted and hungry, Steele's main body of the column entered the town the next day. There was some pillaging initially, but General Steele soon put an end to that and developed a good working relationship with the townspeople. He also sent foraging parties east of the Ouachita to collect livestock for slaughter. A cavalry patrol from the 1st Iowa and 3rd Missouri also captured the Confederate steamer *Homer* 30 miles below Camden and found 3,000 bushels of corn on board. Steele, however, knew that his supply problems were far from over. He was still right in the middle of hostile territory, 120 miles from his main base in Little Rock, and loosely surrounded by tough and experienced Confederate cavalry. He had 12,000 men and 12,000 horses and mules to feed, his supplies were low, and his stock of hardtack was almost exhausted.

---

415 A New York native, General Rice (1828-1864) was a Union College graduate. He moved to Iowa in 1851, where he was known as a brilliant attorney, and was twice elected attorney general of his state. He raised the 33rd Iowa in the summer of 1862 and was promoted to brigadier general on August 4, 1863, due to his excellent performance in battle.

Order Of Battle, Department Of Arkansas
April 13, 1864

Commander: Major General Sterling Price

Fagan's Cavalry Division: Brigadier General James F. Fagan

Cabell's Brigade: Brigadier General William L. Cabell

1st Arkansas Cavalry: Colonel James C. Monroe

2nd Arkansas Cavalry: Colonel Thomas J. Morgan

4th Arkansas Cavalry: Colonel Anderson Gordon

Trader's Regiment, Arkansas State Troops: Colonel W. H. Trader

Gunter's Arkansas Cavalry Battalion: Lieutenant Colonel Thomas M. Gunter

Crawford's Brigade: Colonel William A. Crawford

2nd Arkansas Cavalry: Colonel William F. Slemons

10th Arkansas Cavalry Regiment: Crawford (1)

12th Arkansas Cavalry Regiment: Colonel John C. Wright

Poe's Arkansas Cavalry Battalion: Major James T. Poe

Dockery's Brigade: Brigadier General Thomas P. Dockery

18th Arkansas Mounted Infantry: Colonel D. W. Carroll

19th Arkansas Mounted Infantry: Lieutenant Colonel H. G. P. Williams

20th Arkansas Mounted Infantry: Colonel G. W. King

12th Arkansas Mounted Infantry Battalion: Major William F. Rapley

Marmaduke's Cavalry Division: Brigadier General John S. Marmaduke

Greene's Brigade: Colonel Colton Greene

3rd Missouri Cavalry: Lieutenant Colonel L. A. Campbell

4th Missouri Cavalry: Lieutenant Colonel William J. Preston

8th Missouri Cavalry: Colonel William L. Jeffers

10th Missouri Cavalry: Colonel Robert R. Lawther

Shelby's Brigade: Brigadier General Joseph O. Shelby

5th Missouri Cavalry: Colonel Benjamin Franklin "Frank" Gordon

11th Missouri Cavalry: Colonel Moses W. Smith

12th Missouri Cavalry: Colonel David Shanks

Hunter's Missouri Cavalry Regiment: Colonel DeWitt C. Hunter

Maxey's Cavalry Division: Brigadier General Samuel B. Maxey

Gano's Brigade: Colonel Charles DeMorse, acting commander

29th Texas Cavalry: Major J. A. Carroll

30th Texas Cavalry: Lieutenant Colonel N. W. Battle

31st Texas Cavalry: Major Michael Looscan

2nd Indian Brigade: Colonel Tandy Walker

1st Choctaw Regiment: Lieutenant Colonel James Riley

2nd Choctaw Regiment: Colonel Simpson W. Folsom

NOTES:

(1) Lieutenant Colonel Dawson Kilgore apparently served as acting commander of the regiment at this time

Table 9.2 Order Of Battle, Department Of Arkansas, April 13, 1864

The Battle Of Poison Spring

On April 16, Steele learned that there were 5,000 bushels of Confederate corn in the White Oak Creek area, about 18 miles west of Camden, and he ordered General Thayer to seize it. Thayer, in turn, organized a foraging party under the command of Colonel James M. Williams, the leader of the 1st Kansas Colonel Infantry Regiment. Williams was initially assigned his own regiment (500 men, temporarily under the command of Major Richard G. Ward), 195 horsemen from the 2nd, 6th, and 14th Kansas Cavalry Regiments, and two 6-pounders from the 2nd Indiana Light Artillery Battalion.[416] Williams was also given 198 wagons, each of which was pulled by six mules.

The wagon trains left Camden at 5 a.m. on April 17 and reached White Oak Creek without difficulty. They set up a base camp, and the wagons headed out in various directions, where the men stole everything they could steal. The Rebel cavalry pickets saw them coming and burned about half the corn, but the Union soldiers took the rest. Not only that, they looted smokehouses, private homes, and took baby clothes, women's dresses, shoes, bonnets, bed clothes, blankets, and anything else of value. Meanwhile, 500 more cavalry and infantry from the Kansas cavalry regiments and from the 18th Iowa Infantry joined the camp, and they brought two more cannons with them.[417] The reinforcements were commanded by Captain William M. Duncan. Including teamsters, Colonel Williams now had around 1,300 men.

Their presence did not go unnoticed by the Rebels. On the morning of April 17, scouts informed Colonel Cotton Greene of the presence of the wagon train. He quickly sent dispatch riders to General Marmaduke, who alerted Generals Maxey, Fagan and Sterling Price. Marmaduke immediately began to assemble what we today would call a battle group to destroy the wagon train before

---

416 Edwin C. Bearss, *Steele's Retreat From Camden and the Battle of Jenkins' Ferry* (Little Rock: 1966), pp. 6-7.

417 Gregory J. W. Urwin, "Poison Spring and Jenkins' Ferry: Racial Atrocities During the Camden Expedition," in Mark K. Christ, ed., *"All Cut to Pieces and Gone to Hell:" The Civil War, Race Relations and the Battle of Poison Spring* (Little Rock: 2003), pp. 111-113.

James F. Fagan

it could return to Camden, if he were given the time and opportunity. General Price liked the idea and ordered his other commanders to cooperate with Marmaduke. (Maxey, the senior officer, voluntarily deferred command to Marmaduke, at least for the moment.)

On April 17, General Price had seven cavalry brigades in three cavalry divisions (Marmaduke's, Fagan's, and Maxey's). By dawn the following day, five of them were closing in on the wagon train: Colonel Charles DeMorse's Texans, Colonel Tandy Walker's Indians, Brigadier General William L. "Old Tige" Cabell's Arkansans, Greene's Missourians, and Colonel William A. Crawford's Arkansans. Major Robert C. Wood's 14th Missouri Cavalry (Sterling Price's personal escort battalion) joined them later.

The Yankees played into Marmaduke's hands by spending the night too far from the Camden perimeter and not sending Williams more men. When Colonel Williams marched down the Upper Washington Road on the morning of April 18, he found the road blocked by Cabell and Crawford.[418]

Marmaduke planned for Maxey to attack the Union right flank from the south while he attacked frontally with the rest of his command. The plan was slow in unfolding, however, because of the rough and wooded nature of the terrain, the quick reactions of Williams, and the stubborn resistance of the 1st Kansas Colored—arguably the best

---

418   The 2nd Arkansas Cavalry Regiment (Colonel Thomas J. Morgan) was detached from Cabell's Brigade and was posted two miles to the east, facing east. Its mission was to delay any forces Steele sent from Camden to rescue Williams.

African American regiment to serve in the Civil War. They repulsed the 29th Texas Cavalry in a bitter fire fight, and it was not the first time. They beat them in the Battle of Honey Springs, Indian Territory, on July 17, 1863, when a force of 3,000 Yankees defeated 2,000 Rebels under the command of Brigadier General Douglas H. Cooper.[419] The commander of the 29th Texas Cavalry, Charles DeMorse, was severely wounded in this battle. When Maxey departed the Indian Territory, he left Cooper in charge of the district. DeMorse was now acting commander of the brigade because General Gano was shot in the arm during a skirmish on April 14—an event pregnant with consequences. The straight-laced Church of Christ preacher would never have tolerated abusing or shooting prisoners, even black ones. DeMorse, on the other hand, actually encouraged it. He and his men wanted revenge for Honey Springs.

As soon as he saw the Rebels, Colonel Williams deployed his men with the 1st Kansas Colored covering the front and part of the right flank. The 18th Iowa defended the right flank and rear, and the cavalry covered the extreme left and extreme right. The Yankees, however, were at a severe disadvantage. With 3,600 men, Marmaduke had them outnumbered nearly 3 to 1, and he had a dozen guns, which he positioned extremely well. The blacks were caught in a very effective artillery crossfire. Even so, they repulsed the first Southern attack by DeMorse's brigade. Soon, however, he was joined by Greene, Walker, and Cabell. The fighting was desperate and, in places, hand-to-hand, before the Union line cracked and collapsed. Soon it was "every man for himself." Colonel John Harrell of Cabell's brigade recalled: "Away trotted the poor black men into the forest, clinging to their rifles but not using them, while the pursuing Confederates cut them down right and left."[420]

---

[419] For the story of this battle, see Frank Arey, "The First Kansas Colored at Honey Springs," in Mark K. Christ, ed., cited above.

[420] John M. Harrell, Vol. X, Part 2, *Arkansas*, in Clement Evans, ed., *Confederate Military History* (Atlanta: 1899), pp. 250ff.

Colonel Williams hoped he could hold his positions and delay the Rebels until help arrived from Camden. The sound of the battle could be heard in town, but Steele did not move. The VII Corps did nothing while Williams' command was crushed.

The 29th Texas was not the only unit seeking revenge that day: Colonel Tandy Walker's Choctaws and Cherokees also had blood in their eyes. Unlike the Texans, they were looking for white Yankees, and they found them. The Indians who overran the Union howitzers and chased the survivors beyond the wagon train and into the woods. Colonel Walker recalled: "I feared that the [wagon] train and its contents would prove a temptation too strong for these hungry, half-clothed Choctaws, but had no trouble in pressing them forward, for ... [there was something] more inviting to them than food or clothing—the blood of their despised enemy. They had met and routed the forces of General Thayer, the ravagers of their country, the despoilers of their homes, and the murderers of their women and children ..."[421]

The Rebels and Indians pursued the routed Yankees for two miles before General Maxey ordered them to halt. He was afraid Steele would hear the sound of the battle and rush to their rescue. He should have been right, and certainly his logic is unassailable, but he was wrong. Both he and Steele were severely criticized for their respective decisions (or lack thereof) on April 18. Maxey's decision, at least, had the merit of being sound and prudent. He wanted to secure the captured wagon train.

The Battle of Poison Spring was the greatest military victory the Confederacy won in Arkansas during the Civil War.[422] It was, however, marred by an atrocity.

---

421 O.R., Vol. XXXIV, Part 1, p. 849.

422 Thomas A. DeBlack, "An Overview of the Camden Expedition" in Mark K. Christ, ed., *"All Cut to Pieces and Gone to Hell:" The Civil War, Race Relations and the Battle of Poison Spring.* (Little Rock: 2003): pp. 11-30 (hereafter cited as "DeBlack").

Atrocities take place in almost every war. In the heat of battle, troops sometimes get out of hand—especially if their commanders allow them to or even encourage them to kill enemy prisoners. DeMorse's Texans shot and bayoneted a sizable number of wounded African-Americans. "Where is the 1st N**ger now?" someone would roar.

"Cut to pieces and gone to hell—due to bad management!" came the reply. Then another African American soldier would die. Sometimes they were neither shot nor stabbed. They were simply clubbed to death with the butt of a musket. But the atrocity at Poison Spring (both then and now) was (is) overshadowed by the alleged massacre of African American Union soldiers at Fort Pillow, Tennessee, six days earlier, even though the scale was similar.

The Fort Pillow "Massacre" was an effort on the part of the Lincoln regime to discredit the Confederate commander, Nathan Bedford Forrest. In military parlance, a "massacre" occurs when all or nearly all of the combatants are killed, such as with Custer at Little Big Horn, the Battle of Thermopylae, or the Alamo. It is significant that Poison Spring was never called a massacre, and obviously there was no massacre at Fort Pillow, since half of the Union participants survived.[423] When they surrendered, Forrest had them surrounded on three sides with their backs to the Mississippi River. He could have killed them all had he wished to do so, but he chose not to. He even allowed a truce and had 17 critically wounded African Americans to be placed aboard a Union boat, so they could receive prompt medical attention, along with several white Yankees.

If one wants to discuss a Civil War massacre, I suggest s/he study the Battle of Fort Gregg (April 2, 1865), a/k/a "the Confederate Alamo," where all but about 20 of the roughly 300 defenders were put to death—many after they surrendered. The victims, however, were Southern, so Fort Gregg is never mentioned by mainstream historians, proving that Churchill was right when he declared that the victor writes the history. But I digress.

---

423 I wrote an entire book on General Forrest, *Bust Hell Wide Open: The Life of Nathan Bedford Forrest* (Washington, D.C.: 2016).

In the end, the Confederates captured all 198 wagons at Poison Spring (including about 30 that were burned),[424] all four Union cannons and 125 prisoners. Two hundred four Yankees were killed or missing—117 from the 1st Kansas Colored, which suffered 182 total casualties out of 438 engaged. Colonel Williams later reported that wounded Negroes were "murdered on the spot."[425] Total Confederate casualties were small: 16 killed, 88 wounded and 10 missing—114 total.[426]

When a Union reconnaissance/burial party arrived three days later, they found that all the dead white soldiers were scalped. The officers of the 1st Kansas Colored were left face down on the field, and their soldiers were placed in a circle around them.[427]

Williams and his survivors staggered into the Camden defenses around 11 p.m. Inside the town, morale plummeted after Poison Spring, and there was dissatisfaction in the ranks over the small number of men in Williams' escort. The loss of the corn, bacon, and other captured footstuffs did not help, and the supply situation continued to deteriorate. Meat was still being issued, but there was no more hardtack, and the corn supply was running low. One day, all the 33rd Iowa received to eat was a total ration of four ears of corn per man.[428] A supply train arrived from Pine Bluff on April 20, brought five days' worth of rations (10 days of half rations) and the mail, which improved attitudes somewhat, but the situation was still bad.

Rumors were also circulating in Camden that Banks was defeated, and Kirby Smith was reinforcing Price with 8,000 infantry. On April 18, a courier reported to General Steele. He sent out several, but this man was the only one to reach the Army of the Gulf and return.

---

424 O.R., Vol. XXXIV, Part 1, p. 747.

425 O.R., Vol. XXXIV, Part 1, p. 746. Major Richard G. Ward of the 1st Kansas Colored also reported seeing wounded blacks being shot (p. 754).

426 O.R., Vol. XXXIV, Part 1, pp. 786, 826, 842.

427 Charles H. Lothrop, *A History of the First Regiment Iowa Cavalry Veteran Volunteers.* (Lyons, Iowa: 1890), p. 182.

428 Andrew F. Sherry, *History of the Thirty-Third Iowa Infantry Volunteer Regiment, 1863-6* (Des Moines: 1866), p. 81.

Although Banks tried to convince the courier that he defeated the Rebels and only retreated due to a lack of water, the dispatch rider learned the truth from one of Albert Lee's staff officers. Steele wrote Sherman on April 22: "Although I believe we can beat Price, I do not expect to meet successfully the whole force which Kirby Smith could send against me if Banks should let him go."[429]

The next day, Captain Dunham arrived with a dispatch from Banks, informing Steele that he conducted a retrograde operation and urged him to bring VII Corps to the Red River as soon as possible, so he and Banks could operate against Shreveport from that line. Captain Julius Wheeler, Steele's chief engineer officer, recalled: "To suppose that a force of about 12,000 men, without supplies, ammunition scant, could move over a country nearly barren of forage and exhausted of supplies, in the face of an active and exultant enemy, under the command of one of the most energetic and skillful of the rebel generals [Taylor], and then to cross a river like the Red to make a junction with General Banks' forces, leaving all this country open, was so absurd that General Steele did not consider it for one moment."[430] He sent back an evasive message to Banks, stating that, if the gunboats and transports could travel to the Ouachita via the Red, they might be able to pick up his corps at Arkadelphia, but that would leave Missouri open to invasion.

Meanwhile, on April 19, General Kirby Smith reached the field and assumed active command of the forces operating against Camden. He wanted to bag the entire Yankee army and immediately devised a plan to cut Steele's supply line between Camden, Little Rock, and the large Union garrison/supply base at Pine Bluff. He attached Jo Shelby's brigade to Fagan's division and ordered Fagan to attack Steele's supply lines and bases on the Arkansas River; then he was to position himself between Steele and Little Rock.

---

429   O.R., Vol. XXXIV, Part 1, pp. 663.
430   O.R., Vol. XXXIV, Part 1, p. 676.

Kirby Smith sent instructions to Sterling Price earlier, before he left Shreveport, telling him to initiate similar measures. He was disappointed that Price failed to do so.

In the meantime, Churchill, Parsons, and Walker were marching on Camden. For logistical reasons, they took three different routes. Walker took the easternmost route (to guard against a possible attempt by Steele to join Banks), while Parsons took the central route (from Shreveport to Benton, Louisiana, and then north to Camden), and Churchill took the western approach. By April 23, Churchill and Parsons were in Arkansas and demonstrating against Camden to distract Federal attention away from Fagan.

Kirby Smith's diversion seems to have worked. On April 22, Steele sent a wagon train back to Pine Bluff to get more supplies. Two days later, Fagan learned about it from Shelby's scouts. He was at El Dorado Landing at the time but made a 45-mile forced march to try to cut off the wagons before they reached the Saline River at Mount Elba. At midnight he camped near Marks' Mills on the Camden-Mount Elba-Pine Bluff road.

Before daylight on April 25, James Fagan assembled 4,000 men and learned that the wagon train had not yet passed Marks' Mills, a grist mill complex owned by Hastings Marks, so he set up an ambush there.[431]

The train included 240 government wagons, several sutlers' wagons and private vehicles. It was guarded by three infantry regiments: the 43rd Indiana, the 36th Iowa and the 77th Ohio, all of the 2nd Brigade, 3rd Division, VII Corps, as well as 390 cavalrymen. Its total strength was 1,690 men,[432] excluding a large number of cotton speculators, civilian refugees, assorted other camp followers, and

---

431 James F. Fagan (1828-1893) was born in Kentucky but moved to Arkansas when he was ten. A planter, he served as a lieutenant in the Mexican War. Later elected to the Arkansas legislature, he was an early adherent to the Confederate cause and helped recruit the 1st Arkansas Infantry Regiment. He became its colonel and led it at Shiloh. Fagan was promoted to brigadier general on September 12, 1862, and was transferred to the Trans-Mississippi, where he fought at Prairie Grove.

432 DeBlack, p. 23.

about 300 African Americans. Its commander, Lieutenant Colonel Francis M. Drake, had no idea that there was a large number of Confederate horsemen nearby and despite the fact that he was deep in enemy territory, did not bother to post pickets that night, much less send out reconnaissance parties.

The road was muddy and had deteriorated significantly due to the earlier supply train. Progress was slow the next morning, and the column did not reach Marks' Mills until 8 a.m. Then Fagan sprung his trap.

General Fagan divided his command into two divisions under William Cabell and Jo Shelby.[433] A third force (Colonel William A. Crawford's brigade) blocked the road to the Saline River and Pine Bluff, due east of the wagon train. Cabell struck the Union column first from the southeast and the fighting was fierce. The battle went on for 90 minutes when Colonel Dockery reinforced Cabell with his brigade and forced the Yankees to fall back to the protection of their wagons. At that moment, Shelby struck them from the northeast—right in the rear. Again, the fighting was bitter, but this time, it was brief. Surrounded, the 43rd Indiana and 36th Iowa surrendered, along with Colonel Drake, who was severely wounded. Less than 150 Yankees escaped.[434]

Francis M. Drake

---

433 William L. Cabell was born in Danville, Virginia, on New Years' Day, 1827. He graduated from West Point in 1850 and served in the Quartermaster Department. He became a major in the Confederate Quartermaster Department in 1861 and was on Beauregard's staff at Manassas. He was on Joseph E. Johnston's staff in 1862, where he and two other officers designed the Confederate Battle Flag. Sent to the Trans-Mississippi, he was promoted to brigadier general on January 30, 1863.

434 O.R., Vol. XXXIV, Part 1, 710-715.

Fagan turned his attention to the Union rearguard, the 77th Ohio, which was cut off from the main body during the battle. Realizing that their situation was pretty hopeless (they were on foot and outnumbered 10 to 1), most of the regiment surrendered immediately.

Meanwhile, 500 men from the 1st Iowa Cavalry approached Marks' Mill from the west. They had nothing to do with the wagon train. They were going home on veterans' leave, and their appearance was strictly coincidental. When they saw Fagan deploying against them with thousands of men, they prudently decided to go home another day and returned to Camden at a brisk pace. And that was the end of the Battle of Marks' Mills. The North lost more than 1,400 men captured (including the wounded) and probably more than 100 soldiers killed. Dozens of contrabands were also shot out of hand. Furious at the blacks for supporting the Union, the Rebels fell upon them with a vengeance, and the Southern officers were unable to restrain their men. Estimates of the number killed range from 100 to 250. The truth is probably somewhere in between. Another 150 were made prisoners.[435]

The Northerners also lost all 240 wagons and their teams, dozens of cotton speculators and camp followers, and five guns. The Rebels lost 41 killed, 102 wounded, and 143 missing—283 total casualties.[436]

Finding few supplies in the wagons, the victors went after the prisoners and the dead. One survivors recalled: "The rebs robbed nearly every man of us to our Chaplain & many of our dead they stripped of every stitch of clothes even their shirts & many socks & left them unburyed & the woods on fire & many of the wounded

---

435   O.R., Vol. XXXIV, Part 1, p. 789.
436   O.R., Vol. XXXIV, p. 795.

they jerked off their boots, blouses, pants, and hats."[437] On the other hand, Colonel Drake later reported that he and all the wounded prisoners were "well attended and well cared for."[438]

*

The news of the disaster at Marks' Mills was brought back to Camden by the 1st Iowa Cavalry. The loss of this second wagon train made gathering enough supplies to sustain the VII Corps at Camden clearly impossible. The men were hungry, but forage especially was in short supply. Steele had 9,000 horses and mules remaining, but the area around Camden could only provide forage for about 1,000 of them. His command faced immobilization. If that happened, the Union Army of Arkansas was finished.

That night, Steele had a council of war with his senior officers, Thayer, Saloman, Rice, and Carr. There was little to discuss, since they had only two choices: retreat to Little Rock or starve and surrender.

Rice wanted to retreat to the east, via Mount Elba and Pine Bluff. Steele rejected that route because the road passed through Moro Swamp and would not hold up beneath the Union wagons. The other three generals agreed with this decision. The route of retreat would go through Princeton, cross the Saline River at Jenkins' Ferry, and proceed on to Little Rock.

On April 26, the VII Corps made rapid preparations to evacuate Camden. Everything not to be taken was destroyed, including some bacon and hardtack that should have been distributed to the troops. That afternoon, the men were given the food which would have to last until they got back to the Arkansas capital. It wasn't much. Some men only got two crackers and half a pint of cornmeal.

---

[437] Daniel Sutherland, "1864," in Mark K. Christ, ed., *Rugged and Sublime: The Civil War in Arkansas* (Fayetteville, Arkansas: 1994), p. 119.

[438] O.R., Vol. XXXIV, pp. 715-716. Colonel Francis M. Drake (1830-1903) was for many years after the war president of the Iowa Southern Railroad. He was the Republican governor of Iowa from 1895 to 1898 but did not seek reelection due to declining health. Drake University is named after him.

To deceive the Rebels, taps was sounded at 9 p.m. The retreat began at midnight –very silently. They crossed the Ouachita River over a pontoon bridge and camped a few miles down the road.

The Rebels did not know they were gone until after dawn. Sterling Price (commanding Churchill's and Parsons' divisions) occupied the town at 9 a.m., but pursuit was impossible because they had no pontoon bridge. Kirby Smith had at least two—in Company H, 4th Confederate Engineer Battalion—but he denied them to Taylor before Mansfield and left them in Shreveport, along with the rest of the battalion, when he moved into Arkansas.[439] Kirby Smith's misuse of this engineer unit was one of his worst blunders of the campaign. Meanwhile, the Greyhounds joined Price's forces that afternoon, and Marmaduke's command swam the Ouachita at White Hall that evening. That night, after Price's men finished constructing a floating bridge (raft) at Camden, the pursuit began.

Kirby Smith joined the chase on April 28 and for some reason, sent Maxey's cavalry division (Tandy Walker's Choctaws and Chickasaws and Gano's Texans) back to Indian Territory. Confederate officers at the time and later historians unanimously agree that this move was unjustified and a mistake. With the benefit of hindsight, I disagree. I do not believe the presence of another Confederate division at the Battle of Jenkins' Ferry would have made the slightest difference in the final outcome of the campaign (see below).

Having stolen a march on Kirby Smith and Price, Steele hurried down the Princeton-Jenkins' Ferry-Little Rock road. The going was hard due to the mud, and the road deteriorated underneath the weight of the horses, mules, wagons, caissons, and guns. The hungry and tired Yankees struggled with each step, and the sides of the road were soon littered with discarded clothing, coats, blankets, knapsacks, and other paraphernalia.

---

439 Joiner, *Howling Wilderness*, p. 119. Company H of the 4th Engineers was commanded by Captain Smith Kirby, the general's nephew.

Meanwhile, unaware of the true situation, General Fagan continued up the Saline River, to attack the Arkansas River supply bases, as Kirby Smith ordered. If he knew Steele evacuated Camden, he could have cut off his retreat—a move which would probably have ended in the destruction of the Union army—one of the "might have beens" of history. As events transpired, Fagan pushed to within 10 miles of Benton (just south of Little Rock) and then back to Arkadelphia, looking for supplies and fresh horses.

Steele spent the night of April 28/29 in Princeton. The next day, Marmaduke skirmished with his rearguard. The rain started falling about noon, and by nightfall, the road was very muddy. Early that afternoon, the Army of Arkansas reached the Saline River at a place called Jenkins' Ferry, about 12 miles southwest of the present day town of Sheridan, 55 miles from Camden, and a little more than 40 miles from Little Rock. Here, the pontoon bridge was brought up. It was completed at 4:15 p.m.

Getting the wagons and artillery through the mud and over the bridge was back-breaking work. Captain Julius Wheeler, Steele's chief engineer recalled: "I never saw it rain harder than it did during the night ... It soon became a sea of mud, in which wagons settled to the axles and mules floundered about without a resting place for their feet. Fires were made along the road, pioneers and working details set to work, and every exertion was made to push the impedimenta across before daylight, it being evident that the enemy were [sic] in force in our rear. But we failed. The rain came down in torrents, putting out many of the fires, the men became exhausted, and both they and the animals sank down in the mud and mire, wherever they were, to seek a few hours' repose."[440]

The Confederate infantry stopped to rest that afternoon in Princeton, nine miles from the Saline. They were marching again at midnight, despite the rain. Marmaduke was even closer and, by dawn, was skirmishing with the Yankees.

440　O.R., Vol. XXXIV, Part 1, p. 677.

Both sides knew that April 30 would be the decisive day. If Steele could put the Saline River between himself and Kirby Smith, he would have escaped with his army. On the other side, Kirby Smith knew that this would be his last chance to destroy the Union army. He was determined to do this, even though it meant he would have to fight under distinctly unfavorable circumstances.

"The field of battle at Jenkins' Ferry was a nightmare to both armies," Ludwell Johnson wrote later.[441]

Two miles from the river, the road descended downward to the floodplain of the Saline. Just north of it and running parallel to the road was Toxie Bayou (Creek), north of which lay a swamp and cane thicket. South of the road were two fields divided by a strip of woods which ran parallel to the river. Behind the second field lay the Northerners' final defensive positions and the pontoon bridge. The space between Toxie Bayou on the north and the thick woods to the south was only one quarter of a mile, leaving Kirby Smith no room for maneuver. If he was going to destroy Steele, he would have to do so via frontal assault across a narrow rectangle of a battlefield covered in water and knee-deep mud. On the other side, the Yankees cut trees and constructed wooden breastworks, further strengthening their positions.

After receiving several confusing orders from Price, Churchill began the battle about 7:45 a.m. by sending Tappan's brigade forward. It crossed the first field without significant opposition, reaching the line of trees, and met a heavy volley as it tried to cross the second field. By 8 a.m., Tappan bogged down (no pun intended) and called for help.

Churchill sent Brigadier General Alexander T. Hawthorn's Arkansas brigade into action on Tappan's left but was checked again. Then he sent in his last brigade, Colonel Gause's, in support of Hawthorn and Tappan. Again, the fighting was heavy, but the Union line held.

---
441   Johnson, p. 197.

Brigadier Generals Bill Scurry and Thomas N. Waul. Both were wounded at Jenkins Ferry. Only Waul recovered.

To the north, Kirby Smith sent Lieutenant Colonel H. G. P. Williams' 19th Arkansas Cavalry Regiment along the north bank of Toxie Creek to outflank the Union river. It was a good idea, but it did not work. Williams was checked by the 29th Iowa, which was reinforced by the remnants of Drake's command that was so thoroughly crushed at Marks' Mills.

Price, meanwhile, committed Parsons' division on Churchill's right about 10 a.m. The fighting was heavy all along the line. The field was covered by a thick, low layer of fog that trapped the gunsmoke. Men had to bend down and look under the fog to aim and fire. The fog was so thick that, when the 2nd Kansas Colored Regiment advanced on Captain Samuel T. Ruffner's Missouri Battery, the Rebels did not realize they were Yankees until they were nearly on top of them. The fog was so thick that the Confederates did not know a black Union regiment was advancing on them until it was too late to fire!

Lieutenant John Lockhart was captured by the 2nd Kansas Colored, along with seven of his men. The African Americans then murdered three of the Rebel prisoners. Several of the wounded Texans also had their throats cut this day. The African Americans were extracting revenge for Poison Spring.[442]

Meanwhile, Walker's Texas Division came up. Kirby Smith ordered Scurry's and Randal's brigades to attack the Union left flank. Waul's brigade was initially held in reserve on the bluff, two miles from the river, but was soon sent into action on Randal's left.

Walker's men again attacked with great courage and fury but for once could not break the Union line. Casualties were heavy. Sergeant J. J. Stovall of the 8th Texas recalled that five men were shot down beside him—three on one side, two on the other—"and I tell you I felt as big as a bale of cotton."[443] All three of the Texas brigade commanders went down. Only Waul would recover. He died in bed in 1903, at age 91. Colonel J. R. Walker of the 18th Texas Infantry was also killed, and Colonel Overton Young was seriously wounded. On the Union side, General Rice was wounded when a Southern bullet struck his spur and drove it deep into his foot. His right foot had to be amputated, and he was sent back to Iowa, where he died during surgery on July 6.

Some of the Confederate units retreated in confusion. When the 26th Arkansas retreated, Private John Q. Thompson and four other men in a forward position did not receive the order. They took shelter behind a large oak tree, and "All were shot down except myself." His gun jammed, so he picked up a dead comrade's weapon and kept firing until the enemy charged his position. "I took deliberate aim at a group of the enemy, fired and then retreated in double quick time" (i.e., he ran for friendly lines).[444]

Some members of Company F, 8th Texas Infantry, also ran. His company commander asked one of them: "Mike, what made you run?"

---

442 Johnson, p. 199.
443 Yeary, Vol. II, p. 730.
444 Yeary, Vol. II, p. 748.

He replied: "Captain, because I could not fly."[445]

At 12:30 p.m., the Rebels withdrew to the western edge of the battlefield. The fighting was over.

Meanwhile, Steele completed his pontoon bridge, and by 11 a.m., the entire wagon train and everything except the infantry and a few artillery pieces was over the river. The foot soldiers began to cross as soon as the Confederates withdrew. They had no interest in following, and by 3 p.m., the last Union rearguard successfully crossed the river and reported that there were no unwounded Federals on the west bank. The bridge was then destroyed because there were not enough fit horses left to carry it back to Little Rock. The wounded were at the mercy of the Rebels, who took good care of them—if they were white. Reports again surfaced about wounded blacks being bayoneted.

Edmund Kirby Smith committed about 6,000 men to the Battle of Jenkins' Ferry: 2,000 from Churchill's division, 2,000 from Walker's, 1,200 from Parsons', and perhaps 800 from Marmaduke's cavalry. He lost between 800 and 1,000 men plus three guns.

Steele committed around 4,000 soldiers to the action: most of Saloman's division and the 1st (Union) Arkansas, 2nd Kansas Colored, and 12th Kansas from Thayer's division. The Union losses almost certainly exceeded 700.[446]

Jenkins' Ferry was a battle which should never have been fought. It was also badly handled by Kirby Smith and Price, who sent their infantry in piecemeal (i.e., one unit at a time) across an open, muddy field. The Confederates never launched a single, concentrated assault which alone had a chance of winning the battle. It is doubtful if even this tactic would have been successful, however. Nevertheless, the campaign as a whole was a marginal success from the Southern

---

445   Yeary, Vol. II, p. 730.

446   Johnson, p. 202. The 2nd Kansas Colored reported 15 killed, 55 wounded, and three missing (O.R., Vol. XXXIV, pp. 758-759). During the campaign, Salomon's Division suffered 1,775 casualties, of whom 1,132 were captured or missing. It had 5,226 men when it left Little Rock (O.R., Vol. XXXIV, Part 1, p. 692).

point of view. The expedition as a whole was clearly a Northern failure. Confederate Arkansas was saved, and no Union force would ever again threaten Shreveport.

The North suffered 2,750 military casualties in what became known as the Camden Expedition. The Rebels suffered 2,300 casualties, according to Johnson's estimates.[447] Steele also lost 635 army wagons and 2,500 mules, and these figures do not include sutlers' wagons, trains, and the like. The Southerners lost only 35 wagons—about the normal attrition rate for a major campaign. Steele also lost nine guns at Poison Spring and Marks' Mills. Kirby Smith lost three guns at Jenkins' Ferry.

General Steele, incidentally, was quite pleased with the performance of the 2nd Kansas Colored in the Battle of Jenkins' Ferry. "The conduct of the colored troops of my command proves that the African can be made as formidable in battle as a soldier of any other color," he reported.[448]

The Confederates spent the night of April 30/May 1 on the battlefield. They were cold, wet, and unhappy. That night, General William Scurry, the Texas brigade commander, died of his wounds.[449] He was taken back to the small town of Tulip, where he was given a military funeral. An hour later, his colleague, Brigadier General Horace Randal, succumbed to his wounds.[450] Randal's wife arrived at his side six hours after he passed away. Dr. Cade recalled that her grief was "very great."

---

447 Johnson, p. 203.

448 O.R., Vol. XXXIV, Part 1, p. 671.

449 Scurry was temporarily replaced as brigade commander by Philip Luckett (1824-1869), the commander of the 3rd Texas Infantry, a German unit.

450 Randal was initially buried near the field but was later reinterred in the Old Marshal Cemetery, Marshall, Texas. Kirby Smith assigned Major Robert McClay to duty as a brigadier general, to rank from April 30, and gave him command of Waul's Brigade. After Waul recovered, McClay assumed command of Randal's Brigade. His appointment caused too much dissatisfaction among officers who were bypassed, however, and Kirby Smith sent him home on indefinite leave in January 1865. Richard Waterhouse, the commander of the 19th Texas Infantry, eventually succeeded Scurry.

After the battle, each Rebel soldier was issued two ounces of bacon and one ear of corn. The wounded were carried back to Camden, where they were well cared for by the women of the community, who acted as volunteer nurses.

Kirby Smith quickly issued a proclamation, portraying Jenkins' Ferry as a major Southern triumph. The Confederate civilians naturally believed him, and the fact that Steele was in full retreat to Little Rock lent credibility to his claim. "What a cry of gratitude has gone up to God for our victories," Madison Parish refugee Kate Stone wrote in her journal. "This whole country is in a state of delighted surprise, and as telegram after telegram comes announcing some new success, we can hardly believe our good fortune."[451]

After licking its wounds for two days, Kirby Smith ordered the army to return to Camden. A few days later, on May 7, he ordered the infantry back to Louisiana to rejoin Richard Taylor. Traveling 15 to 20 miles a day, Walker's Greyhounds arrived in Pineville on May 22. By then, it was too late to destroy Napoleon P. Banks and his Army of the Gulf.

*

Meanwhile, Steele's defeated army limped back toward Little Rock.

Once across the Saline and out of the Jenkins' Ferry snare, the suffering of the Union soldiers of the VII Corps was far from over. They were exhausted, hungry, and thirsty, and the road was bottomless. Horses and mules gave out and had to be shot or left to die. Wagons were abandoned and burned. Food was so scarce that one piece of hardtack was sold for $2. It may have been worth $.03 in normal times. Two more pieces of hardtack were traded for a gold watch. They marched all night until 9 a.m. The two miles just east of Jenkins' Ferry were the worst.

He was assigned to duty as a brigadier general on April 30, but unlike McClay, his appointment was confirmed by the Confederate Senate on March 17, 1865 (Warner, *Generals in Gray*, pp. 326-327).

451   John Q. Anderson, ed. *Brokenburn: The Journal of Kate Stone, 1861-1865* (Baton Rouge: 1999 ed.), pp. 280-281.

Steele's column reached the Benton Road on the afternoon of May 1. An hour later, a wagon train full of provisions arrived from Little Rock. The next day, the battered "Army of Arkansas" paraded through the streets of the capital with their prisoners and three cannons that the 2nd Kansas Colored captured near the head of the column, as if they were conquering heroes and these were their trophies of victory. The show rang hollow, however; no one was fooled.

Chapter X

MONETT'S FERRY AND THE RETREAT TO ALEXANDRIA

Back in Louisiana, Banks' Army of the Gulf retreated to the strong defensive positions around Grand Ecore and dug in, preparing for Taylor's next attack. Remarkably enough, the Yankee commanders did not expect another major strike, but the Union soldiers seemed to understand Dick Taylor better than most of their generals, and they knew that a Taylor offensive, *somewhere*, was almost certain. He wasn't going to be satisfied until they were out of Louisiana, prisoners of war, or dead—preferably the latter.

"You don't need any protection," General Franklin told one squad of men from the 56th Ohio as they were digging a trench.

"We have been defeated once, and we think we will look out for ourselves," one of the men replied. The general left and the men kept on digging.[452]

---

[452] Thomas J. Williams, *An Historical Sketch of the 56th Ohio Voluteer Infantry During the Great Civil War from 1861 to 1865* (Columbus, Ohio: 1899), p. 70 (hereafter cited as "Williams.")

Banks, on the other hand, was worried. He was sure that Taylor had 25,000 men. He actually had 5,500, but Banks, nevertheless, summoned all the reinforcements he could muster. Most readily available was Brigadier General Cuvier Grover's 2nd Division, XIX Corps, which was on occupation and garrison duty in Alexandria.[453] On April 9, Banks' chief of staff, General Stone, wrote to Grover and asked him to send as many of his men as possible to Grand Ecore as quickly as he could. A similar order was dispatched on April 11. Grover's men moved rapidly and traveled by steamboats. They faced a few Southern snipers at unexpected places and suffered some discomfort but few casualties.

Banks also ordered Major General John A. McClernand, the commander of the XIII Corps, to bring all except 2,000 men from Pass Cavallo, Texas, to Grand Ecore and to assume command of all XIII Corps units operating with Banks. Simultaneously, Brigadier General Franklin S. Nickerson's brigade was ordered to Alexandria to reinforce Grover. Two of its regiments, however, were on veterans' leave, so it did not amount to much.

On April 13 and 17, Banks wrote to General Grant and put a "spin" on his defeat, to use modern terminology. He claimed his expedition changed the character of the Rebels' operations in the Trans-Mississippi from offensive to defensive in nature and forced Kirby Smith to abort a planned invasion of Missouri. He blamed much of his failure on the low level of the Red River. On April 13, he stated that he intended to resume his offensive on Shreveport immediately; however, his new line of advance would be different and "less dependent upon a river proverbially as treacherous as the enemies we fight."[454] Four days later, however, he was less bellicose and stated that he would have to be reinforced before resuming

---

453   Cuvier Grover was born in Maine in 1828 and graduated fourth in the West Point Class of 1850. He served on the frontier and took part in the expedition against the Mormons in Utah. He served in New Mexico in 1861 and in Virginia in 1862, and was promoted to brigadier general of volunteers on April 14. After the Second Manassas, he was sent to the Department of the Gulf and fought in the Teche and Lafourche campaigns, as well as in the Siege of Port Hudson.

454   O.R., Vol. XXXIV, Part 1, p. 185.

his offensive. He added, however, that Governor Willard P. Hall of Missouri, who was with the expedition, assured him that 10,000 men could be spared from Kansas and Missouri for this purpose.[455] What the governor of Missouri was doing in Grand Ecore, Louisiana, on a cotton fishing expedition when "Bloody Bill" Anderson and his guerrillas were shooting up his state, Banks did not say. Nor was Grant fooled for a moment by this dispatch. He was already looking for a way to replace Napoleon P. Banks.

Meanwhile, Brigadier General John M. Corse arrived at Banks' Headquarters with a message from Sherman: he wanted XVI Corps and Kilby Smith's division from XVII Corps returned to him.[456] This, Banks knew, would be a disaster for the Army of the Gulf. The XIII, XIX, and Cavalry Corps were not yet recovered from the Battle of Mansfield, and Porter's fleet was in serious trouble. Banks, therefore, formally countermanded Sherman's orders to A. J. and Kilby Smith (to return to Vicksburg) and wrote Sherman a letter explaining why. He also declared that their loss would leave him with less than 20,000 men to face Taylor's legions.[457]

David D. Porter, for once, emphatically agreed with Banks. Knowing the commander of the Army of the Gulf had no credibility, the admiral personally wrote to his friend Sherman and begged him to let Banks keep the Smiths, especially A. J. Smith's corps. "His is the only part of the army not demoralized," Porter declared and predicted a major disaster if XVI Corps left.[458]

Confronted with Porter's letter, Sherman let it drop and did not appeal the matter to Grant, who would likely have sided with his favorite lieutenant. Sherman never did get XVI Corps back.

---

455 O.R., Vol. XXXIV, Part 1, p. 188.

456 John M. Corse (1835-1893) was Sherman's inspector general. He already distinguished himself in several battles and later commanded a division in the March to the Sea.

457 O.R., Vol. XXXIV, Part 3, pp. 175, 265-266.

458 O.R.N., Vol. XXVI, pp. 56, 62, 68-69.

Meanwhile, scapegoats were needed to cover up Banks' responsibility for the Mansfield debacle. The first to go was Charles P. Stone, the chief of staff of the Army of the Gulf. He was relieved of his duties on April 16.[459]

Stone was an easy target. A West Pointer, he was placed in charge of the Washington defenses in 1861, but was unjustly held responsible for the Union disaster at Ball's Bluff, Virginia, on October 21-22, 1861.[460] The man actually responsible for the debacle, Colonel (and U.S. Senator) Edward D. Baker, was killed in the action and was not considered a suitable target for disgrace by his fellow Radical Republicans, so Stone was forced to take the fall. He was arrested and thrown in prison without a trial for six months. Stone finally secured a hearing before a court of inquiry, which vindicated him in early 1863. He was restored to active duty and sent to Louisiana as Banks' chief of staff. Their relationship was not good, however, and Banks was making derogatory remarks about Stone as early as the fall of 1863. News of these comments soon reached Stone's ears, so he submitted his resignation. Banks accepted his notice, but for reasons not made clear by the records, Stone did not leave. Banks, however, wrote his wife and told her that Stone was a "very weak" man.[461] The fact that Stone was a friend and supporter of George C. McClellan, a vocal opponent of Abraham Lincoln and the Republicans, made Banks' decision to get rid of Stone even easier. Banks replaced him with his friend, Brigadier General William Dwight, who came from a family of prominent cotton speculators.[462]

---

459 O.R., Vol. XXXIV, p. 3, p. 175.

460 Charles P. Stone was born in Greenfield, Massachusetts, on September 30, 1824, and graduated from West Point in 1845. He served on Winfield Scott's staff in Mexico and was chief of ordnance of the Department of the Pacific from 1851 to 1856, when he resigned to become a surveyor for the Mexican government. He was placed in charge of the Washington defenses in 1861 and was promoted to brigadier general.

461 Johnson, pp. 219-220.

462 Stone was stripped of his volunteer rank by Secretary of War Edwin P. Stanton. He was unemployed until September 1864, when he resigned his Regular Army commission. After the war, he moved to Egypt and became chief of staff to the Army of the Khedive. Later, he was the engineer who lay the foundations for the Statue of Liberty. He died in New York City in early 1887 and is buried at West Point.

Banks also relieved Albert Lee as commander of the Cavalry Corps and sent him back to New Orleans. He later testified that he should not have done this and regretted that he did so. Colonel Nathan A. M. "Gold Lace" Dudley, the commander of the 4th Cavalry Brigade, was also relieved.

Lee was replaced by Brigadier Richard Arnold, a Regular Army soldier who was chief of artillery in the Department of the Gulf since November 1862.[463] Not a cavalry officer, Arnold was probably as astonished by his promotion as anyone else. His performance in his new post would be adequate but hardly impressive.

*

On April 15, Admiral Porter visited Banks in his rather luxurious headquarters tent and was astonished to find him wearing a dressing gown, a velvet cap, and slippers. He was reading Scott's *Tactics*, which was written by General Winfield Scott. Porter was uncharitable enough to remark later that Banks should have read this book *before* the Battle of Mansfield. On this evening, Banks assured Porter that he still intended to capture the capital of the Trans-Mississippi Department. He told the admiral that he was already reinforced by Brigadier General Henry W. Birge, who came up from Alexandria with three regiments on April 13. Banks also sent a dispatch to Steele, asking for his cooperation with the Shreveport offensive.

The former Speaker of the House made it clear to Porter that he thought he won the Battle of Mansfield and only retreated because of a lack of water. What then, the admiral wanted to know, was he doing in Grand Ecore? He was, after all, only six miles from water at Sabine Crossroads, as the bluecoats called the Battle of Mansfield. Before he left, Porter made it plain that he did not intend to steam up the Red again until the river rose; in fact, he intended to get below

---

463   Richard Arnold (1828-1882) was the son of a governor of Rhode Island. He graduated from West Point in 1850 and was associated with the artillery virtually his entire career. He served with distinction in Virginia in 1862, which led to his promotion to brigadier general. He was a lieutenant colonel of the 5th Artillery Regiment on Governors Island, New York, when he died. He was related to the notorious traitor, Benedict Arnold.

the Alexandria Falls as rapidly as possible. He sent the strongest part of the fleet back toward the falls the next morning without bothering to inform the general, although it did not get very far (see below).

Banks, meanwhile, anxiously awaited word from Steele. Without his help, Banks did not believe he could capture Shreveport.

On April 19, realizing that the river was not going to rise and that Steele was not going to arrive anytime soon, Banks decided that it was time to retreat to Alexandria. Porter emphatically agreed with this decision. No further advance on Shreveport was possible, he declared, until there was water in the Red. Banks ordered A. J. Smith to take his entire command to Natchitoches, from which he would cover the retreat of the army.

April 21 was a clear spring day. The retreat began at 5 p.m., with Grover's division in the lead. It was temporarily commanded by General Binge and included his own four regiments plus the remains of Benedict's Brigade, now under the command of Colonel Francis Fessenden. The pontoon and wagon trains followed Binge and were followed by the ammunition wagons and the cavalry trains. The African American engineer regiments and their trains were fifth. Then came Emory's Division (minus Fessenden's Brigade), the XIX Corps, and the XIII Corps, with A. J. Smith's XVI Corps in the rear. Three brigades of cavalry screened the front and flanks of the column, with Colonel Lucas's cavalry brigade (attached to A. J. Smith) bringing up the rear.[464] Banks placed General Franklin in charge of the entire column.

To make the march more rapid, Banks ordered the men to discard all extra clothing, overcoats, and blankets, which were burned in large piles. A large warehouse full of equipment and supplies was also burned. The fires spread to nearby buildings, and the entire Grand Ecore community was burned to the ground. Destroyed, also, was the only chance for secrecy. The Rebels saw the fires and knew exactly what the Union army was up to.

---

464   O.R., Vol. XXXIV, Part 1, pp. 310-312; Part 3, p. 244.

Hamilton P. Bee and his eventual replacement, John A. Wharton.

Dick Taylor spent the night of April 19/20 in Mansfield and rejoined the army on April 20, just in time to direct the pursuit. He had about 5,500 men, including fewer than 2,000 infantry under Polignac; 3,000 cavalry under Hamilton P. Bee; and Brigadier General William Steele's small cavalry brigade, under the command of John A. Wharton, who recently joined him.

Banks' column was long, and the road was dusty. By nightfall, the entire army was moving. The path was lit by the burning houses of Grand Ecore and by the homes along the road heading southeast. Governor Allen recalled: "From Mansfield to the Mississippi River the track of the spoiler was one scene of desolation. The fine estates on Cane and Red rivers, on bayous Rapides, Robert, and De Glaize, were all devastated. Houses, gins, mills, barns, and fences were burned, negroes all carried off, horses, cattle, hogs, every living thing, driven away or killed ... You can travel for miles, in many portions of Louisiana, through a once thickly-settled country, and not see a man, nor a woman, nor a child, nor a four-footed beast. The farm houses have been burned. The plantations are deserted. The once smiling fields now grown up in briars and brakes, in parasites and poisonous vines. A painful melancholy, a death-like silence, broods over the land, and desolation reigns supreme."[465]

One place not desolated, however, was the old French town of Natchitoches, which owed its salvation solely to the speed of Taylor's newest general, John A. Wharton.

Wharton was a member of the planter aristocracy. Born near Nashville, Tennessee, on July 23, 1828, his family moved to Texas when he was an infant. He returned to the east as a student at South Carolina College in 1846. Here, he met Eliza Johnson (the daughter of the governor), whom he married in 1848. He graduated in 1850, returned to Texas, studied law, was admitted to the bar, and set up a practice in Brazoria. Over the next decade, he became a wealthy plantation owner, slave holder, and an ardent secessionist.

John Wharton became a captain in the 8th Texas Cavalry (Terry's Texas Rangers) in 1861. He was elected lieutenant colonel and became colonel when the regimental commander died in January 1862. He committed the worst military blunder of his career on April 5, just before the Battle of Shiloh, when he allowed his men to discard their firearms to load them with fresh charges. This unauthorized shooting should have alerted the Union soldiers and cost the Confederacy the element of surprise in the ensuing battle, but it did not. Wharton partially redeemed himself at Shiloh, where he was wounded. He played an impressive role in the invasion of Kentucky, including the Battle of Perryville. He was promoted to brigadier general on November 18, 1862.

Wharton served under Forrest and "Fighting Joe" Wheeler on the Western Front and took part in several successful raids. He was wounded again at Murfreesboro and so distinguished himself at Chickamauga that he was promoted to major general. He feuded with Wheeler, however, and conspired to replace him. It probably would be better for the South had he succeeded, because he was a better cavalry commander than Wheeler. He was bold without

---

465   Dorsey, *Allen*, pp. 278-279.

Monett's Ferry And The Retreat To Alexandria

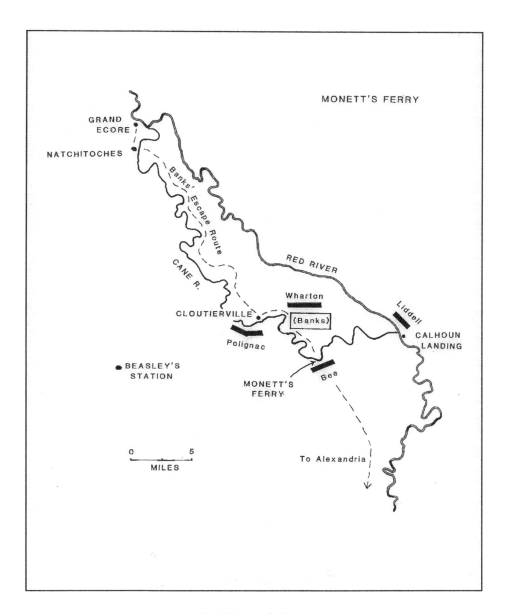

10.1 *Monett's Ferry*

being rash, had a fine touch as a leader of mounted troops and was also loved by his men. He also had a rare talent for being able to communicate with common, uneducated privates and Bourbon aristocrats and have both walk away, thinking they just spoke with a superior personality. In any case, Jefferson Davis ended the Wheeler-Wharton feud in February 1864 by sending Wharton back to Texas. He joined Taylor in Shreveport after the Battle of Mansfield.[466]

During the night of April 21/22, and on many subsequent days and nights, Wharton hung on the Yankee rearguard "like a tic on a mule," to use a 19th Century expression. He dogged the Union rear guard so closely that it did not have time to burn Natchitoches. Some buildings were set on fire, but the Southern cavalry and the civilians put them out before they could be destroyed. Several Federals were captured who actually had torches in their hands when they were surprised by Wharton's horsemen. The present-day Natchitoches, with its old, beautiful buildings, should erect a monument to Wharton's memory.

The Cane River leaves the Red a few miles below Grand Ecore and meanders south and west before it rejoins the Red about 30 miles south of Grand Ecore. The island between the Cane and the Red is called Rigolet du Bon Dieu, or the Isle Breville. The road followed by the Army of the Gulf traversed the length of the island and recrossed the Cane at Monett's Ferry, 40 road miles from Grand Ecore. The ferry became the key to the entire campaign and, momentarily the entire Civil War, because Taylor decided to spring his next trap here. If he could surround the Army of the Gulf and isolate it in the Isle Breville, it would be forced to surrender. Without the army, Porter's fleet would be next. Taylor knew he could not force the fleet to capitulate, but he could force Porter to scuttle it. With both the army and fleet destroyed, Taylor's dream of recapturing New Orleans would no longer seem so unrealistic. At the very least, he could force Lincoln to divert significant forces from Georgia and elsewhere to

---

[466] See Paul R. Scott, "John A. Wharton: The Forgotten General," www.terrstexasrangers.org/biographies/ submitted/Wharton.tml. Accessed 2009. This is an excellent essay.

keep the Mississippi River open. If that occurred, the entire outcome of the war would be in jeopardy, insofar as the United States was concerned. The fact that he was outnumbered 30,000 to 5,500 did not deter Dick Taylor for a moment. He was not the kind of a man to be dissuaded by trifles.

Word reached Banks' Headquarters on April 21 that the Rebels were heading for Monett's Ferry. He knew at once that Taylor was moving to block his retreat, and he did not take the precaution of guarding it.[467] The entire campaign now became a race for the ferry (see Map 10.1).

The retreat was the worst and toughest part of the campaign for most of Banks' men. There was little water and even less rest. They marched all night. Franklin drove his men onward without letting up. Some of the men got only two hours sleep per 24 hours march. Exhaustion soon set in. Officers fell asleep on their horses, and men fell asleep on their feet. There was no time to eat or rest, and daytime made the situation worse. "Through heat and dust the men drive on, taxing their energies almost beyond endurance," one man wrote.[468]

April 22 was a hot day, and exhausted men dropped out of the column. These stragglers were quickly captured by Wharton's cavalry, which took dozens of prisoners. Many times, the Rebel pushed forward and forced A. J. Smith and the rearguard to deploy in line of battle. Wharton, however, refused to charge. He intended to wear the Yankees out without becoming decisively engaged, and he was succeeding masterfully. "The retreat was perilously close to becoming a headlong flight," Johnson wrote later.[469]

---

[467] O.R., Vol. XXXIV, Part 1, p. 190. See pp. 181-218 for Banks' correspondence with Grant and Stanton at this time. Among other things, Banks falsely claims his campaign was a great success, because it forced the Confederates to give up all plans to recapture Arkansas and invade Missouri.

[468] Winter, p. 362.

[469] Johnson, p. 223.

Despite being hard pressed, A. J. Smith's gorillas burned every building they came across, even slave cabins, corn cribs, outhouses, and the homes of free blacks, of which there were many on the Isle Breville. Lieutenant Colonel Francis Richard Lubbock, a former governor of Texas and a member of Wharton's staff, later wrote: "The demoralized enemy in their retreat left no houses or fences, stock or supplies, behind them. Everything of any possible value was taken or destroyed."[470]

Elias P. Pellet of the 114th New York Volunteers agreed with Lubbock when he recalled: "Destruction and desolation followed on the trail of the retreating column. At night, the burning buildings mark our pathway. As far as the eye can reach, we see in front new fires breaking out, and in the rear the dying embers tell the tale of war. Hardly a building is left unharmed ...

"The wanton and useless destruction of property has well earned [A J Smith's] command a lasting disgrace ... In order that the stigma of rendering houseless and homeless innocent women and children, may not rest upon us, be it recorded that not only the Commanders of the army, but our Division and Brigade commanders have issued orders reprobating it, and threatening offenders with instant death."[471]

Rev. James K. Ewer of the 3rd Massachusetts Cavalry recalled that "the country was in flames. Smith's men made a clean sweep. Buildings were burning on every hand."[472]

To deprive both Rebels and civilians of food and water, wells were fouled and animals were shot, including cows, calves, hogs, horses, chickens, and mules. Houses, barns, corn cribs, smokehouses, chicken coups, cotton gins, and Negro cabins were all burned.[473]

---

[470] Francis R. Lubbock, *Six Decades in Texas*, C.W. Raines, ed. (Austin, Texas: 1900), p. 540. Lubbock (1815-1905) was governor from 1861 to 1863, succeeding Sam Houston and Edward Clark. After being narrowly defeated for re-election, he joined the army and became a staff officer. He served as state treasurer from 1878 to 1891.

[471] Pellet, pp. 225, 229.

[472] Ewer, pp. 166-168.

[473] Jefferson Davis Bragg, *Louisiana in the Confederacy* (Baton Rouge: 1941), p. 171; O.R., Vol. XXXIV, Part 1, p. 581.

General Taylor recalled bitterly: "In pursuit, we passed the smoking ruins of homesteads, by which stood weeping women and children. Time for the removal of the most necessary articles of furniture had been refused. It was difficult to restrain one's inclination to punish the ruffians engaged in this work; but they asserted, and doubtless with truth, that they were acting under orders."[474]

Taylor blamed only A. J. Smith's gorillas for these outrages. The Eastern troops were more humane and disciplined, and some of them actually tried to protect the citizens from such acts.[475]

As the Northern vanguard raced down the road toward Monett's Ferry, they found that the Rebels were there already. They felled trees across the road to delay the wagons, and these had to be removed before the main body of the column could proceed. General Birge would not allow them to delay him, however. He pushed the Union vanguard forward as rapidly as possible because he knew the importance of reaching Monett's Ferry before the Secessionists. He covered more than 40 miles in just over 20 hours. When he arrived at the ferry on the morning of April 23, however, he found that the Confederate cavalry had arrived before him.

Taylor now had Polignac holding the crossing site south of Cloutierville, Liddell held the Red River crossing site at Calhoun's Landing (now Colfax, Louisiana), Bee held Monett's Ferry with 1,600 men and four batteries of artillery, and Wharton was cutting up the rearguard (A. J. Smith's XVI Corps), so there was no easy way off the Isle Breville.

The Union army was surrounded.

*

---

474 Taylor, p. 193.
475 Taylor, p. 193.

Confederate Order Of Battle, Monett's Ferry April 23, 1864

Cavalry Corps: Brigadier General Hamilton P. Bee

Major's Cavalry Division: Brigadier General James P. Major

    Lane's Brigade: Colonel George W. Baylor

        1st Texas Partisan Rangers: Lieutenant Colonel R. P. Crump

        2nd Texas Partisan Rangers: Colonel Isham Chisum

        2nd Arizona Cavalry: Lieutenant Colonel John W. Mullen

        3rd Arizona Cavalry: Lieutenant Colonel George T. Madison

    Bagby's Brigade: Brigadier General Arthur P. Bagby

        4th Texas Cavalry: Colonel William P. Hardeman

        5th Texas Cavalry: Major Hugh A. McPhaill

        7th Texas Cavalry: Lieutenant Colonel Gustave Hoffmann

        13th Texas Cavalry Battalion: Lieutenant Colonel Edward Waller, Jr.

    Debray's Brigade: Colonel Xavier B. Debray

        23rd Texas Cavalry: Colonel Nicholas C. Gould

        26th Texas Cavalry: Lieutenant Colonel John L. Meyers

        32nd Texas Cavalry: Colonel Peter C. Woods

    Buchel's Brigade: Colonel Alexander W. Terrell

        1st Texas Cavalry: Lieutenant Colonel William O. Yager

34th (37th) Texas Cavalry: Terrell

Table 10.1 Confederate Order of Battle, Monett's Ferry, April 23, 1864

Monett's Ferry was the only place south of Cloutierville the Cane could be forded in normal times. It was an easy position to defend. A high bluff overlooked the fording point, and here Bee deployed his artillery and most of his men: Brigadier General James P. Major's cavalry division. Table 10.1 shows the Confederate Order of Battle.

To the right of Bee's main position lay a high, abrupt bank which could not be scaled. Like most of the rest of the area, it was covered with woods and thick undergrowth. Brigadier General Arthur P. Bagby's brigade overlooked this sector.[476] On his left flank lay more difficult, woody, hilly terrain and a swamp. This sector was defended by a veteran Indian fighter and former Texas Ranger, Colonel George W. Baylor. Bee also sent Terrell's brigade to Beasley's plantation to defend his supply base—a move for which he was justifiably criticized later, especially in light of the fact that both Taylor and Wharton emphatically impressed upon him the need to hold the ferry at all costs. Sending off his only significant reserves was not a responsible act.

The Confederate Cavalry Corps commander, Hamilton Prioleau Bee, was the older brother of Brigadier General Barnard E. Bee, who gave Thomas Jonathan Jackson his famous sobriquet "Stonewall" during the 1st Battle of Manassas (Bull Run), just before he was mortally wounded.[477] Hamilton was born in Charleston, South Carolina, but moved to Texas with his parents as a boy. He was secretary of the U.S.-Texas Boundary Commission and secretary of

---

476   Arthur Pendleton Bagby (1833-1921) was the son of governor and U.S. senator Arthur P. Bagby of Alabama. He graduated from West Point in 1852 and served in the infantry in New York and Texas. He resigned in 1853 and practiced law with his father in Mobile until 1858, when he returned to Texas. He joined the Confederate Army as a major in the 7th Texas Mounted Volunteers and fought in New Mexico. Promoted to colonel in November 1862, he was accused of drunkenness on duty but was acquitted by a court-martial, in spite of the evidence. He distinguished himself at Galveston, Berwick Bay (where he was shot in the arm on April 13, 1863) and at Mansfield. Kirby Smith, who thought Bagby was "brilliant," assigned him to duty as a brigadier general on April 13, 1864 and as a major general on May 16, 1865. He was never nominated to either rank by President Davis, and he was never confirmed to general officer rank by the Confederate Senate. After the war, he settled in Halletsville, Texas, and established a prosperous law practice. Allardice, *Generals*, pp. 24-25.

477   Barnard Elliott Bee commanded the South Carolina brigade at the First Manassas and was mortally wounded on July 21, 1861. He died the next day.

the Texas Senate before serving in the Mexican War as a lieutenant in the Texas Rangers. He later served in the Texas legislature, where he became speaker of the house. Bee was elected brigadier general in the Texas Militia in 1861 and was named brigadier general in the Confederate army in March 1862. He was commandant of Brownsville until he was called to Louisiana and had little experience in commanding troops; he nevertheless succeeded the late General Green as commander of the Cavalry Corps on April 12. Richard Taylor did not think highly of him because he was a Kirby Smith man, and Bee's stock plunged even lower with Taylor when Bee agreed with Kirby Smith's decision to send Churchill's and Walker's infantry to Arkansas.[478]

Early on the morning of April 23, after a sleepless night, the head of Banks' column reached Monett's Ferry, halted on the north side of the Cane River, and opened up on Bee's positions. Hearing the firing, Nathaniel Banks galloped to the scene with part of his staff to see what was happening. The sizable group of mounted men attracted the attention of the Rebel gunners. One spent shell fragment struck Banks' boot and fell to the ground. Banks calmly asked an aide to hand him the piece of shrapnel before he rode away.[479]

Meanwhile, Major General William Franklin, the commander of the XIX Corps, nursed a painful wound since Mansfield, and the retreat aggravated it further. Unable to go on, he turned command over to Brigadier General William H. Emory. Brigadier General James W. McMillan took charge of Emory's division.

At 4:30 a.m., the Union cavalry and the advanced elements of Emory's division probed the Confederate defenses and were quickly checked. The Yankees could see that the Southerners were in a strong position and were well supported by their horse artillery. Even so, the ferry simply had to be taken if the Army of the Gulf was to continue to exist. Emory ordered his men to advance into the open ground north of the ferry. They were checked within minutes by heavy artillery fire and

---

478   Parrish, p. 379.
479   Hollandsworth, p. 198.

scurried back to the relative safety of the woods. The general realized immediately that this position was too strong to attack frontally. He had to find an alternative crossing point.

Meanwhile, the spirits of many Northern soldiers lagged. They heard Rebel cannon fire to their front and gunfire to their rear, where Wharton—clearly a better general than Whiskey Smith—was pinning down or forcing back an entire Union infantry corps with a handful of Texas cavalrymen. (Banks, in fact, asked Smith for reinforcements to help Emory break out at Monett's Ferry. A. J. Smith replied that he could not spare even a brigade. His entire infantry corps was pinned down by a single cavalry brigade, which he outnumbered about 6 to 1.) The Yankees did not know how few men Taylor had, but they knew that they were surrounded and that the Rebels were better led at the higher levels than they. Emory also knew that, if Union morale collapsed, the end of their weapon was in sight. He ordered Colonel E. J. Davis to take his cavalry brigade and scout to the left. He commanded Brigadier General Henry W. Birge to do the same on the right. A crossing—any crossing—had to be found!

They were saved by a local African American woman. History does not record her name, which is good, because the Ku Klux Klan would have roasted her alive after the war, had her identity became common knowledge. She guided Birge to a spot two miles below Monett's Ferry, where men could cross the Cane in time of low water. The place was not defended by the Confederates, and the hills and woods shielded it from their view. The boys of the 13th Connecticut waded across, holding their muskets above their heads. A group of their NCOs did not want to get wet, so they took a canoe and tried to paddle over; however, the canoe tipped over in midstream and the sergeants were completely immersed, much to the delight of the other enlisted men.[480]

Birge's command on April 23 included the 2nd and 3rd Brigades of Grover's division; the remains of the XIII Corps Detachment, now under Cameron; and Colonel Francis Fessenden's brigade of

---

[480] Homer B. Sprague, *History of the 13th Infantry Regiment of Connecticut Volunteers* (Hartford, Connecticut: 1867), pp. 195-196 (hereafter cited as "Sprague").

Colonel Francis Fessenden.

Emory's division. After crossing the Cane uncontested, the Union troops advanced south and southeast, through dry woodland which would be a swamp in normal years. After pushing forward perhaps a mile, through thick woods, undergrowth, ravines, and hills, they ran into Confederate skirmishers. They found that the Rebel left flank was well protected by a deep lake and a marsh. The right flank of the enemy facing them was covered by a deep ravine. Only the center seemed to offer any hope of success, and even here, the Rebels held the high ground. To make matters worse, one of the few cleared fields in the area lay directly in front of the Confederate position. The bluecoats would have to charge straight across it to get at the enemy.

Monett's Ferry And The Retreat To Alexandria

Birge delegated the planning of the battle to Francis Fessenden. Although he owed his rank to his father's political connections (William Pitt Fessenden was a U.S. senator and would soon become Lincoln's secretary of the treasury), young Fessenden was not without military ability.[481] He placed his brigade on the right and Birge's four regiments on the left, with Cameron's Division in reserve. He then ordered a bayonet attack right across the open field. "Come on, boys!" a Connecticut lieutenant shouted. "The paymaster is on the other side of the hill!"[482]

Fessenden's attack was met by the tough Colonel George W. Baylor, who killed and scalped several braves in this youth.[483] Baylor had mixed two regiments of Arizona and Texas cavalry and two battalions of Texas partisan rangers, supported by a battery of artillery. Union losses were heavy and all they succeeded in doing was to push the Rebels back to the next hill line. Colonel Fessenden was among the casualties. He was so badly wounded that one of his legs had to be amputated. Command of the brigade devolved upon Lieutenant Colonel J. W. Blanchard of the 162nd New York.

The 13th Connecticut and the 1st (Union) Louisiana, spearheaded by a detachment of cavalry, became the vanguard, and they set out in pursuit of Colonel Baylor. But Baylor was not retreating. They soon ran into an ambush. The cavalry was routed and General

---

481   Francis Fessenden was born in Portland, Maine, in 1839. He graduated from Bowdoin College, studied law at Harvard, and was practicing in Maine when the war began. Appointed captain in the 19th U.S. Infantry, he was wounded at Shiloh. After he recovered, Fessenden was given command of the 25th Maine, which was part of the Washington garrison. He assumed command of the 30th Maine in January 1864 and succeeded Lewis Benedict as brigade commander after he was killed at Pleasant Hill.

482   Sprague, p. 196.

483   George W. Baylor was born at Fort Gibson, Indian Territory, in 1832, the son of an army surgeon. He grew up on the frontier and in 1860, along with his brother and a couple of comrades, killed and scalped nine Indian raiders. He was commissioned first lieutenant in the 2nd Texas Cavalry in 1861 but resigned to become senior aide to General Albert Sidney Johnston. After Johnston was killed at Shiloh, Baylor returned to Texas as a lieutenant colonel, took part in the New Mexico campaign, and was elected colonel of the 2nd Arizona Cavalry. He was married and had two daughters. His brother, Colonel John R. Baylor, was governor of the Confederate Territory of Arizona, which included southern Arizona and southern New Mexico. He was also a member of the Confederate Congress.

Birge was swept back with the mob, but Colonel William Fiske of the 1st Louisiana bravely rallied part of his regiment and the 13th Connecticut. From the north bank of the Cane, General Emory took a hand in the battle by concentrating his artillery fire on Baylor's positions. Baylor sent Bee a message, asking for two regiments of reinforcements and requesting counterbattery fire against Emory's guns. Hamilton Bee, however, already decided that the battle was lost. "The critical moment had come," he reported later, "the position turned on both flanks, and a large force close in the front ready to spring on the center."[484] He ordered a general retreat and instructed Baylor to extricate himself as best he could.

Bee's report was inaccurate in every respect. It is true that he received word that the Federals were crossing the Cane on his right, but the report was false. Not one Yankee crossed the river there, and it did not occur to him to have someone check out the validity of this rumor. Also, Emory was not about to attack across the Cane River into the heart of the Rebel defenses. His men would have been slaughtered if he had, and he knew it. Only on the Confederate left flank was there any trouble, and even it was holding. Baylor inflicted six casualties on the Northerners for every one he suffered, and the Union army was still not in possession of a single road out of the Isle Breville. (The Confederates suffered only 50 casualties at Monett's Ferry. Banks lost more than 300 men and several wagons. Bee lost no wagons.) But now General Bee let the cork out of the bottle. He retreated to Beasley's Plantation, 20 miles to the south, on the Fort Jessup Road. Baylor skillfully extricated his men from the action and joined the retreat.

When he realized what was happening, Emory tried to take advantage of the situation and inflict some casualties on the Confederates. He sent three cavalry brigades in pursuit, but they mistook a small Rebel cavalry detachment for Bee's main body and chased it for miles—down the wrong road, so the Confederate Cavalry Corps suffered no more damage.

---

[484] O.R., Vol. XXXIV, Part 1, p. 611.

Dick Taylor held Bee responsible for Banks' escape. And it is true that the Battle of Monett's Ferry was badly handled from the Confederate point of view. Bee should not have sent any forces to Beasley's Plantation, much less Terrell's entire brigade, especially in light of the fact that General Taylor already sent a detachment to guard the place. He also failed to dig in or construct breastworks; failed to improve his position in any way; was deceived by Union demonstrations against his center and right; failed to reinforce Baylor; failed to launch a counterattack; and retreated prematurely. He also did not take cognizance of the fact that both Taylor and Wharton stressed that the position must be held at all costs. After examining the facts, General Taylor relieved Bee of his command three weeks later. He commented later that Bee "displayed great personal gallantry, but no generalship."[485] Taylor also believed that, if at Monett's Ferry he had the three divisions Kirby Smith took with him to Arkansas, he could probably have destroyed the entire Union army. It would be difficult to contradict him on this point.

In any case, after Bee fled, a U.S.C.T. (United States' Colored Troops) engineer brigade constructed a pontoon bridge over the Cane at Monett's Ferry shortly after night descended on April 23.[486] The crossing continued all night and into the next day. The last Union rearguard crossed at 2 p.m., closely pursued (as usual) by Wharton's cavalry.

And so Nathaniel P. Banks wiggled out of Richard Taylor's noose for the second time. Taylor was furious at Kirby Smith, but he put that behind him for the time being. The "might have beens" could be discussed later. At the moment, Dick Taylor was only outnumbered slightly more than 5 to 1, so he took what was for him a characteristic step: he decided to surround the enemy and destroy him. This time, the battlefield would be the area around Alexandria.

*

---

485   Winters, p. 365.

486   The Engineer Brigade was commanded by Colonel George D. Robinson. It included the 97th and 99th Engineer Regiments, U.S.C.T.

With Monett's Ferry behind them, the soldiers of the Army of the Gulf made rapid progress. Its vanguards reached Alexandria on April 25. It left behind a trail of devastation. Taylor reported: "The destruction of this country by the enemy exceeds anything in history. For many miles every dwelling-house, every negro cabin, every cotton-gin, every corn-crib, and even chicken-houses have been burned to the ground; every fence torn down and the fields torn up by the hoofs of horses and wheels of wagons. Many hundreds of persons are utterly without shelter. But for our prompt attacks Natchitoches would have been burned to the ground, and also the little village of Cloutierville."[487]

Governor Allen reported: "They sacked private dwellings ... they grossly and indecently ... insulted the unprotected females ... They shattered crockery, glass-ware, and mirrors, strewing the floor with their fragments ... they dashed to pieces and burned for fuel costly articles of furniture ..." They violated tombs "and stripped the dead," they "fired volleys into peaceful citizens" and even "robbed negroes of watches, food, money, etc."[488]

Some of the bluecoats were also embarrassed by the behavior of the Union Army. Captain Sprague of the 13th Connecticut wrote: "With sorrow and shame it must be recorded that our march was lit up at night with conflagration of buildings burnt by our stragglers. Large rewards were offered by General Banks for the conviction of the perpetrators of those outrages."[489]

---

487 O.R., Vol. XXXIV, Part 1, p. 581.

488 Allen, *The Conduct of Federal Troops*, pp. 13-14, 22-69.

489 Sprague, p. 202. Captain Homer B. Sprague (1829-1918) was married to Antoinette Pardee, heiress to the Winchester Rifle fortune. He was a fervent abolitionist. Sprague joined the 13th Connecticut when it was formed after the First Manassas in 1861. He fought at Labadieville, Irish Bend, Port Hudson, Cane River, the Shenandoah Valley, and other battles and campaigns. He was promoted to lieutenant colonel after the Red River campaign and was captured at Winchester on September 19, 1864. He was in various prisons until April 1865. Highly educated, Sprague served as head of several institutes of higher education, including the University of North Dakota, after the war. He was for a time a professor at Cornell.

Richard Taylor was also angry and not just at the arsonists. He was mad at General Edmund Kirby Smith, this time for taking two siege guns from Brigadier General St. John R. Liddell on the north side of the Red. He was also angry that he took a portion of Liddell's command with him to Arkansas.[490]

On April 27, Taylor received a copy of Kirby Smith's proclamation, congratulating the army for its victories at Mansfield and Pleasant Hill. Taylor himself was not mentioned. The general took this as a personal insult. Taylor wrote Kirby Smith and commented that it was the first time a commanding general was ignored in a victory proclamation, but it was consistent with Kirby Smith's treatment of him.[491]

Taylor was physically ill when he wrote that. His rheumatoid arthritis was acting up again, and he had a low-grade fever. The next day, he wrote Kirby Smith and told him that, had he been given his way, "By this time ... I would have been on my way with the bulk of my army to join Price at Camden, enriched with captured spoils of a great army and fleet; Steele would have been brushed from our path as a cobweb before the broom of a housemaid; we would have reached St. Louis, our objective point, by midsummer and relieved the pressure from our suffering brethren in Virginia and Georgia. All this is true as the living God ... You might have had all the glory."[492] He submitted his resignation on April 28, effective "as soon as it can be done without injury to the service."[493]

Kirby Smith received Taylor's letter of resignation on May 8. He was taken aback but displayed his usual tolerance, calling the Taylor letter "not only improper but unjust." He returned it to Taylor, stating that it must have been written "in a moment of irritation or sickness."[494]

But Taylor meant it, as we shall see.

---

490 Parrish, p. 380.
491 O.R., Vol. XXXIV, Part 1, pp. 541-543.
492 O.R., Vol. XXXIV, Part 1, pp. 541-542.
493 O.R., Vol. XXXIV, Part 1, p. 543.
494 O.R., Vol. XXXIV, Part 1, p. 543.

*

What was happening to the Union fleet while Banks' army was fighting for its life at Monett's Ferry? It also was having more than its share of problems.

The fleet began to fall back on April 16, with the *Eastport* in the lead. It was the pride of the inland fleet—a side-wheeled steamer, 280 feet long, approximately 50 feet at the beam, and armed with four 9-inch Dahlgren smoothbores, two rifled 60-pounder Dahlgrens, and two 100-pounder Parrott guns. It drew six feet three inches of water.[495] Four weeks before, the CSS *Missouri* retreated from Alexandria to Shreveport. On the way, it lay six torpedoes (mines) below the ferry at Grand Ecore. The *Eastport* now found one of them with its hull. The explosion was so muffled that few of the sailors knew what happened. The water, nevertheless, poured in rapidly, and the leak could not be stopped. The river was so low, however, that much of the *Eastport* was still above water when it settled on the soft bed of the river. Unfortunately for the Yankees, she blocked the channel. Porter and the captain, Lieutenant Commander Seth Ledyard Phelps, had two choices: blow up the *Eastport* or refloat her. They decided to refloat and patch her. This involved removing her guns and other equipment to make her lighter. The officers and men of the crew and the pump boat/transport *Champion No. 5*, went to work immediately, and the *Eastport* was finally refloated on April 21.

The Red River, meanwhile, continued to fall. This puzzled the Union naval officers. They had no way of knowing that they had fallen into the most brilliant trap yet laid by William Robertson Boggs, the great military engineer and chief of staff of the Trans-Mississippi Department. He blew up the Hotchkiss Dam, causing about three-quarters of the Red River to flow into the Tones Bayou channel and then into Bayou Pierre and the bayou's floodplain, a bowl which was

---

495 W. Craig Gaines, *Encyclopedia of Civil War Shipwrecks* (Baton Rouge: 2008), pp. 63-64 (hereafter cited as "Gaines"); O.R.N., Vol. XXVI, pp. 62-63, 68, 79, 110, 167-170.

19 miles in diameter.[496] Simply put, if Boggs could not stop the fleet any other way, he would remove the river—or at least most of it. This is why the Red River fell so suddenly, why it stubbornly refused to rise in the spring of 1864, and why Admiral Porter steamed into such serious trouble.

Meanwhile, accompanied by most of the inland fleet, the *Eastport* continued to bounce along the sandy bottom of the Red, still taking on water and running aground or getting stuck on snags eight more times. It made only 20 miles in six days.[497] It grounded on a sand bar on April 22 and could not be freed until the next day. After traveling less than five miles, it grounded again on April 24. It took another day and a half before it could be freed. On April 26, it traveled less than two miles before it grounded yet again. This time, it stuck fast. Hampered by numerous Southern snipers, the combined efforts of the *Fort Hindman*, *Champion No. 3*, and *Champion No. 5* were not enough to free her. With the water level still dropping, Admiral Porter felt he had no choice: he ordered that the *Eastport* be blown up. The sailors placed a ton and a half of gunpowder and tried to detonate it electronically. When this failed to work, Porter had the magazines packed with cotton and tar. (There was always plenty of cotton aboard the Union boats.) Captain Phelps personally applied the match, and the *Eastport* was ripped apart by seven explosions.[498] Its location is currently known, and perhaps one day it will be exhumed, but it is presently under more than 30 feet of sand and silt.

Porter and Captain Phelps were the last to leave the stricken vessel. They were nearly killed by falling debris, which splashed all around the admiral's launch. The debris also landed close enough to frighten several Rebels on shore.

Meanwhile, Brigadier General Prince Camille de Polignac arrived at Monett's Ferry, and Southern scouts informed him that a Union gunboat (the *Eastport*) ran aground. At 2 a.m. on April

---

496 Joiner, *Howling Wilderness*, pp. 69-70.
497 Hollandsworth, p. 199.
498 Porter, *Anecdotes*, p. 239.

26, he dispatched Colonel James Harrison's 15th Texas Cavalry to investigate. After a gallop of 18 miles, Harrison found Polignac's gunboat, along with two other ironclads, two transports which were fitted with guns and another transport, all trying to free the *Eastport*. The sailors were clearly not expecting visitors. Some were sunning themselves on deck, while others were plundering a nearby residence. Harrison led his men through the woods and managed to get within 100 yards of the bank without being seen. It was 9 a.m. when he started a battle by selecting a "portly" captain and personally firing the first shot. The officer tumbled out of his chair "like a Turtle off a log." Then the entire regiment opened up. "Such consternation I never saw," Harrison recalled later. Union shells fell in all directions, above and below the Texans, who dropped to the ground and began firing deliberately. The last efforts to free the *Eastport* were made under enemy fire. When the *Eastport* blew up, timbers fell 200 yards behind the bank. Harrison lost one man killed and five men wounded in the engagement.[499]

His appetite whetted by this victory, Polignac (who was promoted to major general effective April 8) decided that he wanted to sink more Union gunboats. He sent Colonel Caudle and his 34th Texas Cavalry (Dismounted) to set up another ambush at the mouth of the Cane River, 15 miles below the spot Harrison had used. Caudle's 200 dismounted cavalrymen were accompanied by the St. Mary's Cannoneers (the 1st Louisiana Volunteer Battery), which was commanded by a brilliant young Cajun gunner, Captain Florian O. Cornay. This battery was mustered in when the war began but was captured when Fort Jackson surrendered shortly after the fall of New Orleans in April 1862. Its men were exchanged by September and fought in all of Dick Taylor's battles since then. They succeeded in cutting off the Mississippi Squadron's rearguard—the five boats Admiral Porter used when he attempted to free the *Eastport*. They would have to run a gauntlet of Rebel fire to escape.

---

499   Kinard, p. 160.

Porter's flagship, the USS Cricket

Since leaving the ruins of the *Eastport*, Porter traveled 15 miles downriver without incident. Then five miles above the confluence of the Red and the Cane, Cornay opened up on the boats. Admiral Porter's flagship, the sternwheel tinclad *Cricket*, was the first in line. The fire was so precise and rapid that the admiral later reported he was attacked by 18 guns. Actually there were four—two brass 12-pounder howitzers and two 24-pounder howitzers. The fire was so accurate and devastating that the *Cricket* was hit 38 times in five minutes. A shell knocked out the *Cricket*'s aft gun, killing the entire gun crew. Porter replaced them with contrabands.[500] Another shot

---

[500] The term "contrabands" was invented by Union General "Spoons" Butler in New Orleans in 1862. It is basically equivalent to the term "Untermenschen" or "subhumans," which the Nazis used in World War II to describe Jews and other groups they considered ethnically or racially inferior. The Confederates never used this term to describe people.

blew away the forward gun. A third struck the fire room, where the stokers kept the steam pressure up for the boilers. Only one man in that room survived. Admiral Porter personally took charge of the boat. After impressing willing African-Americans into the navy as gunners, he rushed to the engine room and, finding the chief engineer dead, ordered his deputy to take charge and keep the steam pressure up, again using former slaves as necessary. Porter then ran to the pilot house, where he found the pilot wounded and the rest of the bridge crew hiding from Cornay's guns. The admiral took charge of the bridge and drifted past the Rebel battery, which scored several more hits in the process. The *Cricket* was badly damaged, and half of its men were casualties, but at least it escaped.[501]

Next in the Union line was *Champion No. 3* (*New Champion*), a 195-ton side wheel steamer that was a combination tug, pump boat, and transport. It was loaded with 175 African-Americans—former slaves who were taken from upriver plantations, many against their will. One of Cornay's shells hit the boiler, which exploded and scalded 100 contrabands to death. All but three of the remainder died within 24 hours.[502] "The inhumanity of exposing these unarmed people to disaster rests with the Federal commanders," Marie Bankston later wrote.[503] General Taylor agreed with her,[504] and they have a point: transporting unarmed civilians into a combat zone is not a responsible act. Apparently ashamed of the part the navy played in the deaths of these innocents, Admiral Porter did not mention the incident in his report

Captain Stewart and three crewmen were also killed in the explosion. The remainder of the crew abandoned the ship, which sank but was later raised by the Rebels. Only 15 people aboard the *Champion No. 3* survived the battle.[505]

---

501   Porter, *Naval History*, pp. 523-524; O.R.N., Vol. XXVI, pp. 74, 167-169; 176, 781-786.
502   O.R.N., Vol. XXVI, pp. 74-75.
503   Bankston, p. 156.
504   Taylor, p. 223. The general put the total at 187.
505   Gaines, p. 61; Johnson, p. 239;

Next in line was the USS *Juliet*, a stern-wheeled 157-ton tinclad, armed with six 24-pounder howitzers. Cornay's gunfire hit a steam pipe and covered the vessel with steam. More seriously, it cut the tillers, disabling it completely. Yankee sailors reacted swiftly and bravely. They lashed the *Juliet* to *Champion No. 5* and towed her upstream out of range of the Confederate artillery. This left three vessels (the *Juliet*, *Champion No. 5* and *Fort Hindman*) trapped above the Rebel batteries.[506]

Meanwhile, shortly after getting out of range of the Southern gunners, the *Cricket* ran aground, and it took several hours to free her. Fortunately, the Confederates did not know it, or the Union would have lost another vessel as well as one of its more distinguished admirals.

The rest of the inland fleet was also having its problems. Downriver, another four-gun battery under Captain Thomas O. Benton, C.S.A., took up positions on De Loach's Bluff and severely cut up the USS *Lexington*.

As a result of all this, Admiral Porter decided that he could not risk trying to help the three vessels trapped above Cornay's guns. They were on their own.

The USS *Fort Hindman* was a 286-ton side-wheeled tinclad, armed with two 8-inch smoothbores and four 8-inch guns. It was commanded by Lieutenant Selfridge, but the senior officer aboard was Captain Phelps, formerly of the *Eastport*, who had command over all three vessels. Rather than take the risk of running aground in the dark, he decided to run the gauntlet after sunrise on April 27, with the *Fort Hindman* towing the *Juliet*.

The first attempt was aborted because the *Juliet* hit a snag which punctured her hull. The mini-flotilla steamed back upstream, made hasty and temporary repairs, and tried again. Captain Cornay waited until they were within 500 yards and opened up with a heavy and typically accurate fire. The *Juliet* was badly damaged again, as was

---

506 O.R.N., Vol. XXVI, pp. 75, 167, 169, 177.

the *Fort Hindman*, whose tiller ropes were cut. Both tinclads drifted downstream out of control. They were extremely lucky to miss the wreck of *Champion No. 3* and not run aground.

The *Champion No. 5* was not so fortunate. Now without the cover of the tinclads, the Rebel gunners pounded her to bits. The pilothouse was smashed, the pilot was wounded, and the vessel was so badly damaged that it also drifted out of control. It ran aground on the left bank, directly across from the Rebel battery. To remain aboard meant almost certain death. The crew abandoned ship and took to the woods. Most of its survivors were picked up by Caudle's Texans. The steamer itself sank with the hurricane deck and boiler below the water.[507]

The entire effort to save the *Eastport* was a minor disaster for the U.S. Navy. It was also a mistake, as David D. Porter later admitted. He risked five ships to save the *Eastport* and lost two of them as well as the *Eastport*, and the other three were badly shot up. The Confederates lost one rifleman wounded and one artillery officer killed. He was Captain Cornay, who was slain near the end of the fighting.[508] He was succeeded by Captain Minos T. Gordy.

---

507   Gaines, pp. 61-62.

508   Taylor, p. 184.

Chapter XI

Over The Falls

On April 24, 1864, Banks' army was retreating toward Alexandria at a very rapid pace. As they marched, they sang a song to the tune of "When Johnny Comes Marching Home." It went:

> But Taylor and Smith with ragged ranks,
>
> For Bales, For Bales
>
> But Taylor and Smith with ragged ranks
>
> For Bales, Says I
>
> But Taylor and Smith with ragged ranks,
>
> Burned up the cotton and whipped Old Banks
>
> And we'll drink stone blind,
>
> Johnny fill up the bowl![509]

---

509 Robert L. Kerby, *Kirby Smith's Confederacy* (New York: 1972; reprint ed., Tuscaloosa, Alabama: 1991), p. 318.

Another version went:

> In Eighteen Hundred and Sixty-Four
>
> Foot Balls, Foot Balls!
>
> In Eighteen Hundred and Sixty-Four
>
> Foot Balls, Says I,
>
> In Eighteen Hundred and Sixty-Four
>
> We all skedaddled to Grand Ecore,
>
> And we'll drink stone blind,
>
> Johnny fill up the bowl!

Behind them, they left desolation. One Union cavalryman wrote:

> ... the country was in flames. Smith's men were burning on every hand. Dense clouds of smoke could be seen by the rear guard as they fell back.[510]

Trooper Foster of the 32nd Texas Cavalry recalled: "Wherever Banks' army passed through, it was pure desolation. Every house, even the negro cabins, were burned down. The cattle, mules, hogs, any livestock, were driven away or shot. If a well was close, the carcasses were thrown into the well to spoil the water. Many of the people ... . depended on rain water cisterns made of cypress wood. The Yankees shot these full of holes to force the people to drink out of the streams or fouled wells. Many deaths were caused by bad drinking water."[511]

---

[510] Ewen, p. 166.

[511] Duaine, p. 75.

A Texas soldier wrote of the women and children: "Their tear stained faces were heart-rending. We reflected that war seemed to fall heaviest on the innocent and helpless."[512]

General Franklin, for one, was not pleased. On April 27, he issued a General Orders No. 43, which stated:

> The advance of this army in its march from Grand Ecore to this place having been accompanied by indiscriminate marauding and incendiarism, disgraceful to the army of a civilized nation, and no clue having hitherto been found by which the guilty parties can be detected, a reward of $500 is hereby offered for such evidence as will convict the accused of incendiarism before a general court-martial, to be paid to the person furnishing the evidence upon the conviction of the accused.
>
> By order of Major-General Franklin
>
> Wickham Hoffman
>
> Assistant Adjutant General[513]

Despite the devastation, there were acts of mercy. Members of the 32nd Texas Cavalry caught a soldier in a Confederate uniform hiding in the bushes. They took him into custody, questioned him, and as soon as he opened his mouth, they knew he was from New England. It turned out that he was separated from his unit since Mansfield but had followed Taylor's advancing army. After the Battle of Pleasant Hill, he had found a dead Confederate and took his clothes. This was almost a fatal mistake, as now he could legally be hanged or shot as a spy. This, in fact, is what half the regiment wanted to do to him. Others wanted to show compassion; the boy was only 18 years old.

---

512   Duaine, p. 75.
513   O.R., Vol. XXXIV, Part 3, p. 307.

Captain Dye, the commander of Company E, did not want to execute the young man, so he ordered Troopers Foster and Wiley Franklin to guard him. These two men also advocated showing mercy. They let him escape and deliberately fired shots over his head, instead of into his back, as he fled. "No good man enjoys shooting another to satisfy a rule," Foster wrote later. Only after the war did it occur to Foster and Franklin that their captain turned the prisoner over to them in hopes they would act exactly as they did.[514]

*

The vanguard of Banks' army arrived in Alexandria during the afternoon of April 25, while the rear of the column entered the city's defensive perimeter the next day. A. J. Smith received an ovation from his men; his standing with them rose risen considerably since his counterattack saved the army at Pleasant Hill.

When Banks arrived at his new headquarters, he found that his new chief of staff, General Dwight, arranged a magnificent dinner for him, complete with fine champagne. The former speaker of the house invited his senior officers to join him, and by the end of the evening, Banks, Mower, and A. J. Smith got drunk together and were expressing their admiration for each other. (Smith in particular had nothing but contempt for Banks before the corks popped.)[515]

After the Union generals sobered up the next day, however, they found that they were in another Dick Taylor trap. Alexandria was ringed by two lines of entrenchments, complete with bunkers, redoubts, abaits, breastworks, forts, and fortifications. The 1st Brigade of Grover's division arrived from Carrollton, Louisiana, on April 18, and eight days later, McClernand arrived from Texas to take charge of the XIII Corps. He brought with him Brigadier General

---

514   Duaine, pp. 75-76.
515   Johnson, pp. 235-236.

Michael Lawler's brigade (the 16th and 114th Ohio, the 34th Iowa, and the 47th, 49th, and 69th Indiana Infantry Regiments, as well as the 1st Wisconsin Battery), bringing Banks' strength to around 33,500.[516]

General Banks also created more infantry by converting the 1st, 2nd, 3rd, 4th, and 5th Engineer Regiments, Corps d'Afrique, into infantry regiments U.S.C.T., numbered 95 to 99, respectively.[517]

Although Taylor was outnumbered 6 to 1 or more, he realized that the Yankees grossly overestimated his strength. He knew it would be impossible for him to defeat Banks' men by frontal attack; he, therefore, decided to starve them into submission. He kept constant pressure on them with cavalry probes and harassing fire, which generally kept them within their defensive perimeter. To deceive them as to his numbers, Taylor had drummers beating calls where there were no units. Buglers sounded assembly where there were no regiments to assemble. Camp fires could be seen everywhere beyond Federal lines, even though no troops warmed themselves there, other than the men who stoked the fires. Empty wagons rolled over fence rails, so the bluecoats knew the mysterious units were being resupplied, even though there was nothing to resupply. Southern cavalry under men like Wharton and Baylor screened the Rebel lines, so the Northerners could not investigate these sounds of war without running the risk of being shot. The Federals were fooled completely—even the enlisted men. They had no doubt that they were encircled by a major Confederate army, even though that army was 200 miles away, in Arkansas. The Yankees held Alexandria, but the Rebels controlled the countryside, which meant that they controlled the fodder. Taylor's men, meanwhile, removed all the livestock and harvested crops from the area, so any Union foraging parties that did venture out came up empty. "We will play the game the Russians played in the [French] retreat from Moscow," he wrote.[518] General Taylor intended for Mr. Lincoln's army to have two choices: abandon

---

516   As of April 30, 1864. Lawler's Brigade totaled 2,762 men. O.R., Vol. XXXIV, Part 3, pp. 294-296.

517   O.R., Vol. XXXIV, Part 3, p. 296.

518   O.R., Vol. XXXIV, Part 1, p. 589.

the fleet (which could not negotiate the Alexandria Falls) and flee across the Atchafalaya, or starve, in which case he would destroy both the army and the fleet.

Taylor divided his cavalry into three main detachments of 1,000 men each. Brigadier General William Steele held the sector above and west of Alexandria, including the roads along the river; General Bagby held the Boeuf Road sector south of Alexandria; and James Major roamed the sector from David's Ferry on the Red, 25 miles below Alexandria, and points east. Most of the area north of the Red was in the hands of Liddell's brigade, which kept the Yankees pinned down in the town of Pineville, just across the river from Alexandria. Taylor sent Vincent's brigade (the 2nd and 7th Louisiana Cavalry Regiments) on raids far to the south to discourage overland reinforcements from that direction or to provide them early warning if the Yankees tried that (which they did not). Vincent was in his element here. He raided southwest of New Orleans, where he burned the railroad bridges east of Berwick Bay and thoroughly disrupted U.S. communications and supplies.[519] Polignac's infantry was posted on the Bayou Bouef, where it could support either Bagby or Major as necessary.

Taylor now controlled almost all of Louisiana except the New Orleans and Baton Rouge areas. His cavalry ranged as far as Simmesport and Fort DeRussy. The Bayou Teche was clear of Yankees, and Confederate recruiting officers conducted successful campaigns even in the Plaquemines area, which was supposedly far behind Union lines.[520]

Around Alexandria, skirmishes happened every day. Now that the Yankees were in his noose, Taylor proceeded to tighten it. His plan was clearly working. "Taylor orchestrated a masterful exercise in deception and torment," Captain Eustace Surget, the adjutant of the Army of Western Louisiana, wrote to General Walker. "We

---

519 Hollandsworth, p. 200.

520 Johnson, p. 254.

have run the Yankees to earth in Alexandria, which our cavalry now surrounds on all sides and keeps the devils in a constant panic by shooting into their pickets every night at various points."[521]

Porter and A. J. Smith were worried that Banks might abandon the fleet to save his army. Banks promised that he would not, even if his men had to eat mule meat. Porter and Smith did not believe him, but Banks meant every word he said, as the admiral later admitted. And it almost came to that. Alexandria, Taylor wrote on May 10, is "as closely besieged as ever was Vicksburg." Banks' men were "disheartened, sullen, and disinclined to fight." He added that "All captured horses are like scarecrows and show want of forage. From present appearances the end is drawing near."[522]

Confederate soldiers were also hungry. Private W. R. Smith of the 12th Texas Cavalry recalled: "I remember that one of our mess[mates] slipped off to find something to eat and I gave five dollars and he paid it for a pone of corn bread, and it had a thin white crust on it but nevertheless was good." Smith recalled that he and his comrades had no tents. "We had to take the weather just as it came, sleep on the cold wet ground. It was rather hard but we stood it pretty well."[523]

Taylor felt it necessary to issue orders that he would not tolerate his men stealing food. Any officer who attempted to shield thieves would suffer personal consequences. Two men from the 19th Texas Cavalry were caught stealing food from civilians. Taylor had them court-martialed. They were executed on May 3.[524]

---

521 Parrish, p. 384, citing Walker, "Papers."
522 O.R., Vol. XXXIV, Part 1, p. 591.
523 Yeary, Vol. II, pp. 708-709. Smith was born in Aberdeen, Mississippi, in 1845, and enlisted in the Confederate Army in Bastrop, Texas, in 1863. He fought in every battle from Pleasant Hill to Yellow Bayou (see below).
524 Parrish, p. 384.

In Alexandria, General Banks was lonely and frightened. He wrote to his wife: "I have nobody to talk to, nobody to embrace. I am alone."[525] Clearly there would be no bold moves against the Rebels coming from this quarter.

As early as April 28, Banks wrote to Admiral Farragut and asked for more boats to keep the river open. On May 1, he ordered Brigadier General Frank S. Nickerson to take his brigade and travel by boat to Fort DeRussy, to help secure the Union hold on the river. He landed at Wilson's Plantation but was driven off by Rebel forces at Dunn's Bayou. Nickerson asked for reinforcements, but Banks ordered him to return to Alexandria instead.

That same day, at David's Ferry, 30 miles below Alexandria, the transport *Emma* was attacked by Captain John A. A. West's Grosse Tete Louisiana Battery, with sections now commanded by Lieutenants Yoist and W. H. Lyne,[526] which was supported by General Major and elements of his division. Lyne's gunners knocked out the transport's steering, and it drifted onto the southern bank, where it was captured and burned by Major's horsemen.

Three days later, on May 4, the transport *City Belle* was bound for Alexandria with 700 men from the 120th Ohio Volunteer Infantry Regiment on board. It was fired on by Yoist's guns with a particularly devastating effect, as it was crowded with infantry. It was forced to run aground and surrender to Major's cavalrymen. The decks were literally running red with blood. Dozens of Ohio infantrymen were killed or wounded, among them Colonel Mudd, the chief of McClernand's cavalry and a regimental commander, who died of his wounds. Three hundred soldiers and sailors were captured. They spent the rest of the war in Camp Ford.[527]

---

525   Hollandsworth, p. 200.
526   Joiner, p. 150; O.R., Vol. XXXIV, Part 1, p. 622.
527   O.R., Vol. XXXIV, Part 1, pp. 475, 622; Taylor, p. 186. The remnants of the 120th Ohio (i.e., those not aboard the *City Belle* or the *John Warner*) were absorbed by the 114th Ohio.

That same morning, the transport *John Warner* started downriver from Alexandria with the 56th Ohio on board. These men were mustered in in late 1861 and fought at Fort Donelson, Shiloh, Corinth, Helena, and the Vicksburg campaign, where they lost 135 of their comrades killed or wounded at Champion Hill alone. Also, they saw action at Mansfield, Pleasant Hill, and Monett's Ferry. Now they were on their way back home on veterans' furlough. Most of them, however, would spend their leave (and the rest of the war) at Camp Ford, Texas.

They were fired on almost as soon as they left Alexandria, but most of the bullets were stopped by the cotton bales which lined the deck. There always seemed to be plenty of cotton bales. Initially, the *John Warner* was escorted by the tinclad *Covington*, a side-wheeled 224-ton steamer. It had a 76-man crew and was armed with two 30-pounder rifled cannons, two 50-pounder rifles, and two 24-pounder smoothbores. That afternoon, the pair was joined by the tinclad *Signal No. 8*, a stern-wheeled 190-ton steamer. Not as well armored as the *Covington*, the *Signal* was a dispatch vessel and convoy escort, armed with two 30-pounder Parrott rifles, four 24-pounder howitzers, and two 12-pounder Dahlgreen rifled guns. On board the *Signal* was Lieutenant William Simpson of Banks' staff, who was carrying dispatches to Ulysses S. Grant.

The small flotilla traveled 20 miles and tied up for the night on the north bank. The next morning, the boats started out early, but their enemies were also up before sunrise. At 4:45 a.m., the *John Warner* rounded the point opposite Dunn's Bayou when it was struck by fire from two artillery pieces and the muskets of Colonel Baylor's Texans and Arizonians. Her rudders were disabled, and she ran into the bank some distance downstream. Dismounted Rebel cavalrymen fired a heavy volley into the boat from only 100 yards away. They were soon joined by another artillery detachment, which cut the transport to pieces. "... her desks soon became a slaughter pen for the 56th Ohio," Johnson wrote later.[528]

---

528 Johnson, p. 256.

USS Covington.

Trapped with no hope of escape, the transport and the Union infantry regiment surrendered. George P. Lord, the captain of the *Covington*, sent a detachment to burn the *John Warner*, even though this was against the rules of warfare. Colonel W. H. Raynor, the commander of the 56th Ohio, refused to allow it because 125 of his men lay dead or wounded on the decks.

By now, Baylor brought down the artillery from Dunn's Bayou and was blasting the tinclads. Captain Lord ordered Lieutenant Edward Morgan, the captain of the *Signal*, to accompany the *Covington* upriver, out of range. She just started when suddenly, she received direct hits to her port engine and steering gear from Lieutenant Lyne's guns. The *Covington* took her into tow, but just as they got underway, another Rebel shell cut the *Signal*'s port steam pipe. Thinking the boilers had exploded, the *Covington*'s crew cast off the tow line and headed upstream, abandoning the *Signal*. Then a shell hit her rudder and the *Covington* became unmanageable. Somehow, Lord reached the north bank, tied up the tinclad, and began firing broadsides with his port guns as well as his fore and aft guns. The Rebels continued pouring fire into the stricken boat until the *Covington* was riddled with shells. Lord fired until he was out of ammunition; then he spiked his guns, set the boat on fire, and abandoned ship. The survivors headed for Pineville, hoping they could reach Union lines before Liddell's cavalry found them. Thirty two of them eventually made it.

On the southern bank, Baylor's brigade concentrated their musket fire on the *Signal*, which was disabled and without hope of escape. Lieutenant Morgan had no choice but to raise the white flag to save what was left of his crew.

The Battle of Dunn's Bayou cost the North two gunboats and 17 guns. The *Covington* lost 42 out of her 74-man crew. The *Signal* lost 54 men captured, 12 of whom were wounded, and a few dead. The *John Warner*'s losses were not reported but totaled at least 150 killed and wounded, and about 400 captured.[529] The Union also lost another fine infantry regiment.

Admiral Porter reported to Secretary of the Navy Welles that the Confederate force was 6,000 strong and had 25 pieces of artillery. Baylor actually had fewer than 1,000 men, two howitzers, and two 10-pounder Parrott guns. He suffered no casualties.[530]

Nathaniel Banks blamed the navy for the disaster because it did not patrol the river adequately. Porter retorted that the best way to protect the boats was to drive the Rebels away from the river. The result was that the Red River was temporarily closed to Federal shipping. And thus the noose was pulled tighter. Union supplies and reinforcements could no longer reach the Army of the Gulf. At least one Union party tried but was checked by Major and Bagby at Fort DeRussy, which was now back in Rebel hands. Liddell burned all the bridges north and east of Pineville and blocked the roads with trees,

---

529 Williams, pp. 74-78.
530 O.R.N., Vol. XXVI, pp. 114-134; O.R., Vol. XXXIV, Part 1, p. 475.

in case Banks tried to escape to Vicksburg or Arkansas. Rebel cavalry patrolled the Ouachita/Black River sector to prevent communication with the Federal garrison at Natchez, and Taylor continued to probe the Alexandria defenses. There was skirmishing every day.

Inside Alexandria, the supply situation was growing critical. As of May 1, Banks had enough food to last his men three more weeks, but his forage was almost exhausted. His cavalry division could no longer muster horses strong enough to mount a sufficient number of probes against Taylor's cavalry screen, and the forage parties usually came back empty handed, if they came back at all. Dick Taylor knew all this because the horses he captured these days were little more than walking skeletons.[531] Yet Banks could not break out of the encirclement because the Red River stubbornly refused to rise, and the fleet remained trapped above the falls.

Taylor's strategy was clearly working. For the Yankees, the situation was growing very serious indeed.

BAILEY'S DAM

Porter's battered squadron limped into the Alexandria defensive perimeter on April 28. Trapped above the Alexandria Falls was the heart of the Union inland fleet: the *Lexington*, the *Osage*, the *Neosho*, the *Mound City*, the *Louisville*, the *Pittsburg*, the *Chillicothe*, the *Carondelet*, the *Ozark*, and the *Fort Hindman*. The level of the river varied from 3'4" to 4'6." The fleet needed seven feet of water to cross the rapids. One army officer, however, addressed the problem days before.

Lieutenant Colonel Joseph Bailey was from the logging country of Wisconsin, where he became very familiar with raising the water level of streams by constructing dams. Now an engineer officer on Franklin's staff, he knew immediately what would have to be done. As early as April 9, the day of the Battle of Pleasant Hill, he approached General Franklin and proposed the idea of elevating the water level

---

531 Johnson, p. 260.

of the Red by constructing dams to get the fleet over the rapids at Alec. He used the technique at Thompson's Creek near Port Hudson the year before, to salvage a pair of steamers. Franklin—a brilliant engineering officer himself—at once grasped the merits of the idea but was too busy to address it at the moment, for obvious reasons.

When the army and the gunboats were safely entrenched or anchored at Grand Ecore, Franklin sent Bailey to Porter to explain the dam idea to him. Initially, the admiral poked fun at the plan and did not pay much attention to it. "If you can dam better than I can, you must be a good hand at it, for I've been damning all night," he remarked.[532] He would soon change his tune completely.

Meanwhile, on April 27, Major General David Hunter, the emissary of General Grant, arrived at Alexandria, bearing instructions which were completely out of date. Two days later, at Franklin's instigation, Bailey met with Banks and Hunter and explained what he intended to do. Grant's representative was dubious but nevertheless thought that the idea should be tried, mainly because Franklin endorsed it, and he saw no other alternative. Neither, now, did Admiral Porter. Banks issued the necessary orders for wagons, equipment, and men, who came mainly from the woods of Maine, the Corps d'Afrique, and the African American engineer brigade.

Work began on April 30, the same day Franklin applied for a leave of absence due to the injuries he suffered at Mansfield. He was again replaced by General Emory. McMillan took over Emory's division once again.

When work first began, the dam was the subject of a great many jokes. Most people did not think it would work. As the work progressed, however, confidence grew. Buildings in and around Alexandria were torn down and used in the construction of the dam, including the former military academy William T. Sherman once supervised. Quarries were dug, and wagons and flatboats were put to work to carry brick, stone, and filler. Work continued around the clock.

---

532   Hollandsworth, p. 20.

Bailey's Dam under construction, 1864

The escape of Porter's flotilla

At the site of the dam, the river was 758 feet wide and 4 to 6 feet deep. The speed of the current was 10 miles per hour. The dam was built from both sides at once. Every day, thousands of men lined the banks to watch and look for signs of progress, such as a rise in the river. Porter was afraid that Banks might bolt with his army and leave the fleet in the lurch, but the thought apparently never even crossed his mind. Whatever his other military deficiencies, Banks' courage cannot be questioned. Even Admiral Porter later confessed that Banks gave the dam his "whole attention night and day, scarcely sleeping while the work was going on."[533]

General Taylor, meanwhile, expected Brigadier General St. John R. Liddell, the commander of the Sub-District of North Louisiana, to disrupt the dam building from the north bank and simultaneously harass the Union vessels as they traveled downriver. His demands were quite unreasonable. Liddell had only 600 to 700 men of indifferent quality. Parrish said that he looked upon them as "little better than masquerading deserters and draft evaders seeking soft duty."[534] In addition, Kirby Smith took both of Liddell's guns to Arkansas. Liddell did not get any more artillery until the dam was nearly finished; then he was given a two-gun battery. His forces were simply inadequate, and he did good service by driving the Yankee garrison out of Pineville on April 27. Taylor nevertheless relieved him of his command in mid-May for his "failure." The fact that he and Liddell could not stand each other no doubt played a significant role in this decision.[535]

Taylor hoped that Liddell would receive reinforcements from Kirby Smith before the dam was completed, but it was not to be. By May 8, when the dam extended 300 feet from each bank, four

---

[533] O.R.N., Vol. XXVI, pp. 132-133, citing dispatch from Porter to Secretary of the Navy Welles, dated May 16, 1864.

[534] Parrish, p. 389.

[535] Liddell described Taylor as "self-important and self-opinionated." He despised Taylor from the first day they met, and apparently the feeling was mutual. Nathaniel C. Hughes, ed., *Liddell's Record* (Dayton, Ohio: 1985), pp. 172-174.

coal barges were loaded with rocks, placed side by side in the Red, and sunk. There were now only three 20-foot gaps in the dam—the distance between the barges. The water began to rise immediately.

By mid-afternoon, the water was high enough to allow the *Fort Hindman*, *Neosho*, and *Osage* to float over the falls. These gunboats drew four feet of water. The *Pittsburg*, *Carondelet*, *Louisville*, and *Mound City*, which drew six feet, might have escaped at this point but for some reason did not try.[536] Historian Ludwell Johnson described the U.S. Navy as "strangely apathetic" on May 8 and before.[537] They made absolutely no effort to lighten their vessels by removing armor, guns, cargo or cotton. The fact that Admiral Porter was ill at the time may partially explain their lethargy but not entirely.

Shortly after midnight on May 9, Nathaniel Banks personally inspected the dam and concluded that it was likely to give way at any time. He sent word to Porter and urged him to be ready to float at any moment. The admiral did nothing.

Banks was proven right at 5 a.m., when the two barges in the center of the dam were swept aside by the river. As soon as he learned of this, Porter jumped on a horse, rode to the *Lexington*, and ordered it to go straight through the gap, before the river fell too low. The *Lexington* hung up briefly but managed to shoot the rapids, followed by the *Neosho*, *Fort Hindman* and *Osage*. Only the *Osage* was damaged and it only slightly. This, however, still left the *Pittsburg*, *Carondelet*, *Louisville*, and *Mound City* above the falls.

The collapse of the dam disrupted General Banks' plans, for he ordered the army to be prepared to evacuate Alexandria on two hours' notice. As a result, May 9 was a tense day. Porter was worried that Banks might abandon him. A. J. Smith told the admiral that XVI Corps would remain with him, no matter what the Army of the Gulf did.[538]

---

536 Charles B. Boynton, *The History of the Navy During the Rebellion* (New York: 1867), pp. 501-503, 506.

537 Johnson, p. 262.

538 O.R.N., Vol. XXVI, p. 136.

Now thoroughly alarmed, Porter and his men took guns, ammunition, supplies, armor, and cotton off their boats. Everything but the cotton and armor was carried below the falls by wagons. Eleven obsolete 32-pounder smoothbore guns were spiked and dumped into the river. Tar was smeared on the sides of the boats, to keep the Rebels from learning that the timbers were exposed.[539]

On or about May 9, one of Banks' staff officers discovered that the gunboats' holds were full of cotton. He reported to Banks, who took the matter up with Porter. As a result, much of the cotton was thrown overboard.

Nathaniel P. Banks, by this point, had enough of the cotton speculators and their demands for special treatment. He issued orders that only government property was to be evacuated from Alexandria. General McMillan, who was thoroughly disgusted by Banks and the cotton speculators, was given the task of throwing the speculators' cotton off the private riverboats to make room for troops and government property. This assignment thoroughly delighted the general, who turned a deaf ear to the howls of the profiteers.[540] Cotton speculators Samuel Casey and William Butler in particular lost a lot of "white gold." Butler, an old friend of Lincoln, moaned to Colonel J. G. Wilson: "I wish you would take somebody else's cotton. That is very fine cotton!"[541]

Meanwhile, Colonel Bailey began repairing his dam. He also constructed a pair of wing dams on either bank to channel the water above the main dam. Then he constructed bracket dams, to support the wing dams and to pool the water. The wing dams were completed on May 11, and by May 13, the water rose a foot. The

---
539   O.R.N., Vol. XXVI, pp. 132, 149.

540   Johnson, p. 267. James W. McMillan (1825-1903) was described as "a wanderer" by Erza Warner (*Generals in Blue*, p. 305). Born in Kentucky, he was a sergeant in the 4th Illinois during the Mexican War but ended up as a private in a Louisiana battalion. He was engaged in several places until 1861, when he became colonel of the 21st Indiana. He fought in the Battles of Baton Rouge and Berwick Bay and was promoted to brigadier general in late 1862. Later, he served in the Shenandoah Valley. Brevetted major general, he lived in Kansas for a time after the war but died in Washington, D.C.

541   JCCW, p. 81. Colonel Wilson was a member of Banks' staff.

ironclads built up steam, the cribs were dropped, and a torrent of water shot through between the sides of the dams. The ironclads rode the torrent through the falls to safety. They continued downriver and, by May 15, were in the Mississippi River. Taylor's last chance of destroying the fleet vanished.

Alexandria Evacuated

On May 9, a delegation of citizens, led by Dr. G. W. Southwick, appeared at Banks' headquarters, to ask that the city be spared. Banks assured them that it would be. He was afraid that the fire would alert Taylor as to what was happening, as it did at Grand Ecore. He told Southwick that he assigned the task of protecting the city to Colonel Gooding, although he did not inform the colonel of his "mission." Southwick, however, did not take Banks at his word; he took the precaution of getting the promise in writing.

On May 13, it was obvious that the army was leaving, and the citizens became alarmed. The promised protective guard did not arrive. The citizens' delegation went in search of Banks, but he was nowhere to be found. They did, however, find Lieutenant William S. Beebe, Banks' ordnance officer, who joined them and took them to Gooding. The colonel was genuinely surprised to see them. When they showed him the note from Banks, the colonel swore and declared: "This is just like old Banks!"[542] The duplicitous politician left Alexandria without protection.

The evacuation began at 7 a.m. on May 13. General Michael K. Lawler led the army out, followed by Emory's corps. A. J. Smith's corps formed the rearguard. The fires broke out around 8 a.m. Aided by a strong wind, they spread rapidly. Soon, Reverend Ewer recalled, "The city was wrapped in flames."[543]

---

542 Allen, *Report*, pp. 72-73.
543 Ewer, p. 180.

"The Jay-hawkers kept their promise to burn the place rather than have it go into the hands of the enemy again ... " Lieutenant Van Alystyne of the 90th Regiment, U.S.C.T., wrote later. He estimated that there were 100 fires.[544]

The Jayhawkers and the "gorillas" planned their arson well. Union soldiers with buckets and mops were seen smearing a mixture of turpentine and camphene (a forerunner of napalm) on the buildings. One civilian recalled seeing some of the cavalry officers, who were supposed to be protecting the city, helping the arsonists. Some members of Banks' staff tried to stop the pyromaniacs, but without success.[545]

"There was no such thing as saving the buildings ...," Van Alystyne recalled. "Fires were breaking out in new places all the time. All we could do was to help the people get over the levee, the only place where the heat did not reach and where there was nothing to burn. There was no lack of help, but all were helpless to do more than that. Only the things most needful, such as beds and eatables, were saved ... Cows ran bellowing through the streets. Chickens flew out from yards and fell in the streets with their feathers scorching on them. A dog with his bushy tail on fire ran howling through, turning to snap at the fire as he ran ... Crowds of people, men, women, children and soldiers, were running with all they could carry, when the heat would become unbearable, and dropping all, they would flee for their lives, leaving everything but their bodies to burn. Over the levee the sights and sounds were harrowing. Thousands of people, mostly women, children and old men, were wringing their hands as they stood by the little piles of what was left of all their worldly possessions. Thieves were everywhere, and some of them were soldiers. I saw one knocked down and left in the street, who had his arms full of stolen articles ... Nearly all buildings were of wood; great patches of burning roofs would sail away, to drop and start a new fire. By noon the thickly settled portion of Alexandria was a smoking ruin."[546]

---

544   Van Alystne, pp. 320-321.
545   Joiner, p. 169.
546   Van Alystyne, pp. 320-321.

Every building within a 22-block area was burned, including churches and the courthouse. Even the homes of men who enlisted in the Union Army and Alexandria Unionists, whose property was unmolested for three years, were burned. Several families whose men had joined the Federal army rushed to the docks and begged for safe passage behind Union lines. They were turned away.

After the civilians rescued what they could from their burning homes, they were robbed at gunpoint by Jayhawkers, blacks and Union stragglers. A. J. Smith was right in the middle of it, apparently drunk again, cheering on the arsonists, and yelling "Hurrah, boys, this looks like war!" General Banks had not left the city when the fires broke out, so he ordered the Negro engineer brigade to help put out the fires. They attempted to do so, but due to the prolonged drought in Rapides Parish and Boggs' levee cuts, the Red was so low, and the buildings and trees were so dry, they experienced no success.

"Pandemonium reigned," Winters wrote, as frightened old men, women, and children ran through the streets, along with cats, dogs, cows, chickens, and pillaging soldiers.[547] The last elements of the Union fleet had to cast off quickly to escape the flames. When General Taylor entered the city later that day, he found only a smoldering ruin.

The Kent House was the only plantation house in the city to escape destruction. It was originally built from 1796 to 1800 by slaves owned by Pierre Baillio. It was a typical antebellum Creole plantation house, except for the foundations, which are more than 10 feet high instead of the usual five. (All Creole plantation houses are elevated, due to the danger of high water.) Baillio set the slaves to work constructing the foundational pillars and then went out of town on a business trip, leaving them with instructions to continue building until he returned. His return was delayed, but he assumed the slaves would stop at five feet. He was wrong. Rather than start over, he built the house with the foundational pillars "as is."

---

547   Winters, p. 374.

Its owner in 1864 was Robert Henson of Illinois, who purchased it in 1840. During that time, a lonely young officer from Illinois was stationed in the area. The Hensons befriended him, treated him like a son, and he was a frequent and welcome visitor to their home. His name was Lieutenant Ulysses S. Grant. In 1864, Lieutenant General Ulysses S. Grant sent General Banks an emphatic order: burn Alexandria if you wish, but the Kent House and its owners are not to be disturbed. Even A. J. Smith was afraid to disobey such a pointed order from Grant. The general-in-chief, however, neglected to mention the outbuildings (barns, slave quarters, corn cribs, etc.) in his order, so Smith's men burned every single one of them. The house, however, is still extant.[548]

---

548 Dales Genius, Louisiana History Museum, Alexandria, Louisiana, and Alice Scarborough, Director, Kent House Museum, Alexandria, Louisiana, Personal Communications, June 4, 2009.

Chapter XII

Across The Atchafalaya

As Banks retreated on May 13, his rearguard was followed by Brigadier General William Steele's cavalry brigade, while Colonel Isaac F. Harrison's 3rd Louisiana Cavalry, reinforced with Colonel James R. Liken's 35th Texas Cavalry Regiment, harassed the fleet from the north bank.[549] The front of the Union column was harassed by Major and Bagby, and the Yankees were forced to deploy several times in line of battle, but the cavalry refused to be decisively engaged.

The end of the Red River campaign was somewhat anticlimactic. The fleet already escaped, and Taylor no longer had a realistic chance of destroying Banks' army unless the Federal generals made a blunder of incredible proportions. Since they were capable of doing this, Taylor shadowed them until they put the unfordable Atchafalaya

---

[549] Likens, an east Texas lawyer, served under Taylor's father as a private in the Mexican War. William Steele (1819-1885) was a native of New York. He graduated from West Point in 1840, served with distinction in the Mexican War, spent most of his post-war career in Texas, and married a woman from that state. He resigned in 1861, directed the 7th Texas Cavalry in the New Mexico campaign (1861-1862), and commanded the Indian Territory in 1863. After the war, he was a merchant in San Antonio and was adjutant general of Texas from 1873 to 1879.

River (which is considerably deeper than the Mississippi) between him and themselves. This time, the Yankees made no serious mistakes.

On May 13, the Union forces marched down the road toward Fort DeRussy and Marksville, skirmishing with the Rebel cavalry on the way. Every building along the road was put to the torch. The column spent the night on the banks of Bayou Choctaw because the bridge was burned.

The next day, May 14, there was light skirmishing at Wilson's Landing, and the Northerners spanned Bayou Choctaw with a pontoon bridge. They spent the evening camped near the wrecks of the *Covington*, *Signal*, and *John Warner* and were outraged to find letters they wrote to their parents, wives, lady friends, etc., scattered all over the ground. The Rebels had amused themselves by reading their mail!

The next day, May 15, the forward units crossed the Choctaw Swamp and entered the Avoyelles Prairie. Here, the leading troops attacked and were beaten back several times by the 4th, 5th, and 7th Texas Cavalry Regiments. They did not have enough troops to outflank the Rebels until evening. The Union vanguards took and sacked Marksville that night.

General Taylor made a stand near Mansura on the Avoyelles Prairie on May 16. He deployed Bagby and Major on the right flank and backed them with 19 guns. On the left, he positioned Prince de Polignac's infantry division, which was supported by two regiments of Debray's cavalry brigade and 13 guns.

The skirmishing began at dawn, and the scene impressed everyone who witnessed it because it took place on a beautiful, flat prairie where concealment was impossible. It was almost like a parade. Banks formed his army with Mower on the right, then Kilby Smith's division, then Emory's corps in the center, and Lawler on the left. Arnold's cavalry covered both flanks. The Yankees deployed in several lines; Taylor had only enough men to form one. Banks already had 16,000 men or more on the field, as opposed to Taylor's

3,500.⁵⁵⁰ Arnold tried to turn Taylor's right but was easily repulsed. The 34th Wisconsin launched an ill-advised foray and lost 34 men. Mostly the Battle of Mansura was an indecisive artillery duel.

A. J. Smith's corps arrived on the field at 10 a.m., and the Yankees began an advance. Hopelessly outnumbered, Taylor retreated, covered by his cavalry, which kept the Union infantry delayed long enough for him to avoid a general engagement. The entire Battle of Mansura was described as a "spectacular four-hour show," but neither side suffered much in the way of losses.⁵⁵¹

At Moreauville on May 17, General Wharton again tried to outwit Whiskey Smith and, as usual, succeeded. He drove into the Union rearguard, raised havoc, and captured several prisoners. Smith ordered a counterattack against Wharton without realizing that Debray was hiding on his flank with two cavalry regiments. When Smith's men advanced against Wharton, they walked straight into an ambush. Debray's men jumped up all at once and fired a volley into the faces of the surprised Yankees, several of whom were killed. Before the Northerners could recover, both Wharton and Debray escaped. Meanwhile, Colonel William O. Yagar led his own 3rd Texas Cavalry and the 2nd Louisiana Cavalry into the attack, scattered the Union guards, and captured the Federal wagon train near Yellow Bayou. He succeeded in burning some of the wagons but could not bring off the train because the Union infantry was too close. By nightfall on May 17, the entire Union army was across Yellow Bayou.

Banks' vanguard reached the Atchafalaya River near the former site of the town of Simmesport on May 17. He needed time for Colonel Bailey to build a bridge, however, so early on May 18, he ordered A. J. Smith to push back Taylor's pursuit forces. Taylor and Wharton, meanwhile, decided to make one, last attempt to stop Banks before he could escape across the Atchafalaya. The result was the Battle of Yellow Bayou, which the Confederates called the Battle

---

550   O.R., Vol. XXXIV, Part 1, p. 593. General Taylor's report praised Bagby for his skillful use of artillery.

551 Spencer, pp. 49-50.

of Norwood's Plantation. Located only two miles from Simmesport, the battlefield was mostly woods and thickets. Wharton commanded the Confederate forces, which totaled about 5,000 men. Mower had 4,500 men.[552]

While the bulk of the U.S. XVI and XIII Corps crossed the Atchafalaya, Brigadier General Joseph A. Mower led the Union rearguard back across Yellow Bayou and struck Wharton with three infantry brigades and a brigade of cavalry. After advancing two miles, he ran into Wharton's main line of defense, with Major's dismounted cavalry on the left and Polignac's infantry on the right. The result was a see-saw battle that lasted most of the day.

Fighting on foot, General Major succeeded in getting behind the Union left and forcing Mower back. Polignac, however, launched a bayonet charge, which basically amounted to a frontal attack. By this point, Mower brought up his artillery and checked it, firing canister into the Confederate ranks and inflicting severe casualties. He then shifted his fire onto Major, this time firing double-shotted canister.

Among other units, the 32nd Texas Cavalry was heavily engaged against the Union left. The sun was blazing, the woods were on fire, and the heat was terrible. The Rebels and Yankees were so close that they were practically firing into each other's faces.

Captain Joel Stevens of Company C fell mortally wounded when a slug struck him in the upper shoulder near the backbone. He was one of the older men in the regiment, was a doctor of sorts, and was highly respected and very popular with everyone in the 32nd. Unable to move, Stevens asked to be placed under the shade of a tree. Over his dying body, the Texas cavalrymen swore revenge. They decided to start by shooting their prisoners.

Captain Stevens would have none of it. "Boys, most of those Yanks didn't want this war any more than you did ... In this thing, some of us must die. Now it's my turn ..." Speaking with great effort, he ordered his men to spare the lives of their prisoners, to leave him

---

552   Kinard, p. 167.

now, and to do their duty. "I'm at peace with myself, and you must do your duty and live so that you can say the same when the time comes." The men were sobbing as they returned to action. Their prisoners ended up in Camp Ford.[553]

Colonel Dr. Woods, the commander of the 32nd Texas Cavalry, was up front with his men when a Yankee minie ball struck his left hand, ran up his entire forearm, and came out his elbow. After the battle, he took a two-week furlough—the only leave he took during the entire war. His arm was nearly useless for the rest of his life.[554]

Colonel Robert Stone, the commander of the Texas infantry brigade in Polignac's division, was reporting to General Wharton when he was killed, apparently by a piece of shrapnel. He was succeeded by Colonel James E. Harrison of the 15th Texas.[555]

By afternoon, the weather grew even hotter, and the Union troops consumed the last of their water. Several of them suffered sunstroke or collapsed due to heat exhaustion. Major, however, attacked again, and Mower forced him back with a counterattack. The battle set the thickets on fire, and the two sides were separated by a wall of flames. Thus covered, Mower retreated across the bayou. He lost 360 men in the Battle of Yellow Bayou. Taylor's army suffered 500 casualties.

That night, the Confederate forces retreated four to five miles to Bayou Black. The wounded were carried to Norwood Plantation, where the slave cabins were converted into field hospitals.

Richard Taylor now knew that he would not be able to prevent Banks from escaping. He wrote Colonel S. S. Anderson, the assistant adjutant general in Shreveport: "The campaign will probably close today at Simsport [Simmesport] ... Nothing but the withdrawal of Walker's division from me has prevented the capture of Banks's

---

553 Duaine, pp. 80-81.
554 Duaine, p. 82.
555 Kinard, p. 167.

General Joseph Bailey

army and the destruction of Porter's fleet. I feel bitterly about this, because my army has been robbed of the just measure of glory and the country of the most brilliant and complete success of the war."[556]

On May 19, General Taylor reported himself "suffering from sickness and exhaustion."[557]

*

Meanwhile, the Army of the Gulf called upon Lieutenant Colonel Joseph Bailey one last time to get them across the Atchafalaya. He built a bridge by bringing 22 transports into line, anchoring them, lashing them together, and constructing gangplanks to connect them. In this way, he built a continuous bridge to the eastern bank.

---

556 O.R., Vol. XXXIV, Part 1, p. 595.

557 O.R., Vol. XXXIV, Part 1, p.. 595.

The XIII and XIX Corps began to cross on May 19, and A. J. Smith's XVI Corps crossed the next day. The bridge was then dismantled. In the meantime, the sick and wounded were loaded onto the transports and steamed into the Mississippi. The rest of the army marched south to Morganza, on the Mississippi River.

Joseph Bailey was hailed by all the Union factions as a great hero of the campaign. David D. Porter, who once laughed in his face, correctly declared him as a great engineer and presented him with a sword and the thanks of the U.S. Navy. The U.S. Congress also voted him its thanks, along with a promotion to brigadier general of volunteers.

On May 21, A. J. Smith's XVI and XVII Corps troops left the Army of the Gulf. Many of the eastern troops were glad to see them go. They arrived back at Vicksburg on May 23—too late to join Sherman for the summer campaign against Atlanta. They were later sent to Missouri and ended the war in the Shenandoah Valley.

The men in the ranks of both sides were exhausted. Second Lieutenant Van Alystyne of the 90th U.S. Colored Infantry wrote in his diary on May 20, "I was so dead sleepy that I twice fell flat on the ground as I was walking along."[558] The Confederates rested and bathed. Like the Northerners, they also deloused. The 32nd Texas, for example, were not able to wash or change clothes for more than 30 days. They blamed the lice on the Yankees, although exactly how Mister Lincoln's men caused a lice infestation in a Texas cavalry unit was never explained. One unusually filthy man in Company E refused to bathe. The men of the 32nd stripped him, threw him into the bayou, burned his clothes and left him there.[559] How the naked private got out of his fix is not recorded.

*

Meanwhile, both principal commanders of the Red River campaign lost their jobs.

---

558   Van Alystyne, p. 320.
559   Duaine, p. 83.

Dissatisfaction against Nathaniel P. Banks was growing since the Battle of Mansfield. On April 29, Halleck wrote to Sherman: "Banks' operations in the West are about what should have been expected from a general so utterly destitute of military education and capacity. It seems but little better than murder to give important commands to such men as Banks, Butler, McClernand, Sigel and Lew Wallace, and yet it seems impossible to prevent it."[560] Two days before, he had sent orders to Banks, instructing him to hand over command to the next senior officer and to return to New Orleans. This dispatch, however, never reached the Army of the Gulf because it was aboard the *City Belle*, which Confederates sank on May 4.

Secretary of War Stanton, meanwhile, received word of the Mansfield disaster from newspaper reports. He forwarded them to Grant, who telegraphed Halleck, suggesting that Banks be replaced. (Grant never had confidence in Banks.) Halleck showed the telegram to Lincoln, who postponed a decision.[561]

On May 3, Halleck telegraphed Grant:

> General Banks is a personal friend of the President, and has strong political supporters in and out of Congress. There will undoubtedly be a very strong opposition to his being removed or superseded, and I think the President will hesitate to act unless he has a definite request from you to do so, as a military necessity, you designating his superior or superiors in command. On receiving such a formal request (not a mere suggestion) I believe, as I wrote you some days ago, he would act immediately. I have no authority for saying this, but give it simply as my own opinion, formed from the last two years' experience, and the reason, I think, is very obvious. To do an act which

---

560 O.R., Vol. XXXIV, Part 3, p. 333.

561 Hollandsworth, p. 205. Grant's initial choice to succeed Banks was Major General Joseph J. Reynolds, the commander of the New Orleans defenses.

will give offense to a large number of his political friends the President will require some evidence in a positive form to show the military necessities of that act. In other words he must have something in a definitive shape to fall back upon as his justification. You will perceive that the press in New Orleans and in the Eastern States are already beginning to open in General Banks' favor. The administration would be immediately attacked for his removal. Do not understand me as advocating his retention in command. On the contrary, I expressed to the President months ago my own opinion of General Banks' want of military capacity. Whatever order you may ask for on this subject I will do my best to have issued."[562]

Lincoln finally caved in to pressure from Stanton, Halleck, and Grant on May 7, when he gave Major General E. R. S. Canby command of the Military Division of West Mississippi and placed Banks' Department of the Gulf under Canby's command. Banks was, in effect, demoted, and Canby saw to it that he no longer commanded troops. His duties were confined to New Orleans and were strictly civil. Canby arrived on the Atchafalaya and took command of the Army of the Gulf on May 18.

*

Richard Taylor, meanwhile, continued to vent his frustration and anger on Kirby Smith and made his contempt clear. When Kirby Smith offered him a promotion to lieutenant general, Taylor turned it down. The advancement was of dubious legality, and Taylor looked upon it as little more than an attempted bribe. He responded that he preferred to receive his promotions from President Davis and the Confederate Congress. Both complied. They (and the entire South) were delighted by Taylor's victory at Mansfield.

---

562   O.R., Vol. XXXIV, Part 3, pp. 409-410.

General Taylor continued to privately and publicly condemn Kirby Smith's "sheer stupidity and pig-headed obstinacy" for not helping him destroy Banks. "From the first to last, General Kirby Smith seemed determined to throw a protecting shield around the Federal army and fleet," he declared.[563]

The heated correspondence between the two generals reached its climax on June 5, when Taylor wrote Kirby Smith:

> The roads to Saint Louis and New Orleans should now be open to us. Your strategy has riveted the fetters on both. At Jenkins' Ferry the tactical skill which carried Churchill's, Parsons' and Walker's divisions successively into the fight after its predecessor had been driven back, and which failed to use at all, either in the fight or in a pursuit, a force of over 7,000 cavalry, succeeded the strategy which declined the capture of Banks' army and Porter's fleet to march after the comparatively insignificant force of Steele. The same regard for duty which led me to throw myself between you and popular indignation and quietly take the blame of your errors compels me to tell you the truth, however objectionable to you. The grave errors you have committed in the recent campaign may be repeated if the unhappy consequences are not kept before you. After the desire to serve my country, I have none more ardent than to be relieved from longer serving under your command.[564]

This piece of insubordination was too much, even for Kirby Smith. On June 10, Richard Taylor got his wish. Kirby Smith relieved him of his command and placed him under virtual house arrest in Natchitoches. John G. Walker, the former commander

---

563 Taylor, pp. 229-230.
564 O.R., Vol. XXXIV, Part 1, pp. 547-548.

of the Texas Division, succeeded him as commander of the Army of Western Louisiana. Ironically, that same day, a thousand miles away, the Confederate Congress passed a resolution praising Taylor for his "brilliant success" at Mansfield.[565]

For his part, Kirby Smith—a strong Christian—consistently refused to criticize Taylor or to defend himself from Taylor's verbal attacks. Shortly after the campaign ended, Brigadier General St. John R. Liddell visited him and Kirby Smith listened patiently as Liddell berated Taylor for his behavior. After the former subdistrict commander finished, Kirby Smith remarked that Taylor's "mind is affected by the paralysis he had some years since, and he is hardly responsible."[566]

---

565 O.R., Vol. XXXIV, Part 1, p. 597.

566 Nathaniel C. Hughes, ed., *Liddell's Record* (Dayton, Ohio: 1985; reprint ed., Baton Rouge: 1997), p. 184.

Chapter XIII

Epilogue And Postscript: What Happened To The Men Of The Red River Expedition

Historian Ludwell Johnson believed the Red River Expedition prolonged the Civil War by two months.[567] I personally doubt this, although it is certainly possible that he was right, and one would be ill-advised to challenge this distinguished historian too forcefully. In my opinion, however, the Confederacy still had a chance of winning the war politically in 1864, and this campaign improved the South's chances significantly. If the Rebels were able to hold Atlanta until after the November elections, Lincoln would likely have been defeated (according to Lincoln himself), and the Confederacy might have achieved a negotiated peace, given the fact that the Democrats had a "peace at any price" plank in their platform. The fact that Sherman had fewer men in his attempts to take Atlanta than he should have had, and the Southern defenders had more men that they should have had is, in my opinion, the true strategic significance of the campaign. Jefferson Davis and his generals, most notably John B. Hood, blew the opportunity by launching a series of ill-advised attacks. It was here that the fruits of the victory at

---

567 Johnson, p. 278.

Mansfield were lost to the South. After Atlanta fell on September 2, 1864, Lincoln's reelection was assured, and the Confederacy was doomed.

The Red River Expedition cost the U.S. Army of the Gulf at least 5,200 men. The army lost the transports *Emma*, *City Belle* and *John Warner*, and the hospital ship *Woodford*. The U.S. Navy lost the heavy ironclad *Eastport*, the tinclads *Signal* and *Covington*, and the transports *Champion No. 3* and *Champion No. 5*. The navy lost at least 200 men—an estimate this author believes is extremely conservative. Johnson puts the total U.S. losses in Louisiana at 5,412 men—perhaps more. He estimates Taylor's losses at 4,300 men.[568]

Steele lost about 2,750 men in Arkansas against 2,300 for Price and Kirby-Smith. Total losses in Louisiana and Arkansas, therefore, are 6,575 for the Rebels and 8,162 for Steele, Banks, and Porter, if Johnson's estimates are accepted.

The losses in equipment were much more lopsided. Banks and Steele lost 30 guns, while Porter lost 26 heavy naval guns, of which at least eight were salvaged by the Rebels. The Confederates lost 16 guns: 10 at Fort DeRussy, three in the evacuation of Alexandria in March, and three at Jenkins' Ferry. The Northerners also lost 822 government-owned wagons, of which 600 were captured by the enemy. The number of civilian wagons contracted out to the government and lost during the campaign easily pushes this number past the 1,000 mark. The Yankees officially lost 3,502 horses and mules.[569] The actual total was above 5,000 and probably above 6,000. The Rebel equipment losses were negligible. Perhaps 600 horses and mules were lost in battle or through normal attrition.

Who was responsible for the failure of the Red River campaign? Primary blame, of course, must go to Banks, the expedition commander. A share also must go to Secretary of State Seward, who convinced Lincoln and Halleck that great diplomatic advantages could be gained over France in Mexico if Texas were invaded and

---

568   Johnson, p.278.
569   Johnson, pp. 278-279.

who strongly supported Banks for the post of commander of the Department of the Gulf. Halleck must bear a larger share because the overall strategic master plan was his, and it was fundamentally flawed. Abraham Lincoln himself cannot escape some criticism, nor can Porter and Sherman, who sided with Halleck. Finally, Franklin was wrong in insisting that the cavalry wagon train follow the cavalry at Mansfield, a move which certainly was a major contributing factor to the scale of the Union defeat.

The Civil War in Louisiana ended with a whimper, not a bang. There was skirmishing in the Atchafalaya sector in the fall of 1864 but nothing that resembled even a minor battle. As time marched on, both sides became more and more content to remain in their bases. The Confederate cavalry camped in and around Alexandria, while the infantry concentrated at Shreveport. The area between the Atchafalaya and Alexandria became infested by Jayhawkers and outlaws. There were even cases of Union and Confederate cavalry cooperating with each other to suppress the thugs.

In the fall of 1864, John Walker returned to Texas and Major General Simon B. Buckner became commander of the Department of Western Louisiana. During the third week of April 1865, word of Lee's surrender reached the Trans-Mississippi. Kirby Smith announced it to his army on April 21, along with his decision to continue the war and an exhortation to keep fighting. No one listened. They knew that the Confederacy was doomed. More than half his troops went home by May 13, when Guy M. Bryan, the representative of the governor of Texas, met with the governors of Louisiana and Arkansas at Marshall, Texas. (Governor Pendleton Murrah of Texas was too ill to attend.)[570] They unanimously urged Kirby Smith to surrender.

---

570   Pendleton Murrah succeeded Francis R. Lubbock as governor on November 5, 1863. Probably a native of Alabama (some sources say South Carolina), he was an illegitimate child and grew up in a Baptist orphanage. He nevertheless graduated from Brown University and became a prominent attorney in Marshall, Texas. Murrah briefly served in the Texas House of Representatives and before being elected governor. He was commissioned in the 14th Texas Infantry in 1861. A fervent Confederate, he advocated continuing the war, even after General Lee surrendered. He fled to Mexico after the

Throughout the Trans-Mississippi, the Southern units dissolved themselves. On May 14, for example, Lieutenant Colonel Robertson acted on his own initiative and disbanded Terrell's Rangers (the 37th [formerly 34th] Texas Cavalry Regiment) at Wild Cat Bluff on the Trinity River. Colonel Yager disbanded his 1st Texas Cavalry Regiment the same day, as well as the 7th Texas Cavalry (Bagby's old command).[571] When Colonel Terrell, who was promoted to brigade commander, reached Wild Cat Bluff the next day, he discovered that there was nothing left of his old command except his headquarters wagon, its mules, one teamster, and some empty cartridge boxes. He returned to Shreveport, where he learned that he was promoted to brigadier general by Kirby Smith on May 16.

On May 19, Debray's 26th Texas Cavalry and Woods' 32nd made a 50-mile forced march to Houston in 15 hours. They disbanded on May 22.

Acting in Kirby Smith's name, Buckner put an end to the confusion before it became a complete farce. He surrendered the Trans-Mississippi forces to Canby on May 26. The last Rebel army lay down its arms. Shreveport was finally occupied by Union forces on June 6—two months after Appomattox.

*

Nathaniel P. Banks looked "dejected and worn" after the Red River Expedition.[572] Now he was booed and hooted at by the same troops who cheered him in March. He nevertheless continued his political activities and held a Constitutional Convention in New Orleans, which lasted 10 weeks and ended on July 22, 1864. The Convention was noted for its lavish parties and heavy expenditures for liquor, ice, and cigars. It even gave General Banks a $150 cane

---

surrender of the Trans-Mississippi Department leaving Fletcher S. Stockdale as acting governor for five days (June 11-16). Murrah died of tuberculosis in Monterrey, Mexico, on August 4, 1865, and is buried there.

571   Spencer, p. 77.

572   S. C. Jones, *Reminiscences of the 22nd Iowa Infantry* (Iowa City: 1907; reprint ed., Iowa City: 1993), p. 69.

($2,874.27 in 2022 money).[573] The Radical Republicans, who did badly in the contests for delegates, called it a "Convention of Imbeciles." Abraham Lincoln, on the other hand, praised the new Constitution as "excellent" and "better for the poor black than [the one] we have in Illinois."[574]

Since he no longer had combat troops to command, Banks turned his attention to a cause near to his heart: educating African-Americans. As early as 1863, he assigned a lieutenant to each U.S.C.T. regiment as a teacher, to reduce unit illiteracy, which stood at 90%. By the summer of 1864, he set up at least nine military schools in New Orleans, and they were teaching 2,400 students a day. By the end of 1864, he set up 95 schools with 162 teachers, and almost half the African Americans in the Free State of Louisiana between the ages of 5 and 12 attended school, despite white opposition—even from some Republicans. Banks' progressive ideas, however, did not survive the war by long.[575]

In the fall of 1864, Banks applied for a leave of absence and met with Lincoln in Washington later that year. Atlanta had fallen by then, and the election was well in hand, so Banks' previous political leverage was gone. The president refused to restore him to command or give him another one. He did ask Banks, however, to remain in Washington, to lobby for the Louisiana Reconstruction government and to help him check the plans of the Radical Republicans. This naturally annoyed the Radicals, who decided to investigate the Red River campaign in retaliation. The hearings by the Joint Committee on the Conduct of the War lasted from December 14, 1864 to April 21, 1865. Banks, meanwhile, returned to New Orleans, where he continued to engage in Reconstruction politics.

Michael Hahn, Banks' governor of the Free State of Louisiana, resigned in March 1865 to accept a seat in the United States Senate. The Radicals refused to seat him, however, and the new governor

---

573 CPI Inflation Calculator.
574 Hollandsworth, pp. 207-208.
575 Hollandsworth, pp. 211-213.

was J. Madison Wells, a pro-Union planter who (unlike Hahn) was initially opposed to black suffrage and was not a friend of Nathaniel P. Banks.[576] Wells fired Stephen Hoyt, the pro-Banks mayor of New Orleans, and replaced him with Hugh Kennedy, a former secessionist newspaper editor. Banks fired Kennedy and replaced him with Samuel M. Quincy.

Abraham Lincoln was shot on April 14, 1865, and died early the next day, leaving Banks without a major political ally. On May 17, 1865, President Andrew Johnson reorganized the military departments in the South and stripped Banks of what little power he had left. Banks then did what he often did: seeing the political tide turning against him, he joined the Radicals and became a strong advocate of universal black suffrage.

Meanwhile, back in Massachusetts, Banks' successor in Congress resigned to accept a post with the port of Boston. Seeing his chance to return to power, Banks resigned from the army effective September 6, 1865, and hastily returned to Waltham, to resume his political career. He defeated his uncle in a runoff election and returned to the U.S. House of Representatives in December 1865. Here, he became something of a moderate, although he did vote to impeach President Johnson. He also began to take bribes to finance his lavish lifestyle, including one from the Russian ambassador, in exchange for his support for the purchase of Alaska. (He did not take bribes during the war because of his presidential ambitions, which were destroyed at Mansfield.)

Congressman Banks worked hard to pass legislation favorable to big business and the New England capitalists, although he continued to be pro-labor on the issue of the eight-hour work day. He was bitter that President Ulysses S. Grant did not offer him a cabinet post or at

---

576   James Madison Wells (1808-1899) was elected lieutenant governor of the Free State of Louisiana in 1864 and became governor on March 4, 1865, when Michael Hahn resigned. Despite the fact that he advocated Negro suffrage, Wells was removed from office by U.S. General Phil Sheridan for failing to implement reforms vis-à-vis freedmen. Before the war, he was a large slave holder, a prominent Rapides Parish Whig, and the father of 14 children. His plantation was burned by Rebel cavalry during the Red River campaign, in retaliation for Union outrages.

least an ambassadorship. In 1872, he broke with the Republicans, denounced the Grant administration's high taxation rates and corruption, and campaigned for Horace Greeley. As a result, he lost his seat in 1872, but was elected to the Massachusetts state senate as a Democrat in 1873. He succeeded in getting a 10-hour workday bill passed by the Massachusetts legislature, which (along with the corruption of the Grant administration) led to his reelection to Congress as an independent in 1874. His personal charm and skills as an orator also contributed to his victory.

In 1875, Banks again became an advocate of reconciliation with the South but shifted his position yet again in 1876, when he rejoined the Republican Party and waved the bloody shirt. The Republicans were not particularly happy to have him, however, because by now it was obvious to everyone that Banks was a political chameleon. He was, at various times, a Democrat, Republican, Radical Republican, conservative Republican, Democrat, Radical Republican, an Independent, and a Radical Republican again. Also, he was at various times pro-business, pro-labor, pro-reconciliation, anti-reconciliation, pro-universal suffrage, anti-universal suffrage, and pro-Women's suffrage. He said what he thought the voters wanted to hear, which in the end, destroyed his credibility. Gideon Welles wrote that Banks "... has a certain degree of offhand smartness, very good elocution and command of language, with perfect self-possession, but is not profound. He is a pretender, not a statesman ... has great ambition but little fixed principle."[577] This record finally caught up with him. In 1878, he lost the G.O.P. nomination on the 12th ballot, 51 to 50. He did, however, support Rutherford P. Hayes in 1876, and the president did not forget him. He appointed Banks U.S. marshal for the Boston district in March 1879. An investigation into corruption in his office found him guilty of dereliction of duty; as a result, he was not reappointed in 1887.

Banks' had enough left in him for a last hurrah in 1888, when he was again elected to Congress. (After 10 years, the voters apparently forgot why they turned him out.) His mental powers suddenly and

---

577 Welles, Vol. II, pp. 26-27.

quickly declined, however, and it is likely that he was suffering from Alzheimer's Disease. His diminished mental capacity was all too evident by 1890, which led to his final defeat. Nathaniel P. Banks was placed in the McLean Asylum for the Insane in 1893. He died there on September 1, 1894, at the age of 78. His wife joined him in death in 1901.

Richard Taylor was ordered to Natchitoches in June 1864. Here, the Town Council hailed him as a hero and provided him with a large and well-furnished home. He remained here until July 1864, when he was ordered to return to active command. On July 18, Jefferson Davis promoted him to lieutenant general. Of the 17 Confederates to hold this rank during the war, he was the first who was not a West Pointer. (Nathan Bedford Forrest and Wade Hampton followed.)

Acting on his own initiative, Davis' senior military advisor, Braxton Bragg, ordered Taylor to cross the Mississippi River with Walker's and Polignac's divisions. The men—especially the Texans—balked, and two or three Texas companies deserted *en masse*. Taylor had them brought back at gunpoint and had a captain and 10 men court-martialed and shot. The Texans continued to desert in droves. They were perfectly willing to fight—for Texas. They believed that by fighting in Louisiana, they were fighting for Texas. They compared fighting in Louisiana to fighting an intruder. If they had the choice of fighting him in their bedroom (Texas) or their front yard (Louisiana), they preferred to fight in their yard. But crossing to the eastern side of the Mississippi was different. About half the Texas Division deserted by August 28, when Taylor canceled the operation. By then, the secret was out anyway, and the Yankees posted a gunboat every 12 miles. After the operation was scrubbed, the deserters came back.

Taylor crossed the Mississippi via canoe and assumed command of the Department of Alabama, Mississippi, and Eastern Louisiana, headquartered at Meridian, Mississippi, on September 6. He led it until the end of the war. On January 23, 1865, General Beauregard appointed him acting commander of the Army of Tennessee, a post he held (simultaneous with his departmental command) until February

23, when he was superseded by Joseph E. Johnston.[578] On May 4, 1865, he surrendered the last Confederate forces east of the Mississippi to Canby at Citronville, Alabama, about 40 miles north of Mobile. He sold his horse to finance his family's trip from Natchitoches to New Orleans. Stubborn to the end, General Taylor refused to apply for a pardon and thus forfeited his rights of citizenship. He nevertheless worked tirelessly for the South to soften the Reconstruction Acts and to have Jefferson Davis released from prison.

The general's fortune was swept away by the war. He lost his plantation (which is now a subdivision) and had to file for bankruptcy in 1866. He tried to reestablish his fortune by operating the New Basin Canal, which connected New Orleans to Lake Pontchartrain, six miles away, but the venture failed. He then went to Europe, where he represented the business interests of Samuel Barlow. Here, he became a great friend of the Prince of Wales, who later became Edward VII.

Taylor's wife died in 1875, and he spent his last years living with a daughter in Winchester, Virginia, the scene of one of his earlier victories. Here, he wrote a brilliant memoir, *Destruction and Reconstruction*, which was published shortly before his death. Pulitzer Prize winner Dr. Douglas Southall Freeman called Taylor: "the one Confederate general who possessed literary art that approached first rank ... so much literary charm and so observant an analysis of character ..." *Destruction and Reconstruction*, Freeman added, was "written with the unmistakable touch of cultured scholarship."[579] Taylor was in New York City in a business trip when he died on April 12, 1879, at age 53. His pallbearers included a millionaire, a senator, a congressman, and the secretary of state. He is buried in Metairie, a suburb of New Orleans.

*

---

578 Charles P. Roland, "P. G. T. Beauregard" in Gary W. Gallagher and Joseph T. Glatthaar, Leaders of the Lost Cause (Mechanicsburg, Pennsylvania: 2004), p. 1357 of the Kindle Edition.

579 Douglas Southall Freeman, *The South to Posterity* (New York: 1951), pp. 85-86.

After the surrender, Governor **Henry Watkins Allen** fled to Mexico City, where he set up an English-speaking newspaper. In 1865, Louisiana held its first post-war gubernatorial election. Former Confederates were not allowed to vote. Allen did not run, and there was no organized write-in campaign on his behalf. He nevertheless finished second.

Governor Allen died in Mexico City on April 22, 1866. He was still remembered and beloved by the citizens of Louisiana more than 20 years later, when his body was returned to Louisiana and buried on the grounds of the old state capitol in Baton Rouge. He was the only son of the state so honored. For many years after the war, dozens of Louisiana babies were named "Allen."

Arthur P. Bagby was given command of a Texas cavalry division in early 1865. Kirby Smith promoted him to major general on May 16, 1865. He settled in Victoria, Texas, after the war and then moved to Halletsville, where he set up a prosperous legal practice. He died there on February 21, 1921, at the age of 87.

Joseph Bailey, the brilliant Union engineer, took part in the Mobile campaign and was brevetted major general of volunteers at the end of the war. He settled in Vernon County, Missouri, and was elected sheriff in 1866. He was shot and killed in the line of duty on March 21, 1867.

George W. Baylor led his brigade until April 1865. He later became a captain and a company commander in the Texas Rangers and achieved fame as an Indian fighter in actions against the Apaches. He resigned in 1885 and was elected to the Texas House of Representatives that same year. Baylor got along well with Mexicans and lived in Mexico from 1898 to 1913. He died in San Antonio on March 17, 1916, and is buried there in the Confederate Cemetery.

Kirby Smith gave **Hamilton P. Bee** the cavalry division Tom Green commanded after Taylor resigned. He was severely criticized for this action. Bee ended the war commanding a brigade of infantry in Maxey's division. He went to Mexico after the war but returned to

San Antonio in 1876. He died there in 1897 at the age of 75 and is buried there in the Confederate Cemetery. He and his wife Mildred had six children.

As a result of a palace intrigue, **William Robertson Boggs** was replaced as chief of staff of the Trans-Mississippi Department by Colonel Dr. Sol Smith in 1865. He returned to Georgia after the war but soon moved to St. Louis, where he worked as a civil engineer. He was a professor of mechanical engineering at Virginia Tech from 1875 to 1881. He retired to Winston-Salem, North Carolina, where he wrote his reminiscences, which are historically very valuable. He died in 1911, at age 82.

After leaving New Orleans, **Benjamin F. Butler** rose to the command of the Army of the James in Virginia. Despite being bottled up by Beauregard in the Bermuda Hundred area, even though he outnumbered the rebel by 3 to 1, Lincoln refused to allow Grant to relieve the inept Butler until after the 1864 elections. Grant sent him home shortly after. Now one of the most radical Republicans, Butler resumed his political career and served in Congress from 1867 to 1875 and from 1877 to 1879. He wrote the Civil Rights Acts of 1871 and 1875. The 1875 act was far ahead of its time and would have outlawed racial discrimination in public places but was declared unconstitutional. After being defeated twice, Butler was elected governor of Massachusetts in 1882 but served only a single one-year term. He died in 1893.

Xavier B. Debray commanded his brigade until the end of the war. He lived in Houston and Galveston, where he worked as a teacher, accountant, secretary of the produce exchange, and a member of the city council. He relocated to Austin in 1880 and became translator for the state land office. He died on January 6, 1895, at age 77, and is buried in the State Cemetery in Austin.

William Dwight, Banks' second chief of staff, was given command of a division in Emory's XIX Corps and led it in the Shenandoah Valley. Here, he was arrested for leaving the battlefield for a place of safety so that he could eat his lunch. The charges died of inertia, but Dwight's military career was over. He was discharged in early 1866 without receiving the normal brevet promotion to major general. He settled in Cincinnati, where he and his brothers were employed in the railroad business. He died in Boston in 1888.

William H. Emory assumed command of the XIX Corps and led it in the Shenandoah Valley. He was commander of the District of West Virginia at the end of the war. Breveted major general of volunteers in September 1865, he remained in the Regular Army until 1876, when he retired as a brigadier general. He died in Washington, D.C., in 1887, at the age of 76, and is buried in the Congressional Cemetery.

James F. Fagan was promoted to major general effective April 25, 1864, for his victory at Marks' Mills. He was a post-war planter and was made a U.S. marshal by President Grant in 1875. He died in Little Rock in 1893 and is buried in Mount Holly Cemetery.

William B. Franklin recovered from the wounds he suffered at Mansfield, but his career was ruined. He was never restored to command. Confederate raiders captured him during Early's drive on Washington in July 1864, but he managed to escape. He ended the war as president of a board for retiring disabled officers. Franklin resigned from the army in 1865 and became president of the Colt Fire Arms Manufacturing Company, where he was highly successful. He also supervised the construction of the Connecticut state capitol, was a Democratic presidential elector in 1876, and represented the United States at the Paris Exposition of 1888. He died in Hartford in 1903 at age 80.

After recovering from his wounds at Camden, **Richard M. Gano** returned to Indian Territory. He defeated a sizable Union force at Cabin Creek in September 1864, where he was wounded again. He was one of the last Confederate generals, being promoted to brigadier on March 17, 1865. He resumed his Church of Christ ministry after the war, started numerous churches over the next 45 years, and baptized some 8,000 people. His other passion was livestock, and he was responsible for bringing fine-blooded cattle, horses, sheep, and hogs into Texas. He also formed a real estate and livestock company with his two sons and at one time owned

50,000 acres. Successful at everything he tried, Richard Gano died a millionaire in Dallas on March 27, 1913. Howard Hughes, the eccentric millionaire and aviation pioneer, was one of his grandsons.

Henry Gray, the commander of the Louisiana Brigade, was elected to the Confederate Congress by the voters of north Louisiana in 1864, despite the fact that he was not a candidate for the office and did not even know that he was on the ballot until after the election. He took his seat but was nevertheless promoted to brigadier general on March 17, 1865—two weeks before the fall of Richmond. After the war, General Gray resumed his law practice and except for a term in the Louisiana Senate, retired from public service. Following the death of his wife, Gray spent his last years in virtual seclusion and died in Coushatta, Louisiana, in 1892, at age 76.

Cuvier Grover later served in the Shenandoah Valley campaign of 1864, where he performed better than he had in Louisiana by a wide margin. He was brevetted major general for his gallantry at Cedar Creek, where he was wounded. He commanded the District of Savannah in 1865. After the war, he remained in the Regular Army as lieutenant colonel of the 38th Infantry, a Negro unit, and later as colonel of the 1st Cavalry. He died in Atlantic City, New Jersey, in 1885.

Albert L. Lee was later restored to the command of the cavalry division by General Edward R. S. Canby, but the two did not get along, and on April 2, 1865, Canby ordered Lee not to leave New Orleans without his permission. After the war, Lee engaged in business in New York and Europe. He died in New York City on New Year's Eve, 1907, at the age of 73.

St. John R. Liddell, the former Confederate commander of the Subdistrict of North Louisiana, was contentious by nature, as we have seen, and the years did not improve his disposition. In 1870, he was murdered by a neighbor and his two sons while he was eating on a steamboat. His death was the continuation of a feud which pre-dated the war.[580]

---

580 Kinard, p. 119.

It took **Louisiana** almost a century to recover from the war, and it has yet to recover its previous position. In 1860, it was ranked second in the Union in per capita income, and half of all American millionaires lived along the Natchez-New Orleans axis. Today, it ranks 41st in per capita income. Its overall political leadership since 1865 has given the residents of the state little to brag about.

"Prince John" Magruder fled to Mexico after the war and joined the Imperial Army as a major general. He escaped the fall of Emperor Macmillian and returned to Texas, where he died in poverty on February 18, 1871. He is buried in Galveston. Contrary to the popular myth that he was never married, he did, in fact, wed Henrietta von Kapff in Baltimore in 1831, and she had at least three children.[581] He did not always act married, however.

John S. Marmaduke followed Sterling Price into Missouri in 1864 and during the retreat, was captured at Mine Creek, Kansas, on October 25, 1864. Although he spent the rest of the war in prison, he was nevertheless promoted to major general of March 18, 1865—the last Confederate to reach that rank. After the war, he engaged in business and edited an agricultural journal. He was elected governor of Missouri in 1884 and died in office in Jefferson City on December 28, 1887.

Samuel B. Maxey, the Confederate commander of Indian Territory, returned to Texas and practiced law at Paris until 1875, when he was elected to the U.S. Senate. He was reelected in 1881 but was defeated in 1887. He died in Eureka Springs, Arkansas, in 1895, at the age of 70. He is buried in Paris, Texas.

Joseph A. Mower was promoted to major general on August 12, 1864. He led a division during the Atlanta campaign, in Sherman's March to the Sea, and in the Carolinas. At the end of the war, he was commanding the XX Corps in the Army of Georgia. When the army was reorganized in 1866, Mower was given command of the newly formed 39th Infantry, an African-American regiment. Later, he commanded the 25th Infantry, another black regiment. He was

---

581   Warner, *Generals in Gray*, pp. 207-208.

in New Orleans as commander of the District of Louisiana in 1869, when he came down with pneumonia and died on January 6, 1870, at age 42. He is buried in Arlington National Cemetery.

Ormand F. Nims, the commander of the 2nd Massachusetts Light Artillery, was sent home with his battery, which was disbanded. Nims injured his ankle while at home and when he returned to New Orleans, was assigned to a staff position in the Quartermaster Department, since he was physically unable to handle another field command. He was brevetted colonel in 1865 and returned to Boston after the war. He ran his small drug store until 1910, when he retired. He died at home in Boston on May 23, 1911, at age 91.[582]

Prince Camille de Polignac was sent to France on a secret diplomatic mission in early 1865 and never returned because the South surrendered shortly after he arrived in Europe. He lived on his family's estate and studied mathematics for the next five years. When the Franco-Prussian War began in 1870, Polignac was commissioned major in the French Army. Here, his experience in the Confederate Army became immediately apparent, as he was one of the few French officers who could actually defeat the Germans. In less than a year, he earned the Cross of the Legion of Honor and rose to the rank of major general. He was a corps commander when Paris surrendered.

In 1874, he married Marie Langenberger in Frankfurt/Main, Germany. The marriage lasted only 14 months, because his wife died in childbirth. The prince, however, proved to be an excellent father and delighted in his daughter. He remarried in 1883 to 18-year-old Margaret Elizabeth Knight of London. They had three children, and he was, by all accounts, a loving and faithful husband. He instilled in his children Southern values, Southern hospitality, and a love for the Confederacy. He praised Southerners for their courage and generosity at every opportunity and was an unrepentant Rebel until the end. He named his only son Victor Mansfield.

---

582 Whitcomb, pp. 88-90.

In 1883, he bought Podwein, a large estate in the Austrian Alps, where he spent his remaining years playing his violin and studying mathematics. His wife, who was an accomplished pianist, usually accompanied him.

Camille de Polignac died of a cerebral edema while working on a math problem at his daughter's home in Paris on November 15, 1913, the last of the Confederate major generals to pass away. He was 81 years old. He was buried in the family vault with his first wife in Frankfurt-am-Main, Germany.

David D. Porter was named commander of the North Atlantic Blockading Squadron shortly after the Red River campaign. He testified against Nathaniel Banks before the Joint Congressional Committee, where he stated: "I am happy to say that I have never been afflicted with the mania" of trying to profit from cotton speculation. Porter was promoted to vice admiral in 1866, making him the senior naval officer of the post-war era. He was superintendent of the U.S. Naval Academy from 1866 to 1870. He lived in Washington, D.C., after that and wrote several naval history books and novels. He died on February 13, 1891, and is buried in Arlington National Cemetery.

Sterling Price invaded Missouri in 1864. Although he threatened Jefferson City and St. Louis, he was ultimately defeated and lost more than half his command. After the war, he fled to Mexico but returned to Missouri in 1866. He died in St. Louis on September 29, 1867, nine days after his 57th birthday. He is buried in Bellefontaine Cemetery not far from A. J. Smith.

Thomas E. G. Ransom took command of a division in the XVI Corps near Atlanta in August but was soon commanding the corps, as General Grenville Dodge was wounded. Brevetted major general, Ransom was given command of the XVII Corps after the city fell, but he never fully recovered from the wound he suffered at Mansfield. Active campaigning proved too much for his health, and he died near Rome, Georgia, on October 29, 1864. His body was returned to Chicago for burial.

Epilogue And Postscript

Joseph J. Reynolds, who Banks left in charge of New Orleans, Baton Rouge, and the Lafourche region, while he conducted the Red River campaign, was eventually named commander of the XIX Corps and in 1865, commander of the VII Corps in Arkansas. The carpetbagger legislature of Texas elected him to the U.S. Senate in 1871, but his seat was successfully contested by Morgan C. Hamilton, the brother of the former governor. He later returned to the West, but his career was ruined when he ordered a premature retreat at Powder River in 1876, allowing the Sioux to capture a wounded private, whom they immediately dismembered. Reynolds was court-martialed and forced to retire. He was born in 1822 and died in 1899.

A. J. Smith led the XVI Corps for the rest of the war. He took the town of Tupelo, Mississippi, from Major General Stephen D. Lee in July 1864 but was unable to hold it and retreated rapidly to Memphis. Although he won a tactical victory of sorts and burned Tupelo, Smith failed in his primary objective: destroy Nathan Bedford Forrest's cavalry. A. J. Smith later fought in Missouri and Tennessee with greater success and was involved in capturing Mobile at the end of the war. He commanded the 7th Cavalry (1866-69) in the post-war army and was named postmaster of St. Louis by President Grant in 1869. He became city auditor in 1877 and served until his retirement in 1889. He died in St. Louis in 1897 at age 81.

Edmund Kirby Smith fled to Mexico in June 1865, riding a mule, with a revolver in his belt and carrying a shotgun. He wrote his wife that he "had left everything behind except a clear conscience and a sense of having done my duty."[583] One of his last acts was to order Captain Erneste Cucullu to turn over the last $3,300 in Confederate Secret Service funds to Major General Canby. This turned out to be $3,209 after expenses. "That is just like Kirby Smith," Canby remarked. "Always the soul of honor."[584]

---

583   Cassidy and Simpson, p. 136.
584   Noll, pp. 267-268.

After a brief stay in Mexico, Kirby Smith moved on to Havana. He returned to the United States and was president of an insurance company, and then he ran the Atlantic and Pacific Telegraph Company, located in Louisville, Kentucky. He established a military school at New Castle, Kentucky, but it was destroyed by a fire. In 1870, he became chancellor of the University of Nashville, where he served until 1875. He was named professor of mathematics at the University of the South in 1875, a position which he held until his death on March 28, 1893. He is buried in Sewanee.

A Christian his entire life, Kirby Smith was hurt by General Taylor's attacks, which he considered unjustified, but he steadfastly refused to respond to them. One of his grandsons, also named Edmund Kirby-Smith, was a West Point graduate and, during World War II, fought in North Africa, Italy, France, and Germany. He retired as a colonel. He is buried in the University of the South Cemetery, near his grandfather.

Thomas Kilby Smith performed well in the Red River campaign, but like most of the Union officers who fought there, he was looked upon as a bit of a failure—guilt by association. He was sent to Mississippi to chase Nathan Bedford Forrest, which he did without success. He was nevertheless brevetted major general. After the war, he was briefly U.S. consul to Panama but settled in Torresdale, Pennsylvania. He died in New York City in 1887 and was buried in Torresdale.

After the Camden Expedition, **Frederick Steele** was demoted from a corps to a division commander, although he remained a major general. He commanded a division under E. R. S. Canby during the Mobile campaign in 1865. He remained in the army after the war, was named colonel of the 20th Infantry Regiment in 1867, and became commander of the Department of Columbia later that year. He was killed in a buggy accident in California on January 12, 1868.

Alexander W. Terrell resumed his law practice after the war and served as U.S. ambassador to Turkey from 1893 to 1897 under President Grover Cleveland, despite a famous poem he wrote lavishing praise on John Wilkes Booth. When Northerners were considering exhuming Booth's body and dumping it in the Atlantic Ocean, Terrill professed to believing this was a fine idea. The Atlantic Ocean, he declared, would be suitable memorial for a man as great as John Wilkes Booth.[585]

General Terrill visited relatives in Virginia in 1912 and stopped off at the Crazy Water Building, a hotel in Mineral Wells, Texas, on September 9. He went automobile riding that day and was in a very cheerful mood when he went to his room. He was found dead the next morning, the apparent victim of a heart attack. He is buried in the State Cemetery at Austin, near Colonels Hardeman, Debray, and Buchel.[586]

John M. Thayer commanded the District of the Frontier until early 1865, when he was named commandant of St. Charles, Arkansas—a definite demotion. He was nevertheless mustered out as a brevet major general in 1865. When Nebraska was admitted to the Union, Thayer became one of its first two U.S. senators. A Radical Republican and an ardent Grant supporter, he was defeated for reelection in 1871. President Grant named him governor of Wyoming Territory that same year. Thayer was elected governor of Nebraska in 1886 and 1888. Not a candidate for reelection in 1890, Thayer filed a law suit against his successor, claiming that he was not a U.S. citizen. This enabled him to remain in office until 1892, when the U.S. Supreme Court finally ousted him. He retired to Lincoln, where he died in 1906 at age 86.

Colonel **William G. Vincent** continued to lead a cavalry brigade until the end of the war. He was a highly successful merchant after the conflict and served on the board of directors of several corporations and banks. A generous and compassionate man, he was active in civic affairs and charitable organizations in New Orleans, especially

---

585 Although many Southerners were appalled when they first heard that Lincoln had been assassinated, many later came to believe that Lincoln had gotten what he deserved. A popular toast in the Reconstruction and New South eras went: "Here's to the man who pulled the trigger, and killed the man who freed the n**ger."

586 Spencer, pp. 92-99.

in helping educate the deaf and the blind. He also played a major role in suppressing the notoriously corrupt Louisiana Lottery. He retired in 1896 and died around 1922. In his will, he left $60,000 ($1,074,428.in 2023 money) to Tulane University to establish a medical chair in tropical diseases and hygiene, as well as $30,000 to the charity hospital in New Orleans—a huge amount of money in those days.

Major General **John G. Walker** was commander of the District of Texas, New Mexico and Arizona from August 4, 1864 to March 31, 1865, when he was replaced by Magruder. He commanded Wharton's Cavalry Corps from April 6, 1865 until the end of the war. After briefly going to Mexico, he returned to the United States and then went to South America as U.S. consul general to Bogata, Columbia, and as a special commissioner to South America. He died of a stroke in Washington, D.C., on July 20, 1893, and is buried in the Stonewall Jackson Cemetery in Winchester, Virginia. He was survived by a wife, a son, and four daughters.

John A. Wharton's cavalry corps took part in Price's disastrous raid into Missouri in 1864 and was downgraded to a 5,400-man division by General Kirby Smith in November but became a corps again in early 1865. By February, he had a paper strength of 10,169 men, but only 5,944 were present for duty. By then, he was headquartered in Hempstead, Texas.

Wharton commanded his cavalry corps until April 6, 1865. That day, he was preparing to leave Houston following a meeting with General Magruder. Brigadier General James E. Harrison drove him to the railroad yard in a carriage when they ran into Colonel George W. Baylor. Wharton and Baylor hated each other since the Red River campaign, when Baylor blamed Wharton for needlessly sacrificing some of his men. Wharton retaliated by rejecting Baylor's request for a furlough, even though he approved others. Wharton also placed Baylor's brigade (which was being dismounted) under the command of Colonel David S. Terry, who was junior to Baylor. The chance encounter led to harsh words and ended with Wharton calling Baylor a "damned liar." Baylor swung at the general with his fist, but Harrison moved the carriage forward just in time, so the blow missed. Wharton then ordered Baylor to report to his headquarters in Hempstead under arrest. Baylor replied that he would report to General Magruder. Wharton replied that he could report to Magruder's headquarters at the Fannin House, but he was still under arrest.

After Baylor left, Wharton got on the train but decided that he needed to settle the matter with Magruder first, so he went to the Fannin House.

Baylor, meanwhile, reported to Magruder in tears. The general took him to a private room upstairs, told him to compose himself, and then come back down. Wharton and Harrison arrived shortly thereafter and, looking for Magruder, entered the same room and found Baylor on the bed, crying. More angry words followed and Wharton moved toward Baylor, his fists clenched. Harrison stepped between them, but it was too late. Wharton swung at Baylor and the colonel drew his pistol and, even though Harrison was grabbing at his hand, fired a single shot, which struck the general just below the ribs. He died almost instantly.

Baylor was arrested for the murder of General Wharton but the Confederacy died before he could be tried. He was placed on trial in late 1868 but was acquitted, as the jury determined that it was an affair of honor. Baylor recalled later that the incident, to him, was a source of lifelong regret.

George W. Baylor lived in Mexico, Dallas, and El Paso after the war, working as an insurance agent and a farmer. He also served in the Texas state legislature. Born at Fort Gibson, Indian Territory, in 1832, he died in San Antonio in 1916, and is buried there in the Confederate Cemetery.

Appendix 1

Order Of Battle, The Army Of Western Louisiana

April 8, 1864

Commander: Major General Richard Taylor

1st Division: Major General John G. Walker

1st Brigade: Brigadier General Thomas N. Waul

    12th Texas Infantry: Colonel Overton C. Young

    18th Texas Infantry: Colonel Wilburn H. King

    22nd Texas Infantry: Colonel Richard B. Hubbard

    13th Texas Cavalry (Dismounted): Colonel Anderson F. Crawford

2nd Brigade: Colonel Horace Randal

    11th Texas Infantry: Colonel Oran M. Roberts

    14th Texas Infantry: Colonel Edward Clark

28th Texas Cavalry (Dismounted): Lieutenant Colonel Eli H. Baxter, Jr.

6th Texas Cavalry Battalion: Lieutenant Colonel Robert S. Gould

3rd Brigade: Brigadier General William R. Scurry

3rd Texas Infantry: Colonel Phillip N. Luckett

16th Texas Infantry: Colonel George Flournoy

16th Texas Cavalry (Dismounted): Colonel William Fitzhugh

17th Texas Infantry: Colonel Robert T. P. Allen

19th Texas Infantry: Colonel Richard Waterhouse

2nd Division: Brigadier General Alfred Mouton (K); Brigadier General Prince Camille de Polignac

1st (Louisiana) Brigade: Colonel Henry Gray

18th Louisiana Infantry: Colonel Leopold L. Armant (K); Lieutenant Colonel Joseph Collins

28th Louisiana Infantry: Lieutenant Colonel William Walker (K); Major Thomas W. Pool

Consolidated Crescent Regiment: Colonel James Beard (K); Major Mercer Canfield (K); Captain William C. C. Claiborne, Jr. **

2nd (Texas) Brigade: Polignac; Colonel James R. Taylor (K); Lieutenant Colonel Robert D. Stone (K); Lieutenant Colonel James E. Harrison

15th Texas Infantry: Lieutenant Colonel Harrison; Major John W. Daniel

17th Consolidated Texas Cavalry (Dismounted): Colonel James R. Taylor; Lieutenant Colonel Sebron M. Noble (K); Major Thomas F. Tucker

Appendix 1

22nd Texas Cavalry (Dismounted): Lieutenant Colonel Stone; Major George W. Merrick

31st Texas Cavalry (Dismounted): Major Frederick J. Malone

34th Texas Cavalry (Dismounted): Lieutenant Colonel John H. Caudle

Cavalry Corps: Brigadier General Thomas Green; Brigadier General Hamilton P. Bee; Major General John Wharton

Bee's Division: Brigadier General Hamilton P. Bee

Debray's Brigade: Colonel Xavier B. Debray

    23rd Texas Cavalry: Colonel Nicholas C. Gould

    26th Texas Cavalry: Lieutenant Colonel John J. Meyers

    32nd Texas Cavalry: Colonel Peter C. Woods *

Buchel's Brigade: Colonel Augustus C. Buchel

    1st Texas Cavalry: Lieutenant Colonel William O. Yager

    35th Texas Cavalry: Colonel James B. Likens *

    37th (34th) Texas Cavalry: Colonel Alexander W. Terrell

Major's Division: Brigadier General James P. Major

Lane's Brigade: Colonel Walter P. Lane (wounded, April 8); Colonel George W. Baylor

    1st Texas Partisan Ranger Battalion: Lieutenant Colonel Richard P. Crump

    2nd Texas Partisan Ranger Battalion: Colonel Isham Chisum

    2nd Arizona Cavalry: Colonel Baylor; Lieutenant Colonel John W. Mullen

3rd Arizona Cavalry: Lieutenant Colonel George T. Madison

Bagby's Brigade: Colonel Arthur P. Bagby

4th Texas Cavalry: Colonel William P. Hardeman

5th Texas Cavalry: Major Hugh A. McPhaill

7th Texas Cavalry: Lieutenant Colonel Philemon T. Herbert, Jr. (mortally wounded, April 8); Lieutenant Colonel Gustave Hoffman

13th Texas Cavalry Battalion: Lieutenant Colonel Edward Waller

Vincent's Brigade: Colonel William G. Vincent

2nd Louisiana Cavalry: Vincent; Major Winter O. Breazeale

7th Louisiana Cavalry: Colonel Louis Bush

NOTES:

* Did not arrive in time to participate in the Battle of Mansfield

** Colonel Abel W. Bosworth was also with the Crescent Regiment and was killed in action on April 8. It is unclear if he ever commanded the regiment; if so, it was only for a few minutes.

Appendix 2

Order Of Battle, The Army Of The Gulf April 8, 1864

Commander: Major General Nathaniel P. Banks

XIII Corps Detachment: Brigadier General Thomas E. G. Ransom (W)

3rd Division: Brigadier General Robert A. Cameron

1st Brigade: Lieutenant Colonel Aaron M. Flory

- 46th Indiana
- 29th Wisconsin

2nd Brigade: Colonel William H. Reynor

- 24th Iowa
- 28th Iowa
- 56th Ohio

4th Division: Colonel William J. Landrum

1st Brigade: Colonel Frank Emerson (W and C)

    77th Illinois

    67th Illinois

    19th Kentucky

    23rd Wisconsin

2nd Brigade: Colonel Joseph W. Vance (W and C)

    130th Illinois

    48th Ohio

    83rd Ohio

    96th Ohio

2nd Brigade, 1st Division: Brigadier General Michael K. Lawler (3)

    49th Indiana

    69th Indiana

    34th Iowa

    22nd Kentucky

    16th Ohio

XIX Corps: Major General William B. Franklin (W)

1st Division: Brigadier General William H. Emory

1st Brigade: Brigadier General William Dwight

    29th Maine

    114th New York

Appendix 2

    116th New York

    153rd New York

    161st New York

2nd Brigade: Brigadier General James W. McMillan

    15th Maine

    160th New York

    47th Pennsylvania

    13th Maine

3rd Brigade: Colonel Lewis Benedict

    30th Maine

    162nd New York

    173rd New York

    165th New York

2nd Division: Brigadier General Cuvier Grover (3)

2nd Brigade: Colonel Edward L. Molineaux

    13th Connecticut

    1st Louisiana

    90th New York

    159th New York

3rd Brigade: Colonel Jacob Sharpe

    38th Massachusetts

    128th New York

156th New York

175th New York

3rd Maryland Cavalry

Cavalry Division: Brigadier General Albert L. Lee

1st Brigade: Colonel Thomas J. Lucas

14th New York Cavalry

16th Indiana Mounted Infantry

2nd Louisiana Mounted Infantry

3rd Brigade: Colonel Harai Robinson

1st Louisiana Cavalry

87th Illinois Mounted Infantry

4th Brigade: Colonel Nathan A. M. Dudley

2nd Illinois Cavalry

3rd Massachusetts Cavalry (1)

2nd New Hampshire Cavalry (2)

5th Brigade: Colonel Oliver R. Gooding

18th New York Cavalry

3rd Rhode Island Cavalry

2nd New York Cavalry

XVI Corps: Brigadier General Andrew J. Smith (3)

1st Division

Appendix 2

2nd Brigade: Colonel Lucius Hubbard
- 47th Illinois
- 5th Minnesota
- 8th Wisconsin

3rd Brigade: Colonel Sylvester G. Hill
- 35th Iowa (4)
- 33rd Missouri (5)

3rd Division: Brigadier General Joseph A. Mower

1st Brigade: Colonel William F. Lynch
- 58th Illinois
- 119th Illinois
- 89th Indiana (6)

2nd Brigade: Colonel William T. Shaw
- 14th Iowa
- 27th Iowa
- 32nd Iowa
- 24th Missouri (7)

3rd Brigade: Colonel Risdon M. Moore
- 49th Illinois
- 117th Illinois
- 178th New York

2nd Division, XVII Corps: Brigadier General Thomas Kilby Smith (8)

1st Brigade: Colonel Jonathan B. Moore

    41st Illinois

    3rd Iowa

    33rd Wisconsin

2nd Brigade: Colonel Lyman M. Ward

    81st Illinois

    95th Illinois

    14th Wisconsin

Marine Brigade: Brigadier General A. W. Ellet

  Infantry Regiment

  Cavalry Battalion

Corps d' Afrique (U.S. Colored Troops [USCT])

1st Brigade: Colonel William Dickey

    73rd Regiment, USCT

    75th Regiment, USCT

    84th Regiment, USCT

    92nd Regiment, USCT

Engineer Brigade: Colonel George D. Robinson

    97th Regiment, USCT

    99th Regiment, USCT

Appendix 2

(1) Formerly the 31st Massachusetts Mounted Infantry

(2) Formerly the 8th New Hampshire Mounted Infantry

(3) Not present at the Battle of Mansfield

(4) With elements of the 8th and 12th Iowa attached

(5) With elements of the 11th Missouri attached

(6) With elements of the 52nd Indiana attached

(7) With elements of the 21st Missouri attached

(8) Attached to XVI Corps

Bibliography

Aiken, Charles. Lecture delivered at the University of Tennessee, 1981.

Alceneaux, William. *Lafayette of the South: Prince Camille de Polignac and the American Civil War*. College Station, Texas: 2001.

Allardice, Bruce S. *Confederate Colonels*. Columbia, Missouri: 2008.

Allardice, Bruce S. *More Generals in Gray*. Baton Rouge: 1995.

Allen, Henry Watkins. *The Conduct of Federal Troops in Louisiana During the Invasions of 1863 and 1864*. Shreveport: 1865.

Anderson, John Q. *A Texas Surgeon in the Confederate States Army*. Tuscaloosa, Alabama: 1957.

Anderson, John Q. *Brockenburn: The Journal of Kate Stone: 1861-1868*. Baton Rouge: 1955.

Andrews, J. Cutler. *The North Reports the Civil War*. Pittsburgh: 1955.

Andrus, Onley. *The Civil War Letters of Sergeant Onley Andrus*, Fred Albert Sharmon, ed. Urbana, Illinois: 1947.

Anonymous. *An Historical Sketch of the 162nd Regiment, New York Volunteer Infantry.* Albany, New York: 1867.

Arceneaux, William. *Acadian General: Alfred Mouton and the Civil War*. Lafayette: University of Southwestern Louisiana Press, 1981.

Arey, Frank. "The First Kansas Colored at Honey Springs" in Mark K. Christ, ed., *"All Cut to Pieces and Gone to Hell:" The Civil War, Race Relations and the Battle of Poison Springs*. Little Rock: 2003.

Armstrong, Fred C., and Joseph W. Kirkley, comp. *The War of the Rebellion: A Compilation of the Official Records of the Union and Confederate Armies*. Series 3. Washington, D.C.: 1900. This series deals with prisons and prisoners of war.

Ayres, Thomas. *Dark and Bloody Ground: The Battle of Mansfield and the Forgotten Civil War in Louisiana*. Lanham, Maryland: 2001.

Babcock, Willoughby M. *Selections from the Letters and Diaries of Brevet-Brigadier General Willoughby Babcock of the Seventy-Fifth New York Volunteers*. Albany: 1922.

Bailey, Anne J. *Between the Enemy and Texas: Parsons's Texas Cavalry in the Civil War*. Ft. Worth: 1989.

Baker, William D. *The Camden Expedition of 1864*. Little Rock: 1964.

Bankston, Marie Louise Benton. *Camp-Fire Stories of the Mississippi Valley Campaign*. New Orleans: 1914.

Barr, Alwyn, ed. "The Civil War Diary of James Allen Hamilton, 1861-1864." *Texana*. Vol II, No. 2 (Summer 1964).

Bartlett, Napier. *Military Record of Louisiana: Including Biographical and Historical Papers Relating to the Military Organization of the State*. New Orleans: 1875. Reprint ed., Baton Rouge: 1964.

"Battle of Yellow Bayou." *Confederate Veteran*. Vol XXV (February 1917).

Bearss, Edwin C., ed. *A Louisiana Confederate: Diary of Felix Pierre Poche*. Eugenie Watson Somdal, trans. Natchitoches, Louisiana: 1972.

Bearss, Edwin C. *Steele's Retreat from Camden and the Battle of Jenkins' Ferry*. Little Rock: 1967.

Bee, Hamilton P. "Battle of Pleasant Hill—An Error Corrected." *Southern Historical Society Papers*. Vol. VIII (April 1880).

Beecher, Harris H. *Record of the 114th Regiment, New York State Volunteers: Where It Went, What It Saw and What It Did*. Norwich, New York: 1866.

Benedict, Henry M. *A Memorial of Brevet Brigadier General Lewis Benedict*. Albany, New York: 1866.

Bentley, W. H. *History of the 7th Illinois Volunteer Infantry*. Peoria, Illinois: 1883.

Bering, John A., and Thomas Montgomery. *History of the Forty-Eighth Ohio Veteran Volunteer Infantry*. Hillsboro, Ohio: 1880.

Blessington, J. P. *The Campaign of Walker's Texas Division*. New York: 1875.

Boggs, William R. *Military Reminiscences of General William R. Boggs, C.S.A*. Durham, North Carolina: 1913.

Bonner, Thomas R. "Sketches of the Campaign of 1864." *The Land We Love*. Volume V, No. VI (October 1868).

Booth, A. B. "Louisiana Confederate Military Records." *Louisiana Historical Quarterly*. Vol. IV (July 1921).

Bowman, Thomas H. *Reminiscences of an Ex-Confederate Soldier or Forty Years on Crutches*. Austin, Texas: 1904.

Boynton, Charles B. *The History of the Navy During the Rebellion*. New York: 1967.

Bragg, Jefferson Davis. *Louisiana in the Confederacy*. Baton Rouge: 1941.

Bringhurst, Thomas H., and Frank Swigart. *History of the Forty-Sixth Regiment, Indiana Volunteer Infantry*. Logansport, Indiana: 1888.

Britton, Wiley. *The Civil War on the Border*. New York: 1899. 2 Volumes.

Brooksher, William Riley. *War Along the Bayous*. Washington, D.C.: 1998.

Brown, Norman, D., ed. *Journey to Pleasant Hill: The Civil War Letters of Captain Elijah P. Petty, Walker's Texas Division, C.S.A.* San Antonio: 1982.

Bryner, Cloyd. *The Story of the Illinois 47th*. Springfield: 1905.

Cassidy, Vincent H., and Amos E. Simpson. *Henry Watkins Allen of Louisiana*. Baton Rouge: 1964.

Cawthon, John A., ed. "Letters of a North Louisiana Private to His Wife, 1962-1865." *Mississippi Valley Historical Review*. Vol. XXX (March 1944).

Chandler, Luther E. "The Career of Henry Watkins Allen." Unpublished Ph.D. Dissertation, L.S.U., Baton Rouge: 1940.

Christ, Mark. *All Cut to Pieces and Gone to Hell: The Civil War, Race Relations and the Battle of Poison Springs*. Little Rock: 2003.

_____, ed. *Rugged and Sublime: The Civil War in Arkansas*. Fayetteville, Arkansas: 1994.

_____. "Who Wrote the Poison Spring Letter?" in Mark K. Christ, ed., *"All Cut to Pieces and Gone to Hell:" The Civil War, Race Relations and the Battle of Poison Springs*. Little Rock: 2003.

Clark, Orton S. *The One Hundred and Sixteenth Regiment of New York State Volunteers*. Buffalo: 1868.

Connelly, Thomas L. *Autumn of Glory: The Army of Tennessee, 1862-1865*. Baton Rouge: 1971.

Coulter, E. Merton. "Commercial Intercourse with the Confederacy in the Mississippi Valley." *Mississippi Valley Historical Review*. Vol. IV (1918-19).

Davis, Jackson Beauregard. "The Life of Richard Taylor." *Louisiana Historical Quarterly*. Vol. XXIV (Jan 1941).

Davis, William C., ed. *The Confederate General*. Harrisburg, Pennsylvania: 1991-92. 6 Vol.s.

DeBlack, Thomas A. "An Overview of the Camden Expedition" in Mark K. Christ, ed., *"All Cut to Pieces and Gone to Hell:" The Civil War, Race Relations and the Battle of Poison Springs*. Little Rock: 2003.

Debray, Xavier B. "A Sketch of Debray's Twenty-Sixth Regiment of Texas Cavalry." *Southern Historical Society Papers*. Vol. XII (Oct-Dec 1884) and Vol. XIII (Jan-Dec 1885).

DiLorenzo, Thomas. Interview on Confederate Broadcasting. Aired April 18, 2018, and periodically before and since.

DiLorenzo, Thomas. *Lincoln Unmasked*. New York: 2006.

DiLorenzo, Thomas. *The Real Lincoln*. New York: 2002.

Dimitry, John. "Louisiana," in *Confederate Military History*. Clement A. Evans, ed. Vol X. Atlanta: 1899.

Dorsey, Sarah A. *Recollections of Henry Watkins Allen, Brigadier General, Confederate States Army, Ex-Governor of Louisiana*. New York: 1866.

Douglas, Kyd. *I Rode With Stonewall*. Chapel Hill, North Carolina: 1940. Reprint ed., Chapel Hill, North Carolina: 1968.

Douglass, Frederick. *Douglass' Monthly*. Vol. IV (September 1861).

Duaine, Carl L. *The Dead Men Wore Boots: An Account of the 32nd Texas Volunteer Cavalry, C.S.A*. Austin, Texas: 1966.

Dufour, Charles L. *Nine Men in Gray*. Garden City, New York: 1969.

Dufour, Charles L. *Ten Flags in the Wind: The Story of Louisiana*. New York: 1967.

Dupree, Stephen A. *Campaigning with the 67th Indiana*. Bloomington, Indiana: 2006.

Dupree, Stephen A. *Planting the Union Flag in Texas: The Campaigns of Major General Nathaniel P. Banks*. College Station, Texas: 2008.

Edmonds, David C. *Yankee Autumn in Acadiana*. Lafayette: 1979.

Edwards, John W. *Shelby and His Men: or, the War in the West*. Cincinnati: 1867.

Eicher, David J. *The Longest Night*. New York: 2002.

Eicher, John H. and David J. Eicher. *Civil War High Commads*. Stanford, California: 2001.

Erikson, Edgar L., ed. "Hunting for Cotton in Dixie: From the Diary of Captain Charles E. Wilcox." *Journal of Southern History*. Vol. IV (1938).

Evans, Clement A., ed. *Confederate Military History*. Atlanta: 1899. 12 Volumes.

Ewer, James K. *The 3rd Massachusetts Cavalry in the War for the Union*. Maplewood, Mass.: 1903.

Faulk, Odie. *Tom Green*. Waco, Texas: 1963.

Find-A-Grave Memorials. Various people, find-a-grave.com.

Fiske, John. *The Mississippi Valley in the Civil War*. Boston: 1900.

Fitzhugh, Lester N. *Texas Batteries, Battalions, Regiments, Commanders and Field Officers, Confederate States Army, 1861-1865*. Midlothian, Texas: 1959.

Flinn, Frank M. *Campaigning with Banks in Louisiana in '63 and '64 and with Sheridan in the Shenandoah Valley in '64 and '65*. 2nd ed. Boston: 1889.

Forsyth, Michael J. *The Camden Expedition*. Jefferson, North Carolina: 2007.

Forsyth, Michael J. *The Red River Campaign of 1864 and the Loss by the Confederacy of the Civil War.* Jefferson, North Carolina: 2002.

Forty Sixth Indiana Volunteer Infantry Regimental Association. *Forty-Sixth Regiment, Indiana Volunteer Infantry.* Indianapolis: 1888.

Fox, William F. *Regimental Losses in the American Civil War.* Dayton, Ohio: 1985.

Freeman, Douglas Southall. *Lee's Lieutenants.* New York: 1942-44. 3 Vol.s.

Freeman, Douglas Southall. *R. E. Lee: A Biography.* New York: 1934-36. 4 Vol.s.

Freeman, Douglas Southall. *The South to Posterity.* New York: 1951.

Gaines, W. Craig. *Encyclopedia of Civil War Shipwrecks.* Baton Rouge: 2008.

Gallagher, Gary W. and Joseph T. Glatthaar. *Leaders of the Lost Cause.* Mechanicsburg, Pennsylvania: 2004.

Gallaway, B. P. *The Ragged Rebel: A Cannon Soldier in W. H. Parsons's Texas Cavalry, 1861-1865.* Austin: 1988.

Garland, Albert N. "E. Kirby Smith and the Trans-Mississippi Confederacy." Unpublished M.A. Thesis, L.S.U., Baton Rouge: 1947.

Genius, Dale. Louisiana History Museum. Personal communication, June 24, 2009.

Glatthaar, Joseph T. *Forged in Battle; The Civil War Alliance of Black Soldiers and White Officers.* New York: 1990.

Goff, Richard D. *Confederate Supply.* Durham, North Carolina: 1969.

Gosnell, H. Allen. *Guns on the Western Waters: The Story of the River Gunboats in the Civil War.* Baton Rouge: 1949.

Govan, Gilbert, and James W. Livingood, ed.s. *The Haskell Memoirs: The Personal Narrative of a Confederate Officer.* New York: 1960.

Groce, William Wharton. "Major General John A. Wharton." *Southwestern Historical Quarterly.* Vol. XIX (January 1916).

Hall, Winchester. *The Story of the 26th Louisiana Infantry Regiment.* N.p, n.d.

Hamilton, Holman. *Zachary Taylor: Soldier in the White House.* Norwalk, Connecticut: 1941.

Hammond, Paul E. "General Kirby Smith's Campaign in Kentucky in 1862." *Southern Historical Society Papers.* Volume 9 (July-August 1881).

Hanaburgh, D. H. *History of the One Hundred and Twenty-eighth Regiment, New York Volunteers.* Poughkeepsie, New York: 1894.

Harrell, John M. "Arkansas" in Vol. X, *Confederate Military History.* Clement A. Evans, ed. Atlanta: 1899. 12 Vol.s.

Harrington, Fred H. *Fighting Politician: Major General N. P. Banks.* Philadelphia: 1948.

Hatton, Roy O. "Prince Camille de Polignac and the American Civil War, 1863-1865." *Louisiana Studies*, Vol. 3, No. 2 (Summer 1964).

Heartsill, W. W. *Fourteen Hundred and 91 Days in the Confederate Army.* Bell I. Wiley, ed. Jackson, Tennessee: 1954.

Henry, Robert S. *The Story of the Confederacy.* New York: 1931. Reprint ed., Old Saybrook, Connecticut: 1999.

Hewitt, J. E. "The Battle of Mansfield, Louisiana." *Confederate Veterans.* Vol. XXXIII (May 1925).

Hewitt, J. E. 1864, *Battle of Mansfield.* Mansfield, Louisiana: 1925. Reprint ed., Mansfield, Louisiana: 1949.

Hewitt, Lawrence L. *Port Hudson: Confederate Bastion on the Mississippi.* Baton Rouge: 1994.

Hoffman, Wickman. *Camp, Court and Siege: A Narrative of Personal Adventure and Observation During Two Wars, 1861-1865, 1870-1871*. New York: 1877.

Hollandsworth, James G., Jr. *Pretense of Glory: The Life of General Nathaniel P. Banks*. Baton Rouge: 1998.

Homans, John. "The Red River Expedition" in *Mississippi Valley, Tennessee, Georgia, Alabama, 1861-1964*. Boston: The Military History Society of Massachusetts, 1910. Vol. VIII of The Papers of the Military History Society of Massachusetts. 1895-1913.

Huffstodt, Jim. *Hard Men Dying*. Bowie, Maryland: 1991.

Hughes, Nathaniel C., ed. *Liddell's Record*. Dayton, Ohio: 1985. Reprint ed., Baton Rouge: 1997.

Irwin, Richard B. *History of the Nineteenth Army Corps*. New York and London: 1892.

Joiner, Gary D. *Little to Eat and Thin Mud of Drink: Letter, Diaries and Memoirs from the Red River Campaign, 1863-1864*. Knoxville, Tennessee: 2007.

Joiner, Gary D. *One Damn Blunder From Beginning to End*. Wilmington, Delaware: 2003.

Joiner, Gary D. *Through the Howling Wilderness: The 1864 Red River Campaign and Union Failure in the West*. Knoxville, Tennessee: 2006.

Johnson, Ludwell H. *Red River Campaign*. Baltimore: 1958.

Johnson, Robert U., and Clarence C. Buel, ed.s *Battles and Leaders of the Civil War*. New York: 1887-1888. 4 Vol.s.

Johnston, David E. *Confederate Boy in the Civil War*. Portland, Oregon: 1914.

Johnston, Joseph E. *Narrative of Military Operations*. New York: 1874.

Jones, Joseph, and Samuel Cooper. "Confederate Losses During the War: Correspondence between Dr. Joseph Jones and Gen. Cooper." Southern Historical Society *Papers*, Vol. VII (1879).

Jones, S. C. *History of the Twenty-second Iowa Volunteer Infantry.* Iowa City: 1907.

Jones, Terry L. *Lee's Tigers.* Baton Rouge: 1987.

Kennedy, James Ronald and Walter Donald Kennedy. *The South Was Right*! 3rd ed. Columbia, South Carolina: 2021.

Kerby, Robert L. *Kirby Smith's Confederacy.* New York: 1972. Reprint ed., Tuscaloosa, Alabama: 1991.

Kirby Smith, Edmund. "The Defense of the Red River" in Volume IV, Robert U. Johnson and Clarence C. Buel, ed.s. *Battles and Leaders of the Civil War.* New York: 1887-1888. 4 Vol.s.

Knox, Thomas W. *Camp Fire and Cotton-field: Southern Adventures in Time of War.* New York and Chicago: 1865.

Landers, H. L. "Wet Sand and Cotton—Banks' Red River Campaign." *Louisiana Historical Quarterly*, Vol. XIX (January 1936).

Lane, Walter P. *Adventures and Recollections of General Walter P. Lane.* Austin: 1970.

Leland, Edwin A. "Organization and Administration of the Louisiana Army During the Civil War." Unpublished M.A. thesis, L.S.U., Baton Rouge: 1938.

Livermore, Thomas L. *Numbers and Losses in the Civil War.* Boston and New York: 1900.

Lonn, Ella. *Foreigners in the Confederacy.* Chapel City, North Carolina: 1940.

Lothrop, Charles A. *A History of the First Regiment Iowa Cavalry Veteran Volunteers.* Lyons, Iowa: 1890.

Lubbock, Francis R. *Six Decades in Texas or Memoirs of Francis Richard Lubbock*. C. W. Raines, ed. Austin: Ben C. Jones and Company, Printers, 1900.

Lufkin, Edwin B. *History of the Thirteenth Maine Regiment*. Bridgton, Maine: H. A. Shorey and Son, 1898.

Marshall, T. B. *History of the Eighty-third Ohio Volunteer Infantry*. Cincinnati: 1913.

Lyman, Theodore. *Meade's Headquarters, 1863-1865*. George R. Agassiz, ed. Boston: 1922.

Massey, Mary Elizabeth. *Ersatz in the Confederacy*. Columbia, South Carolina: 1952.

Maury, Dabney H. Reminiscences of General Taylor." *Appleton's Journal*, Volume 6 (June 1879).

Maury, Dabney H. "Sketch of General Richard Taylor." *Southern Historical Society Papers*. Vol. VII (1879).

Mayeux, Steven M. *Earthen Walls, Iron Men: Fort De Russy, Louisiana, and the Defense of the Red River*. Knoxville, Tennessee: 2007.

Meiners, Fredericka. "Hamilton P. Bee in the Red River Campaign." *Southwestern Historical Quarterly*. Vol. LXXVIII, No. 1 (July 1974).

Mendes, Thomas C. "Blacks, Jews Fight on the Side of the South." *Washington Times*. June 15, 2002.

Mitcham, Samuel W., Jr. *Bust Hell Wide Open: The Life of Nathan Bedford Forrest*. Washington, D.C.: 2016.

Mitcham, Samuel W., Jr. *Encyclopedia of Confederate Generals*. Washington, D.C.: 2022.

Mitcham, Samuel W., Jr. *It Wasn't About Slavery: Exposing the Great Lie of the Civil War*. Washington, D.C.: 2020.

Mitcham, Samuel W., Jr. "Louisiana's Warrior Governor." *Abbeville Institute*: https://www.abbevilleinstitute.org/louisianas-warrior-governor. August 26, 2019.

Moneyhon, Carl H. "White Society and African-American Soldiers" in Mark K. Christ, ed., *"All Cut to Pieces and Gone to Hell:" The Civil War, Race Relations and the Battle of Poison Springs*. Little Rock: 2003.

Moore, Frank, ed. *The Rebellion Record: A Diary of American Events*. New York: 1862-1871. 12 Volumes.

Nichols, Ronnie A. "The Changing Role of Blacks in the Civil War" in Mark K. Christ, ed., *"All Cut to Pieces and Gone to Hell:" The Civil War, Race Relations and the Battle of Poison Springs*. Little Rock: 2003.

Noel, Theophilus. *Autobiography and Reminiscences of Theophilus Noel*. Chicago: 1904.

Noll, Arthur H. *General Kirby-Smith*. Sewanee, Tennessee: 1907.

Oates, Stephen B. *Confederate Cavalry West of the River*. Austin: 1961.

O.R.: see Scott, Robert N.

O.R.N.: see Rush, Richard.

Official Records of the Union and Confederate Navies in the War of the Rebellion. Washington, D.C.: 1894-1927. 31 Vol.s.

Parks, Joseph H. *General Edmund Kirby Smith, C.S.A*. Baton Rouge: 1954.

Papers. City Court House Museum. Vicksburg, Mississippi.

Parrish, T. Michael. *Richard Taylor: Soldier Prince of Dixie*. Chapel Hill, North Carolina: 1992.

Pellet, Elias P. *History of the 114th Regiment, New York State Volunteer*. Norwich, New York: 1866.

BIBLIOGRAPHY

Pittman, Rickey. "Louisiana Jayhawkers." Presentation Before the Major Thomas McGuire Camp 1714, Sons of Confederate Veterans: January 10, 2023.

Plummer, Alonzo H. *Confederate Victory at Mansfield.* Mansfield: 1969.

Porter, David D. *Incidents and Anecdotes of the Civil War.* New York: 1885.

Porter, David D. *The Naval History of the Civil War.* New York and San Francisco: 1887.

Porter, David D. "The Opening of the Lower Mississippi," in Vol. II, Robert U. Johnson and Clarence C. Buel, ed.s. *Battles and Leaders of the Civil War.* New York: 1887-1888. 4 Vol.s.

Post, Lydia M., ed. *Soldiers' Letters from Camp, Battlefield and Prison.* New York: 1865.

Powers, George W. *The Story of the Thirty Eighth Regiment of Massachusetts Volunteers.* Cambridge: 1966

Prushankin, Jeffery S. *A Crisis in Confederate Command: Edmund Kirby Smith, Richard Taylor, and the Army of the Trans-Mississippi.* Baton Rouge: 2005.

Rainwater, Percy L., ed. "Excerpts from Fulkerson's 'Recollections of the War Between the States.'" *Mississippi Valley Historical Review.* Vol. XXIV (1937-38).

Report of the Proceedings of the Society of the Army of the Tennessee. Volume 28 (1896). Cincinnati: 1897.

Richardson, Frank L. "War As I Saw It." *Louisiana Historical Quarterly.* Vol. VI (January 1923) and Vol. VII (April 1923).

Roberts, A. Sellew. "The Federal Government and Confederate Cotton." *American Historical Review*, Volume 32 (January 1927): pp. 262-75.

Robins, Glenn. *The Bishop of the Old South: The Ministry and Civil War Legacy of Leonidas Polk.* Macon, Georgia: 2006.

Rogers, Henrietta G. History of the Committees of Vigilance in the Attakapas Country. Unpublished M.A. thesis, L.S.U., Baton Rouge: 1936.

Roland, Charles P. "P. G. T. Beauregard" in Gary W. Gallagher and Joseph T. Glatthaar, *Leaders of the Lost Cause*. Mechanicsburg, Pennsylvania: 2004.

Rollins, Richard. "Black Southerners in Gray" in Richard Rollins, ed., *Black Southerners in Gray: Essays on Afro-Americans in Confederate Armies*. Murfreesboro, Tennessee: 1994.

Rollins, Richard, ed. *Black Southerners in Gray: Essays on Afro-Americans in Confederate Armies*. Redondo Beach, California: Rank and File Publications, 1994.

Rush, Richard, and Robert H. Woods. *Official Records of the Union and Confederate Navies in the War of the Rebellion*. Washington, D.C.: 1880-1891. Series 1. 31 volumes.

Scott, John. *Story of the Thirty Second Iowa Infantry Volunteers*. Nevada, Iowa: 1896.

Scott, R. B. *The History of the 67th Regiment, Indiana Infantry*. Bedford, Indiana: 1892.

Scott, Robert N., chief compiler. *The War of the Rebellion: A Complication of the Official Records of the Union and Confederate Armies*. Washington, D.C.: 1880-1901. Series 1. 52 Vol.s, 132 parts. Vol. XXXIV., Part 1 (Red River campaign reports); Parts 2, 3 and 4 (Red River campaign correspondence).

Selfridge, Thomas O. *Memoirs of Thomas O. Selfridge, Jr., Rear Admiral, U.S.N.* New York and London: 1924. Reprint ed., Columbia, South Carolina: 1987.

Sherry, Andrew F. *History of the Thirty-Third Iowa Infantry Volunteer Regiment, 1863-6*. Des Moines, Iowa: 1866.

Shorey, Henry A. *The Story of the Maine Fifteenth*. Bridgton, Maine: 1890.

Sliger, J. E. "How General Taylor Fought the Battle of Mansfield, Louisiana." *Confederate Veteran*. Vol. XXXI (December 1923).

Smith, Rebecca W., and Marion Mullins, ed. "The Diary of H. C. Medford, Confederate Soldier, 1864 (Part 2)." *Southwestern Historical Quarterly*. Vol. XXXIV (1930-31).

Smith, Walter G. *The Life and Letters of Thomas Kilby Smith*. New York and London: 1898

Spencer, John W. *Terrell's Texas Cavalry*. Burnett, Texas: 1982.

Sperry, A. F. *History of the 33rd Iowa Infantry Volunteer Regiment*. Des Moines: 1866.

Sprague, Homer B. *History of the 13th Infantry Regiment of Connecticut Volunteers*. Hartfort, Connecticut: 1867.

Stanyan, John M. *A History of the Eighth Regiment of New Hampshire Volunteers*. Concord, New Hampshire: 1892.

Stephens, Robert W. *August Buchel, Texas Soldier of Fortune*. Privately published, 1970.

Sutherland, Daniel. "1864" in Mark K. Christ, ed. *Rugged and Sublime: The Civil War in Arkansas*. Fayetteville: 1994.

Taylor, Richard. "A Chapter of History." *Southern Historical Society Papers*. Vol. XXXI (January-December 1903): pp. 48-52.

Taylor, Richard. *Destruction and Reconstruction*. New York: 1890.

Thirty-Eighth Congress. Report of the Joint Committee on the Conduct of the War: Red River Expedition, Fort Fisher Expedition, Heavy Ordnance. Washington, D.C.: 1865.

Thomas, David Y. *Arkansas in War and Reconstruction, 1861-1874*. Little Rock: 1926.

Report of the Joint Committee on the Conduct of the War. , see Thirty-Eighth Congress.

Urwin, Gregory J. W. "Poison Spring and Jenkins' Ferry: Racial Atrocities during the Camden Expedition" in Mark K. Christ, ed., *"All Cut to Pieces and Gone to Hell:" The Civil War, Race Relations and the Battle of Poison Springs.* Little Rock: 2003.

Vandiver, Frank E., ed. "A Collection of Louisiana Confederate Letters." *Louisiana Historical Quarterly*, Vol. XVII (October 1943).

Visco, Stephen G. *The Red River Campaign: An Analysis.* Carlises Barracks, Pennsylvania: 2001

Warmoth, Henry C. *War, Politics and Reconstruction: Stormy Days in Louisiana.* New York: 1930.

Warner, Ezra J. *Generals in Blue.* Baton Rouge: 1964.

Warner, Ezra J. *Generals in Gray.* Baton Rouge: 1959.

Watkins, Samuel R. *Co. Aytch.* Chattanooga, Tennessee: 1900.

Weddle, Robert S. *Plow-Horse Cavalry: The Caney Creek Boys in the Thirty-Fourth Texas.* Austin, Texas: 1974.

Welsh, Jack D. *Medical Histories of Confederate Generals.* Kent, Ohio: 1995.

Welsh, Jack D. *Medical Histories of Union Generals.* Kent, Ohio: 1996.

Welles, Gideon. *Diary of Gideon Welles.* Boston and New York: 1911. 3 Volumes.

West, Richard S., Jr. *The Second Admiral: A Life of David Dixon Porter, 1813-1891.* New York: 1937.

Whitcomb, Caroline E. *History of the Second Massachusetts Battery (Nims' Battery) of Light Artillery, 1861-1865.* Concord, New Hampshire: 1912.

Wiley, Bell Irvin. *"The Infernal War," The Confederate Letters of Sergeant Edwin H. Foy.* Austin: 1959.

Williams, E. Cort. "Recollections of the Red River Expedition" in *Sketches of War History 1861-1865, Papers Read Before the Ohio Commandery of the Military Order of the Loyal Legion of the United States, 1886-1888*. Vol. II. Cincinnati: Ohio: 1888.

Williams, J. M. *"The Eagle Regiment," 8th Wisconsin Infantry Volunteers*. Belleville, Wisconsin: 1890.

Williams, Robert W., Jr., and Ralph A. Wooster, ed.s. "Camp Life in Civil War Louisiana: The Letters of Private Isaac Dunbar Affleck." *Louisiana History*. Vol. V (Spring 1964).

Williams, Thomas J. *An Historical Sketch of the 56th Ohio Volunteer Infantry Regiment*. Columbus: 1899.

Wills, Brian Steele. *A Battle from the Start: The Life of Nathan Bedford Forrest*. New York: 1992.

Winn Parish Historical Society. *Winn Parish History*. Dallas, Texas: 1985.

Winters, John D. *The Civil War in Louisiana*. Baton Rouge: 1963.

Wright, B. Giraud. *A Southern Girl in 1861*. Garden City, New York: 1906.

Woods, J. T. *Services of the Ninety-sixth Ohio Volunteers*. Toledo: 1874.

Yeary, Mamie. *Reminiscences of the Boys in Gray, 1861-1865*. Dallas: 1912. 2 volumes.

INTERNET SOURCES:

Morgan Friedman Inflation Calculator. https://westegg.com/inflation/

Scott, Paul R. "John A. Wharton: The Forgotten General," at www.terrstexasrangers.org/ biographies/submitted/wharton.html. Accessed 2009.

www.forrestsescort.org/blacks/htm.

www.jewishworldreview.com.

www.sv.c-kirby.smith.org/Black%20Confederate.htm

Latest Releases & Best Sellers

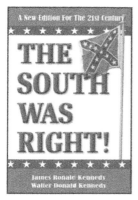

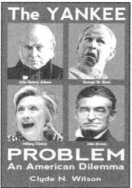

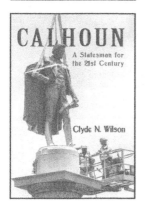
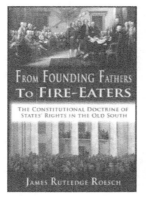
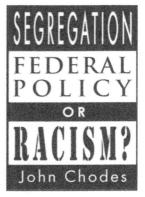

Over 70 Unapologetically Southern
titles for you to enjoy

SHOTWELLPUBLISHING.COM

Free Book Offer

DON'T GET LEFT OUT, Y'ALL.
Sign-up and be the first to know about new releases, sales, and other goodies
—plus we'll send you TWO FREE EBOOKS!

*Lies My Teacher Told Me:
The True History of the War for
Southern Independence*
by Dr. Clyde N. Wilson

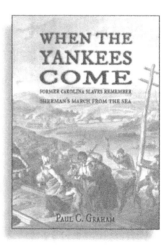

*When The Yankees Come
Former Carolina Slaves Remember
Sherman's March From the Sea*
by Paul C. Graham

FreeLiesBook.com

Southern Books. No Apologies.
We love the South — its history, traditions, and culture — and are proud of our inheritance as Southerners. Our books are a reflection of this love.

Made in United States
Orlando, FL
20 August 2024